Five-a-Day
Fruit & Vegetable
Cookbook

Five-a-Day Fruit & Vegetable Cookbook

Over 200 recipes to ensure you achieve the health experts' recommended five-portion daily minimum for you and your family

KATE WHITEMAN • MAGGIE MAYHEW • CHRISTINE INGRAM

HERMES
HOUSE

This edition is published by Hermes House
an imprint of Anness Publishing Ltd
Hermes House, 88–89 Blackfriars Road,
London SE1 8HA
tel. 020 7401 2077; fax 020 7633 9499

www.hermeshouse.com; www.annesspublishing.com

If you like the images in this book and would like to
investigate using them for publishing, promotions or
advertising, please visit our website
www.practicalpictures.com for more information.

Publisher: Joanna Lorenz
Project Editor: Linda Fraser
Designers: Nigel Partridge and Patrick McLeavey
Photography and styling: William Lingwood (fruit
recipes),
Don Last (fruit reference) and Patrick McLeavey
(vegetable reference and recipes)
Food for photography: Bridget Sargeson (fruit recipes),
Christine France (fruits) and Jane Stevenson (vegetables)
Indexer: Hiliary Bird
Production Controller: Pedro Nelson

© Anness Publishing Ltd 2004, 2008

ETHICAL TRADING POLICY

At Anness Publishing we believe that business should
be conducted in an ethical and ecologically sustainable
way, with respect for the environment and a proper
regard to the replacement of the natural resources
we employ.
As a publisher, we use a lot of wood pulp to make
high-quality paper for printing, and that wood
commonly comes from spruce trees. We are therefore
currently growing more than 750,000 trees in three
Scottish forest plantations: Berrymoss (130
hectares/320 acres), West Touxhill (125 hectares/305
acres) and Deveron Forest (75 hectares/185 acres).
The forests we manage contain more than 3.5 times the
number of trees employed each year in making paper
for the books we manufacture.
Because of this ongoing ecological investment program,
you, as our customer, can have the pleasure and
reassurance of knowing that a tree is being cultivated
on your behalf to naturally replace the materials used to
make the book you are holding.
Our forestry programme is run in accordance with the
UK Woodland Assurance Scheme (UKWAS) and will be
certified by the internationally recognized Forest
Stewardship Council (FSC). The FSC is a non-
government organization dedicated to promoting
responsible management of the world's forests.
Certification ensures forests are managed in an
environmentally sustainable and socially responsible
way. For further information about this scheme, go to
www.annesspublishing.com/trees

NOTES

Standard spoon and cup measures are level.

Large eggs are used unless otherwise stated.

Electric oven temperatures in this book are for
conventional ovens. When using a fan oven, the
temperature will probably need to be reduced by about
20–40°F. Since ovens vary,
you should check with your manufacturer's instruction
book for guidance.

The diets and information in this book are not intended to
replace advice from a qualified medical practitioner,
doctor or dietician. Always consult your health practitioner before adopting any of the suggestions in this book.
Neither the author nor the publishers can accept any lia-
bility for failure to follow this advice.

CONTENTS

MAKE IT FIVE   6

FRUIT

DISCOVERING FRUIT   10
EQUIPMENT   12
PURCHASING, PREPARING AND COOKING   14
APPLES, PEARS, QUINCES AND MEDLARS   18
APPLE, PEAR AND QUINCE RECIPES   38
STONE FRUITS   58
STONE FRUIT RECIPES   72
BERRIES AND CURRANTS   92
BERRY AND CURRANT RECIPES   112
CITRUS FRUITS   134
CITRUS FRUIT RECIPES   148
EXOTIC FRUITS   170
EXOTIC FRUIT RECIPES   198
MELONS, GRAPES, FIGS AND RHUBARB   226
MELON, GRAPE, FIG AND RHUBARB RECIPES   240

VEGETABLES

DISCOVERING VEGETABLES   254
EQUIPMENT   256
PURCHASING, PREPARING AND COOKING   258
ONIONS AND LEEKS   262
ONION AND LEEK RECIPES   274
SHOOTS AND STEMS   286
SHOOT AND STEM RECIPES   298
ROOTS   312
ROOTS RECIPES   332
GREENS   348
GREENS RECIPES   366
BEANS, PEAS AND SEEDS   382
BEAN, PEA AND SEED RECIPES   394
SQUASHES   406
SQUASH RECIPES   418
VEGETABLE FRUITS   430
VEGETABLE FRUIT RECIPES   446
SALAD VEGETABLES   460
SALAD VEGETABLE RECIPES   472
MUSHROOMS   484
MUSHROOM RECIPES   492
INDEX   504

MAKE IT FIVE

Research has shown that eating a balanced diet with at least five portions of fruit and vegetables a day can significantly reduce the risk of many chronic diseases such as heart disease, cancer and stroke as well as offering many other health benefits. Eating more of them can also help you to increase fibre intake, reduce fat intake and maintain a healthy weight.

Frozen fruit and vegetables are just as good as fresh, and are sometimes even better because they are frozen so soon after picking. Canned fruit and vegetables make a good substitute, but try to buy ones canned in water or fruit juice rather than brine or sugar syrup.

Balance and Variety

Eating a healthy diet doesn't have to mean giving up all your favorite foods. It's all about balance and making sure you eat the right proportions of the right foods. Balance, moderation and variety are the key words.

There are five main food groups: starchy foods such as potatoes, pasta and bread; fruit and vegetables; dairy foods such as milk, yogurt and cheese; protein foods such as meat, chicken, fish and tofu; and foods high in fat and sugar such as cakes and cookies.

Starchy foods and fruit and vegetables should make up the largest part of each meal. Protein foods and dairy products are important, but should be eaten in moderation. Fatty and sugary foods should be enjoyed only as an occasional treat.

As with all foods, different types of fruit and vegetables contain different combinations of fibre and nutrients. To ensure you obtain the maximum benefit, make sure you eat a variety.

How Big is a Portion?

The size of a portion, and how many times you can count it in a single day, varies depending on the type of fruit or vegetable. Use the table below to check whether you're eating enough.

ONE PORTION	HOW MUCH IS THAT?	HOW DOES IT COUNT?
Fruit (fresh, frozen or canned)	• 1 medium-size piece of fruit such as an apple or banana • 2 smaller pieces of fruit such as satsumas or figs • a handful of small fruits such as grapes or strawberries • 3 heaped tablespoons of fruit salad • half a larger piece of fruit such as a grapefruit • 2-inch slice of very large fruit such as melon	Every portion of fruit you eat counts towards your daily five.
Dried fruit	• 3 small fruits such as apricots • 1 tablespoon very small dried fruits such as raisins	Dried fruit counts as only one portion a day, no matter how much of it you eat.
100% pure fruit or vegetable juice	• 1 glass	Juices count as only one portion a day, no matter how many glasses of juice you drink.
Vegetables	• 3 heaped tablespoons cooked vegetables such as carrots or peas	Every portion of vegetables you eat counts towards your daily five. **But remember** – potatoes are counted as a starchy food, not a vegetable, so they can't be included in your daily five portions.
Salad	• 1 cereal bowl	Every portion of salad you eat counts towards your daily five.
Beans and lentils	• 3 tablespoons cooked beans or lentils such as kidney beans or chickpeas	Beans and lentils count as only one portion a day, no matter how many portions you eat.

Easy Ways to Five

If you don't usually eat five portions of fruit and vegetables a day, achieving this target can sometimes seem like an unmanageable task. The good news is that it doesn't need to be a struggle. There are so many delicious ways to prepare fruit and vegetables, and clever ways to "sneak" them into your diet that you'll find it a pure pleasure achieving your daily target. Listed below are some simple ways to work more fruits and vegetables into your diet.

• Enjoy a fresh fruit smoothie at any time of day. Simply blend soft fruits such as raspberries or mangoes with milk to make a rich, creamy drink that is packed with nutrients. Unlike fruit juices, smoothies still contain all the fibre of the original fruit.
• Add a chopped banana, or a handful of strawberries or raisins to a bowl of cereal in the morning. It will taste like a special breakfast but it's actually helping you on your way to five-a-day.
• When you feel like a sweet treat, eat a few dried apricots or figs instead of reaching for the cookie jar. They taste just as sweet, but they're healthier and can count as one of your portions.

Above: Snacking on raw vegetables is an easy way to eat more fruit and veg. They taste great and are low in fat too.

Above: Drink your way to five portions a day with a delicious, healthy blend of ripe strawberries, yogurt and milk.

• Instead of spreading jam on toast, use a mashed banana instead. It tastes great and is so much healthier than a sugar-packed spread.
• Desserts and cakes don't need to be all bad. Although they are high in fat and sugar so should be eaten in moderation, choosing a slice of cake packed with dried fruit, or a dessert containing lots of fruit will contribute to your five daily portions—rather than just offering empty calories.
• When making sandwiches, add plenty of extra salad. They will look more appealing and taste much nicer.
• Chopped raw vegetables such as carrots, cucumber and peppers make a great snack at any time of day and are so much healthier than a packet of potato chips or a cookie.
• Add a few extra chopped vegetables to non-vegetable dishes such as meat stews, or stir baby spinach into mashed potatoes just before serving.

About this Book

The recipes in this book have been specially designed to make the most of the delicious fruits and vegetables that are available in the supermarket, helping you to enjoy a tastier, healthier diet. There is a huge choice of recipes for every occasion—from healthy salads and low-fat desserts, to rich and creamy risottos, spicy curries, golden pies and pizzas and indulgent cakes. No matter what your mood, you are sure to find the perfect recipe to help you on your way to five-a-day.

Left: Eating a variety of different fruits and vegetables every day is essential to good health.

FRUIT

DISCOVERING FRUIT

FRUITS ARE NATURE'S most bountiful and versatile creation. No other foods offer such a variety of colors, textures, scents and flavors. Almost all fruits are pleasing to the senses of sight, smell and taste. Just think of the crispness of an apple, the velvety skin of a peach, the jewellike colors of red currants, the juicy tartness of citrus fruits. There is nothing like the sight of a glorious display of fruit in a market to lift the spirits and whet the appetite. Without colorful, health-giving fruits, our diet would be infinitely more dull.

Fruit is not only good for the soul; it is a supremely healthy food, bursting with natural energy-giving sugars, minerals and vitamins. When energy levels are low, a few grapes, a banana or an apple revitalize us in moments. Fruit provides the perfect guilt-free snack, since most varieties are completely fat-free and contain very few calories. Nearly all fruits have a high proportion of water—between 75 and 90 percent—which makes them wonderfully thirst-quenching in hot weather. Picture the pleasure of eating a large wedge of chilled watermelon or a

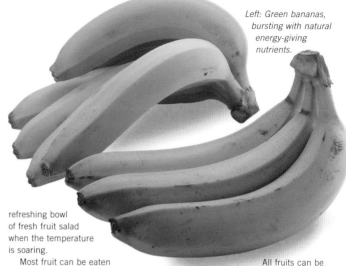

Left: Green bananas, bursting with natural energy-giving nutrients.

refreshing bowl of fresh fruit salad when the temperature is soaring.

Most fruit can be eaten raw, just as it is (be sure to wash it first), although some varieties may need peeling. Nothing beats a simple dessert of perfectly ripe juicy fruit, perhaps served with a scoop or two of vanilla ice cream or a dollop of cream, or with some good cheese—try crisp apples with a wedge of farmhouse Cheddar or Lancashire cheese, juicy, ripe pears with either blue Stilton or Gorgonzola, or raspberries and sliced peaches with mascarpone cheese.

All fruits can be served on their own, or used to create sweet and savory dishes of infinite variety, from pies to puddings, cakes, muffins, ice creams, mousses, soufflés and featherlight fruit-topped meringues.

You could easily base an entire meal on fresh fruit without repeating any colors, textures or flavors. The meal might begin with the classic combination of melon with prosciutto, or a refreshing fruit soup, followed by Normandy pheasant with apples and cider, then a platter of cheese, fresh and dried fruit and nuts and finally a tropical fruit salad, a bowl of bright red berries or a lemon tart.

Fruit is enormously rewarding to cook with and is very versatile. Almost all fruits complement each other, so you can create all manner of interesting combinations. Although the recipes in this book concentrate on the use of fruits in sweet dishes, they have an important role to play in savory ones too. Tart fruits like gooseberries, rhubarb and cranberries cut the richness of fatty fish like mackerel and can also enhance the sometimes insipid flavor of poultry. Dried fruits are used extensively in North African and Middle Eastern cooking—the combination of meat and sweet, sticky dates, prunes or

Below: The vibrant seeds from ripe pomegranates can be eaten raw as they are or added to both sweet and savory dishes.

dried apricots is superb. Most fruits also marry well with exotic spices, such as cinnamon, ginger and vanilla, and even those fruits that are relatively bland can be lifted by the addition of a squeeze of lemon or lime juice.

The hundreds of different kinds of fruit can be divided into four main categories: soft fruits, such as raspberries, strawberries, blueberries and red, black, and white currants; stone fruits, including peaches, apricots, cherries and plums; "pome" fruits of the apple and pear families; and citrus fruits. In addition there are several that do not fit into any other category. These include figs, grapes, melons and rhubarb (which is actually a vegetable, but is always treated as a fruit).

Fruits are no longer the seasonal produce they once were. Nowadays, thanks to sophisticated transportation methods, all types of fruit from every country are available almost all year round. Travelers who have enjoyed exotic produce abroad now find it gracing the shelves of their local

Above: Orleans Reinette apples—one of the pome fruits.

Left: Watermelons, like other melon varieties, are in a category of their own.

greengrocer or supermarket, giving less fortunate stay-at-homes a taste of the tropics. The disadvantage of this is that we no longer wait with eager anticipation for a particular fruit to come into season; somewhere in the world it will be grown year-round. So strawberries, raspberries and peaches have ceased to be exclusively summer treats, but can be bought in almost any season, although they will never taste as good as when freshly picked, and are still always at their best and cheapest in the summer.

There are many other ways of savoring fruits throughout the year. They can be frozen, canned, or preserved in other ways—as juices, liqueurs or macerated in alcohol; dried or candied; or made into jams, jellies, curds, chutneys and relishes. There is no time of year when fruit is not readily available in one form or another, so you need never go without nature's most precious bounty.

EQUIPMENT

Although most fruits can be prepared with the aid of a good sharp knife, a wide variety of special implements is available to make the task easier, safer and more efficient. The following items are very useful—provided you have space for them in your kitchen.

Peeling and Coring

Paring knife The most useful item in any kitchen. Choose a really sharp knife with a short blade and a handle that is comfortable to hold. Always use a stainless steel knife for preparing fruit; the acids may damage other metals.

Apple corer This utensil removes apple and pear cores in one easy movement. Place over the core at the stem end and push down firmly right through the fruit, then twist slightly and pull out the core and seeds.

Apple segmenter Use this handy device to core and slice an apple into twelve even-size segments in one simple operation.

Apple peeler Perfect for people with a huge glut of home-grown apples, this hand-cranked implement peels, cores and neatly slices the fruit into rings in seconds. This tool is expensive to buy, but worth it if you have apple trees that bear abundantly.

Above right: Apple corer
Below left: Paring knife
Below right: Apple segmenter

Above: Fixed- and swivel-blade vegetable peelers

Pineapple slicer Cores and slices a pineapple in one easy corkscrewlike action. This simple-to-operate utensil is useful for keeping the pineapple shell intact for use as a serving container, but only works with smaller pineapples.

Swivel-blade vegetable peeler Use this tool to pare off the thinnest possible layer of peel or skin so that no nutrients are lost.

Fixed-blade vegetable peeler This type of peeler takes a thicker strip of peel or skin than the swivel-blade version.

Grating and Zesting

Box grater Choose a stainless steel grater with four different grating

Below: Citrus zester and channel knife
Right: Box grater

Left:
Pineapple slicer

surfaces and make sure it will stand firmly on a chopping board or in a bowl. Most include a flat blade suitable for slicing lemons or limes.

Citrus zester The row of holes at the top of the zester shaves off thin shreds of zest, leaving behind the bitter pith.

Channel knife This tool has a toothlike blade that pares off the zest in ribbons or julienne strips. Combined zesters/channel knives are available.

Juicing

Lemon squeezer Hand-operated squeezers catch the juice in the base. Basic models can also be used for limes and small oranges. Some have interchangeable heads to accommodate citrus fruits of various sizes.

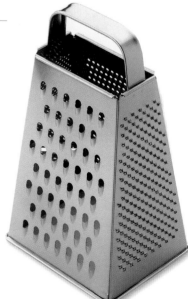

Left: Citrus press
Below: Reamer

Citrus press

These hand-operated chrome juicers have a geared mechanism to enable as much juice as possible to be extracted. When the handle is pulled forward, the juice is squeezed into a container.

Electric juice extractor These machines will extract juice from other fruits besides citrus. They take up a lot of space, but are invaluable for lovers of fresh fruit juice.

Pitting and Preparing

Cherry pitter The bowl of this implement has a hole through which the cherry pit is ejected when the fruit is pressed. Useful for large quantities.

Grapefruit knife A curved knife serrated on both sides. Run it between the membranes and pulp to release the segments.

Left: Cherry pitter

Below: Grapefruit knife

Reamer This wooden device enables you to squeeze the fruit directly into a bowl or pan. Insert into the cut fruit and twist.

Lemon tap A simple gadget that turns citrus fruit into a "juice jug." If only a small amount of juice is required, leave the tap inserted in the fruit to keep the juice fresh between squeezings.

Below: Lemon squeezer

Grapefruit segmenter This curved implement has a V-shaped blade. Position with the point against the inside of the rind and push down, around and inward to cut out the segments.

Melon baller Insert this small, round scoop into the melon flesh and twist to remove neat balls of fruit. It comes in various sizes and can also be used for other fruits. Tiny ones sometimes double as a cherry pitter.

Preserving

Funnel Essential for pouring hot jams and jellies into jars. Stainless steel funnels will withstand heat better than plastic ones.

Jelly bag A heavy muslin filter bag for straining jellies and juices. Suspend it from the legs of a chair placed upside down or, far better, buy one on a stand.

Preserving pan Especially designed for preserving, this is a thick-bottomed double-handled pan. The heavy bottom prevents the fruit preserve from burning and sticking.

Sugar thermometer Use this for checking the temperature of a syrup or to determine whether the setting point of a jam and jelly has been reached.

Above: Sugar thermometer
Below: Funnel with strainer

Above: Melon baller

PURCHASING, PREPARING AND COOKING

BUYING FRUIT

Obviously, the best time to buy fruit is when it is fully ripe and at its peak. The exceptions are fruits, such as bananas and pears, that ripen quickly and should therefore be bought at different stages of maturity so that they are not all ready at the same time. You are most likely to find top-quality fruits in markets and shops that have a quick turnover of fresh produce, preferably with a daily delivery. Although most fruits are now available almost year-round, they are best and cheapest when in season in the country of origin. Only buy as much fruit as you need at one time so that it remains fresh and appetizing.

PREPARING FRUIT

For some fruits, the only preparation needed is washing or wiping with a damp cloth; others must be peeled or skinned, cored, pitted or seeded. Wash fruit only just before using. If necessary, cut away any bruised or damaged parts.

Firm Fruit

Peeling

Some firm fruits, such as dessert apples and pears, can be eaten raw without peeling. For cooking, peeling is often necessary. Pare off the skin as thinly as possible to avoid losing the valuable nutrients under the skin.

1 Wash the fruit and pat dry using paper towels. Use a small, sharp paring knife or a vegetable peeler to pare off the skin in long, thin vertical strips. Pears are best peeled by this method.

2 Alternatively, for apples, thinly peel all around the fruit in a spiral.

Coring

1 To core whole apples and pears, place the sharp edge of a corer over the stem end of the fruit.

2 Press down firmly, then twist slightly; the core, complete with seeds, will come away in the center of the corer. Push out the core from the handle end.

Storing
Storage methods depend on the type of fruit, but there are some basic guidelines:
• Do not wash fruit before storing, but only when ready to use.
• Store fruit at the bottom of the refrigerator in the salad crisper.
• Do not refrigerate unripe fruit; keep it at room temperature or in a cool, dark place, depending on the variety (see individual fruits).
• Fragile fruits, such as berries, are easily squashed, so spread them out in a single layer on a tray lined with paper towels.

Segmenting

1 Halve the fruit lengthwise, then cut into quarters or segments.

2 Cut out the central core and seeds with a small, sharp knife.

Preventing discoloration
Some fruits, such as apples, pears and bananas, quickly oxidize and turn brown when exposed to the air. To prevent discoloration, brush cut fruits with lemon juice. Alternatively, acidulate a bowl of cold water by stirring in the juice of half a lemon. Drop the cut fruits into the bowl immediately after preparing.

Citrus Fruit

Peeling

It is very important to remove all of the bitter white pith that lies just beneath the rind of citrus fruits.

1 To peel firm-skinned fruits, hold the fruit over a bowl to catch the juice and use a sharp knife to cut off the rind.

2 For loose-skinned fruit, such as tangerines, pierce the skin with your forefinger at the stem end and peel off the rind. Pull off all the white shreds adhering to the fruit.

Segmenting

Use a small serrated knife to cut down between the membranes enclosing the segments; carefully ease out the flesh.

Grating

Citrus zest adds a wonderful flavor to many dishes. If it is to be eaten raw, grate it finely, using the fine side of a grater. Remove only the colored zest; if you grate too deeply into the peel, you will be in danger of including the bitter white pith. For cooking, pare off long, thin strips of zest using a zester.

Garnishing

1 To make thick julienne strips of zest, cut downward, using a channel knife.

2 To make twists, slice the fruits thinly, cut to the center, then twist the ends in opposite directions to make an S-shape.

Soft Fruit

Peeling

Fruits such as peaches, nectarines and apricots can be peeled with a sharp paring knife, but this may waste some of the delicious flesh. It is better to loosen the skins by dipping them *briefly* in boiling water.

1 Make a tiny nick in the skin.

2 Cover with boiling water and leave for 15–30 seconds, depending on the ripeness of the fruit. Remove the fruit with a slotted spoon and peel off the skin, which should come away easily.

Removing pits and seeds

1 To pit peaches, apricots etc., cut all around the fruit through the seam. Twist the halves in opposite directions, then lever out the pit with a knife.

2 To pit cherries, put the fruit in a cherry pitter and push the bar into the fruit. The pit will be ejected.

3 To remove grape seeds, cut the grapes in half, then pick out the seeds with the tip of a small, sharp knife.

COOKING FRUIT

Most fruits can be cooked and in a great variety of ways.

Poaching

Apples and pears, stone fruits, figs, rhubarb and even grapes can be poached whole, halved or in segments. The classic poaching liquid is a syrup and usually consists of 1 part sugar boiled with 2 parts water for about 2 minutes, or until clear. The syrup can be flavored with lemon, orange or spices, such as cinnamon or vanilla. Red or white wine can also be used for poaching, usually with added sugar. Alternatively, use fruit juice.

Bring the poaching liquid to a boil. Lower the heat and add the fruit. Simmer gently until the fruit is just tender.

Stewing

This method is suitable for all fruits that can be poached.

Cut up the fruit. Put in a saucepan with just enough water, wine or fruit juice to cover. Add sugar to taste. Simmer gently until tender. Stir only if you want the fruit to become a pulp.

Broiling

Any firm fruits can be broiled, with or without sugar. Tropical fruits, such as pineapple and bananas, are particularly good for grilling. For desserts, they can be cut into 1-inch wedges or chunks and threaded onto skewers to make kebabs. Brush the fruit with honey before broiling.

For savory dishes, halve the fruit or cut into pieces, removing the core if necessary. Brush with melted butter and broil under medium heat, turning occasionally, until tender and browned on all sides.

Baking

Apples and pears; stone fruits such as peaches, nectarines, apricots and plums; and figs and rhubarb can be baked whole or in halves, wedges or slices, according to type.

1 Put the fruit in a shallow ovenproof dish, add a little water and sprinkle with sugar to taste.

2 Top the fruit with small pieces of butter. Bake in a preheated oven at 350°F until tender.

Microwave Cooking

All fruits that can be conventionally cooked can be microwaved with excellent results, although the skins on some fruits, such as plums, may not soften sufficiently in the short cooking time. Whole fruits, such as apples, should be scored, or they may burst. Place the fruit in a suitable dish, cover and cook on High for the time recommended, or until tender.

Sautéing

Slice or dice the fruit (peel it or not, as you wish) and toss quickly in hot butter until lightly browned all over. Add sugar and flavorings to taste.

Deep-Frying

For fruit fritters, such as pineapple, apple or banana, peel the fruit and cut into chunks.

Heat oil for deep-frying to 360°F, or until a cube of dried bread sizzles when it is added to the pan. Coat the pieces of fruit in batter and deep-fry until the fritters rise to the surface of the hot oil and are golden brown. Drain the fritters on paper towels and sprinkle with sugar.

Puréeing

Fruit can be puréed for sauces, fools, ice creams and sorbets. Some types must be cooked first; others, like berries, can be puréed raw.

1 For berries, wash briefly and push through a fine nylon sieve, using the back of a large spoon or ladle. If you prefer, purée the berries in a food processor, then strain the purée to remove any seeds.

2 For cooked peeled fruit, mash with a potato masher for a coarse purée.
3 For a finer purée, process cooked, peeled fruit in a food processor or push through a food mill.

Caramelizing

Fruits look pretty when caramelized. Small fruits like cherries can be used whole. Larger fruits should be cubed.

1 Combine scant 1 cup sugar and ¼ cup water in a small, heavy saucepan. Stir over low heat until the sugar has dissolved. When the mixture boils, add 1 teaspoon lemon juice and boil until the syrup turns a deep golden brown.

2 Carefully add 1 tablespoon hot water (protecting your hand with an oven mitt, as the mixture will "spit") and shake the pan to mix.
3 Spear a piece of fruit on a fork and dip it into the caramel to coat. Place on an oiled baking sheet until the caramel cools and hardens.

Candying

Also known as crystallized or glacé fruits, candied fruits make a delicious end to a meal. Suitable fruits include citrus (slices and peel), cherries and other stone fruits, physalis (cape gooseberries) and pineapple. For professional results, the candying process is a lengthy one, but this simplified method works well for candied citrus zest or for fruit that is to be eaten within a few days.

1 Cut the fruit into slices or chunks. Make a syrup using 1 cup sugar and ²⁄₃ cup water; follow the instructions under Caramelizing. Immerse the pieces of fruit in the syrup. Set aside in a cool, dry place to soak for 2 weeks. Drain.

2 Place the fruit on a rack over a baking sheet. Dry for 3–6 hours in a very low oven (no higher than 125°F). Cool, then store in an airtight container.

Frosting

Try this technique with grapes, red and black currants and cranberries. Eat on the day they are prepared.

1 Leave the fruit on the stem. Dip in lightly beaten egg white, then roll in sugar until frosted all over. Let dry before serving.

Drying

Suitable fruits include apples, pears, stone fruits, figs, grapes and bananas. Commercial dehydrators are available, but you can dry the fruit in a low oven.
    Prepare the fruit: Peel, core and slice apples; peel, core and halve pears; halve and pit peaches or similar fruits. Leave smaller fruits whole. Lay the fruit on clean wooden slatted trays, cut side up. Dry in an oven preheated to the lowest possible temperature. Cool completely before storing.

Preserving in Alcohol

All fruits can be preserved in alcohol. In the eighteenth century, seafarers discovered that their cargoes of exotic fruits could be preserved in barrels of rum. Dark rum is still the classic preserving spirit, but brandy and other spirits can also be used.
    The ideal container is a purpose-made *rumtopf*, but a wide-mouthed preserving jar will do. Start with summer fruits, then add other fruits as they come into season.

1 Wash and dry the fruit. Place in a bowl and cover with an equal weight of sugar. Set aside for 1 hour.

2 Tip the fruit mixture into a *rumtopf* or preserving jar. Pour in just enough rum to cover the fruit completely. Cover the jar with plastic wrap and store in a cool, dark place.
3 Continue to fill the jar with fruits as they come into season, using only half as much sugar by weight as fruit; cover the fruit with rum each time. When the jar is full, leave for at least two months before using the fruit.

APPLES, PEARS, QUINCES AND MEDLARS

A bowlful of apples, polished to shiny perfection, is one of life's pleasures—beautiful to behold, delicious and healthy to eat. Pears are almost as popular, with juicy flesh whose scent is almost as tempting as its taste. Quinces are even more aromatic, while medlars are intriguing—not least because they can only be eaten when they are on the verge of rotting. They are all pome fruits, with an indentation in the stem end and the coarse brown remains of a flower at the other, and a tough central core containing a number of brown seeds.

APPLES

Ever since Adam bit into the fruit of the Tree of Knowledge, apples have been the stuff of myth and legend. The ancient Greeks and Romans believed them to be aphrodisiacs, and for the Celts crab apples were a symbol of fertility. In the Middle Ages, the cult of the apple continued in such customs as apple bobbing at Halloween and wassailing at Christmas.

The most popular of all fruits, apples are also convenient, perfect for eating raw as a nutritious snack and ideal for making into a multitude of hot and cold desserts. There are thousands of named varieties worldwide, but the choice of those available to buy is, sadly, decreasing year by year. However, because apples are now grown in every temperate country in the world, some varieties can be found in the shops all year round. Delicious as they may be, no store-bought apples can ever beat the flavor and crisp texture of local apples that have been freshly picked.

Apples come in many shapes and sizes, from tiny cherry-sized crab apples to huge cooking varieties like Howgate Wonder, Reverend W. Wilkes and the unbelievably warty Knobby Russet, which looks remarkably like a huge toad. They can be round, oval, or "cornered," with four distinct corners around the calyx, like the Catshead, which is shaped like the face of a Siamese cat.

Left: Granny Smith apples—first cultivated in Australia in the nineteenth century.

Colors range from bright, shiny red through vivid greens, yellows and pale creamy-white to golden russet, while the skins may be ultra-thin or unpalatably thick. As for taste and texture, there is an almost infinite variety—something to suit every palate, from crisp and sour to soft and sweet.

History

Apples have been eaten since prehistoric times, when only crab apples existed. The Romans adored apples and were the first people to cultivate the fruit; by the first century AD they were growing at least a dozen varieties throughout the Roman Empire.

The most famous of all British apple growers was the nineteenth-century English nurseryman Thomas Laxton. With his sons, he hybridized hundreds of varieties of apples, many of which still exist today and bear his name.

The Pilgrims introduced apples to the New World, planting seeds that they had taken with them from England. They proved so popular that in the eighteenth century John Chapman (popularly known as "Johnny Appleseed") planted apple orchards across about 10,000 square miles of North America, using discarded apple seeds from cider-making plants.

A century later, apple growing in Australia took off when Mrs. Maria Smith cultivated the first Granny Smith apple in her garden in Sydney.

Above: Laxton's Fortune

Below: Braeburn—crisp, juicy apples that make excellent eating.

EATING APPLES

Ashmead's Kernel: These late-variety apples were first cultivated in Gloucestershire in the seventeenth century. Their flesh has a good acid/sugar balance and develops a strong, spicy, aniseed flavor in some seasons.

Beauty of Bath A beautiful, small, flattish green apple extensively flushed with red, with sharp, sweet, juicy flesh. Beauty of Bath apples should be eaten straight from the tree, as they rot almost as soon as they are picked. Consequently, you are unlikely to find this apple in stores.

Blenheim Orange This apple was discovered growing out of a wall in Blenheim Palace in England in the nineteenth century and was named by permission of the Duke of Marlborough, but it also has sixty-seven other names! It is a dual-purpose apple, good for both cooking and eating, with a pleasantly nutty flavor. It is suitable for cooking in dishes, such as apple charlotte and apple crumble, and for serving as a dessert fruit.

Braeburn This crisp, juicy apple with a smooth, pale green skin, heavily flushed with red, makes excellent eating. Braeburn apples need plenty of daylight to grow.

Varieties

With over 7,000 named varieties of apples, it would be impossible to list more than a tiny fraction. In any case, only about a dozen varieties are readily available in stores, although nurseries can supply many more to people who wish to grow apples in their gardens.

Growing your own apples will allow you to enjoy exotically flavored fruit, like the pineapple-flavored Pine Golden Pippin or Ananas Reinette, or the Winter Banana, which develops a creamy texture and a banana flavor when stored. D'Arcy Spice is a small golden apple with the flavors of cinnamon and allspice, while Anisa is one of several aniseed-flavored apples. Other apples are redolent of melon, strawberries, raspberries, peaches, lemon, and even fennel.

In some countries, including Britain and the United States, apples are categorized as eating or dessert fruit, or cooking apples. Other countries regard all apples as suitable for both eating or cooking. As for cider apples, many are disagreeably sour, but some are very pleasant to eat.

Below: Beauty of Bath

Above: Empire

Above left: Egremont Russet—this sweet, crisp apple is delicious served at the end of a meal with a wedge of strong-tasting cheese, such as farmhouse Cheddar or Lancashire.

Cox's Orange Pippin A greenish yellow apple of medium size, with some orange-red russeting. The firm, crisp, juicy flesh of this sweet fruit, with its overtones of acidity, make it one of the world's best and most popular apples. Cox's Orange Pippins are excellent for cooking as well as eating raw.

Crispin Large, pale yellowish green apples with firm and juicy creamy-white flesh and a pleasant mild flavor.

Discovery Bred from the Worcester Pearmain, Discovery was the first apple to be commercially grown in Britain. It is particularly attractive for its highly colored bright red skin and contrasting hard, crisp white flesh. Best eaten straight from the tree.

Egremont Russet Russet apples have rough, porous skins that allow the water to evaporate, giving a denser flesh and intensifying the nutty flavor. Egremont Russet is the most readily available. It is golden russet in color, sometimes with a bright orange flush, and has a crisp texture and very sweet taste. It can be used for eating or cooking and goes superbly with cheese.

Elstar This sweet, crisp and juicy apple is a cross between Ingrid Marie and Golden Delicious. Originally bred in Holland, it is now grown extensively throughout Europe and in North America. Picked in mid-autumn, Elstar apples will keep for 3–4 months.

Empire A dark red American apple with a shiny skin, best for eating raw, but suitable for cooking. It has crisp, green, juicy flesh and a slightly tart flavor.

Above: Cox's Orange Pippin

Left: Jonagold—these dual-purpose apples have a superb flavor.

Fuji This sweet apple has greenish yellow skin with a rosy blush and crisp, juicy white flesh. It is also suitable for cooking.

Gala This colorful eating apple from New Zealand has a yellow ground color flushed with bright orange and red. The yellow flesh is very sweet, juicy and crisp. It is at its best when absolutely fresh. Good for either cooking or eating. **Royal Gala** is similar, but red all over.

Golden Delicious Originally grown from a chance seedling in the United States, this conical, freckled, golden apple has become ubiquitous. At its peak, the cream flesh is juicy and crisp with a mild flavor; unfortunately, most commercially grown Golden Delicious are sold when they are under- or overripe and are consequently tasteless and mealy in texture. Golden Delicious are suitable for cooking or eating.

Granny Smith First grown in Australia by the eponymous "Granny" Smith, this largish

Right: Golden Delicious

all-purpose apple is bright green, becoming yellow as it ripens. Usually sold underripe, it has firm, crunchy flesh and a tart flavor.

Greensleeves This James Grieve/Golden Delicious cross has more flavor than a James Grieve and better acidity. It is an early-fruiting variety, which should be eaten immediately after picking.

Idared By far the favorite North American apple for making applesauce. American-grown fruits have a good acid flavor that is often lacking in European-grown apples.

James Grieve A Scottish apple raised in Edinburgh in the late nineteenth century, with tart, juicy flesh that bruises easily when handled. James Grieve is good for cooking and eating, but, like most early varieties, it does not store well and should be kept for no more than 2–3 weeks after picking.

Jonagold A hybrid of Jonathan and Golden Delicious, this large, round, green-tinged yellow apple has creamy

Above: Gala are best eaten very fresh, when the flesh is crisp and juicy.

Left: Katy

Right: Orleans Reinette

Above:
Pink Lady

white flesh and a superb flavor. It can be used for cooking or eating.

Jonathan This smallish, round orange-red North American apple has white, juicy flesh and a fragrant, slightly acidic flavor. It can be used for cooking.

Katy A highly colored early apple bred in Sweden from the Worcester Pearmain. Its small size appeals to children, and its flesh is crisp, sweet and juicy. Katy apples are best eaten immediately after picking.

Kidd's Orange Red A New Zealand apple bred from Cox's Orange Pippin. These deliciously crisp apples are highly aromatic, but need many hours of sunshine to develop their full flavor and color, so they cannot be successfully grown in Northern Europe.

Laxton's Fortune A cross between Cox's Orange Pippin and Wealthy, these apples have yellowish skin heavily tinged with red, and sweet, juicy, lightly aromatic flesh. You are most likely to find them at farm stands.

Laxton's Superb Greenish yellow and partially covered with red, this all-purpose apple has crisp, very juicy flesh. It is sweet, with some acidity.

McIntosh A Canadian apple that is popular throughout North America. It is wonderfully decorative, with deep red waxy skin that can be polished to a superb sheen, but the skin is quite tough. The pale flesh is melting (and sometimes mushy), with a hint of fresh strawberry flavor.

Orleans Reinette One of the best apples of all, this large orange-flecked russet has a rough skin but juicy, sweet, aromatic flesh. Orleans Reinette is ideal for cooking and eating.

Pink Lady A pretty Australian cross between Golden Delicious and Lady Williams, this large all-purpose apple has a mild flavor and is becoming increasing available in supermarkets and greengrocers.

Pomme d'Apis Also known as Lady Apple, this very attractive fruit has a yellow skin suffused with a bright red blush. Pomme d'Apis is a late apple with good keeping qualities.

Red Delicious This North American apple was first grown in the nineteenth century. It has an exceptionally sweet flavor,

Above: Spartan—a Canadian apple with a tough skin, but delicious, floral-scented flesh.

Left: Grown mostly in the United States, colorful Red Delicious is another apple with a tough skin that hides juicy, sweet flesh.

but tough skin. Red Delicious apples can be grown in Europe, but not always successfully.

Spartan Another Canadian apple raised in 1926 from McIntosh and Newton's Pippin. It inherits a tough skin from McIntosh, but tastes highly aromatic, with a floral perfume.

Worcester Pearmain A conical yellow apple flushed with bright red. The juicy white flesh has a hint of strawberry flavor. Worcester Pearmain are best eaten straight from the tree, but can also be used for cooking.

Above: Worcester Pearmain

Above: Greensleeves

Below left: With their shiny, bright red skin and crisp cream flesh, Washington Red apples are worth looking for at farmers' markets.

Above: Lord Lambourne

Other eating varieties of note
Less well known apple varieties worth looking for include Lord Derby, Lord Lambourne, Red Pippin, Rome Beauty, Starking, Sturmer Pippin, Tydeman's Late Orange, Washington Red, Winesap and Winston.

Above: Originally bred in Holland, Elstar apples are now grown throughout Europe and in North America.

Below right: Red Pippin—a tasty Cox's Orange Pippin cross.

Below left: Royal Gala—sweet, juicy and crisp, this apple is good for either cooking or eating.

Above: Bramley's Seedling

Below: Howgate Wonder

COOKING APPLES

Bramley's Seedling The nonpareil of cookers, this large, flattish green apple (sometimes faintly flushed with red) has coarse, white, juicy, acid flesh that cooks into a frothy purée. Bramleys are perfect for baking or as the basis for applesauce.

Grenadier An irregularly shaped conical apple with yellow skin. The acid flesh is faintly green, firm and juicy. It breaks down during cooking. Grenadiers do not keep well.

Howgate Wonder This apple can grow to an enormous size—in 1997, the world record was achieved with a specimen

weighing 3 pounds, 14 ounces! The juicy white flesh breaks up during cooking and has an uninspiring flavor, so this variety is grown mainly for exhibition.

Reverend W. Wilkes A very large conical apple with pale greenish-white skin. The fine, very white flesh is crisp, juicy and acidic. The apple can be eaten raw, but it is best as a cooker. It keeps well.

Nutrition

Apples were once believed to be the most nutritious of fruits, giving rise to the saying "an apple a day keeps the doctor away." In fact, they have fewer vitamins than many other fruits (although they contain some vitamins C and A), but are high in pectin and are a good source of dietary fiber. They provide 52 calories per 3¾ ounces.

Buying and Storing

Choose apples with undamaged skins, and never buy bruised fruits. If possible, smell the fruits to determine their fragrance (not easy when they are prebagged) and squeeze gently to make sure that they are firm. Do not be seduced by the skin color of an apple; those gorgeous-looking specimens with thick, vivid red, waxy skins often have mealy, tasteless flesh.

Apples continue to ripen after they have been picked, so their color and texture may change during storage. For short-term storage, they can be kept in a ventilated plastic bag in the refrigerator. To store pick-your-own apples, wrap each one in newspaper and place, folded side down, in a single layer in wooden or fiber trays. Keep in a cool, dry, dark place and check occasionally to make sure none has rotted. A bad fruit will taint all the others, so remove it immediately.

Dried Apples These have a sweet, concentrated flavor and are an

Below: Dried apple rings

Drying apples at home

1 Peel the apples, remove the cores and slice the fruit into rings. Soak in salted water for a few minutes to prevent discoloration.

2 Thread the apple rings onto string. Hang them from the ceiling or suspend across the room until they are completely dry.

3 Alternatively, arrange the rings in a single layer on a wire rack on a baking sheet, making sure that they are not touching. Place in an oven set to 150°F for several hours, until dried.

extremely useful pantry ingredient. Eat them straight from the package as a nutritious snack, add them to homemade muesli or soak them in water, then cook them in sweet and savory dishes like fruit compotes, applesauce or casseroles. Dried apples are available commercially, but it is easy to dry your own when there is a glut, and you can choose your favorite varieties. Russets are particularly delicious when dried.

Preparing

Most apples can be eaten with the skin on. To peel, use a vegetable peeler or small, sharp knife, either in a spiral following the circumference of the apple, or peeling downward in strips from stem to calyx. Peeled apples turn brown very quickly; brush them with lemon juice or drop them into water acidulated with lemon juice or cider vinegar immediately.

Cooking

Some apples are suitable only for eating raw, but most can be cooked in such classic sweet dishes as apple pies, crumbles and tarts, baked apples and strudel. Sweet apples combine well with other fruits, like blackberries, quinces and lemon, and dried fruits like raisins or cranberries. Aromatic spices like cinnamon, nutmeg and cloves highlight their flavor. Their high pectin content will help other fruit jellies and jams to set, or they can be made into apple jelly, apple cheese and chutney.

Tart apples make excellent accompaniments for game birds, sausages and rich meats like pork, duck and goose. They go well with red cabbage and are a vital ingredient in Waldorf salad.

To bake apples, core them with an apple corer and score around the circumference to prevent the skin from bursting. Stuff with dried fruit, nuts, butter and sugar and bake in a preheated oven at 350°F until soft.

To cook sliced apples and rings, sauté in butter and sugar to help them keep their shape. To stew, cook in the minimum amount of water or with butter and seasonings.

Making applesauce

1 Peel, core and thickly slice the apples, immediately dropping the pieces into a bowl of cold water acidulated with lemon juice or cider vinegar.

2 Barely cover the bottom of a saucepan with cold water. Add the apple pieces and cook to a purée, adding sugar to taste toward the end.

3 If you are using firmer dessert apples, which will not disintegrate to a purée, cook until very tender, then rub through a coarse strainer.

CRAB APPLES AND CIDER APPLES

Crab apples have grown wild for thousands of years and were eaten in prehistoric times. The fruits are smaller and often more colorful than cultivated varieties. Nowadays crab apples are often grown for their ornamental qualities. The fruits can be vivid yellow, green, orange or bright red.

Crab apples are seldom worth eating raw (and may be completely inedible), although some are perfectly palatable for those without too sweet a tooth. You may find larger self-seeded wild apples, which have grown from the seeds of cultivated apples that have become wild; these can be eaten.

Thanks to their high pectin content, all crab apples make wonderful jellies, either on their own or mixed with other wild fruits, such as hawthorn berries.

Cider apples are closer to eating apples than crab apples, but usually have a bitter or sour flavor due to their high tannin content. There

Below: Crab apples are almost always too sour to eat raw.

are hundreds of different varieties with wonderful names like Strawberry Norma and Foxwhelp, and each local grower will insist that his is the best. Some, like Tom Putt, are sweet enough to eat; these are used to make sweet cider.

Apple Drinks

Apple juice and sweet apple cider, hard (alcoholic) cider and apple brandies, such as Calvados, are the main drinks made from apples. Apple juice is made by crushing dessert apples; the best is pressed from a single variety, such as Cox's Orange Pippin or Russet, but most commercial apple juices are made from a mixture of varieties or, worse, from concentrate.

Cider may have been brought to Britain by the Phoenicians or the Celts; it has certainly been around for thousands of years. It is a fermented drink made from the juice of cider apples and, depending on the variety of fruit and

Left: Cider—the best is still made by artisan producers.

Right and far right: Calvados and applejack are both types of apple brandy.

pressing technique, can range from sweet and bubbly to cloudy and flat. The best ciders are still made by small producers using artisanal methods; some of these ciders can be very strong. The strongest and crudest cider is scrumpy. It is made from the apples of the poorest quality, but can certainly pack a punch!

Apple brandy is made from fermented and distilled apple juice. The best of all is Calvados, the famous apple brandy from Normandy, which is double-distilled and aged in oak. Calvados may only be produced within a defined area; other apple brandies must be labeled *eau-de-vie de cidre* or simply "apple brandy" ("applejack" in North America).

Fermented apple juice can also be made into cider vinegar, which has a strong apple taste and is excellent for making fruit chutneys or adding extra flavor to casseroles containing apples.

PEARS

There are almost as many varieties of pears as there are apples, but only a dozen or so are available commercially. Pears are related to apples, but are more fragile and are more often eaten raw than cooked. They have fine, white, granular flesh and a central core containing the seeds. Most pears have the familiar shape, wider at the bottom than the top, but some are apple-shaped, while "calabash" pears have an elongated neck, like a gourd. Pears are less vividly colored than apples, generally varying from bronze to gold, green or yellow, but there are some beautiful red varieties, too.

Right: Anjou pears are sweet, juicy and aromatic.

History

Wild pears are native to Europe and Asia, where they have grown since prehistoric times. They were cultivated by the ancient Phoenicians and the Romans, and they became a royal delicacy for the ancient Persian kings. Their popularity spread so fast that in medieval Italy over 200 varieties of

Below: Beurré Bosc

pear were cultivated. By the seventeenth century, the French were growing 300 different varieties, inspired by Louis XIV's passion for the fruit. There are now said to be more than 5,000 named varieties throughout the world.

Varieties

Cooking pears (which cannot be eaten raw) do exist, but almost all the pears available in stores are dessert fruit, which can also be cooked. Pears are seasonal, so only a few varieties are available at any one time.

Anjou These large pears have greenish yellow skin with brown speckles or russeting. The flesh is juicy and sweet. Suitable for eating and cooking.

Bartlett These irregularly shaped pears are generally swollen on one side of the stem. The speckled skin is golden yellow with russet patches and sometimes a red tinge. The delicious tender flesh is creamy white and very juicy, and the flavor is sweet and slightly musky. Unfortunately, these superb pears do not keep well. Bartletts are suitable for cooking and eating. (Bartlett is an old English pear also known as Williams Bon Chrétien.)

Beth This modern pear variety resembles the Bartlett in flavor and texture but has the added advantage of keeping longer.

Beurré Bosc and **Beurré Hardi** These elongated pears have an uneven green-gold skin, which becomes yellow and completely russeted as the fruit ripens. The creamy white flesh is firm and juicy with a buttery texture (hence the name, which means

"buttered"), and the flavor is deliciously sweet and aromatic, with some acidity. Both varieties are excellent for eating and cooking.

Beurré Superfin These medium-to-large pears are round-conical in shape. Their uneven, almost knobbly skin is pale greenish yellow, which changes to yellow with bronze russeting as they ripen. The creamy-white flesh is firm and buttery and extremely juicy, with a sweet flavor and a hint of acidity. A truly delicious pear.

Comice This large, roundish pear (also know as Doyenné du Comice) is one of the finest of all, with creamy white, melting, very juicy flesh and a sweet, aromatic flavor. The thick, yellowish green skin is covered with speckles and patches of russeting. Comice are best eaten raw, and are delicious with Brie or Camembert.

Conference First cultivated in Berkshire in 1770, these long, conical pears have remained a favorite in Britain, largely because they keep so well. The yellowish green skin with extensive

Below: Conference are one of the best-loved English pears.

russeting turns yellower when the pears are mature. The granular flesh is tender, sweet and juicy. Excellent for eating and cooking.

Forelle A beautiful golden pear with a dark red flush on one side. The grainy flesh is crisp, with a fresh flavor that goes well with cheese, but is at its best when cooked.

Josephine de Malines A French pear, first raised in 1830. The medium-size fruits are round-conical in shape, with yellowish green skin flushed with red and some russeting, The tender flesh can be white or pinkish and is very juicy, with an aromatic flavor. It has good keeping qualities.

Merton Pride An exceptionally sweet and juicy pear with a superb flavor. The conical fruits have yellow skin with brown freckles.

Onward A cross between Laxton's Superb and Comice, these roundish pears are best peeled before eating, as they have ribbed skin. The yellowish green skin is flushed with red and mottled with pale russeting. The creamy white flesh is exceptionally good—soft, melting, juicy and very sweet.

Above: Doyenné du Comice, also known simply as Comice, are very juicy and aromatic.

Right: Forelle are ideal pears to use for cooking.

Packham's Triumph The first successful Australian pear was produced by Charles Packham in 1896 and remains a favorite. A largish dessert pear, it has a smooth, green, lightly russeted skin, which changes to yellow as it ripens. The soft white flesh is succulent and sweet, with a touch of acidity.

Passacrena Very plump, roundish pears with russeted greenish yellow skin. The flesh can sometimes be rather gritty, but is very juicy and sweet.

Red Bartlett These pears have shiny, speckled skins, at first green with a red blush, turning to yellow flushed with red. The flesh is sweet and juicy.

Rocha A Portuguese pear with greenish yellow skin with russet spotting and brown markings at the stem end. The firm white flesh has a sugary flavor and unlike many other pears, which pass their prime almost as soon as they reach it, the fruit remains in excellent condition for several days.

Winter Nelis This roundish medium-size pear has thick but tender greenish-yellow skin with cinnamon brown russeting and sometimes a pink flush. The creamy white flesh is soft and very juicy, and the flavor is sweet. These pears can be cooked or eaten raw.

Left: Packham's Triumph

Nutrition

Pears contain a small amount of vitamins A and C and some potassium and riboflavin. They provide about 60 calories per 3¾ ounce.

Pears should always be bought when they are in perfect condition, as they deteriorate quickly. Once past their best, they become mealy or soft and unpleasant. Test for ripeness by pressing the stem end between your forefinger and thumb; it should give a little, but the pear should still be quite firm. Once ripe, pears should be eaten within a couple of days, or they will become overripe. Keep ripe fruit in the bottom of the refrigerator.

Above: Suitable for both eating and cooking, Bartletts have delicious creamy white flesh. They don't keep well, so use them as soon as they are ripe.

Below: Juicy, with a red blush, Red Bartletts make excellent eating.

Above left: The firm-fleshed Rocha will remain in good condition for several days in your fruit bowl.

Dried pears Although dried pears are most often used in winter fruit compotes and savory casseroles, they have a delicate flavor and are delicious eaten raw. They are readily available in stores, but it is easy to prepare your own.

Canned pears Pears are among the most successful of all canned fruit and can be used to make almost any dessert that calls for cooked pears. They are often canned in heavy syrup, but are now available in the healthier alternative of apple juice. Purée drained canned pears, flavor them with pear liqueur, lemon or preserved ginger syrup and freeze for a quick and easy sorbet.

Right: Dried pears

Preparing and Cooking

Most pears are eaten raw, by themselves or with a robust cheese, such as Gorgonzola, Parmesan, Stilton or Roquefort. They also make a good addition to winter salads. Whether or not to peel pears before eating raw is a matter of preference, but they should always be peeled before cooking. Pears discolor quickly once they are peeled, so immediately rub the cut surface with a little lemon juice or place in a bowl of acidulated water. For whole poached pears, simply peel,

leaving on the stem. Use an apple corer to core the pears if you want to stuff them with nuts or dried fruit. Poach in port or red wine spiced with cinnamon, cloves and thinly pared lemon rind, or in a vanilla-flavored syrup. For sautéed or grilled pears, peel and quarter or halve the fruit and scoop out the cores with a melon baller.

Dessert or cooking pears can also be cooked in compotes, tarts, terrines, trifles and the famous Poires Belle Hélène (poached pears with vanilla ice cream and hot chocolate sauce). They make marvelous fritters and go very well with ingredients such as nuts and spices, port and marsala. Cooked pears are also excellent in savory dishes—with game and duck, for example—either made into chutney or braised with game birds or venison. They can be preserved with sugar and vinegar, or pickled with mustard seeds and horseradish. If you are cooking dessert pears, use them while they are still slightly underripe.

Pears can also be dried, canned, crystallized and distilled into spirits like *eau-de-vie de poires* and Poire William. The bottle in which this liqueur is sold sometimes contains a whole pear, an apparent illusion, as the neck is too narrow to allow the pear to pass. The effect is achieved by placing the bottle necks over the infant fruits on the tree so that each pear grows inside a bottle. When it has ripened, the bottle is topped up with the pear-flavored liqueur.

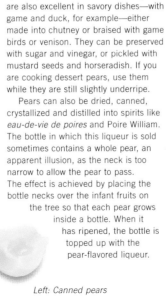

Left: Canned pears

Drying pears

1 Peel the pears and cut them in half lengthwise.

2 Scoop out the cores with a small melon baller, removing all the fibrous part of the fruit.

3 Brush them with lemon juice to prevent discoloration. Spread out in a single layer on a rack over a baking sheet and dry in an oven set to 150°F for several hours, until dried.

ASIAN OR NASHI PEARS

There are many varieties of Asian pear, but their characteristics are very similar. Round rather than pear-shaped, the fruits have a golden brown–russet skin and very crisp, white, juicy flesh. The crunchy texture resembles that of an apple but is more granular. It would be a shame to spoil the crisp texture by cooking. Asian pears are best eaten straight from the refrigerator, to be enjoyed as a "drink on a stalk." They also make excellent additions to fruit salads or savory winter salads.

HOSUI PEARS

These pears have much the same crunch and juiciness of Tientsin pears but look much more like apples, with greeny brown mottled flesh that tastes like a cross between an apple and an unripe pear.

PERRY PEARS

With the demise of the most famous of the sparkling alcoholic pear drinks, perry pears have largely fallen into disfavor. A few small producers still press perry pears into juice, wine or "champagne" perry, but although there

Left: Tientsin pears are best eaten chilled.

are still about 300 known varieties, you will never find these fruit in stores. Perry pears are smaller than their dessert counterparts. Although they look delicious, they contain large quantities of tannin and taste bitter and astringent, whether they are eaten raw or cooked.

TIENTSIN PEARS

These Asian pears from China and Korea are very similar to Asian Nashi pears in taste and texture. They are available when Asian pears are out of season. They look rather like elongated apples, tapering gently at both ends, The skin is pale yellow, slightly speckled with light brown. The pure white flesh is exceptionally juicy and crunchy—perfect for a hot day. Tientsin pears are best eaten chilled to appreciate their refreshing quality, and make the perfect healthy alternative to popsicles.

Left: Asian pears are round rather than pear-shaped, and their crunchy texture resembles that of apples too.

QUINCES

These highly aromatic fruits are known as "apple" or "pear" quinces, according to their shape. Unripe fruits have a downy skin, while ripe quinces have the smooth texture of a pear. Raw quinces are inedible, but they make excellent natural air fresheners—a quince kept in the glove compartment will shrivel but not rot, and will fill your car with the most delicious aroma for up to six months.

History

Quinces originated in Turkestan and Persia. It is said that they were the mythical golden apples of the Hesperides and that the golden apple Paris gave to Aphrodite, the goddess of love, was in fact a quince. To the

Above: Quinces may have been the mythical golden apples of the Hesperides.

ancient Greeks and Romans, quinces were a symbol of happiness, love and fruitfulness. The fruits were widely grown in Britain from the sixteenth to the eighteenth century, but their popularity has declined. In Spain, however, they are still highly prized and are used to make a thick fruit paste called *membrillo*.

Choosing and Storing

Quinces are available in stores in October and November. The skin of ripe quinces should be uniformly golden yellow; unripe fruit may still have patches of down, which can be rubbed off. Quinces keep well—the best way to store them is in a bowl in your kitchen or living room. They will fill the room with their delicious scent.

Preparing and Cooking

Quinces are always cooked. They are prepared in much the same way as pears. For jellies and fruit pastes, the skin is left on, as it contributes valuable pectin, as do the seeds (the word "marmalade" comes from the Portuguese word for quince, *marmelo*). Quince jelly can be spread on bread or served with pork and game. Quinces can be baked whole like apples or pears, stuffed with a rich mixture of butter, sugar and cream. One or two quinces also make a good addition to

---

Quince jelly
Makes about 4½ pounds

1 Roughly chop 2¼ pounds quinces. Put in a large, heavy pan with 8 cups of water.

2 Bring to a boil, then simmer until the quinces are very tender.

3 Pour into a jelly bag set over a bowl; let the juice run through, but do not squeeze the bag or the finished jelly will be cloudy.

4 Measure the strained juice and pour into a large, heavy pan. Add 2½ cups preserving sugar for each 2½ cups of the juice. Bring to a boil, stirring until the sugar has dissolved completely. Boil rapidly until the setting point is reached.

5 Skim the jelly and pour into sterilized jars. Cover the jars while the jelly is still hot, then label once the jars are cool enough to handle.

an apple pie. Peel and slice the quinces (this will be easier to achieve if you parboil them for 10 minutes), then toss them with the apple slices, sugar and cinnamon before layering them in the pie.

In Spain, quince pulp is boiled with sugar to make the fruit paste *membrillo*, which is then cooled, cut into squares and served with soft cheeses or as a sweet. The French equivalent is known as *cotignac*, while quince cheese is similar, but softer and more spreadable.

Quinces marry well with almost all meats, from poultry to beef and game, and also make a wonderful scented addition to spirits such as vodka, grappa or eau-de-vie.

Japonica Quince

As the name suggests, this cultivated quince came originally from Japan. The hard yellowish fruits are virtually inedible raw, but can be cooked and used like quinces. Their perfume is less intense, but they are still sufficiently aromatic to make an excellent addition to pies and tarts. They can also be made into both quince jelly and quince cheese.

Above: Japonica quinces are not edible raw, but they make a wonderful jelly.

MEDLARS

Medlar trees resemble pear trees, but the fruits are quite different. They look rather like large, golden brown rose hips with a russeted skin and a distinctive open five-pointed calyx end. They are eaten when overripe, almost rotten. The process is known as "bletting" and is traditionally achieved by spreading out unripe fruit on straw and leaving it to decay for several weeks, by which time the flesh can be spooned out. To speed up the bletting process, whole unripe medlars can be frozen to break up the cell structure, then left to decay at room temperature. The flesh has a dry, sticky texture. It tastes a little like the flesh of dried dates, but is tarter. Medlars are not to everyone's taste; the nineteenth-century horticulturalist George Bunyard described several different varieties of medlar as "all of equal unpleasantness."

Left: Medlars are seldom sold in stores these days, nor eaten much either.

History

Medlars originated in the Transcaucasus, but are found growing wild in Asia Minor and southern Europe. They were cultivated by the Assyrians, who introduced them to ancient Greece. In Victorian times in England, they were often enjoyed at the end of a meal with the port, but they are seldom eaten today.

Choosing and Storing

Medlars are not available in stores in the United States, but are sometimes cultivated or found growing wild. They are extremely hard and, if left on the tree, are unlikely to ripen sufficiently to be eaten. They are therefore picked in their unripe state and left to "blet." A bletted medlar will be soft and yielding to the touch.

Preparing and Cooking

To eat bletted medlars raw, peel back the skin from the five points of the calyx and suck out the flesh, leaving the five seeds behind, or scrape it out with a spoon. Unripe medlars can be used with bletted fruits to make medlar jelly, or baked to make a thick sauce that goes well with rich meats. Medlar jelly is made in the same way as quince jelly.

APPLE, PEAR AND QUINCE RECIPES

*Apples, pears and quinces are
wonderfully versatile. Dutch Apple Cake and
Chocolate Pear and Pecan Pie are just two of the
tempting treats in store, while Hot Quince Soufflés
and Iced Pear Terrine make memorable desserts.*

ICED PEAR TERRINE WITH CALVADOS AND CHOCOLATE SAUCE

THIS TERRINE, BASED ON A CLASSIC FRENCH DESSERT, MAKES A REFRESHING AND IMPRESSIVE END TO ANY MEAL. FOR FLAVOR, BE SURE THE PEARS ARE RIPE AND JUICY.

SERVES EIGHT

INGREDIENTS
   3–3½ pounds ripe Bartlett pears
   juice of 1 lemon
   ½ cup sugar
   10 whole cloves
   6 tablespoons water
   julienne strips of orange zest,
      to decorate
For the sauce
   7 ounces semisweet chocolate
   ¼ cup hot strong black coffee
   1 cup heavy cream
   2 tablespoons Calvados or brandy

1 Peel, core and slice the pears. Place them in a saucepan with the lemon juice, sugar, cloves and water. Cover and simmer for 10 minutes. Remove the cloves. Allow the pears to cool.

2 Process the pears with their juice in a food processor or blender until smooth. Pour the purée into a freezerproof bowl, cover and freeze until firm.

3 Meanwhile, line a 9 x 5 x 3 inch loaf pan with plastic wrap. Allow the wrap to overhang the sides of the pan. Remove the frozen pear purée from the freezer and spoon it into a food processor or blender. Process until smooth. Pour into the prepared pan, cover and freeze until firm.

4 Make the sauce. Break the chocolate into a large heatproof bowl. Place the bowl over a saucepan of hot water. When the chocolate has melted, stir in the coffee until smooth. Gradually stir in the cream and then the Calvados or brandy. Set the sauce aside.

5 About 20 minutes before serving, remove the pan from the freezer. Invert the terrine onto a plate, lift off the plastic wrap and place the terrine in the refrigerator to soften slightly. Warm the sauce over hot water. Place a slice of terrine on each dessert plate and spoon some of the sauce over. Decorate with julienne strips of orange zest and serve at once.

QUINCE AND GINGER MOUSSE WITH ALMOND COOKIES

QUINCES AND GINGER ARE PERFECTLY MATCHED FLAVOR PARTNERS. AS WITH ANY QUINCE RECIPE, YOU CAN SUBSTITUTE PEARS OR APPLES WITH EQUALLY DELICIOUS RESULTS.

SERVES FOUR

INGREDIENTS
  1 pound quinces
  ⅓ cup sugar
  grated zest of ½ lemon
  6 tablespoons water
  2 pieces preserved ginger in syrup,
    finely chopped, plus 1 tablespoon
    syrup from the jar
  1 tablespoon powdered gelatin
  ⅔ cup heavy cream
  2 egg whites
  mint leaves and blackberries dusted
    with sugar, to decorate
For the cookies
  4 tablespoons butter
  2 tablespoons sugar
  ½ cup all-purpose flour
  ½ cup ground almonds
  a few drops of pure almond extract

1 Grease four ⅔-cup ramekins and line the bottoms with baking parchment. Peel the quinces, core and put in a saucepan with the sugar, lemon zest and ¼ cup of the water. Bring to a boil, lower the heat, cover and simmer for 10 minutes, or until softened. Remove the lid; continue cooking until the liquid has almost evaporated.

2 Cool the quince mixture slightly, then purée in a food processor or blender. Press the purée through a strainer into a large bowl, then stir in the ginger and ginger syrup and set aside.

3 Pour the remaining 2 tablespoons water into a small heatproof bowl and sprinkle the gelatin on top. Let soak for 5 minutes. Stand the bowl in a pan of hot water, stirring occasionally, until the gelatin has dissolved.

4 Lightly whip the cream. Stir the gelatin into the quince purée, then fold in the whipped cream. In a greasefree bowl, beat the egg whites to stiff peaks; fold into the quince mixture. Divide among the prepared ramekins, level the tops and chill until firm. Preheat the oven to 375°F.

5 Make the cookies. Line a baking sheet with baking parchment. Cream the butter and sugar until smooth. Add the flour, almonds and almond extract and mix to a dough with a knife. Roll out thinly on a lightly floured surface; cut into rounds with a 3-inch cutter. Transfer to the baking sheet. Chill for 10 minutes, then bake for 10–12 minutes.

6 Cool slightly on the paper, then lift onto a wire rack to cool. Run a knife around each mousse; turn out onto dessert plates. Discard the paper. Decorate and serve with cookies.

SPICED APPLE CRUMBLE

ANY FRUIT CAN BE USED IN THIS POPULAR DESSERT, BUT YOU CAN'T BEAT THE COMBINATION OF BLACKBERRY AND APPLE. HAZELNUTS AND CARDAMOM SEEDS GIVE THE TOPPING EXTRA FLAVOR.

SERVES FOUR TO SIX

INGREDIENTS
    butter, for greasing
    1 pound cooking apples
    1 cup blackberries
    grated zest and juice of 1 orange
    ⅓ cup light brown sugar
    custard, to serve
For the topping
    1½ cups all-purpose flour
    ⅓ cup butter
    ⅓ cup sugar
    ¼ cup chopped hazelnuts
    ½ teaspoon crushed cardamom seeds

VARIATIONS
This wonderfully good-natured dessert can be made with all sorts of fruit. Try plums, apricots, peaches or pears, alone or in combination with apples. Rhubarb makes a delectable crumble, especially when mixed with bananas.

1 Preheat the oven to 400°F. Generously butter a 5-cup baking dish. Peel and core the apples, then slice them into the prepared baking dish. Level the surface, then scatter the blackberries over. Sprinkle the orange zest and light brown sugar evenly over the top, then pour the orange juice over. Set the fruit mixture aside while you make the crumble topping.

2 Make the topping. Sift the flour into a bowl and rub in the butter until the mixture resembles coarse bread crumbs. Stir in the sugar, hazelnuts and cardamom seeds. Scatter the topping over the top of the fruit.

3 Press the topping around the edges of the dish to seal in the juices. Bake for 30–35 minutes, or until the crumble is golden. Serve hot, with custard.

BAKED STUFFED APPLES

THIS TRADITIONAL APPLE DESSERT IS EXCEPTIONALLY SIMPLE AND SPEEDY. BAKE THE APPLES IN THE OVEN ON THE SHELF UNDER THE SUNDAY ROAST FOR A DELICIOUS END TO THE MEAL.

SERVES FOUR

INGREDIENTS
    4 large cooking apples
    ½ cup light brown sugar
    6 tablespoons butter, softened
    grated zest and juice of ½ orange
    ¼ teaspoon ground cinnamon
    2 tablespoons crushed ratafia biscuits
      (almond-paste cookies) or other
      dessert cookies
    ½ cup pecans, chopped
    ½ cup deluxe mixed glacé fruit, chopped

COOK'S TIP
Use a little butter or oil to grease the baking dish, if you like, or pour a small amount of water around the stuffed apples to keep them from sticking to the dish during baking.

1 Preheat the oven to 350°F. Wash and dry the apples. Remove the cores with an apple corer, then carefully enlarge each core cavity to twice its size by shaving off more flesh with the corer. Score each apple around its equator, using a sharp knife. Stand the apples in a baking dish.

2 Mix the brown sugar, butter, orange zest and juice, cinnamon and ratafia crumbs. Beat well, then stir in the nuts and glacé fruit. Divide the filling among the apples, piling it high. Shield the filling in each apple with a small piece of foil. Bake for 45–60 minutes, until each apple is tender.

APPLE CREPES WITH BUTTERSCOTCH SAUCE

THESE WONDERFUL DESSERT CREPES ARE FLAVORED WITH SWEET CIDER, FILLED WITH CARAMELIZED APPLES AND DRIZZLED WITH A RICH, SMOOTH BUTTERSCOTCH SAUCE.

3 Make the filling. Core the apples and cut them into thick slices. Heat 1 tablespoon of the butter in a large frying pan. Add the apples to the pan. Cook until golden on both sides, then transfer the slices to a bowl with a slotted spoon and set them aside.

4 Add the rest of the butter to the pan. As soon as it has melted, add the brown sugar. When the sugar has dissolved and the mixture is bubbling, stir in the cream. Continue cooking until it forms a smooth sauce.

5 Fold each pancake in half, then fold in half again to form a cone; fill each with some of the fried apples. Place two filled pancakes on each dessert plate, drizzle some of the butterscotch sauce over and serve at once.

SERVES FOUR

INGREDIENTS
    1 cup all-purpose flour
    pinch of salt
    2 eggs
    ¾ cup whole milk or half-and-half
    ½ cup apple cider
    butter, for greasing pan
For the filling and sauce
    4 crisp eating apples
    7 tablespoons butter
    1⅓ cups light brown sugar
    ⅔ cup heavy cream

1 Make the crêpe batter. Sift the flour and salt into a large bowl. Add the eggs and milk and beat until smooth. Stir in the cider; set aside for 30 minutes.

2 Heat a small, heavy nonstick frying pan. Add a pat of butter and ladle in enough batter to coat the pan thinly. Cook until the crêpe is golden underneath, then flip it over and cook the other side until golden. Slide the crêpe onto a plate. Repeat with the remaining mixture to make seven more.

VARIATIONS
You could just as easily use plums, pears, strawberries or bananas to fill the crêpes. If you like, add a touch of Grand Marnier to the apples toward the end of cooking.

PEAR AND CINNAMON FRITTERS

IF YOU DON'T LIKE DEEP-FRYING AS A RULE, MAKE AN EXCEPTION FOR THIS DISH. FRITTERS ARE IRRESISTIBLE, AND A WONDERFUL WAY OF PERSUADING CHILDREN TO EAT MORE FRUIT.

SERVES FOUR

INGREDIENTS
    3 ripe, firm pears
    2 tablespoons sugar
    2 tablespoons kirsch
    peanut oil, for frying
    1 cup finely crushed amaretti cookies
For the batter
    ¾ cup all-purpose flour
    ¼ teaspoon salt
    ¼ teaspoon ground cinnamon
    ¼ cup milk
    2 eggs, separated
    3 tablespoons water
To serve
    2 tablespoons sugar
    ¼ teaspoon ground cinnamon
    clotted cream or crème fraîche

1 Peel the pears, cut them into quarters and remove the cores. Toss the wedges in the sugar and kirsch. Set aside for 15 minutes.

2 Make the batter. Sift the flour, salt and cinnamon into a large bowl. Beat in the milk, egg yolks and water until smooth. Set aside for 10 minutes.

3 Beat the egg whites in a greasefree bowl until they form stiff peaks; lightly fold them into the batter. Preheat the oven to 300°F.

4 Pour oil into a deep, heavy saucepan to a depth of 3 inches. Heat to 360°F, or until a bread cube added to the oil browns in 45 seconds.

5 Toss a pear wedge in the amaretti crumbs, then spear it on a fork and dip it into the batter until evenly coated. Lower it gently into the hot oil and use a knife to push it off the fork. Add more wedges in the same way, but do not overcrowd the pan. Cook the fritters for 3–4 minutes, or until golden. Drain on paper towels. Keep hot in the oven while cooking successive batches.

6 Mix the sugar and cinnamon and sprinkle some over the fritters. Sprinkle a little cinnamon sugar over the cream or crème fraîche; serve with the hot fritters.

VARIATIONS
Also try apples, apricots and bananas.

POACHED PEARS IN PORT SYRUP

THE PERFECT CHOICE FOR AUTUMN ENTERTAINING, THIS SIMPLE DESSERT HAS A BEAUTIFUL, RICH COLOR AND FANTASTIC FLAVOR THANKS TO THE PORT AND LEMON.

SERVES FOUR

INGREDIENTS
  2 ripe, firm pears, such as Bartlett or
    Comice
  pared zest of 1 lemon
  ¾ cup ruby port
  ¼ cup sugar
  1 cinnamon stick
  ¼ cup cold water
  whipped cream, to serve
To decorate
  2 tablespoons sliced hazelnuts, toasted
  fresh mint, pear or rose leaves

COOK'S TIP
Choose pears of similar size, with the stems intact, for the most attractive effect when fanned on the plate.

1 Peel the pears, cut them in half and remove the cores. Place the lemon zest, port, sugar, cinnamon stick and water in a shallow pan. Bring to a boil over low heat. Add the pears, lower the heat, cover and poach for 5 minutes. Let the pears cool in the syrup.

2 When the pears are cool, transfer them to a bowl with a slotted spoon. Return the syrup to the heat. Boil rapidly until it has reduced enough to lightly coat the back of a spoon. Remove the cinnamon stick and lemon zest and let the syrup cool.

3 To serve, place each pear in turn on a board, cut side down. Keeping it intact at the stem end, slice it lengthwise, then, using a metal spatula, carefully lift it off and place on a dessert plate. Press gently so that the pear fans out. When all the pears have been fanned, spoon the port syrup over them. Top each portion with a few hazelnuts and decorate with fresh mint, pear or rose leaves. Serve with whipped cream.

APPLE CHARLOTTES

THESE TEMPTING LITTLE FRUIT CHARLOTTES ARE A WONDERFUL WAY TO USE WINDFALLS.

SERVES FOUR

INGREDIENTS

12 tablespoons (1½ sticks) butter
1 pound cooking apples
8 ounces eating apples
¼ cup water
scant ⅔ cup sugar
2 egg yolks
pinch of grated nutmeg
9 thin slices white bread,
  crusts removed
whipped cream or custard, to serve

COOK'S TIP
A mixture of cooking and eating apples gives the best flavor, but there's no reason why you can't use only cooking apples; just sweeten the pulp to taste.

1 Preheat the oven to 375°F. Put a pat of the butter in a saucepan. Peel and core the apples, dice them finely and put them in the pan with the water. Cover and cook for 10 minutes, or until the cooking apples have pulped down. Stir in ½ cup of the sugar. Boil, uncovered, until any liquid has evaporated and what remains is a thick pulp. Remove from the heat, beat in the egg yolks and nutmeg and set aside.

2 Melt the remaining butter in a separate saucepan over low heat until the white milk solids start to separate from the clear yellow liquid. Remove from the heat. Let stand for a few minutes, then strain the clear, clarified butter through a cheesecloth-lined sieve.

3 Brush four ⅔-cup individual charlotte or pudding molds with a little of the clarified butter; sprinkle with the remaining sugar. Cut the bread slices into 1-inch-wide strips. Dip the strips into the remaining clarified butter; use to line the molds. Overlap the strips on the bottom to give the effect of a swirl and let the excess bread overhang the tops of the molds.

4 Fill each lined mold with apple pulp. Fold the excess bread over the top of each mold to make a lid; press down lightly. Bake for 45–50 minutes, or until golden. Run a knife between each charlotte and its mold, then turn out onto dessert plates. Serve with whipped cream or custard.

HOT QUINCE SOUFFLES

THESE DELICIOUS FRUITS ARE BEGINNING TO BE MORE WIDELY AVAILABLE IN SHOPS AND MARKETS.
YOU CAN USE PEARS INSTEAD, BUT THE FLAVOR WILL NOT BE AS INTENSE.

SERVES SIX

INGREDIENTS
    2 quinces, peeled and cored
    ¼ cup water
    ½ cup granulated sugar,
        plus extra for sprinkling
    5 egg whites
    melted butter, for greasing
    confectioners' sugar, for dusting
For the pastry cream
    1 cup milk
    1 vanilla bean
    3 egg yolks
    ⅓ cup granulated sugar
    ¼ cup all-purpose flour
    1 tablespoon Poire William liqueur

1 Cut the quinces into cubes. Place in a saucepan with the water. Stir in half the granulated sugar. Bring to a boil, lower the heat, cover and simmer for 10 minutes, or until tender. Remove the lid; boil until most of the liquid has evaporated.

2 Cool slightly, then purée the fruit in a blender or food processor. Press through a strainer into a bowl; set aside.

3 Make the pastry cream. Pour the milk into a small saucepan. Add the vanilla bean and bring to a boil over low heat. Meanwhile, beat the egg yolks, granulated sugar and flour in a bowl until smooth.

4 Gradually strain the hot milk onto the yolks, whisking frequently until the mixture is smooth.

5 Discard the vanilla bean. Return the mixture to the clean pan and heat gently, stirring, until thickened. Cook, for another 2 minutes, whisking constantly, to ensure that the sauce is smooth and the flour is cooked.

6 Remove the pan from the heat and stir in the quince purée and liqueur. Cover the surface of the pastry cream with plastic wrap to prevent it from forming a skin. Allow to cool slightly while you prepare the ramekins.

7 Preheat the oven to 425°F. Place a baking sheet in the oven to heat up. Butter six ⅔-cup ramekins and sprinkle the inside of each with granulated sugar. In a greasefree bowl, beat the egg whites to stiff peaks. Gradually beat in the remaining granulated sugar, then fold the egg whites into the pastry cream.

8 Divide the mixture among the prepared ramekins and level the surface of each. Carefully run a sharp knife between the side of each ramekin and the mixture, then place the ramekins on the hot baking sheet and bake for 8–10 minutes, until the tops of the soufflés are well risen and golden. Generously dust the tops with confectioners' sugar and serve the soufflés at once.

COOK'S TIP
Poire William is a clear, colorless pear eau-de-vie, which sometimes is sold with a ripe pear in the bottle. Kirsch, made from cherries, also works well in this recipe to complement the flavor of the quinces.

TARTE TATIN

IF YOU USE FROZEN PUFF PASTRY, THIS TASTY TART CAN BE MADE VERY EASILY.

SERVES SIX TO EIGHT

INGREDIENTS
   3 crisp eating apples
   juice of ½ lemon
   4 tablespoons butter, softened
   ⅓ cup sugar
   9 ounces frozen puff pastry, thawed
   whipped cream or créme fraîche,
     to serve

1 Preheat the oven to 425°F. Cut the apples into quarters and remove the cores. Toss the apple quarters in the lemon juice to prevent them from discoloring.

2 Spread the butter over the bottom of a heavy 8-inch omelet pan that can safely be used in the oven. Sprinkle the sugar over the bottom of the pan and add the apple wedges, rounded side down.

3 Cook over medium heat for 15–20 minutes, or until the sugar and butter have melted and the apples are golden. Cut the pastry into a 10-inch round and place on top of the apples; tuck the edges in with a knife. Place the pan in the oven and bake for 15–20 minutes, or until the pastry is golden. Carefully invert the tart onto a plate. Cool slightly before serving with cream.

COOK'S TIP
To turn out the Tarte Tatin, place the serving plate upside down on top of it, then, protecting your arms with oven mitts, hold both pan and plate firmly together and carefully turn them over. Lift off the pan.

FILO-TOPPED APPLE PIE

WITH ITS CRUNCHY FILO PASTRY TOPPING AND MINIMAL BUTTER, THIS MAKES A LIGHT DESSERT, A GOOD CHOICE FOR AN APPLE PIE ADDICT WATCHING HIS OR HER FAT INTAKE.

SERVES SIX

INGREDIENTS

2 pounds cooking apples
⅓ cup granulated sugar
grated zest of 1 lemon
1 tablespoon lemon juice
½ cup golden raisins
½ teaspoon ground cinnamon
4 large sheets filo pastry, thawed
  if frozen
2 tablespoons butter, melted
confectioners' sugar, for dusting

VARIATION
To make phyllo "Christmas crackers," cut the buttered filo into 8-inch-wide strips. Spoon a little of the filling along one end of each strip, leaving the sides clear. Roll up and twist the ends. Brush with more butter; bake for 20 minutes.

1 Peel, core and dice the apples. Place them in a saucepan with the granulated sugar and lemon zest. Drizzle the lemon juice over. Bring to a boil, stir well, then cook for 5 minutes, or until the apples have softened. Stir in the golden raisins and cinnamon. Spoon the mixture into a 5-cup pie dish and level the top. Let cool.

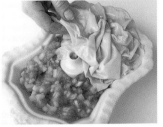

2 Preheat the oven to 350°F. Place a pie funnel in the center of the fruit. Brush each sheet of filo with melted butter. Crunch up loosely and place on the fruit to cover it completely.

3 Bake for 20–30 minutes, until the filo is golden. Dust with confectioners' sugar before serving with custard or cream.

CHOCOLATE, PEAR AND PECAN PIE

THE RICHNESS OF DEEP, DARK CHOCOLATE COUPLED WITH JUICY PEARS GIVES A CLASSIC PECAN PIE AN OUT-OF-THE-ORDINARY TWIST. THE RESULT IS UTTERLY DELICIOUS—AND UTTERLY IRRESISTIBLE.

SERVES EIGHT TO TEN

INGREDIENTS

    11 ounces shortcrust pastry, thawed
      if frozen
    3 small pears
    scant ¾ cup sugar
    ⅔ cup water
    pared zest of 1 lemon
    2 ounces good-quality semisweet
      chocolate
    4 tablespoons unsalted butter, diced
    ¾ cup golden syrup or light corn syrup
    3 eggs, beaten
    1 teaspoon pure vanilla extract
    1¼ cups pecans, chopped
    1 tablespoon maple syrup (optional)
    ice cream, to serve

1 Preheat the oven to 400°F. Roll out the pastry on a lightly floured surface and line a deep 9-inch fluted tart pan. Chill the pastry shell for 20 minutes, then line it with baking parchment and baking beans. Bake for 10 minutes. Lift out the paper and beans and return the pastry shell to the oven for 5 minutes. Set aside to cool.

2 Peel the pears, cut them in half and remove the cores with a small spoon. Place ¼ cup of the sugar in a pan with the water. Add the lemon zest and bring to a boil. Add the pears. Cover, lower the heat and simmer for 10 minutes. Remove the pears from the pan with a slotted spoon and set aside to cool. Discard the cooking liquid.

3 Break the chocolate into a large heatproof bowl. Melt over a pan of barely simmering water. Beat in the butter until combined. Set aside. In a saucepan, heat the remaining sugar and golden or corn syrup together over low heat until most of the sugar has dissolved. Bring to a boil, lower the heat and simmer for 2 minutes.

4 Whisk the eggs into the chocolate mixture until combined, then whisk in the syrup mixture. Stir in the vanilla extract and pecans.

5 Place the pear halves flat side down on a board. Using a fine, sharp knife, make lengthwise cuts all along each pear, taking care not to cut all the way through. Using a spatula, lift the pear halves and arrange in the pastry shell. Pour the pecan mixture over the top, so the pears are visible through the mixture.

6 Bake for 25–30 minutes, or until the filling is set, then let cool on a wire rack. If you like, glaze the surface of the pie with maple syrup before serving with ice cream.

FRENCH APPLE TART

THIS GLORIOUS TART MAKES A TRULY INDULGENT DESSERT. FOR AN EARLY MORNING TREAT, TRY A SLICE FOR BREAKFAST WITH A CUP OF STRONG BLACK COFFEE.

SERVES EIGHT

INGREDIENTS
    12 ounces sweet shortcrust pastry,
      thawed if frozen
    whipped cream, to serve
For the filling
    8 tablespoons (1 stick) butter, softened
    ½ cup sugar
    2 large eggs, beaten
    1 cup ground almonds
    ¼ cup all-purpose flour
For the topping
    3 eating apples
    ¼ cup apricot jam
    1 tablespoon water

1 Preheat the oven to 375°F. Place a baking sheet in the oven to heat up. Roll out the pastry on a lightly floured surface and use it to line a 9-inch fluted tart pan.

2 Beat all the ingredients for the filling together until light and fluffy. Spoon into the pastry shell and level the surface.

3 Make the topping. Peel the apples, remove the cores, and cut the apples in half. Place each half, cut side down, on a board. Using a fine, sharp knife, slice the apples thinly, keeping the shape, then press down lightly to fan each apple half in a row.

VARIATION
A red currant glaze would also look good on this tart. Warm red currant jelly with a little lemon juice and brush it over the apples. Straining is not needed.

4 Using a spatula, carefully transfer each row of apple slices to the tart, arranging them on the filling so they resemble the spokes of a wheel. You may need to overlap the slices slightly in the middle to fit. Press the slices down well into the filling. Warm the apricot jam with the water, then press the mixture through a strainer into a small bowl.

5 Using a pastry brush, brush half this apricot glaze over the apples. Place the pan on the hot baking sheet and bake the tart for 45 minutes, or until the pastry is golden and the apples have started to singe slightly.

6 Warm the remaining apricot glaze and brush it over the apples. Let the tart cool slightly before serving with cream.

DUTCH APPLE CAKE

THE APPLE TOPPING MAKES THIS CAKE REALLY MOIST. IT IS JUST AS GOOD HOT AS IT IS COLD.

MAKES EIGHT TO TEN SLICES

INGREDIENTS
    2¼ cups self-rising flour
    2 teaspoons baking powder
    1 teaspoon ground cinnamon
    generous ½ cup sugar
    4 tablespoons butter, melted
    2 eggs, beaten
    ⅔ cup milk
For the topping
    2 crisp, juicy eating apples
    1 tablespoon butter, melted
    ¼ cup demerara sugar
    ¼ teaspoon ground cinnamon

VARIATION
Add a few golden raisins or raisins to the apples if you like.

1 Preheat the oven to 400°F. Grease and line an 8-inch round cake pan. Sift the flour, baking powder and cinnamon into a large mixing bowl. Stir in the sugar. In a separate bowl, whisk the melted butter, eggs and milk together, then stir the mixture into the dry ingredients.

2 Pour the cake mixture into the prepared pan, smooth the surface, then make a shallow hollow in a ring around the edge of the mixture.

3 Make the topping. Peel and core the apples, slice them into wedges and slice the wedges thinly. Arrange the slices around the hollow in the cake mixture. Brush with the melted butter, then scatter the demerara sugar and ground cinnamon over the top.

4 Bake for 45–50 minutes, or until the cake has risen well, is golden and a skewer inserted into the center comes out clean. Serve immediately with cream, or remove from the pan, peel off the lining paper and cool on a wire rack before slicing.

PEAR AND POLENTA CAKE

POLENTA GIVES THE LIGHT SPONGE THAT TOPS THE SLICED PEARS A NUTTY CORN FLAVOR THAT COMPLEMENTS THE FRUIT PERFECTLY. SERVE WITH CUSTARD OR CREAM.

MAKES TEN SLICES

INGREDIENTS
    ¾ cup turbinado sugar
    4 ripe pears
    juice of ½ lemon
    2 tablespoons honey
    3 eggs
    seeds from 1 vanilla bean
    ½ cup sunflower oil
    1 cup self-rising flour
    ⅓ cup instant polenta

1 Preheat the oven to 350°F. Generously grease and line an 8½-inch round cake pan. Scatter 2 tablespoons of the turbinado sugar over the bottom of the prepared pan.

COOK'S TIP
Use the tip of a small, sharp knife to scrape out the vanilla bean seeds. If you do not have a vanilla bean, use 1 teaspoon pure vanilla extract instead.

2 Peel and core the pears. Cut them into chunky slices and toss in the lemon juice. Arrange them on the bottom of the prepared cake pan. Drizzle the honey over the pears and set aside.

3 Mix together the eggs, seeds from the vanilla bean and the remaining turbinado sugar in a bowl.

4 Beat the egg mixture until thick and creamy, then gradually beat in the oil. Sift together the flour and polenta and fold into the egg mixture.

5 Pour the mixture carefully into the pan over the pears. Bake for about 50 minutes, or until a skewer inserted into the center comes out clean. Cool in the pan for 10 minutes, then turn the cake out onto a plate, peel off the lining paper, invert and slice.

APPLE <u>AND</u> CIDER SAUCE

*THIS SAUCE COULDN'T BE SIMPLER TO MAKE. IT TASTES GREAT
WITH ROAST PORK, DUCK OR GOOSE.*

MAKES 1 POUND

INGREDIENTS
    1 pound cooking apples
    ⅔ cup apple cider
    ½ teaspoon cider vinegar
    2 tablespoons butter
    2 whole cloves
    a few sprigs of fresh thyme
    1 tablespoon honey
    2 teaspoons Dijon mustard

1 Peel, core and slice the apples.
Place them in a saucepan with the
cider, cider vinegar, butter, cloves and
thyme. Simmer over low heat, stirring
occasionally, for 10 minutes, or until the
apples are soft and pulpy, then raise the
heat and cook until most of the liquid
has evaporated.

2 Remove the cloves and thyme sprigs
and beat in the honey and mustard.
Taste and add more honey if necessary,
but the sauce is best when slightly tart.

COOK'S TIP
Press the sauce through a strainer if you
prefer it to be perfectly smooth.

APPLE <u>AND</u> RED ONION
MARMALADE

*THIS MARMALADE CHUTNEY IS GOOD ENOUGH TO EAT ON ITS OWN.
SERVE IT WITH PORK SAUSAGES OR IN A HAM SANDWICH INSTEAD
OF MUSTARD.*

MAKES 1 POUND

INGREDIENTS
    ¼ cup extra virgin olive oil
    2 pounds red onions, thinly sliced
    ½ cup demerara sugar
    2 crisp, juicy eating apples
    6 tablespoons cider vinegar

1 Heat the oil in a large, heavy
saucepan and add the onions.

2 Stir in the sugar and cook, uncovered,
over medium heat, stirring occasionally,
for about 40 minutes, or until the
onions have softened and become a
rich golden color.

3 Peel, core and grate the apples. Add
them to the pan with the vinegar and
continue to cook for 20 minutes, until
the chutney is thick and sticky. Spoon
into a sterilized jar and cover.

4 When cool, label and store in the
refrigerator for up to 1 month.

STONE FRUITS

One of life's greatest joys is to bite into a perfectly ripe, juicy stone

fruit and savor the wonderful sweetness of the sticky juices.

Stone fruits herald summer—the season starts with cherries,

continues with sun-drenched peaches and apricots, and ends with

plums, from gorgeous greengages to fat, juicy Victorias. Although

stone fruits (or "drupes") may seem very different, they are all

members of the prunus family and share the characteristics of soft,

juicy flesh and a single pit. Stone fruits are often grown in

greenhouses, but nothing beats the taste of a sun-ripened fruit,

so it is worth waiting until they are in season.

PEACHES

Sometimes known as the "queen of fruits," peaches are certainly among the most beautiful. Their downy, velvety skin is yellow flushed with red, and they are voluptuously curvaceous—the French call one variety *tétons de Venus* (the breasts of Venus).

The most familiar peaches are round or "beaked" with a pointed end, but they can also be flat and disk-shaped. The delicate fine-textured flesh, which can be yellow, white or tinged with red, encloses a heavily ridged pit. In some peaches, the flesh clings firmly to the pit; these are known as "clingstone." In "freestone" fruit, the flesh comes away easily and cleanly from the pit.

Peaches and nectarines originated from the same species and are very similar, except that peaches have fuzzy skin, while nectarines are smooth. So alike are they that peach trees sometimes spontaneously produce nectarines and vice versa.

History

Peaches have been grown in China since the fifth century BC and are regarded as a symbol of longevity and immortality. Even today, some Chinese families place peach trees or branches outside their front doors to ward off evil spirits. Peaches were taken along the old silk routes to Persia, where they were discovered by Alexander the Great, who introduced them to the Greeks and Romans; the word "peach" comes from the Latin *Persicum malum* (Persian apple). Immensely popular in Europe, peaches were introduced to America by Christopher Columbus and spread so profusely that they were once thought to be indigenous. Nowadays, so many are grown in Georgia that it is known as "the Peach State."

Varieties

Peaches are seldom sold by variety, but by the color of their flesh—yellow or white. Which you choose is a matter of preference; some people believe that white peaches have the finer flavor.

Above: Mireille, a white-fleshed peach.

Yellow varieties include Elegant Lady, Royal George and Bellegarde. Mireille is a popular white peach. The finest peaches of all are the *pêches de vigne,* small red-fleshed fruits that are grown in vineyards. They do not look particularly attractive, being covered in grayish down, but the flavor is superb. You are unlikely to find them outside markets in France.

Nutrition

Peaches are a source of vitamins A, B and C and provide about 60 calories per 3¾ ounces.

Buying and Storing

Peaches do not ripen successfully after picking, so always buy ripe fruit. The fruits should be handled carefully. Press gently to make sure that they are firm, with some "give." Never buy greenish peaches, except for chutney making, and avoid fruit with bruised skin. Peaches do not keep well. Firm fruit can be kept at room temperature for a day or two to soften; ripe peaches can be kept in the refrigerator for not more than two days.

Left: Elegant Lady—a popular yellow variety of peach.

Dried peaches These are not as widely available as dried apricots, but are becoming increasingly popular. Use them in compotes and cakes, or eat them on their own. Peaches are also crystallized or glacéed (candied).

Canned peaches Available in syrup or apple juice, canned peaches are fine for cooking, but lack the delicate texture and flavor of the fresh fruit.

Above: Dried peaches

Pitting a peach or nectarine

1 Slice through the seam line all around the peach.

2 Twist the two halves in opposite directions to separate them.

3 Lever out the pit with a knife.

Glacé peaches The fruits are coated in a thick syrup, which hardens to a shiny glaze. Glacé peaches are often included in boxes of assorted glacé fruits. They are very sweet, with a melting texture.

Preparing and Serving

A really ripe peach is delicious eaten on its own or in a fruit salad. Peaches combine well with most other fruits and nuts, particularly raspberries, a marriage that inspired Escoffier to create his famous dessert Peach Melba, in honor of the great singer Dame Nellie Melba.

Above: Glacé peaches are coated in a thick sugar syrup and are very sweet.

Left: Canned peaches, available in halves or slices, are fine for cooking but lack the flavor of the fresh fruit.

Fresh peaches feature in ice cream sundaes and can be used to make luxurious drinks like the Bellini (Champagne, peach liqueur and crushed peach pulp) or Champagne cocktails. They are also made into liqueurs and peach wine and brandy.

The fuzzy skin of a peach is not particularly pleasant to eat, so the fruit is best peeled. Nick the fruit, place it in a heatproof bowl and pour boiling water over. Leave for 15–30 seconds, depending on how ripe the fruits are, then drain and refresh in cold water. The skins will peel off easily.

Cooking and Serving

Peaches can be cooked in a multitude of ways—poached whole in vanilla-flavored syrup or wine; macerated in alcohol; in compotes, soufflés, pies,

tarts, pancakes, ice creams and sorbets. They make very good jams and jellies, while spiced peaches are delicious with cured or cold meats. Underripe green-tinged peaches can be made into excellent relishes and chutneys.

Peaches are also good, raw or cooked, in salads, and are natural partners for ham and duck. They can be substituted for mangoes in Southeast Asian dishes and are particularly good with crab and lobster.

To poach peaches in syrup, put 4 cups water in a pan. Add 2 cups sugar, 2 strips of pared lemon rind, a piece of cinnamon and half a split vanilla bean. Bring to a boil, stirring to

dissolve the sugar. Boil for about 5 minutes, then add six to eight peeled peaches (whole or halved) and poach gently until tender, turning occasionally. Let the fruit cool in the syrup.

Peaches make a delicious sweet after-dinner liqueur, Crème de Peche, which can be drunk on its own or combined with Champagne or sparking white wine to make an unusual cocktail. To make a classic Bellini, put some fresh peach pulp in a champagne glass, add a teaspoon of peach liqueur and top up with Champagne.

Left: Peach liqueur

NECTARINES

The botanical name for nectarines is *Prunus persican*, meaning "Persian plum," although these smooth-skinned fruits are a variant of peaches and natives of China. They taste very similar to peaches, with a touch more acidity. The flesh can be yellow, white or pinkish and is delicate and sweet. Unlike peaches, they

do not require peeling, so some people prefer them as a dessert fruit. They can be prepared and cooked in exactly the same way as peaches. Nectarines are sometimes crossed with peaches, but the fuzzy peach skin is generally dominant, so the hybrids are often actually peaches.

Left: Smooth-skinned white nectarines

Nutrition

Nectarines have a lower calorie count than peaches (containing only about 45 calories per 3¾ ounces). They are a good source of potassium and phosphorus, dietary fiber and vitamins A and C.

Buying and Storing

Like peaches, nectarines do not continue to mature after picking, so choose ripe fruit. The skins should be bright and smooth, with no blemishes or wrinkles. Nectarines can be kept at room temperature or in the refrigerator for two or three days.

Left: Yellow nectarines

APRICOTS

These round, yellow-orange fruit have velvety skins flushed with pink. The flesh is firm, sweet and fragrant, and contains little juice. The kernel of the pit (poisonous until it is cooked) is used to flavor jams, cookies and Amaretto liqueur.

Left: Ripe apricots are deliciously fragrant.

History

Apricots grew wild in China thousands of years ago and were introduced to Persia and Armenia, from where they got their Latin name, *Prunus armeniaca*. Alexander the Great brought apricots to Southern Europe; they were prized by the Romans and Greeks, who called them "golden eggs of the sun." They were first successfully cultivated in Northern Europe in the sixteenth century.

Nutrition

Apricots contain the antioxidant beta-carotene, and are a rich source of minerals and vitamin A. An average 2¹/₂-ounce apricot provides only 20 calories.

Above: Turkish sun-dried apricots

Below: Dried apricots

Buying and Storing

Apricots do not travel well, nor do they continue to ripen after picking, so those that you buy may be disappointing. Look for plump fruit with a rich color and smooth skin. Do not buy dull-looking or greenish fruit, as their flesh will be mealy. Keep apricots at room temperature for a couple of days, or store in a plastic bag in the refrigerator for up to five days.

Dried and canned apricots Because apricots are so delicate, they are often preserved by drying or canning. The best dried apricots come from Turkey; they are burnished orange and have a rich flavor. Dried apricots can be substituted for fresh apricots and make excellent jams. Use them just as they are in slow-cooked dishes that contain plenty of liquid, like stews and casseroles, but, unless they are plump, soak them in warm water for a couple of hours before using them in sweet dishes.

Preparing and Cooking

Ripe apricots are delicious raw and can be used in fruit salads and platters. Because the flesh is dry, they will not

Right: Canned apricots

disintegrate during cooking, which makes them ideal for tarts and Danish pastries. Apricots can be poached in syrup or sweet white wine and served with yogurt or spice-flavored ice cream; they are also very tasty when halved, stuffed with crushed amaretti cookies and baked, or caramelized and served over French toast. Apricots make wonderful jams and conserves.

Both fresh and dried apricots make frequent appearances in Middle Eastern and North African recipes, where they go particularly well with lamb, poultry and rice dishes.

PLUMS

There are thousands of varieties of plum, all differing in size, shape, color and flavor. These members of the rose family originate from three main types—European, Japanese and Western Asian. The skins can vary from blue-black to purple, red, green and yellow. They have a long season, and one variety or another is available almost all year round. All plums have smooth skins with a bloom and juicy flesh with plenty of acidity.

Dessert plums can be eaten on their own; they are usually larger than cooking plums (up to 4 inches long) and are sweet and very juicy. Cooking plums are drier, with tart flesh that is ideal for pies, tarts and cakes.

History

Wild plums originated in Asia at least 2,000 years ago. They were first cultivated by the Assyrians, then adopted by the Romans, who hybridized them with great enthusiasm; the historian Pliny wrote of the huge numbers of plum crossbreeds available. The Crusaders brought plums to Europe, where they became highly prized. Nowadays they are grown in almost all temperate countries.

Varieties

There are over 2,000 varieties of plum, ripening at different times throughout summer and autumn, although only a dozen or so are available in stores. Japanese varieties are large, round and juicy; they can be purplish red with orange flesh, or orangey yellow

Right: Victorias are the most prolific dessert plum.

with yellow flesh. On the whole, dark-colored plums have bitter skins, while the red and yellow varieties tend to be sweeter. Most dessert plums can be cooked as well as eaten raw.

DESSERT PLUMS

Denniston's Superb An early variety of plum, with medium-size green fruits flushed with red. These plums have an excellent, sweet flavor.
Gaviota These large, round plums have yellow skins deeply tinged with scarlet, and sweet, juicy red flesh. They are best eaten raw.
Marjorie's Seedling These small purple plums with a green flush have bitter skins and sweet, green, almost translucent flesh. They are good for eating and cooking.
Santa Rosa and **Burbank** Large and round, with bright red skins, these two North American varieties of plum are mainly grown in California. They have juicy, deep yellow flesh and a pleasantly tart flavor, which makes them good for both cooking and eating.

Above: Mirabelles—the golden-skinned variety of these small wild plums, which grow on long stems like cherries, are best cooked.

Victoria The most prolific of all dessert plums, Victorias were first cultivated in 1840 from a stray seedling found in Sussex, England. Since then, these large oval fruits with yellow skins flushed with scarlet and sweet, juicy flesh have become ubiquitous. They are good for canning, stewing or eating raw.

Left: Marjorie's Seedlings have sweet, almost translucent green flesh and are good for cooking and eating.

COOKING PLUMS

Beach plums These small plums grow wild along the Atlantic coast of North America, especially near Cape Cod. They have dark purplish black skins and tart flesh that makes them unsuitable for eating raw, but they make excellent jams and jellies.

Cherry plums or **mirabelles** These very small wild plums are round and grow on long stems like cherries. They have black, red or yellow skins, which can taste rather bitter, but all have sweet, juicy flesh. These plums can be eaten raw, but are best stewed or baked, or made into jams, sauces and jellies. Golden mirabelles are delicious in tarts and soufflés, and are also made into a plum eau-de-vie, called *mirabelle*.

Czar Large, rather acidic dark blue-black plums with golden flesh, these can be eaten raw but are more usually used for cooking. They are best eaten straight from the tree.

Nutrition

Plums contain more antioxidant than any other fruit. They provide about 40 calories per 3¾ ounces.

Buying and Storing

Plums are delicate, so make sure that the ones you buy are unblemished. They should be plump and firm, with some "give" (but never squashy), and they should be fully colored for their variety. Plums should always have a pleasant aroma.

These fruit ripen fast and quickly become overripe, so store them in the refrigerator for only a day or two. For cooking at a

Above: Angelino—the skin color varies from red to almost black, but the flesh of these plums is always yellow.

Left: Sweet-tasting Avalon plums

Below: Red-fleshed Spanish Autumn Rose plums

Quetsch Also known as *svetsch* or *Zwetschen,* these small purplish black plums have a beautiful bloom. Although their flesh is sweet, they are seldom eaten raw, but are used in Eastern Europe to make plum breads and *pflaumenkuchen, a* yeast bread topped with purple plums. Quetsch plums are also used for making slivovitz and other plum brandies.

Other varieties of note

Angelino, Autumn Rose, Avalon, Circiela Queen Rose, Reeves Seedling, Stanley and Sungold.

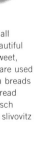

later date, plums can be frozen: Halve the fruit and remove the pits. Place on trays and open-freeze, then pack the fruit into freezer bags and seal.

Preparing and Cooking

Dessert plums are delicious eaten on their own. Dual varieties (suitable for eating and cooking) and cooking plums make excellent pies and tarts, compotes, crumbles, dumplings, sauces, mousses and soufflés. They can be poached, baked or stewed, either whole or in halves or slices. It is not recommended that plums with tough skins be cooked in the microwave, as they will not soften in the short cooking time. Cook plums until just tender; do not let them disintegrate. Plums make tasty ice cream, and the poached fruit goes very well with ice creams flavored with spices like cardamom, nutmeg and cinnamon.

Plums work extremely well in savory dishes. The Chinese make them into a thick sweet-sour sauce to serve with Peking duck, lamb or pork. Spiced stewed plums are good with ham, cured meats, terrines and poultry. Plums add a special flavor to beef or lamb casseroles.

Plums also make superb jams and jellies. They can be preserved in many different

Above: Circiela Queen Rose

Below: Reeves Seedling

Below: Stanley

ways: dried (as prunes), crystallized and candied, bottled or made into wine and liqueurs like slivovitz and plum brandy.

Preserved plums There are many ways of preserving plums, the best known being by drying them as prunes. In Spain, Elvas plums are partially dried, then rolled in sugar. The Portuguese candy sweet greengages, while Carlsbad plums (named after the spa town, now Karlovy Vary) are a speciality of the Czech Republic. These plums (usually Quetsch) are candied in hot syrup until shriveled, then halved and stuffed into dried damsons. The process gives them a very intense flavor. Carlsbad plums are considered a great delicacy and are packed in attractive wooden boxes.

Soaking prunes

Prunes must be soaked for at least 4 hours before using. Place in a bowl and cover with cold water or tepid weak tea for added flavor. Leave overnight if possible to plump up. For compotes and purées it is not necessary to soak the prunes; cook them directly in wine, water or fruit juice until they are very tender.

Prunes These wrinkled dried purple or red plums can be prepared in various ways. The plums can be left to dry naturally on the tree, but are more often sun-dried. They can also be desiccated in a low oven. The finest variety of "pruning" plum is the Agen, which is grown in France and California. These prunes are sold complete with pits and must be soaked overnight before being cooked.

Left: Chinese plum sauce has a wonderful sweet-sour flavor and is classically served with Peking duck.

Nowadays, pitted no-soak prunes are also widely available, but they tend to be flabbier than the traditional variety. Apart from their famed laxative qualities, prunes have other healthful properties. They are said to be an excellent cure for hangovers, give a great energy boost, and are purported to be an aphrodisiac.

Culinary Uses

Cooked prunes are traditionally served with custard, but they are equally good with thick cream. They make excellent ice cream, especially when combined with Armagnac. Prunes are often used in savory dishes, particularly in Middle Eastern cooking, and they go extremely well with pork and chicken. They are an essential ingredient in Scottish cock-a-leekie soup. They go well with citrus flavors and can be made into a compote with red wine and orange or lemon zest.

Below: California prunes

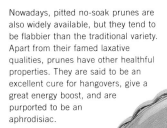

Left: Slivovitz—black Madjarka plums are crushed with their pits and slowly fermented to make this eau-de-vie from Croatia.

Puréed prunes can be sweetened, then spiced with a little ground cinnamon or nutmeg and served as a sauce with vanilla ice cream.

Below: French Agen prunes

GREENGAGES

These small members of the plum family have green skins, sometimes tinged with yellow or rose pink, which turn golden as the fruit ripens. There are many varieties of greengage; all have firm flesh and a delicious honeyed flavor. "Transparent" gages have fine, translucent flesh; if you hold the fruit up to the light, you can clearly see the shadow of the pit. These golden gages have a particularly sweet flavor.

History

Wild greengages from Asia Minor were probably introduced to Britain by the Romans, but disappeared from cultivation until Sir Thomas Gage brought them from France in the eighteenth century (and gave them his name). In France, they are known as Reine-Claude after the wife of François I, who adored their sweet flavor.

Preparing and Cooking

The deliciously sweet flavor of greengages makes them ideal for eating raw. They can also be gently poached in syrup, puréed for mousses and fools or made into excellent compotes and jam.

Below: Greengages, named after Sir Thomas Gage, have firm flesh with a deliciously sweet flavor.

DAMSONS

These small, plumlike fruits take their name from Damascus, which is probably where they originated. They have deep blue-black skins with an attractive bloom. The flavor is very strong and tart, which makes them more suitable for cooking than eating raw. Damsons grow wild, but are sometimes commercially available.

Preparing and Cooking

Damsons can be stewed and used in pies, tarts, ice creams and fools, but they are most commonly used for canning or for jams and jellies. Once cooked with sugar, they develop a pleasantly spicy flavor. A traditional old English sweetmeat is damson cheese, very thick fruit pulp boiled with sugar to make a solid jam similar to quince cheese, which can be eaten with bread and butter or biscuits.

The tart flavor of damsons makes them particularly suitable for savory dishes, such as pork or lamb casseroles. The fruit can also be made into wine or damson gin.

Above: Once cooked, damsons have a pleasantly spicy flavor.

Damson cheese

Damson cheese is a traditional English country dish with a very distinctive flavor that is an acquired taste. The "cheese" is potted and aged for several months before being eaten. To make 5½ pounds of damson cheese, put 3½ pounds of damsons in a saucepan, barely cover with water and simmer until the flesh is so tender that it falls off the pits. Strain the pulp, weigh it and return it to the pan with three-quarters of its weight in light brown sugar. Boil until the jam is clear, skimming the surface frequently. Pot the jam in oiled straight-sided containers, seal and store in a cool, dark place for at least two months. Serve with bread and butter, and eat with a knife and fork.

BULLACES

The small round plums known as "black bullaces" have bluish purple skins and mouth-puckeringly acid flesh. So-called "white" bullaces are pale greenish yellow. They can be found throughout Europe in late autumn growing in thorny hedgerows long after the other wild fruits like sloes and blackberries have finished. Although very tart and virtually inedible when raw, bullaces can be cooked with sugar to make pies and tarts. They are also good for jams and other preserves.

Right: The pale greenish yellow fruits known as "white" bullaces are almost inedible raw, but can be cooked with sugar to make delicious jams and jellies or a filling for pies.

SLOES

Sloes are the fruit of the blackthorn, a thorny shrub that grows wild throughout Europe (hence its botanical name, *Prunus spinosa*, which means "spiny plum"). These small wild fruits resemble tiny plums. The blue-black skins have a slight bloom. The flesh is highly astringent and cannot be eaten raw. Sloes ripen late and can be picked from the hedgerows in autumn, but they only become edible after the first frosts. They can be made into jams, jellies, sloe wine and liqueurs, but their chief claim to fame is that they are the principal ingredient of the irresistible sloe gin.

Make sloe gin as soon as the fruit is ripe, and with any luck you'll have a bottle ready in time for Christmas. For each 1¼ pint bottle of gin, you will need 2 cups sloes and a generous ½ cup sugar. Wash the sloes and prick them all over with a darning needle. Pack them loosely into a perfectly clean flagon or bottle, add the sugar and top up with gin. If you like, add two or three drops of pure almond extract and shake well. Seal and store for at least three months before drinking, shaking the bottles three times a week. If pricking the sloes seems like too much trouble, freeze them for several hours to crack the skin. Purists, however, allege that this compromises the flavor of the gin.

Left: Sloes are small wild fruits that grow in hedgerows throughout Europe. They are best picked in late autumn, after the first frosts.

CHERRIES

Cherry trees in blossom are one of the great delights of spring, followed in summer by clusters of bright, shiny fruit hanging in pairs from long, elegant stems. The skin of these small round stone fruits can vary in color from pale creamy yellow to deepest red to almost black. The firm, juicy flesh can be sweet or sour, depending on the variety, of which there are hundreds. Cherries are categorized into three main groups: sweet (for eating), sour (for cooking) and hybrids such as the nobly named Dukes and Royals, which are suitable for eating raw or cooking.

History

The original wild sweet cherries, known as *mazzards,* were found in Asia Minor and were cultivated by the Chinese 3,000 years ago. Mazzards were known to the ancient Egyptians, Greeks and Romans, and still exist today. Sour cherries were brought to Rome from Greece, and all modern varieties derive from these early specimens.

Varieties

Sweet cherries fall into two main groups: **bigarreaus,** with firm, crisp flesh, and **geans** or **guines,** with a softer texture. Today, there are also many hybrids. Sour cherries range from almost sweet to bitter and tart; they are full of flavor and are mainly used for preserving or in the manufacture of liqueurs.

SWEET CHERRIES

BIGARREAUS The best-known of these are the **Napoleons,** large pale yellow cherries tinged with light red. Their crisp fragrant flesh is slightly tart. **Bing** cherries are large, heart-shaped deep red fruit with a superb flavor. They are widely grown in North America.
GEANS/GUINES These fruits have soft, juicy flesh and come in many colors. **Black Tartarian** are deep purplish black from the skin right through to the pit. **Early Rivers** have dark purple skins and flesh, and very small pits. They are fragrant, sweet and juicy. **Ranier** has golden skin with a pink blush. The famous Swiss black cherry jam is made from intensely dark guines.

Above: Bright red Colney cherries.

Left: Napoleons are one of the sweet cherry varieties, with slightly crisp, tart, fragrant flesh.

Left: Widely grown in North America, sweet Bing cherries have a superb flavor.

SOUR CHERRIES

Most sour cherries are too tart to eat but are ideal for cooking. The two main types are **morello** and **amarelle**. Morellos have dark juice, and amarelles have light, almost colorless juice. The small, dark red morello cherries (known in France as *griottes*) are inedible raw, but are delicious preserved in either brandy or syrup.

Montmorency These are bright red cherries with a sweet-sour flavor. They have given their name to a range of dishes that include the fruit, from duck to pastries and ice creams.

English cherries are small, bright orange-red fruit with soft translucent flesh. They are mainly used for preserving in brandy.

Right: Morello cherries, which are often preserved in brandy.

Maraschino cherries

These small wild fruit from Dalmatia are *damasca* or *amaresca* cherries. They are distilled into a colorless sweet, sticky Italian liqueur called Maraschino. The familiar bottled Maraschino cherries beloved of bartenders were originally damasca cherries preserved in Maraschino liqueur; nowadays, the vibrant red fruits sold as "maraschino" tend to be ordinary cherries tinted with artificial coloring and steeped in syrup flavored with bitter almonds. Check the label before buying.

Nutrition

Cherries contain vitamins A and C and some dietary fiber. Their calorie content varies with the type; sweet cherries provide about 77 calories per 3¾ ounces, while the same quantity of sour fruit provides about 56 calories.

Buying and Storing

Choose plump cherries with shiny, unblemished skins. It is best to buy them still on the stem. As a rule of thumb, pale cherries are very sweet, while dark cherries tend to be more acidic; if possible, taste before you buy.

Unwashed cherries will keep for a few days in the refrigerator; wash them just before serving. They can also be removed from their stems and frozen.

Preparing and Cooking

Sweet cherries often need no preparation other than washing and are best eaten on their own or in fruit salads. They make unusual sweets when left on the stem and dipped into melted dark chocolate. Pitted fresh cherries make a delicious filling for sponge cakes and meringues, or an attractive decoration for cakes and desserts. There is no reason not to cook with sweet cherries, but they may not have much flavor, due to their low acidity. Although fresh cherries can be served as they are, for cooking they should be pitted.

Cherries can be preserved by drying in the sun or in a low oven, by preserving in sugar or in brandy. Candied—or glacé—cherries are a popular ingredient in baking.

Dual-purpose and sour cherries can be cooked in tarts, pies, compotes and sauces. They go well with sweet spices, citrus flavors and chocolate; the classic combination of cherries and chocolate is found in Black Forest Cake. In Eastern Europe, they are made into a sweet-sour soup or pickled in spiced vinegar as an accompaniment for rich meats. Cherries go well with all game and are classically served with duck. Amarelle and morello cherries are used for making jam and preserves, or for crystallizing as glacé cherries.

Below: Brightly colored, sweet and sticky glacé cherries are a popular baking ingredient.

Above: Dried sour Montmorency and Bing cherries

Left and below: Maraschino cherries may be bottled with their stems.

STONE FRUIT RECIPES

Juicy and full of flavor, peaches, plums, apricots,
cherries and nectarines make perfect partners for crisp
pastry. Try the irresistible Baked Peaches with a
Lattice Crust or Plum and Marzipan Pastries.
For simpler but equally delicious desserts,
choose Peach Melba Syllabub or
Plum and Custard Creams.

PLUM AND CUSTARD CREAMS

THIS SOPHISTICATED VERSION OF STEWED PLUMS AND CUSTARD, A STANDARD ENGLISH NURSERY DESSERT, IS PRETTILY LAYERED IN A PARFAIT GLASS AND TASTES AS GOOD AS IT LOOKS.

SERVES SIX

INGREDIENTS

1½ pounds red plums, pitted
    and sliced
grated zest and juice of 1 orange
¼ cup sugar
about 2 cups custard sauce (crème
    anglaise), prepared in advance
1¼ cups heavy cream
2 tablespoons water
1 tablespoon powdered gelatin
1 egg white
plum slices and fresh mint sprigs,
    to decorate

COOK'S TIP
Use a long metal skewer or thin metal spoon handle to marble the custard and plum purée mixtures together.

1 Put the plums in a saucepan with the orange zest and juice. Add the sugar and heat, stirring constantly, until the sugar has dissolved. Cook the plums for 5 minutes, until tender. Cool slightly, then purée in a food processor until smooth. Press through a strainer into a bowl and set aside to cool.

2 Put the custard in a saucepan, add half the cream and heat until boiling. Meanwhile, pour the water into a heatproof bowl and sprinkle the gelatin on top; set aside for 5 minutes, until softened. Whisk the soaked gelatin into the hot custard until it has dissolved. Allow the mixture to cool.

3 Whip the remaining cream to soft peaks, then fold it into the custard mixture. In a grease-free bowl, beat the egg white to soft peaks, then fold it into the custard too. Set aside, stirring occasionally, until just starting to set.

4 Quickly spoon alternate spoonfuls of the custard and the plum purée into six tall parfait glasses. Marble the mixtures together. Chill for 2–3 hours, or until the custard has set. Decorate each dessert with plum slices and fresh mint sprigs just before serving.

SPICED FRUITS JUBILEE

BASED ON THE CLASSIC CHERRIES JUBILEE, THIS IS A GREAT WAY TO USE A GLUT OF ANY STONE FRUIT. THE SPICED SYRUP IS A DELICIOUS BONUS. SERVE WITH THE BEST VANILLA ICE CREAM YOU CAN FIND.

SERVES SIX

INGREDIENTS
½ cup sugar
thinly pared zest of 1 unwaxed lemon
1 cinnamon stick
4 whole cloves
1¼ cups water
8 ounces tart red plums, pitted
  and sliced
8 ounces nectarines, pitted
  and chopped
1½ cups cherries, pitted
1 teaspoon arrowroot
5 tablespoons brandy
vanilla ice cream, to serve

1 Put the sugar, lemon zest, cinnamon stick, cloves and water in a pan. Bring to a boil, stirring. Lower the heat and simmer for 5 minutes, then lift out the spices with a slotted spoon and discard.

2 Add the fruit, cover the pan and simmer for 5 minutes. Drain the fruit, reserving the syrup, and set it aside; return the syrup to the pan. Boil it, uncovered, for 2 minutes, or until thick.

3 Put the arrowroot in a small bowl and stir in 2 tablespoons of the brandy. Stir the mixture into the syrup. Continue cooking and stirring until the sauce thickens. Return the fruit to the pan.

4 Place scoops of ice cream in serving bowls and spoon the hot fruit on top. Warm the remaining brandy in a small pan, then set it alight. Ladle it over the fruit at the table for maximum effect.

PEACH MELBA SYLLABUB

IF YOU ARE MAKING THIS SOPHISTICATED DESSERT FOR A DINNER PARTY, COOK THE PEACHES AND RASPBERRIES THE DAY BEFORE TO ALLOW THE FRUIT TO CHILL. WHIP UP THE SYLLABUB AT THE VERY LAST MINUTE TO MAKE A DELICIOUS, LIGHT-AS-A-CLOUD TOPPING.

SERVES SIX

INGREDIENTS
    4 peaches, peeled, pitted and sliced
    1¼ cups blush or red grape juice
    ⅔ cup raspberries
    raspberry or mint leaves, to decorate
    ratafia biscuits or other dessert
      cookies, to serve
For the syllabub
    ¼ cup peach schnapps
    2 tablespoons blush or red grape
      juice
    1¼ cups heavy cream

VARIATIONS
Use dessert pears and sliced kiwi fruit instead of peaches and raspberries. Instead of the syllabub, top the fruit with whipped cream flavored with Advocaat and finely chopped preserved ginger.

1 Place the peach slices in a large saucepan. Add the grape juice. bring to a boil, then cover, lower the heat and simmer for 5–7 minutes, or until tender.

2 Add the raspberries and remove from the heat. Set aside in the refrigerator until cold. Divide the peach and raspberry mixture among six dessert glasses.

3 For the syllabub, place the peach schnapps and grape juice in a large bowl and beat in the cream until it forms soft peaks.

4 Spoon the syllabub on top of the fruit and decorate each portion with a fresh raspberry or mint leaf. Serve with dessert cookies.

NECTARINE AND HAZELNUT MERINGUES

IF IT'S INDULGENCE YOU'RE SEEKING, LOOK NO FURTHER. SWEET NECTARINES AND CREAM SYLLABUB PAIRED WITH CRISP HAZELNUT MERINGUES MAKE A SUPERB DESSERT.

SERVES FIVE

INGREDIENTS
    3 egg whites
    ¾ cup superfine sugar
    ½ cup chopped
      hazelnuts, toasted
    1¼ cups heavy cream
    ¼ cup sweet dessert wine
    2 nectarines, pitted and sliced
    fresh mint sprigs, to decorate

VARIATIONS
Use apricots instead of nectarines if you prefer, or try this with a raspberry filling.

1 Preheat the oven to 275°F. Line two large baking sheets with baking parchment. Beat the egg whites in a greasefree bowl until they form stiff peaks when the whisk or beaters are lifted. Gradually beat in the superfine sugar, a spoonful at a time, until the mixture forms a stiff, glossy meringue.

2 Fold in two-thirds of the chopped toasted hazelnuts, then spoon five large ovals onto each lined baking sheet. Scatter the remaining hazelnuts over five of the meringue ovals. Flatten the tops of the remaining five ovals.

3 Bake the meringues for 1–1¼ hours, until crisp and dry, then carefully lift them off the baking parchment and cool completely on a wire rack.

4 Whip the cream with the dessert wine until the mixture forms soft peaks. Spoon some of the cream syllabub onto each of the plain meringues. Arrange a few nectarine slices on each. Put each meringue on a dessert plate with a hazelnut-topped meringue. Decorate each portion with mint sprigs and serve the meringues immediately.

Black Cherry Clafouti

This favorite recipe has been reproduced with all manner of fruit, but you simply can't beat the classic version using slightly tart black cherries.

SERVES SIX

INGREDIENTS
    2 tablespoons butter, for greasing
    2 cups black cherries, pitted
    ¼ cup all-purpose flour
    ½ cup confectioners' sugar, plus
        extra for dusting
    4 eggs, beaten
    1 cup whole milk or half-and-half
    2 tablespoons kirsch

1 Preheat the oven to 350°F. Use the butter to grease a 5-cup gratin dish thickly. Scatter the cherries over the bottom.

2 Sift the flour and confectioners' sugar together into a large mixing bowl and gradually beat in the eggs until the mixture is smooth. Beat in the milk until blended, then stir in the kirsch.

3 Pour the batter carefully over the cherries, then bake for 35–45 minutes, or until just set and lightly golden.

4 Allow the clafouti to cool for about 15 minutes. Dust liberally with confectioners' sugar just before serving.

VARIATIONS
Try other liqueurs in this dessert. Almond-flavored liqueur is delicious teamed with cherries. Hazelnut, raspberry or orange liqueur would also work nicely.

ICED GIN AND DAMSON SOUFFLES

FOR AN UNFORGETTABLE TASTE SENSATION, USE SLOE GIN FOR THESE DELICIOUS INDIVIDUAL FROZEN SOUFFLES. THEY ARE PERFECT FOR A PARTY AND CAN BE MADE AHEAD.

MAKES SIX

INGREDIENTS
1¼ pounds damsons
1 cup water
1¼ cups sugar
2 tablespoons gin or sloe gin
4 large egg whites
1¼ cups heavy cream, whipped
fresh mint leaves, to decorate

1 You will need six ⅔-cup ramekins. Fit each with a collar of greased baking parchment that extends about 2 inches above the rim.

2 Slice two damsons and set aside for the decoration. Put the rest of the damsons in a pan with half the water and ¼ cup of the sugar. Cover and simmer the mixture for about 7 minutes, or until the damsons are tender. Press the pulp through a strainer placed over a bowl to remove all the pits and skin, then stir in the gin and set aside.

3 Combine the remaining sugar and water in the clean pan and heat gently until the sugar has dissolved. Bring to a boil and cook the syrup until it registers 238°F on a sugar thermometer, or until a small amount of the mixture dropped into a cup of cold water can be molded to a soft ball.

4 Meanwhile, beat the egg whites in a grease-free bowl until they form stiff peaks. Still beating, slowly pour in the hot syrup until the meringue mixture is stiff and glossy. Fold in the whipped cream and fruit purée until combined.

5 Spoon into the dishes to come 1 inch above the rim of each. Freeze until firm. Remove from the freezer 10 minutes before serving. Remove the collars, then decorate each with damson slices and mint leaves.

CARAMELIZED APRICOTS WITH FRENCH TOAST

PAIN PERDU IS THE FRENCH NAME FOR FRENCH TOAST WHICH LITERALLY TRANSLATES AS "LOST BREAD." A BRITISH VERSION IS KNOWN AS POOR KNIGHTS.

SERVES FOUR

INGREDIENTS
    6 tablespoons unsalted butter, clarified
    1 pound apricots, pitted and
        thickly sliced
    ½ cup sugar
    ⅔ cup heavy cream
    2 tablespoons apricot brandy or brandy
For the French toast
    2½ cups milk
    1 vanilla bean
    ¼ cup sugar
    4 large eggs, beaten
    8 tablespoons (1 stick) unsalted
        butter, clarified
    6 brioche or challah slices,
        diagonally halved
    ½ teaspoon ground cinnamon

1 Heat a heavy frying pan, then melt 1½ tablespoons of the butter in it. Add the apricots and cook for 2–3 minutes, until golden. Using a slotted spoon, transfer to a bowl. Add the rest of the butter to the pan with the sugar and heat gently, stirring, until golden.

2 Pour in the cream and brandy and cook gently until the mixture forms a smooth sauce. Boil for 2–3 minutes, until thickened, then pour the sauce over the apricots and set aside.

3 To make the French toast, pour the milk into a saucepan and add the vanilla bean and half the sugar. Heat gently until almost boiling, then set aside to cool.

4 Remove the vanilla bean and pour the flavored milk into a shallow dish. Beat in the eggs. Heat a sixth of the butter in the clean frying pan. Dip each slice of brioche in turn into the milk mixture, add it to the pan and cook until golden brown on both sides. Add the remaining butter as needed. As the French toast is cooked, remove the slices; keep hot.

5 Warm the apricot sauce and spoon it onto the French toast. Mix the remaining sugar with the cinnamon and sprinkle a little of the mixture over each portion.

COOK'S TIP
To clarify the butter, melt it in a small saucepan, then let it stand for a few minutes. Carefully pour the clear butter on the surface (the clarified butter) into a small bowl, leaving the milky solids behind in the pan.

FRESH CHERRY AND HAZELNUT STRUDEL

SERVE THIS WONDERFUL OLD-WORLD TREAT AS A WARM DESSERT, OR ALLOW IT TO COOL AND OFFER IT AS AN AFTERNOON SNACK WITH TEA OR COFFEE.

SERVES SIX TO EIGHT

INGREDIENTS
    6 tablespoons butter
    6 tablespoons light brown sugar
    3 egg yolks
    grated zest of 1 lemon
    ¼ teaspoon grated nutmeg
    generous 1 cup ricotta cheese
    8 large sheets phyllo pastry, thawed
      if frozen
    3 ounces ratafia biscuits or other
      dessert cookies, crushed
    2½ cups cherries, pitted
    2 tablespoons chopped hazelnuts
    confectioners' sugar, for dusting
    crème fraîche, to serve

1 Preheat the oven to 375°F. Soften 1 tablespoon of the butter. Place it in a bowl and beat in the sugar and egg yolks until light and fluffy. Beat in the lemon zest, nutmeg and ricotta, then set aside.

2 Melt the remaining butter in a small pan. Working quickly, place a sheet of phyllo on a clean dish towel and brush it generously with melted butter. Place a second sheet on top and repeat the process. Continue until all the phyllo has been layered and buttered, reserving some of the melted butter.

3 Scatter the crushed cookies over the top, leaving a 2-inch border around the outside. Spoon the ricotta mixture over the cookies, spread it lightly to cover, then scatter the cherries over the top.

4 Fold in the phyllo pastry border and use the dish towel to carefully roll up the strudel, jelly-roll style, beginning from one of the long sides of the pastry. Grease a baking sheet with the remaining melted butter.

5 Place the strudel on the baking sheet and scatter the hazelnuts over the surface. Bake for 35–40 minutes, or until the strudel is golden and crisp. Dust with confectioners' sugar and serve with a dollop of crème fraîche.

BAKED PEACHES WITH A LATTICE CRUST

IF YOU WOULD RATHER USE NECTARINES FOR THE RECIPE, THERE'S NO NEED TO PEEL THEM FIRST.

MAKES SIX

INGREDIENTS
  3 peaches
  juice of ½ lemon
  scant ½ cup white marzipan
  13 ounces prepared puff pastry,
    thawed if frozen
  a large pinch of ground cinnamon
  beaten egg, to glaze
  sugar, for sprinkling
For the caramel sauce
  ¼ cup sugar
  2 tablespoons cold water
  ⅔ cup heavy cream

1 Preheat the oven to 375°F. Place the peaches in a large bowl and pour boiling water over to cover. Leave for 60 seconds, then drain the peaches and peel off the skins. Toss the skinned fruit in the lemon juice to prevent them from turning brown.

2 Divide the marzipan into six pieces and shape each to form a small round. Cut the peaches in half and remove their pits. Fill the pit cavity in each with a marzipan round.

3 Cut the puff pastry in half. Set one half aside, then cut out six rounds from the rest, making each round slightly larger than a peach half. Sprinkle a little cinnamon on each pastry round, then place a peach half, marzipan side down, on the pastry.

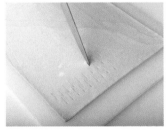

4 Cut the remaining pastry into lattice pastry, using a special cutter if you have one. If not, simply cut small slits in rows all over the pastry, starting each row slightly lower than the last. Cut the lattice pastry into six equal squares.

COOK'S TIP
Take care when adding the cream to the hot caramel, as the mixture is liable to spit. Pour it from a cup, protecting your hand with an oven mitt, and use a long-handled wooden spoon for stirring.

5 Dampen the edges of the pastry rounds with a little water, then drape a lattice pastry square over each peach half. Press around the edge to seal, then trim off the excess pastry and decorate with small peach leaves made from the trimmings. Transfer the peach pastries to a baking sheet. Brush with the beaten egg and sprinkle with the sugar. Bake for 20 minutes, or until the pastries are golden.

6 Meanwhile, make the caramel sauce. Heat the sugar with the water in a small pan until it dissolves. bring to a boil and continue to boil until the syrup turns a dark golden brown. Stand back and add the cream. Heat gently, stirring until smooth. Serve the peach pastries with the sauce.

PEACH AND RED CURRANT TARTLETS

TART RED CURRANTS AND SWEET PEACHES MAKE A WINNING COMBINATION IN THESE SIMPLE TARTLETS.

MAKES FOUR

INGREDIENTS
  2 tablespoons butter, melted
  16 × 6-inch squares of phyllo pastry,
    thawed if frozen
  confectioners' sugar, for dusting
  red currant sprigs, to decorate
For the filling
  ⅔ cup heavy cream
  4¼ ounces mixed peach and
    mango yogurt
  a few drops of pure vanilla extract
  1 tablespoon confectioners' sugar
For the topping
  2 peaches
  ½ cup red currants

COOK'S TIP
To strip red currants from their stalks, pull
the stems through the tines of a fork.

1 Preheat the oven to 375°F. Use a little of the butter to grease four cups of a standard muffin pan or four tartlet pans. Brush the pastry squares with butter, stack them in fours, then place in the pans to make four pastry shells.

2 Bake for 12–15 minutes, until golden. Cool the phyllo cases on a wire rack.

3 Make the filling. Whip the cream to soft peaks, then lightly fold in the yogurt, vanilla extract and confectioners' sugar. Divide among the pastry shells.

4 Slice the peaches and fan them out on top of the filling, with a few red currants. Decorate with red currant sprigs and dust with confectioners' sugar.

PLUM <u>AND</u> MARZIPAN PASTRIES

THESE DANISH PASTRIES CAN BE MADE WITH ANY PITTED FRUIT. TRY APRICOTS, CHERRIES OR DAMSON OR GREENGAGE PLUMS INSTEAD OF RED ONES, ADDING A GLAZE MADE FROM HONEY OR JAM.

MAKES SIX

INGREDIENTS
    13 ounces prepared puff pastry
    6 tablespoons plum jam
    ½ cup white marzipan, coarsely
        grated
    3 red plums, halved and pitted
    1 egg, beaten
    ½ cup sliced almonds
For the glaze
    2 tablespoons plum jam
    1 tablespoon water

1 Preheat the oven to 425°F. Cut the pastry into six equal squares and place on one or two dampened baking sheets.

2 Spoon 1 tablespoon jam into the center of each pastry square. Divide the marzipan among them. Place half a plum, hollow side down, on top of each marzipan mound.

3 Brush the edges of the pastry with beaten egg. Bring up the corners and press them together lightly, then open out the pastry corners at the top. Glaze the pastries with a little beaten egg, then press a sixth of the flaked almonds on each.

4 Bake the pastries for 20–25 minutes, or until lightly golden.

5 Meanwhile, make the glaze by heating the jam and water in a small pan, stirring until smooth. Press the mixture through a strainer into a small bowl, then brush it over the tops of the pastries while they are still warm. Let cool on a wire rack.

YELLOW PLUM TART

IN THIS TART, GLAZED YELLOW PLUMS SIT ATOP A DELECTABLE ALMOND FILLING IN A CRISP PASTRY SHELL. WHEN THEY ARE IN SEASON, GREENGAGE PLUMS MAKE AN EXCELLENT ALTERNATIVE.

SERVES EIGHT

INGREDIENTS
    1½ cups all-purpose flour
    pinch of salt
    6 tablespoons butter, chilled
    2 tablespoons sugar
    a few drops of pure vanilla extract
    3 tablespoons ice water
    whipped cream or custard, to serve
For the filling
    ⅓ cup sugar
    6 tablespoons butter, softened
    ¾ cup ground almonds
    1 egg, beaten
    2 tablespoons all-purpose flour
    1 pound yellow plums, halved
      and pitted
For the glaze
    3 tablespoons apricot jam, strained
    1 tablespoon water

1 Sift the flour and salt into a bowl, then rub in the chilled butter until the mixture resembles fine bread crumbs. Stir in the sugar, vanilla extract and enough of the ice water to make a soft dough.

COOK'S TIP
Ceramic baking beans are ideal for baking blind, but any dried beans will do. You can use them over and over again, but make sure you keep them in a special jar, separate from the rest of your dried beans, as you cannot use them for conventional cooking.

2 Knead the dough gently on a lightly floured surface until smooth, then wrap in plastic wrap and chill for 10 minutes.

3 Preheat the oven to 400°F. Roll out the pastry and use it to line a 9-inch fluted tart pan, allowing excess pastry to overhang the top. Prick the bottom with a fork and line with baking parchment and baking beans.

4 Bake for 10 minutes, remove the paper and beans, then return the pastry shell to the oven for 10 minutes. Remove and allow to cool. Trim off any excess pastry with a sharp knife.

5 To make the filling, beat together all the ingredients except the plums. Spread on the bottom of the pastry shell. Arrange the plums on top, placing them cut side down. Make a glaze by heating the jam with the water. Stir well, then brush a little of the apricot glaze over the top of the fruit.

6 Bake the tart for 50–60 minutes, until the almond filling is cooked and the plums are tender. Warm any remaining apricot glaze and brush it over the top. Cut into slices and serve with whipped cream or custard.

APRICOT PARCELS

THESE LITTLE PHYLLO PARCELS CONTAIN A SPECIAL APRICOT AND MINCEMEAT FILLING. A GOOD WAY TO USE UP ANY MINCEMEAT AND MARZIPAN THAT HAVE BEEN IN YOUR PANTRY SINCE CHRISTMAS!

MAKES EIGHT

INGREDIENTS

12 ounces phyllo pastry, thawed
   if frozen
4 tablespoons butter, melted
8 apricots, halved and pitted
4 tablespoons mincemeat
12 ratafia (almond paste) or other
   dessert cookies, crushed
2 tablespoons grated marzipan
confectioners' sugar, for dusting

COOK'S TIP

Phyllo pastry dries out quickly, so keep any squares not being used under a clean, damp dish towel. Work as quickly as possible. If the phyllo turns dry and brittle, brush it with melted butter to moisten.

1 Preheat the oven to 400°F. Cut the phyllo pastry into thirty-two 7-inch squares. Brush four of the squares with a little melted butter and stack them, giving each layer a quarter turn so that the stack acquires a star shape. Repeat to make eight stars.

2 Place an apricot half, hollow side up, in the center of each pastry star. Mix together the mincemeat, crushed cookies and marzipan and spoon a little of the mixture into the hollow in each apricot.

3 Top with another apricot half, then bring the corners of each pastry together and squeeze to make a gathered purse.

4 Place the purses on a baking sheet and brush each with a little melted butter. Bake for 15–20 minutes, or until the pastry is golden and crisp. Lightly dust with confectioners' sugar to serve. Whipped cream, flavored with a little brandy, makes an ideal accompaniment.

CRUNCHY-TOPPED FRESH APRICOT CAKE

ALMONDS ARE PERFECT PARTNERS FOR FRESH APRICOTS, AND THIS IS A GREAT WAY TO USE UP FIRM FRUITS. SERVE COLD AS A SNACK OR WARM WITH CUSTARD FOR A DESSERT.

MAKES EIGHT SLICES

INGREDIENTS
   1½ cups self-rising flour
   12 tablespoons (1½ sticks) butter,
   softened
   ¾ cup granulated sugar
   1 cup ground almonds
   3 eggs
   1 teaspoon pure almond extract
   ½ teaspoon baking powder
   8 firm apricots, pitted and chopped
For the topping
   2 tablespoons demerara sugar
   ½ cup slivered almonds

1 Preheat the oven to 325°F. Grease a 7-inch round cake pan and line with baking parchment. Put all the cake ingredients, except the apricots, in a large mixing bowl and beat until creamy.

2 Fold the apricots into the cake mixture, then spoon into the prepared cake pan. Make a hollow in the center with the back of a large spoon, then scatter 1 tablespoon of the demerara sugar over for the topping, with the slivered almonds.

3 Bake for 1½ hours, or until a skewer inserted into the middle comes out clean. Sprinkle the remaining demerara sugar over the top of the cake and let cool for 10 minutes in the pan. Remove from the pan, peel off the paper and finish cooling on a wire rack.

PICKLED PEACH AND CHILI CHUTNEY

THIS IS A SPICY, RICH CHUTNEY THAT IS GREAT SERVED WITH COLD ROAST MEATS SUCH AS HAM, PORK OR TURKEY. IT IS ALSO GOOD WITH A STRONG FARMHOUSE CHEDDAR CHEESE.

MAKES 1 POUND

INGREDIENTS
2 cups cider vinegar
1⅔ cups light brown sugar
1 cup dried dates, pitted and finely
  chopped
1 teaspoon ground allspice
1 teaspoon ground mace
1 pound ripe peaches, pitted and cut
  into small chunks
3 onions, thinly sliced
4 fresh red chilies, seeded and finely
  chopped
4 garlic cloves, crushed
2-inch piece of fresh ginger root,
  finely grated
1 teaspoon salt

1 Place the vinegar, brown sugar, dates and spices in a large saucepan and bring to a boil, stirring occasionally.

2 Add all the remaining ingredients and return to a boil. Lower the heat and simmer for 40–50 minutes, or until thick. Stir often to prevent the mixture from burning on the bottom of the pan.

3 Spoon into clean, sterilized jars and seal. When cool, store the jars in the refrigerator and use within 2 months.

COOK'S TIP
To test the consistency of the finished chutney before canning, spoon a little of the mixture onto a plate: The chutney is ready once it holds its shape.

NECTARINE RELISH

THIS SWEET AND TANGY FRUIT RELISH GOES VERY WELL WITH HOT ROAST MEATS AND GAME BIRDS, SUCH AS GUINEA FOWL, PHEASANT AND PORK. MAKE WHILE NECTARINES ARE PLENTIFUL AND KEEP TIGHTLY COVERED IN THE REFRIGERATOR TO SERVE AT CHRISTMAS FOR A SPECIAL TREAT.

MAKES 1 POUND

INGREDIENTS
3 tablespoons olive oil
2 Spanish onions, thinly sliced
1 fresh green chile, seeded and finely
  chopped
1 teaspoon finely chopped
  fresh rosemary
2 bay leaves
1 pound nectarines, pitted and cut
  into chunks
1 cup raisins
2 teaspoons crushed coriander seeds
2 cups demerara sugar
scant 1 cup red wine vinegar

1 Heat the oil in a large pan. Add the onions, chile, rosemary and bay leaves. Cook, stirring often, for 15–20 minutes, or until the onions are soft.

COOK'S TIP
Jars of this relish make a welcome gift. Add a colorful tag reminding the recipient to keep it in the refrigerator.

2 Add all the remaining ingredients and bring to a boil slowly, stirring often. Lower the heat and simmer, stirring occasionally, for 1 hour, or until the relish is thick and sticky.

3 Spoon into sterilized jars and seal. Cool, then chill. The relish will keep in the refrigerator for up to 5 months.

BERRIES AND CURRANTS

Small wonders—that sums up the splendor of berries.
The glowing colors and delectable flavors of strawberries and
raspberries, gooseberries, currants, loganberries and blackberries
(to name but a few of the many varieties) give us immense
pleasure. Whether you brave the brambles or pick up a basket
at your local supermarket, these wonderful treats
are there for the taking.

STRAWBERRIES

For centuries, strawberries have been the most highly prized soft fruit. A sixteenth-century enthusiast, on tasting his first strawberry, summed up their eternal appeal: "Doubtless God could have made a better berry, but doubtless He never did." Nowadays, greenhouse-grown strawberries are available all year round, but these fruits are at their seductive best when grown outdoors.

History

Cultivated strawberries derive from the small wild fraises des bois, tiny fragrant woodland fruits that grow in all temperate countries and were transplanted into kitchen gardens as early as Roman times. By the fourteenth century, the French had become strawberry enthusiasts, but it was another hundred years before the first bowls of strawberries and cream were served in England, at a banquet given by Cardinal Wolsey in 1509.

The cultivated strawberries we enjoy so much today were developed in the nineteenth century from small, scarlet wild strawberries from Virginia. These were crossed with the larger yellow Chilean pine strawberries, which the aptly named French Captain Frézier (the French word for strawberry is *fraise*) had brought to Brittany in 1712. Once the perfect balance of flavor and size had been achieved, enthusiasm for cultivated strawberries blossomed, and they remain one of the world's favorite fruits.

Varieties

Strawberries come in many different sizes, colors and shapes, ranging from conical to globular to oval or heart-shaped. New varieties are constantly being developed.

Left: Fraise des Bois liqueur is a wild-strawberry version of crème de fraise.

Above: These tiny wild woodland fruits, fraises des bois, have a lovely perfumed flavor.

Below: Cultivated strawberries like these are now one of the world's favorite fruits.

Below: Fragrantly scented and vanilla-flavored white fraises des bois.

Above: Gorella—conical-shaped and deep red when ripe.

Left: Cambridge Favorite—medium-size strawberries that are popular with both commercial growers and gardeners.

Below: Elsantas have a great flavor.

FRAISES DES BOIS

The smallest wild strawberries are the **Hautbois** (or wood) varieties, whose tiny red fruits taste wonderfully fragrant. **Alpine** strawberries are generally a little larger and less juicy, with a highly perfumed flavor. Yellow and white varieties look less appealing, but have a delicious flavor of vanilla.

SUMMER STRAWBERRIES

Cambridge Favorite Medium-size berries with an attractive color and flavor, this variety is indeed a favorite with strawberry growers large and small.
Elsanta Largish, firm berries with attractive glossy flesh and an excellent sweet flavor.
Elvira These Dutch strawberries were developed in the 1970s. The oval berries are a deep glossy red.
Gorella A deep red conical berry with paler red flesh. This is an extremely consistent variety.
Perpetual and remontant strawberries As their name implies, these late-season strawberries go on to fruit continuously throughout the autumn. Although they are juicier than summer berries, they are not as sweet, so are better for cooking than other varieties. They can be picked while they are still green and made into jams, sauces and compotes.

Preparing strawberries

1 Wipe the strawberries with a piece of damp paper towels.

2 Hold the strawberry between your thumb and forefinger and twist off the green frill and stem. Try to remove the central hull in the same movement.

Below: Chocolate-dipped strawberries make a delectable after-dinner treat, or a delightful decoration for chocolate cakes and desserts.

Nutrition

Strawberries are rich in vitamins B and C and contain considerable amounts of potassium, iron and fiber. Three and three-fourths ounces of strawberries provide fewer than 30 calories.

Buying and Storing

Size and color are not necessarily indications of quality. Some smaller, greenish varieties taste succulent and delicious. Try always to buy locally grown fruits and check those at the bottom of the pint, making sure they are not squashed or moldy.

Strawberries should ideally be eaten the day they are bought. If necessary, keep the berries in the refrigerator for a day or two, covering them with plastic wrap to prevent them from drying out and from permeating other foods with their scent. Remove from the refrigerator at least an hour before serving.

Frozen strawberries are never as good as fresh, as the texture collapses after freezing, but they are fine for sauces and ice cream. To freeze whole strawberries, sprinkle with a little sugar and pack in a single layer in a plastic box, or open-freeze on a tray, then pack in a rigid container. Puréed strawberries can be frozen with or without added sugar.

Preparing and Serving

It is best not to wash strawberries, as they easily become waterlogged. If they are very dirty, wipe them gently.

Really ripe strawberries need no other accompaniment than cream or crème fraîche and perhaps a little sugar. Improbable though this may sound, a grinding of black pepper or sprinkling of balsamic vinegar will bring out the flavor of the fruit. Strawberries are seldom improved by cooking, although they make delicious jam. They are best used in their raw state in such desserts as strawberry tartlets, shortcake and meringues. They have an affinity with chocolate and make a fine decoration for chocolate terrines and mousses, or they can be dipped into melted chocolate and served as petits fours.

To "dress up" strawberries, macerate them in red wine, Champagne or orange juice. The classic dish Strawberries Romanov simply consists of fresh strawberries macerated in orange juice and orange liqueur. Puréed strawberries can be served as a coulis or made into ice creams and sorbets.

Arbutus (tree strawberry)
The arbutus is a tall shrub whose bright red fruits look like strawberries but have a different taste. The sweet, spiky berries have a soft, slightly mushy texture and a faint flavor of vanilla. You will not find arbutus berries in stores, but the shrubs can be found growing in Europe, as far north as western Ireland (where they are known as Killarney strawberries), and in the United States and China. The berries are unexciting to eat raw, but are used to make jellies and liqueurs.

RASPBERRIES

Perhaps surprisingly, raspberries are a member of the rose family, as you might guess if you have ever been pricked by a raspberry thorn. Native to hilly areas of Europe and Asia, they grow best in a cool, damp climate and can be found even in Alaska. The deep red (or sometimes yellow) jewellike fruits have a sweet, intense flavor, and indeed many people prefer them to strawberries.

Above: Raspberries—deep red fruits, with a wonderfully intense flavor.

History

Wild raspberries have been eaten since prehistoric times, but perhaps because they were so plentiful in the wild, the fruits were not cultivated until the Middle Ages. Nowadays, in colder climates, raspberries are cultivated from native European raspberry varieties, while in North America, they derive from an indigenous species better suited to the drier, hotter conditions that prevail there.

Varieties

Although there are many different varieties of raspberry, and new ones are constantly being developed, those sold in stores and markets are not identified specifically. Gardeners have their own favorites:
Heritage is a late-fruiting variety with outstanding flavor.
Malling Jewel, which fruits in mid-season, is a heavy cropper.
Wild raspberries You will often find these tiny, fragrant fruits growing in

Above: Arctic raspberries, grown in the chilly climes of Alaska.

Below: Yellow or golden raspberries are worth seeking out, because they have a delectable flavor.

cool, damp areas of woodland. They are full of seeds, but their exquisite flavor makes up for this deficiency.
Yellow and golden raspberries Clear golden berries, not widely available, but worth seeking out for their fine flavor.

Nutrition

Raspberries are a valuable source of vitamin C, potassium, niacin and riboflavin, and dietary fiber. They contain 25 calories per 3¾ ounces. Raspberry juice is said to be good for the heart, while the leaves have long been renowned for their beneficial effects during childbirth; raspberry-leaf tea is said to prevent miscarriages, ease labor and help the uterus to contract after the birth.

Buying and Storing

Raspberries are ripe when they are brightly and evenly colored. They are always sold hulled, but if you are picking your own, they should slide easily off the hulls. When buying raspberries in a basket, check the bottom to make sure it is not stained red or leaking—a sure sign that the fruit is soft and past its best.

If possible, always eat raspberries the day they are bought or picked; if necessary, they can be stored for up to two days in the bottom of the refrigerator, but bring them out at least an hour before serving.

Raspberries freeze very well; whole berries emerge almost as good as fresh. Open-freeze the fruit in a single layer

Left: Raspberry vinegar makes a sharp, yet refreshingly fruity addition to home-made salad dressing.

on a baking sheet, then pack into rigid cartons. Less than perfect raspberries can be puréed and strained, then sweetened with a little granulated sugar or confectioners' sugar before being frozen.

Preparing and Serving

Do not wash raspberries unless this is unavoidable; they are seldom very dirty, and washing will ruin the texture and flavor. All you need do is gently pick off any bits of leaf or stem.

Good raspberries have such a wonderful flavor that they are best eaten on their own, with a little sugar and cream. They go well with other fruits, like oranges, apples, pears, figs and melon. In the classic dish Peach Melba, raspberries are used as a coulis to coat a lightly poached peach. They also make delicious fillings for pastries, meringues and tartlets, and, because they look so attractive, they are ideal for decoration.

Raspberries can be crushed with a little confectioners' sugar, then pushed through a nylon or stainless strainer strain to make sauces, coulis or bases for ice creams and sorbets. They can be cooked in pies; apple and raspberry is a classic combination. They are rich in pectin, so make excellent jams and jellies. Raspberry vinegar is delicious and makes delectable dressings and sauces.

Preparing a raspberry coulis
1 Put the raspberries in a bowl and crush to a purée with a fork.

2 Pour the purée into a strainer set over a clean bowl. Rub through, using the back of a large spoon.

3 Sweeten to taste with granulated or confectioners' sugar; stir well.

CLOUDBERRIES

These deep golden relatives of the raspberry grow on boggy land in the cold northern climates of Scandinavia, Siberia, Canada and even the Arctic Circle. Because they lack warmth, the berries ripen slowly, allowing the flavor

Left: Popular in Scandinavia, cloudberry jam makes a colorful topping for chocolate mousse or soufflé.

to develop to an extraordinary intensity and sweetness, almost like honeyed apples (Canadians call cloudberries "baked apple berries"). These unusual berries are particularly highly prized in Scandinavian countries, where they are made into excellent jams and desserts, and also into wonderful fruit soups.

Cloudberries are also distilled into a nectarlike liqueur that tastes delicious with bitter chocolate. The berries have a particular affinity for chocolate; try topping a chocolate mousse or soufflé with a spoonful of cloudberry jam.

Above: Brightly colored cloudberries have an amazingly intense flavor.

BLACKBERRIES AND DEWBERRIES

These two relations of the raspberry and the rose are virtually indistinguishable, the main difference being that blackberries are larger and grow on thorny upright bushes or brambles, while dewberries trail. The shiny purplish black berries are made up of a number of segments (drupelets), each containing a hard seed. They grow wild almost everywhere in the world, but are also cultivated to give a larger, juicier berry with better keeping properties. Buying cultivated blackberries, however, is not nearly as much fun as picking your own.

Below: Large, cultivated blackberries

History

Archaeological excavations show that man has eaten blackberries since Neolithic times. The ancient Greeks prized them as much for the medicinal properties of their leaves as for the fruit, and they have remained popular throughout the centuries. Not everyone appreciates the qualities of wild brambles, though; after they had been introduced to Australia by the early settlers, they were declared a noxious weed in some areas!

Nutrition

Blackberries are rich in dietary fiber and vitamin C and are often used to make health drinks. They also contain some calcium, phosphorus and potassium. Blackberries typically contain about 30 calories per 3¾ ounces.

Choosing and Storing

Whether you pick or buy blackberries, they should be plump and tender, but not wet or mushy. Look for large, shiny fruit, and if you are buying a basket, check that the underside is not stained. Legend has it that blackberries should not be picked after September, or the Devil will be in them and they will taste impossibly sour.

Blackberries do not keep well. If you cannot eat them immediately, store them for no more than one day in the bottom of the refrigerator.

Preparing and Cooking

If you must wash blackberries, do so just before serving and drain them well on paper towels.

Freezing blackberries

Blackberries freeze well. Open-freeze perfect specimens in a single layer on a baking sheet, then pack into rigid containers. Damaged berries can be puréed and strained, then sweetened with sugar or honey.

Above: Wild blackberries—also known as brambles.

Right: Crème de mûre— this richly flavored blackberry liqueur is seldom drunk on its own. It is more often used as a colorful flavoring for cocktails.

Left: Dewberries— smaller than but very similar to blackberries—grow on long, trailing branches.

Blackberry Kir Royale

Ripe, juicy blackberries are best eaten just as they are, with sugar and cream. They make a tasty addition to breakfast cereal or a fruit salad. Blackberries can be puréed and strained to make coulis, ice cream, sorbets and fools. They make delicious jam or jelly and in England are the classic partner for apples in a pie or crumble. There is no need to cook them before using them in a pie or a pudding.

Left: English Bramble liqueur

Above: Dewberry flowers, which appear before the fruits develop.

Blackberries go well with many other fruits besides apples, and can be used in savory game dishes. Use them to flavor spirits, such as vodka or eau-de-vie, or make a cordial to combat a cold. Commercially produced *crème de mûre* (blackberry liqueur) enhances the flavor of any dessert that incorporates fresh uncooked blackberries.

For a delicious variation on the classic Kir Royale, which is usually made with crème de cassis (black currant liqueur), pour a little crème de mûre into a champagne flute and top up with Champagne or sparkling white wine. Alternatively, to make an exceptionally luxurious cocktail, put some blackberries in a champagne flute, add a dash of orange liqueur, such as Cointreau, and top up with Champagne or sparkling white wine.

HYBRID BERRIES

There are a wide variety of raspberry/blackberry crossbreeds. Some of these occurred naturally, like the loganberry; others have been cultivated to produce a more robust or better-flavored fruit. All these hybrids can be cooked and frozen in the same way as raspberries or blackberries.

Loganberries The first loganberry appeared in 1881 at Santa Cruz in California in the garden of Judge J.H. Logan. It was a natural hybrid, probably derived from a cross between a native dewberry and a raspberry. Since then, loganberries have been

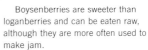

Right: Tayberries were bred in Scotland.

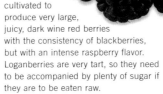

cultivated to produce very large, juicy, dark wine red berries with the consistency of blackberries, but with an intense raspberry flavor. Loganberries are very tart, so they need to be accompanied by plenty of sugar if they are to be eaten raw.

Youngberries These dewberry/loganberry hybrids resemble a dark red, elongated blackberry, but taste rather like a sweeter loganberry.

Boysenberries An even more elaborate hybrid—a cross between a youngberry and a raspberry, but resembling a large reddish purple blackberry.

Left: Large, sweet boysenberries are mostly used to make jam.

Boysenberries are sweeter than loganberries and can be eaten raw, although they are more often used to make jam.

Tayberries Tayberries are arguably the finest hybrids of all. Bred in Scotland, they are a cross between the American blackberry Aurora and a tetraploid raspberry. They grow on long, spiny canes. The bright red, elongated berries have a slightly tart, aromatic flavor and although they can be eaten raw, tayberries are better cooked.

Tummelberries are similar to tayberries, but fruit later in the season. Other, similar crossbreeds include **sunberries** and **wineberries.**

Above: Loganberries, which look more like reddish blackberries, have an intense raspberry flavor.

Left: Dark red youngberries are a hybrid of the dewberry and loganberry, but taste rather like a sweeter version of loganberry.

MULBERRIES

Mulberries grow on magnificent dome-headed trees, which can often be very ancient and grow up to 30 feet across, so they are rarely found in small modern yards! Silkworms feed on the leaves, but the berries are left to drop to the ground as they ripen and have a delicious, slightly musky flavor. Luscious black mulberries taste very good but beware—they stain everything with which they come into contact. Legend has it that rubbing a stain created by a ripe mulberry with an unripe mulberry (if you can reach one) will remove it.

Right: Mulberries taste very good, but the juice stains terribly.

dark wine red berries resemble loganberries.

History

Black mulberries are native to Western Asia. They were known to the ancient Greeks, but it was the Roman emperor Justinian who deliberately encouraged their propagation as part of an enterprise in silk production.

In the sixteenth century, it was discovered that silkworms preferred to feed on the white mulberry leaves, and many of these trees were planted in Europe in the vain hope of stimulating a silk trade. Some of these white mulberry trees still survive today.

Varieties

White mulberries are actually pinkish or pale red. There is also an American red mulberry, whose leaves turn beautifully yellow in autumn.

Black mulberries are considered finer than the white variety. The elongated,

Preparing and Serving

Ripe mulberries can be eaten just as they are, with or without the addition of cream, and are usually sweet enough not to need sugar. They also make a good addition to summer pudding.

Overripe fruit is best used for jams, jellies and sauces. Mulberries make excellent ice creams, fools and sorbets. Mulberry sauce goes well with richly flavored roast meats, such as game, duck and lamb.

HUCKLEBERRIES

These berries, which gave their name to Mark Twain's famous character Huckleberry Finn, are quite similar to blueberries, but have a tougher skin and hard internal seeds. They have a sharper flavor than blueberries, but can be eaten and cooked in exactly the same way.

Another variety of huckleberry is the **tangleberry**, which grows on the coast of North America. These purplish blue berries are sweeter than huckleberries and have a subtle tang of the sea.

Right: Huckleberries, which are similar to blueberries, have fairly tough skins and a sharp flavor.

BLUEBERRIES AND BILBERRIES

Blueberries and bilberries (also known as blaeberries, whortleberries or whinberries) are both small, round blue-black berries with a silvery bloom. They grow on shrubs on inhospitable, peaty moors and uplands. The flavor is mild and sweet and the texture firm.

American blueberries are generally larger and sweeter than bilberries. Today they are often cultivated, resulting in large, perfect berries that sometimes lack the distinctive flavor of the wild fruit.

Right: Blueberries— mild and sweet-flavored.

Nutrition

Blueberries and bilberries are a source of vitamin C, iron and dietary fiber. They provide about 60 calories per 3¾ ounces.

Buying and Storing

The best blueberries and bilberries are those you pick yourself. If you buy them, look for plump berries of uniform size. Reject shriveled specimens, or those without the characteristic bloom. Unwashed berries will keep for up to a week in the bottom of the refrigerator.

Blueberries and bilberries can be frozen just as they are, provided they are in a sealed bag. Alternatively, poach them in a little lemon-flavored syrup and then freeze.

Above: Bilberries are smaller and less sweet than blueberries, but have a distinctive flavor.

Above: Dried blueberries are available in specialty food shops and greengrocers. They make a tasty addition to homemade fruit cakes and muesli, and are delicious scattered into fresh fruit salads or over breakfast cereal.

Preparing and Cooking

Blueberries and bilberries have soft seeds, so they can be eaten raw. Simply rinse and drain them first. However, they are more usually baked in pies or muffins, or used as a jamlike topping for cheesecake. To cook, make a light sugar syrup and flavor it with lemon, orange and cinnamon or allspice, and poach the berries until tender.

Blueberry pie is a classic dessert, as is blueberry grunt, which consists of blueberries stewed with lemon and spice, baked with a dumpling-like topping. Blueberries can also be made into a sauce to serve with game.

ELDERBERRIES

Although you can seldom buy elderberries, you will find them growing all over the countryside in the summer. First come the creamy white flowerheads, whose flavor goes very well with gooseberries. These are followed by flat, wide clusters of small, sweet, almost black berries, which must be cooked before eating.

History

Elderberries have grown in Europe and Asia since prehistoric times. The bushes themselves were little loved, perhaps because of their unattractive smell, but the berries provided sustenance for the poor. People often used elderberries as a fabric dye and to make wine; later the berries were used to add color and extra flavor to thin, cheap wines.

Nutrition

Elderberries are an excellent source of vitamin C.

Choosing and Storing

Never pick elderberries growing close to a road, as they will be contaminated by dust and pollution. Good elderberries should be shiny and black. For elderflower syrup, choose creamy flowerheads that are fully open, but whose petals have not begun to drop. Use both flowers and berries as soon as possible after picking.

Below: Elderberries can be cooked with other fruits in pies and tarts or used to make jellies and sauces.

Preparing and Cooking

Use a fork to strip the berries from the stems. Elderberries can be cooked in the same way as red currants or other berries. Flowers should be shaken to dislodge any insects or loose petals and briefly rinsed in cold water.

Sprigs of elderflowers can be dipped in batter to make fritters, or made into an intensely flavored syrup. The berries can be made into jellies, or used to bulk out other berries in pies, tarts and fools.

Elderberries can be made into a savory sauce for pork and game. They are often used to make vinegar, and are excellent for making wine.

Elderflowers can be made into a refreshing summer drink. To make eight 1¼ pint bottles, you will need about 12 large elderflower heads. Choose blossoms that are fully open, but not shedding their petals, and wash thoroughly. Place in a large pan and pour 6 quarts boiling water over. Add a generous 1 cup sugar, 2 thinly sliced lemons and ½ cup white wine or cider vinegar. Stir and leave to macerate in a cool place for three days, stirring twice a day. Strain the liquid and pour into sterilized wine bottles. Cork very firmly and leave for at least a week before drinking.

Left: Elderflowers can be made into fritters and intensely flavored drinks.

Stripping elderberries

Hold the stem in one hand and run a fork through the berries.

ROWANBERRIES

These bright orangey red berries are the fruit of the mountain ash. They grow in large clusters and are a great favorite with wild birds. Rowanberries are not available commercially.

Nutrition

Rowanberries are very rich in vitamin C and pectin.

Preparing and Cooking

The best-known use for rowanberries is in a glorious deep orange jewellike jelly with a bittersweet flavor, which goes particularly well with rich meats and game. Rowanberries are also used to add color to sweet apple dishes, such as pies and crumbles, or they can be made into compotes and sauces. Cook them in the same way as other berries. They cannot be eaten raw.

Right: Rowan-berries can be made into a vibrant jelly.

ROSE HIPS

These are the seed pods of roses, and appear after the plants have finished flowering. They vary in color from orange to deep red and make a beautiful sight in autumn in gardens and hedgerows. Hips contain extremely hairy seeds, which must be removed before they can be eaten.

Nutrition

Rose hips are so rich in vitamin C that in wartime Britain they were picked by both children and adult volunteers and used in vast quantities to make bright pink rose hip syrup for pregnant women and babies. A single rose hip typically contains twenty times more vitamin C than an orange.

Right: Rose hips are enormously rich in vitamin C.

Preparing and Cooking

Very ripe rose hips can be eaten raw, but they do not taste particularly pleasant. Plump rose hips can be made into a bittersweet jelly to serve with poultry or game, or sweetened with sugar or honey and boiled to a syrup. Rose hips can also be used to flavor vinegar, and make an attractive garnish for salads.

Before cooking rose hips, trim them, cut them in half and scoop out every trace of the seeds and prickly hairs. If making jelly or syrup, strain the liquid twice through a double layer of cheesecloth.

HAWS

The fruit of the hawthorn or May tree, the white spring blossom is followed by these small, wine red berries with a bitter, pungent taste.

Preparing and Cooking

Haws cannot be eaten raw, but make a delicious jelly when combined with crab apples. Elderberries can be added to the mixture to make a hedgerow jelly. Haws also make a good sauce for rich meats and game.

Right: Wine red haws are pretty to look at, but have a bitter, pungent taste.

GOOSEBERRIES

The gooseberry, a botanical cousin of the black currant, is native to Europe and North America. The fruits, which grow on dauntingly spiny bushes, come in many varieties—hard and sour, succulently soft and sweet, smooth and hairy—and in a range of colors, from vivid green to luscious purple.

History

Gooseberries were popular all over Britain well before Tudor times, when they grew wild in many kitchen gardens. The Tudors served them in savory sauces and in all manner of sweet dishes. They were first cultivated in the sixteenth century and became so popular that in the nineteenth century competitors formed gooseberry clubs to see who could grow the biggest berry (some are reputed to have been grown to the size of a bantam's egg).

For some reason, their popularity did not spread abroad; even today the French use them only in a sauce to cut the richness of oily fish. There is no specific French word for gooseberry; it shares its name with the red currant and is known as *groseille de maquereau* ("red currant for mackerel").

Varieties

Gooseberries have a very long season. Early gooseberries are usually bright green and rather hard. They cannot be eaten raw, but taste wonderful cooked. These are followed by the softer, mid-season fruits, which are not generally identified by variety when sold in supermarkets and greengrocers, but which you may find in gardens and farm stands.

Early Sulphur A very early variety with golden, almost transparent berries and a lovely sweet flavor.

Goldendrop As attractive as its name, this small, round yellow gooseberry has a fine rich flavor, which makes it ideal for eating

raw as a dessert fruit. Ready to pick in midsummer.

Langley's Industry A large, red, hairy berry with a lovely sweet flavor. Ideal for the less green-thumbed gardener, it will grow vigorously anywhere and can be picked early for cooking, or left to ripen fully on the bush to eat raw like grapes.

Above: Huge, deep red London berries are sweet enough to eat raw.

Leveller A mid-season yellowish green berry with a sweet flavor.

London This huge mid-season berry is deep red or purple. For thirty-seven years, between 1829 and 1867, it was the unbeaten British champion in major gooseberry competitions! These dessert gooseberries can be eaten fresh, just as they are.

Left: Green gooseberries—these early-cropping fruits cannot be eaten raw, but are delicious cooked.

Right: Fully ripe red gooseberries are sweet enough to be eaten just as they are.

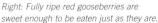

Nutrition

Gooseberries are high in vitamin C and also contain vitamins A and D, potassium, calcium, phosphorus and niacin. They are rich in dietary fiber and provide only 17 calories per 3¾ ounces.

Buying and Storing

Choose slightly unripe green gooseberries for cooking. Check that they are not rock hard. Dessert varieties should be yielding and juicy (if possible, taste before you buy). Gooseberries will keep in the refrigerator for up to a week.

To freeze whole gooseberries, trim them and open-freeze on baking sheets. Pack the frozen berries in bags. Alternatively, purée and strain them, sweeten and freeze in rigid containers.

Below: You may find Leveller berries, which have a lovely sweet flavor, in garden centers, pick-your-own farms and farm stands.

Preparing

For recipes using whole gooseberries, wash, then trim them (this is not necessary if you are making jam or jelly, or are going to strain the cooked fruit).

Cooking

Gooseberries are rich in pectin, particularly when they are slightly unripe, which makes them ideal for jams and jellies. Their tartness makes an excellent foil for oily fish and rich poultry or meat.

Cook gooseberries very gently with a little water and sugar to taste until all the fruit has collapsed. If you like, flavor them with cinnamon, lemon or herbs. A few fennel or dill seeds will enhance a gooseberry sauce for fish.

In England, the first gooseberries of the season were traditionally used to make a Whitsun pie. They also make a good filling for suet pudding or crumble.

Worcestershire berries
A North American species of gooseberry that grows on a bush with wicked spines. The small purplish red berries are hardly much bigger than blackberries, but have the distinctive veining of gooseberries and a gooseberry flavor. Worcestershire berries can be eaten raw or cooked.

Trimming gooseberries
1 Hold the gooseberry between your forefinger and thumb.
2 Snip off the stem and flower end with sharp scissors or trim with a knife.

Puréed, strained and mixed with whipped cream, they make the perfect fruit fool. Gooseberries have an extraordinary affinity for elderflowers, which come into season at the same time as the early fruit and add a delicious muscat flavor to the berries.

Below: Sweet-tasting Early Sulphur are golden and almost translucent.

CRANBERRIES

These tart, bright red berries grow wild on evergreen shrubs in peaty marshland all over northern Europe and North America. They are closely related to blueberries and bilberries, but are much more sour and are always served cooked. **Cowberries** and **lingonberries** are very similar, but smaller.

Cranberries are sometimes known as "bounceberries," since they were traditionally tested for firmness by being bounced seven times. Any that failed the bounce test were too squashy and were therefore discarded. Because of their waxy skins, cranberries keep for much longer than other berries, which helps to explain their popularity.

History

For centuries before the first settlers arrived in America, the native American Indians prized wild cranberries for their nutritional and medicinal value, and used them to make a dye for fabric and for decorative feathers. Although cranberries were already known in Britain, the Pilgrims found that the American berries were larger and more succulent.

Right: Bright red cranberries can be used in sweet and savory dishes.

Below: Dried cranberries

Cranberry sauce

1 Thinly pare an orange with a swivel-bladed vegetable peeler, taking care to remove only the zest. Squeeze the juice and put it in a saucepan with the zest.

2 Add 3 cups cranberries and cook gently for a few minutes, until the cranberry skins pop.

3 Stir in sugar to taste and simmer for 5 minutes. Stir in 2 tablespoons port (optional). Pour the cranberry sauce into a bowl, then cool and chill before serving.

They called them "craneberries" because the pink blossoms resembled a crane's head, or possibly because the cranes, which lived in the marshlands, were partial to the berries.

Cranberries featured in the first-ever Thanksgiving feast in 1620 and have been a traditional part of the celebrations ever since. Commercial cultivation began in the nineteenth century, and today cranberries are available frozen, canned, dried, as juice and in jellies and relishes.

Nutrition

Cranberries contain vitamins C and D, potassium and iron. They were considered to be a good protection against scurvy. They are naturally very low in calories (but need sweetening to make them palatable).

Buying and Storing

Look for plump, firm, bright red berries and make sure that those at the bottom of the package are neither squashed nor shriveled. Fresh cranberries will keep in the refrigerator for four weeks, or they can be frozen in freezer bags and used without being thawed.

Preparing and Cooking

Cranberries can be used in sweet or savory dishes. Their most famous incarnation is as cranberry sauce, which is served with turkey or game. Their distinctive tartness even adds zest to firm-fleshed fish. The berries are high in pectin, so they make excellent jams and jellies. They combine well with oranges and apples, and can be mixed with blackberries and raspberries to make an autumnal variation on summer pudding.

Cranberries should be stewed slowly with sugar to taste and a little water or orange juice until the skins pop. Dried cranberries can be used in the same way as raisins. Cranberry juice can be mixed with soda water and white wine or grape juice to make a refreshing drink. It is also good with orange juice and vodka.

Cranberry and chestnut stuffing

The traditional Christmas accompaniments of cranberries and chestnuts can be combined to make the perfect stuffing for turkey or other poultry. To make about 1 pound (enough to stuff a 10–12-pound bird), soften 4 ounces (⅔ cup) finely chopped onion in 2 tablespoons butter in a saucepan. Stir in 6 ounces unsweetened chestnut purée and 2 tablespoons cooked cranberries or chunky cranberry sauce. Season to taste with salt and pepper and mix thoroughly. Take the pan off the heat and stir in 8 ounces fresh white bread crumbs. Coarsely crumble or chop 4 ounces cooked chestnuts (canned chestnuts are fine) and fold into the stuffing mixture. Let cool completely before stuffing the bird.

Below: Cranberry juice and soda water makes a refreshing drink.

BLACK CURRANTS, RED CURRANTS AND WHITE CURRANTS

These native European berries, with their glowing colors, make a beautiful sight in summer, hanging like tiny bunches of grapes on the bush. Each berry contains a mass of small seeds. Currants can be eaten whole, but because they are highly acidic, this is seldom the preferred option.

History

Currants grow wild all over Europe and even as far north as Siberia. For some inexplicable reason, they were not cultivated by the Romans, but became popular only in the sixteenth century, when they were prized for their health-giving properties.

Nutrition

All currants, particularly black currants, are very rich in vitamin C. Black currants are used in cordials, cough drops and other remedies designed to ward off colds; in the past, they were often used as a cure for quinsy. They are also high in pectin.

Buying and Storing

Choose plump, firm currants with shiny skins. They will keep in the refrigerator for several days. They can be frozen very successfully: Strip the currants

Below: Buffalo currants are a type of black currant with larger berries.

Right: Black currants grow wild all over Europe. The fruits have a tart flavor and are usually cooked.

from the stems, then rinse and drain them. Freeze in rigid containers. Sweetened or unsweetened black currant purée also freezes well.

Preparing

Strip the currants from the stems, unless this has already been done. If you wish, pick off the calyx tops before cooking the currants by pinching them between the nails of your forefinger and thumb. This is a tedious process and is seldom necessary.

BLACK CURRANTS

Although they are often combined with other currants in cooking (as in summer pudding), black currants are different from other types. They have tougher skins and, unlike other currants, which grow on old wood, they fruit on new wood. Both the bushes and the currants themselves are highly aromatic and the fruits have a luscious, tart flavor.

Cooking

Black currants can be added raw to fruit salads if they are not too tart, but are usually cooked in a little water, with sugar to taste. Simmer until just tender—do not overcook them, or they will lose their fresh flavor. Black currants make wonderful jams and jellies and combine well with soft cheeses, rich meats and game. To serve black currants with meat, sauté them lightly

Stripping currants off the stem

Hold the bunch of currants by the stem and strip off the berries with the tines of a fork.

Right: White currants are less tart than other currants and can be eaten raw.

in butter, adding a pinch of sugar. They adapt well to other flavorings, such as mint and lemon, and are used to make the liqueur crème de cassis, which is the basis for Kir Royale and similar drinks.

RED CURRANTS

Red currants can be eaten raw. Small bunches look very decorative if frosted with egg white and sugar. They are an essential ingredient for summer pudding and make a good addition to creamy desserts, such as crème brûlée. For a refreshing summer drink, purée 4 cups red currants with 2 cups water and sugar to taste, then press the purée gently through a strainer placed over a pitcher. Serve with sparkling water or soda water, or add a dash of vodka or gin.

The most familiar use of red currants, however, is in the jewellike red currant jelly that goes so well with lamb and venison. Cumberland sauce (for game, ham and rich meats) is made by heating red currant jelly with lemon zest, port and sometimes mustard.

WHITE CURRANTS

These beautiful, translucent, silvery golden currants are an albino strain of red currants. They are less tart than other types and can be eaten raw. They look wonderfully decorative frosted with egg white and sugar. **Pink currants** are an even more attractive variety, with a beautiful pink flush.

Above: Red currant jelly

Left: Red currants are an essential ingredient for summer pudding.

Red currant jelly

1 Put the red currants (as many as you have) in a preserving pan with just enough water to cover. Simmer for 8–10 minutes, or until the currants are very soft.

2 Strain through a jelly bag, then measure the liquid. Pour it back into the pan and add 1 1/2 cups sugar for every 2 1/2 cups liquid. Stir over medium heat until dissolved.

3 Boil briskly for 10 minutes, or until setting point is reached, skimming off any scum as it rises to the surface. Pour the jelly into sterilized jars, seal and label.

BERRY AND CURRANT RECIPES

For sheer beauty, berries are hard to beat.
Make the most of their tantalizing colors and flavors
by serving them simply, as a topping for shortcakes
or in a summer pudding. Fresh Blueberry Muffins,
Berry Brûlée Tarts, Blackberry Jelly—
these are berries at their best.

SUMMER PUDDING

NO FRUIT BOOK WOULD BE COMPLETE WITHOUT THIS WELL-LOVED CLASSIC RECIPE. DON'T RESERVE IT SOLELY FOR SUMMER: IT FREEZES WELL AND PROVIDES A DELICIOUS DESSERT FOR CHRISTMAS DAY, AS A LIGHT AND REFRESHING ALTERNATIVE TO THE TRADITIONAL PLUM PUDDING.

SERVES FOUR TO SIX

INGREDIENTS
½-inch-thick slices of day-old white
  bread, crusts removed
6–7 cups mixed berries, such as
  strawberries, raspberries, black
  currants, red currants and
  blueberries
¼ cup turbinado sugar
lightly whipped heavy cream or crème
  fraîche, to serve

3 Fold over the excess bread, then cover the fruit with the remaining bread slices, trimming them to fit. Place a small plate or saucer directly on top of the pudding, fitting it inside the bowl or mold. Weight it with a 2-pound weight or a couple of full cans.

4 Leave the pudding in the refrigerator for at least 8 hours or overnight. To serve, run a knife between the pudding and the bowl or mold and turn it out onto a plate. Spoon any reserved juices over the top and serve with whipped cream or crème fraîche.

1 Trim a slice of bread to fit in the bottom of a 5-cup pudding bowl or mold, then trim another 5–6 slices to line the sides.

2 Place all the fruit in a saucepan with the sugar. Cook gently for 4–5 minutes, until the juices begin to run—it will not be necessary to add any water. Allow the mixture to cool slightly, then spoon the berries and enough of their juices to moisten into the bread-lined pudding bowl or mold. Save any leftover juice to serve with the pudding.

HOT BLACKBERRY AND APPLE SOUFFLES

AS THE BLACKBERRY SEASON IS SO SHORT AND THE APPLE SEASON SO LONG, IT'S ALWAYS WORTH FREEZING A BAG OF BLACKBERRIES TO HAVE ON HAND FOR TREATS LIKE THIS ONE.

2 Cook the blackberries and diced apple with the orange zest and juice in a pan for 10 minutes, or until the apple has pulped down well. Press through a strainer into a bowl. Stir in ¼ cup of the superfine sugar. Set aside to cool.

3 Put a spoonful of the fruit purée into each prepared dish and smooth the surface. Set the dishes aside.

4 Beat the egg whites in a large, greasefree bowl until they form stiff peaks. Very gradually beat in the remaining superfine sugar to make a stiff, glossy meringue mixture.

5 Fold in the remaining fruit purée and spoon the flavored meringue into the prepared dishes. Level the tops with a spatula, and run a table knife around the edge of each dish.

6 Place the dishes on the hot baking sheet and bake for 10–15 minutes, until the soufflés have risen well and are lightly browned. Dust the tops with confectioners' sugar and serve immediately.

MAKES SIX

INGREDIENTS
- butter, for greasing
- ⅔ cup superfine sugar, plus extra for dusting
- 3 cups blackberries
- 1 large cooking apple, peeled, cored and finely diced
- grated zest and juice of 1 orange
- 3 egg whites
- confectioners' sugar, for dusting

COOK'S TIP
Running a table knife around the edge of the soufflés before baking helps them to rise evenly without any part sticking to the rim of the dishes.

1 Preheat the oven to 400°F. Generously grease six ⅔-cup individual soufflé dishes with butter and dust with superfine sugar, shaking out the excess. Put a baking sheet in the oven to heat.

SUMMER BERRY CREPES

THE DELICATE FLAVOR OF THESE FLUFFY CRÊPES CONTRASTS BEAUTIFULLY WITH TANGY BERRIES.

INGREDIENTS
   1 cup self-rising flour
   1 large egg
   1¼ cups milk
   a few drops of pure vanilla extract
   1 tablespoon butter
   1 tablespoon sunflower oil
   confectioners' sugar, for dusting
For the fruit
   2 tablespoons butter
   ¼ cup sugar
   juice of 2 oranges
   thinly pared zest of ½ orange
   3 cups mixed summer berries,
     such as sliced strawberries,
     yellow raspberries, blueberries
     and red currants
   3 tablespoons Grand Marnier or other
     orange liqueur

1 Preheat the oven to 300°F. To make the crêpes, sift the flour into a large bowl and make a well in the center. Break in the egg and gradually whisk in the milk to make a smooth batter. Stir in the vanilla extract. Set the batter aside in a cool place for up to half an hour,

2 Heat the butter and oil together in a 7-inch nonstick frying pan. Swirl to grease the pan, then pour the excess fat into a small bowl.

3 If the batter has been allowed to stand, whisk it thoroughly until smooth. Pour a little of the batter into the hot pan, swirling to cover the bottom of the pan evenly. Cook until the mixture comes away from the sides and the crêpe is golden underneath.

4 Flip over the crêpe with a large metal spatula and cook the other side briefly until golden.

5 Slide the crêpe onto a heatproof plate. Make seven more crêpes in the same way, greasing the pan with more butter and oil mixture as needed. Cover the crêpes with foil or another plate and keep them hot in the oven.

COOK'S TIP
For safety, when igniting a mixture for flambéing, use a long taper or long wooden match. Stand back as you set the mixture alight.

6 To prepare the fruit, melt the butter in a heavy frying pan, stir in the sugar and cook gently until the mixture is golden brown. Add the orange juice and zest and cook until syrupy.

7 Add the fruits and warm through, then add the liqueur and set it alight. Shake the pan to incorporate the liqueur until the flame dies down.

8 Fold the crêpes into quarters and arrange two on each plate. Spoon some of the fruit mixture over and dust with the confectioners' sugar. Serve the remaining fruit mixture separately.

FRESH BERRY PAVLOVA

PAVLOVA IS THE SIMPLEST OF DESSERTS, BUT IT CAN ALSO BE THE MOST STUNNING. FILL WITH A MIXTURE OF BERRIES IF YOU LIKE—RASPBERRIES AND BLUEBERRIES MAKE A MARVELOUS COMBINATION.

SERVES SIX TO EIGHT

INGREDIENTS
  4 egg whites, at room temperature
  1 cup superfine sugar
  1 teaspoon cornstarch
  1 teaspoon cider vinegar
  ½ teaspoon pure vanilla extract
  1¼ cups heavy cream
  ⅔ cup crème fraîche
  1½ cups blueberries
  fresh mint sprigs,
    to decorate
  confectioners' sugar, for dusting

COOK'S TIP
To begin, invert a plate on the baking parchment and draw around it with a pencil. Turn the paper over and use the circle as a guide for the meringue.

1 Preheat the oven to 275°F. Line a baking sheet with baking parchment. Beat the egg whites in a large greasefree bowl until they form stiff peaks. Gradually beat in the sugar to make a stiff, glossy meringue. Sift the cornstarch over and fold it in with the vinegar and vanilla.

2 Spoon the meringue mixture onto the paper-lined sheet, using the circle drawn on the paper as a guide (see Cook's Tip). Spread into a round, swirling the top, and bake for 1¼ hours, or until the meringue is crisp and very lightly golden. Switch off the oven, keeping the door closed, and allow the meringue to cool for 1–2 hours.

3 Carefully peel the parchment from the meringue and transfer it to a serving plate. Whip the cream in a large mixing bowl until it forms soft peaks, fold in the crème fraîche, then spoon the mixture into the center of the meringue shell. Top with the raspberries and blueberries and decorate with the mint sprigs. Sift confectioners' sugar over the top and serve at once.

GOOSEBERRY AND ELDERFLOWER FOOL

GOOSEBERRIES AND ELDERFLOWERS ARE A MATCH MADE IN HEAVEN, EACH BRINGING OUT THE FLAVOR OF THE OTHER. SERVE WITH AMARETTI OR OTHER DESSERT COOKIES FOR DIPPING.

SERVES SIX

INGREDIENTS
  4 cups gooseberries, cleaned
  2 tablespoons water
  ¼–⅓ cup sugar
  2 tablespoons elderflower cordial
  about 2 cups custard sauce (crème
    anglaise), prepared in advance
  1¼ cups heavy cream
  crushed amaretti cookies, to decorate
  amaretti cookies, to serve

1 Put the gooseberries and water in a pan. Cover and cook for 5–6 minutes, or until the berries pop open.

2 Add the sugar and elderflower cordial to the gooseberries, then stir vigorously or mash until the fruit forms a pulp. Remove the pan from the heat, spoon the gooseberry pulp into a bowl and set aside to cool.

3 Stir the custard into the fruit. Whip the cream to soft peaks, then fold it into the mixture and chill. Serve in dessert glasses, decorated with crushed amaretti and accompanied by amaretti.

FRUITS OF THE FOREST WITH WHITE CHOCOLATE CREAMS

COLORFUL FRUITS MACERATED IN A MIXTURE OF WHITE COCONUT RUM AND SUGAR MAKE A FANTASTIC ACCOMPANIMENT TO A DELIGHTFULLY CREAMY WHITE CHOCOLATE MOUSSE.

SERVES FOUR

INGREDIENTS
3 ounces white cooking chocolate, in squares
⅔ cup heavy cream
2 tablespoons crème fraîche
1 egg, separated
1 teaspoon powdered gelatin
2 tablespoons cold water
a few drops of pure vanilla extract
1 cup small strawberries, sliced
½ cup raspberries
¾ cup blueberries
3 tablespoons superfine sugar
5 tablespoons white coconut rum
strawberry leaves, to decorate (optional)

1 Melt the chocolate in a heatproof bowl set over a pan of hot water. Heat the cream in a separate pan until almost boiling, then stir into the chocolate with the crème fraîche. Cool slightly, then beat in the egg yolk.

2 Sprinkle the gelatin over the cold water in another heatproof bowl and set aside for a few minutes to soften.

COOK'S TIP
For a dramatic effect, decorate each white chocolate cream with dark chocolate leaves, made by coating the veined side of unsprayed rose leaves with melted chocolate. Let them dry before gently pulling off the leaves.

3 Set the bowl in a pan of hot water until the gelatin has dissolved completely. Stir the dissolved gelatin into the chocolate mixture and add the vanilla extract. Set aside until starting to thicken and set.

4 Brush four dariole molds or individual soufflé dishes with oil; line the bottom of each with baking parchment.

5 In a greasefree bowl, beat the egg white to soft peaks, then fold into the chocolate mixture.

6 Spoon the mixture into the prepared molds or soufflé dishes, then level the surface of each and chill for 2–3 hours, or until firm.

7 Meanwhile, place the fruits in a bowl. Add the superfine sugar and coconut rum and stir gently to mix. Cover and chill until required.

8 Ease the chocolate cream away from the rims of the molds or dishes and turn out onto dessert plates. Spoon the fruits around the outside. Decorate with the strawberry leaves, if you like, then serve at once.

FRESH STRAWBERRY ICE CREAM

YOU CAN MAKE THE ICE CREAM BY HAND IF YOU FREEZE IT OVER A PERIOD OF SEVERAL HOURS, WHISKING IT EVERY HOUR OR SO, BUT THE TEXTURE WON'T BE AS GOOD.

SERVES SIX

INGREDIENTS

1¼ cups whole milk or half-and-half
1 vanilla bean
3 large egg yolks
8 ounces (1½–2 cups) strawberries
juice of ½ lemon
¾ cup confectioners' sugar
1¼ cups heavy cream
sliced strawberries, to serve

1 Put the milk into a pan, add the vanilla bean and bring to a boil over low heat. Remove from the heat. Set aside for 20 minutes, then remove the vanilla bean. Strain the warm milk into a bowl containing the egg yolks; whisk well.

2 Return the mixture to the clean pan and heat, stirring, until the custard just coats the back of the spoon. Pour the custard into a bowl, cover the surface with plastic wrap and set aside to cool.

COOK'S TIP
Use free-range eggs if possible, bought from a reputable supplier.

3 Meanwhile, purée the strawberries with the lemon juice in a food processor or blender. Press the strawberry purée through a strainer into a bowl. Stir in the confectioners' sugar and set aside.

4 Whip the cream to soft peaks, then gently but thoroughly fold it into the custard with the strawberry purée. Pour the mixture into an ice-cream maker. Churn for 20–30 minutes, or until the mixture holds its shape. Transfer the ice cream to a freezerproof container, cover and freeze until firm. Soften briefly before serving with the strawberries.

BLACK CURRANT SORBET

THIS LUSCIOUS SORBET IS EASILY MADE BY HAND, BUT IT IS IMPORTANT TO ALTERNATELY FREEZE AND BLEND OR PROCESS THE MIXTURE FIVE OR SIX TIMES TO GET THE BEST RESULT. IF YOU MAKE LOTS OF ICE CREAM AND SORBETS, IT IS WORTH INVESTING IN AN ICE-CREAM MAKER.

SERVES SIX

INGREDIENTS

    1¼ cups water, plus
    2 tablespoons
    ½ cup sugar
    2 cups black currants
    2 tablespoons crème de cassis or
    other black currant liqueur
    1 teaspoon lemon juice
    2 egg whites

1 Pour 1¼ cups of the water into a saucepan and add the sugar. Place over low heat until the sugar has dissolved. Bring to a boil and boil rapidly for 10 minutes, then set the syrup aside to cool.

2 Meanwhile, cook the black currants with the remaining 2 tablespoons water over low heat for 5–7 minutes. Press the black currants and juice through a strainer placed over a bowl, then stir the black currant purée into the syrup with the liqueur and lemon juice. Allow to cool completely, then chill for 1 hour.

3 Pour the chilled black currant syrup into a freezerproof bowl; freeze until slushy, whisking occasionally. Beat the egg whites in a greasefree bowl until they form soft peaks, then fold into the half-frozen black currant mixture.

4 Freeze the mixture again until firm, then spoon into a food processor or blender and process. Alternately freeze and process or blend until completely smooth. Serve the sorbet straight from the freezer.

RASPBERRY AND ROSE PETAL SHORTCAKES

ROSE WATER—SCENTED CREAM AND FRESH RASPBERRIES FORM THE FILLING FOR THIS DELECTABLE DESSERT. THOUGH THEY LOOK IMPRESSIVE, THESE SHORTCAKES ARE EASY TO MAKE.

MAKES SIX

INGREDIENTS
    8 tablespoons (1 stick) unsalted
    butter, softened
    ¼ cup granulated sugar
    ½ vanilla bean, split, seeds reserved
    1 cup all-purpose flour, plus extra for
    dusting
    ⅓ cup semolina
    confectioners' sugar, for dusting
For the filling
    1¼ cups heavy cream
    1 tablespoon confectioners' sugar
    ½ teaspoon rose water
    4 cups raspberries
For the decoration
    12 miniature roses, unsprayed
    6 mint sprigs
    1 egg white, beaten
    sugar, for dusting

1 Cream the butter, sugar and vanilla seeds in a bowl until pale and fluffy. Sift the flour and semolina together, then gradually work the dry ingredients into the creamed mixture to make a cookie dough.

VARIATIONS
Other soft red summer berries, such as mulberries, loganberries and tayberries, would be equally good in this dessert.

COOK'S TIP
For best results, serve the shortcakes as soon as possible after assembling them. Otherwise, they are likely to turn soggy from the berries' liquid.

2 Gently knead the dough on a lightly floured surface until smooth. Roll out quite thinly and prick all over with a fork. Using a 3-inch fluted cutter, cut out 12 rounds. Place these on a baking sheet and chill for 30 minutes.

3 Meanwhile, make the filling. Whisk the cream with the confectioners' sugar until soft peaks form. Fold in the rose water and chill until required.

4 Preheat the oven to 350°F. To make the decoration, paint the roses and leaves with the egg white. Dust with sugar; dry on a wire rack.

5 Bake the shortcakes for 15 minutes, or until lightly golden. Lift them off the baking sheet with a metal spatula and cool on a wire rack.

6 To assemble the shortcakes, spoon the rose-water cream onto half the cookies. Add a layer of raspberries, then top with a second shortcake. Dust with confectioners' sugar. Decorate with the frosted roses and mint sprigs.

FRESH CURRANT BREAD AND BUTTER PUDDING

MIXED FRESH CURRANTS ADD A TART TOUCH TO THIS SCRUMPTIOUS HOT DESSERT.

SERVES SIX

INGREDIENTS
    8 medium-thick slices day-old bread,
       crusts removed
    4 tablespoons butter, softened
    1 cup red currants
    1 cup black currants
    4 eggs, beaten
    6 tablespoons granulated sugar
    2 cups whole milk or half-and-half
    1 teaspoon pure vanilla extract
    freshly grated nutmeg
    2 tablespoons demerara sugar
    light cream, to serve

1 Preheat the oven to 325°F.
Generously butter a 5-cup oval
baking dish.

VARIATION
A mixture of blueberries and raspberries
would work just as well as the currants.

2 Spread the slices of bread generously
with the butter, then cut them in half
diagonally. Layer the slices in the dish,
buttered side up, scattering the currants
between the layers.

3 Beat the eggs and granulated sugar
lightly together in a large mixing bowl,
then gradually beat in the milk, vanilla
extract and a large pinch of freshly
grated nutmeg.

4 Pour the milk mixture over the bread,
pushing the slices down. Scatter the
demerara sugar and a little nutmeg over
the top. Place the dish in a baking pan
and fill with hot water to come halfway
up the sides of the dish. Bake for
40 minutes, then increase the oven
temperature to 350°F and bake for
20–25 minutes more, or until the top is
golden. Cool slightly, then serve with
light cream.

CRANBERRY AND BLUEBERRY STREUSEL CAKE

CRANBERRIES ARE SELDOM USED IN SWEET DISHES, BUT ONCE THEY ARE SWEETENED, THEY HAVE
A GREAT FLAVOR, AND ARE PERFECT WHEN PARTNERED WITH BLUEBERRIES.

MAKES TEN SLICES

INGREDIENTS

¾ cup butter, softened
½ cup granulated sugar
3 cups all-purpose flour
2 large eggs, beaten
1 teaspoon baking powder
1 teaspoon pure vanilla extract
1 cup cranberries
1 cup blueberries
⅓ cup light brown sugar
½ teaspoon crushed cardamom seeds
confectioners' sugar, for dusting

1 Preheat the oven to 375°F. Grease and line an 8½-inch springform pan.

2 Cream the butter and granulated sugar together until smooth, then rub in the flour with your fingers until the mixture resembles fine bread crumbs. Take out a generous 1 cup of the mixture and set aside.

3 Beat the eggs, baking powder and vanilla extract into the remaining mixture until soft and creamy. Spoon onto the bottom of the prepared pan and spread evenly. Arrange the cranberries and blueberries on top, then sprinkle the brown sugar over them.

4 Stir the cardamom seeds into the reserved flour mixture, then scatter evenly over the top of the fruit. Bake for 50–60 minutes, or until the topping is golden. Cool the cake in the pan for 10 minutes, then remove the sides. Slide the cake onto a wire rack, lifting it off the bottom of the pan. Let the cake cool, then dust with confectioners' sugar and serve with whipped cream.

FRESH BLUEBERRY MUFFINS

MAKE THESE POPULAR AMERICAN TREATS IN PAPER LINERS FOR MOISTER MUFFINS—IF YOU CAN'T FIND THEM, JUST GREASE THE PAN WELL BEFORE FILLING. THESE ARE BEST SERVED SLIGHTLY WARM.

MAKES TWELVE

INGREDIENTS
    2½ cups all-purpose flour
    1 tablespoon baking powder
    6 tablespoons sugar
    1 cup milk
    3 eggs, beaten
    8 tablespoons (1 stick) butter, melted
    a few drops of pure vanilla extract
    2 cups blueberries
For the topping
    ½ cup pecans, coarsely chopped
    2 tablespoons demerara sugar

COOK'S TIP
Don't be tempted to beat the muffin mixture; it should be fairly wet and needs to be quite lumpy. Overmixing will create tough muffins.

1 Preheat the oven to 400°F. Stand 12 paper liners in a muffin pan, or simply grease the pan well (or use lined individual pans, set on a baking sheet). Sift the flour and baking powder into a large bowl. Stir in the sugar. Mix the milk, eggs, melted butter and vanilla in a bowl and whisk lightly. Add to the flour mixture and fold together lightly.

2 Fold in the blueberries, then divide the mixture among the muffin liners. Scatter a few nuts and a little demerara sugar over the top of each. Bake for 20–25 minutes, or until the muffins are well risen and golden.

3 Remove the warm muffins from the pan; cool slightly on a wire rack.

BLUEBERRY PIE

AMERICAN BLUEBERRIES OR EUROPEAN BILBERRIES CAN BE USED FOR THIS PIE. YOU MAY NEED TO ADD A LITTLE MORE SUGAR IF YOU ARE LUCKY ENOUGH TO FIND BILBERRIES.

SERVES SIX

INGREDIENTS

2 × 8-ounce prepared shortcrust
pastry sheets, thawed if frozen
7 cups blueberries
6 tablespoons sugar, plus extra for
sprinkling
3 tablespoons cornstarch
grated zest and juice of ½ orange
grated zest of ½ lemon
½ teaspoon ground cinnamon
1 tablespoon unsalted
butter, diced
beaten egg, to glaze
whipped cream, to serve

1 Preheat the oven to 400°F. Use one
sheet of pastry to line a 9-inch pie pan,
leaving the excess pastry hanging over
the edges.

2 Mix the blueberries, sugar,
cornstarch, orange zest and juice,
lemon zest and cinnamon in a large
bowl. Spoon into the pastry shell and
dot with the butter. Dampen the rim of
the pastry shell with a little water and
top with the remaining pastry sheet.

VARIATION
Substitute a crumble topping for the top
crust. The contrast with the juicy
blueberry filling is sensational.

3 Cut the pastry edge at 1-inch
intervals, then fold each section over
on itself to form a triangle and create
a sunflower edge. Trim off the excess
pastry and cut out decorations from the
trimmings. Attach them to the top crust
with a little of the beaten egg.

4 Glaze the pastry with the egg
and sprinkle with sugar. Bake for
30–35 minutes, or until golden. Serve
warm or cold with whipped cream.

BERRY BRULEE TARTS

THIS QUANTITY OF PASTRY IS ENOUGH FOR EIGHT TARTLETS, SO FREEZE HALF FOR ANOTHER DAY.
THE BRÛLÉE TOPPING IS BEST ADDED NO MORE THAN TWO HOURS BEFORE SERVING THE TARTS.

MAKES FOUR

INGREDIENTS
   2¼ cups all-purpose flour
   pinch of salt
   ¼ cup ground almonds
   1 tablespoon confectioners' sugar
   10 tablespoons unsalted butter,
      chilled and diced
   1 egg yolk
   about 3 tablespoons cold water
For the filling
   4 egg yolks
   1 tablespoon cornstarch
   ¼ cup granulated sugar
   a few drops of pure vanilla extract
   1¼ cups whole milk or half-and-half
   2 cups mixed berries, such as small
      strawberries, raspberries, black
      currants and red currants
   ½ cup confectioners' sugar

1 Mix the flour, salt, ground almonds and confectioners' sugar in a bowl. Rub in the butter by hand or in a food processor until the mixture resembles fine bread crumbs. Add the egg yolk and enough cold water to form a dough. Knead the dough gently, then cut it in half and freeze half for use later.

2 Cut the remaining pastry into four equal pieces and roll out thinly.

COOK'S TIP
If you possess a culinary blowtorch—and are confident about operating it safely—use it to easily melt and caramelize the brûlée topping.

3 Use the pastry rounds to line four individual tartlet pans, letting the excess pastry hang over the edges. Chill for 30 minutes.

4 Preheat the oven to 400°F. Line the pastry with baking parchment and baking beans. Bake for 10 minutes. Remove the paper and beans and return the tartlet shells to the oven for 5 minutes, until golden. Allow the pastry to cool, then carefully trim off the excess.

5 Beat the egg yolks, cornstarch, granulated sugar and vanilla extract in a bowl.

6 Warm the milk in a heavy pan, pour it onto the egg yolks, whisking constantly, then return the mixture to the clean pan.

7 Heat, stirring, until the custard thickens, but do not let it boil. Remove from the heat, press a piece of plastic wrap directly onto the surface of the custard and allow to cool.

8 Scatter the berries in the tartlet shells and spoon the custard over them. Chill the tarts for 2 hours.

9 To serve, sift confectioners' sugar generously over the tops of the tartlets. Preheat the broiler to the highest setting. Place the tartlets under the hot broiler until the sugar melts and caramelizes. Allow the topping to cool and harden for about 10 minutes before serving the tarts.

BLACKBERRY JELLY

THIS JELLY IS ONE OF THE BEST. IT HAS TO BE MADE WITH HAND-PICKED WILD BLACKBERRIES FOR THE BEST FLAVOR. MAKE SURE YOU INCLUDE A FEW RED UNRIPE BERRIES FOR A GOOD SET.

MAKES 2 POUNDS

INGREDIENTS
    8 cups blackberries
    1¼ cups water
    juice of 1 lemon
    about 4 cups sugar
    hot buttered toast or English muffins,
       to serve

VARIATION
Red currant jelly is made in the same way, but with less sugar. Reduce the quantity to 1½ cups for every 2½ cups juice.

1 Put the fruit, water and lemon juice into a large saucepan. Cover the pan and cook for 15–30 minutes, or until the blackberries are very soft.

2 Ladle into a jelly bag or a large strainer lined with cheesecloth and set over a large bowl. Let drip overnight to obtain the maximum amount of juice.

3 Discard the fruit pulp. Measure the juice and allow 2 cups sugar to every 2½ cups juice. Place both in a large, heavy pan and bring the mixture slowly to a boil, stirring all the time until the sugar has dissolved.

4 Boil rapidly until the jelly registers 220°F on a sugar thermometer, or test for setting by spooning a small amount onto a chilled saucer. Chill for 3 minutes, then push the mixture with your finger; if wrinkles form on the surface, it is ready. Cool for 10 minutes.

5 Skim off any scum and pour the jelly into warm sterilized jars. Cover and seal while the jelly is still hot and label when the jars are cool. Serve the jelly with hot buttered toast or English muffins.

STRAWBERRY JAM

CAPTURE THE ESSENCE OF SUMMER IN A JAR OF HOMEMADE STRAWBERRY JAM.

MAKES ABOUT 3 POUNDS

INGREDIENTS
  8 cups small strawberries
  4 cups sugar
  juice of 2 lemons
  scones and crème fraîche, to serve

1 Layer the strawberries and sugar in a large bowl. Cover and leave overnight.

2 The next day, scrape the strawberries and their juice into a large, heavy pan. Add the lemon juice. Gradually bring to a boil over low heat, stirring until the sugar has dissolved.

COOK'S TIPS
For best results when making jam, don't wash the strawberries unless absolutely necessary. Instead, brush off any dirt, or wipe the strawberries with a damp cloth. If you have to wash any, pat them dry and then spread them out on a clean dish towel to dry further.
  To sterilize jam jars, wash in hot soapy water, then rinse thoroughly and drain. Place the jars on a baking sheet and dry in a warm oven for 15–20 minutes.

3 Boil steadily for 10–15 minutes, or until the jam registers 220°F on a sugar thermometer. Alternatively, test for setting by spooning a small amount onto a chilled saucer. Chill for 3 minutes, then push the jam with your finger; if wrinkles form on the surface, it is ready. Cool for 10 minutes.

4 Pour the strawberry jam into warm sterilized jars, filling them right to the top. Cover and seal while the jam is still hot and label when the jars are cool. Serve with scones and crème fraîche, if you like. This jam can be stored in a cool dark place and should keep for up to 1 year.

CITRUS
FRUITS

No family of fruits seems to store up sunshine more successfully than citrus fruits. Golden oranges and tangerines, yellow lemons, deep green limes—their glowing colors light up a room, and the wonderful scent of their essential oils tempts the taste buds. Wonderfully versatile, they can be juiced, enjoyed just as they are or used in both sweet and savory dishes. All citrus fruits have a tough, bitter peel that is highly scented and contains aromatic essential oils. Inside, the fruit is segmented and encloses juicy flesh, with a more or less acid flavor. The fruits ripen on the tree and do not continue to develop after picking, so they have excellent keeping qualities.

GRAPEFRUIT

One of the largest citrus fruits, grapefruit can vary in diameter from 4 to 7 inches. Most have deep yellow skins, but the flesh can range from very pale yellow (confusingly called "white") through rosy pink to deep pink (known as "ruby"). Generally speaking, the pinker the flesh, the sweeter the grapefruit will be.

History

Grapefruit are descended from the Malaysian **pomelo** or **shaddock**, a large, sour fruit (the pomelos sold today are a cross between a grapefruit and a shaddock). These fruits were brought to Europe from the West Indies in the seventeenth century and are now grown in every subtropical country of the world.

Varieties

The main varieties of grapefruit are white, pink or ruby, but you may also find the green-skinned **Sweetie,** whose flesh, as the name implies, is so sweet that it needs no sugar.

Nutrition

One of the most filling fruits, yet very low in calories (about 43 calories per 3¾ ounces), grapefruit are an excellent source of dietary fiber and vitamin C; one fruit provides one and a half times the adult daily requirement.

Above: Sweetie is a very sweet variety of grapefruit that needs no sugar.

Buying and Storing

Choose fruits that feel heavy for their size; they will be juicy. The skin can be thin or thick, depending on the variety, but it should be plump and firm; if it is puffy and coarse, the flesh will be dry. Avoid grapefruit with bruised or damaged skin. You cannot ripen grapefruit once they have been picked, but they can be kept in a cool place or in the refrigerator for a week or more.

Preparing and Serving

Grapefruit are best eaten raw and chilled, although in the 1960s it was fashionable to sprinkle them with brown sugar or brush with melted butter and caramelize them under the grill. They constitute the perfect breakfast food; perhaps the easiest way to enjoy them is freshly squeezed into a glass, but half a grapefruit on its own or with a little sugar is more satisfying. The fruits can also be used to make delicious marmalade to round off your breakfast.
Grapefruit can be used to start or finish a meal. The tart flavor goes well with seafood;

Above: White grapefruit have pale yellow flesh.

Segmenting grapefruit

1 Cut the grapefruit in half and remove the seeds.

2 Using a curved, serrated grapefruit knife, cut between the skin and flesh.

3 Using a small, sharp paring knife, cut carefully between the membrane that separates the segments. Start at the center, work out to the skin, then around the segment and back to the center again.

4 Finally, cut out the central core of the grapefruit with a sharp knife and remove the membrane.

grapefruit segments mixed with shrimp and avocado make a refreshing appetizer. They combine well with smoked fish and poultry, and segments are sometimes served as a garnish to cut the richness of liver or sweetbreads. The segments can also be used in fruit salads, mousses and sorbets. Grapefruit juice makes an unusual addition to salad dressings, and the peel can be candied to be used in cakes or coated with chocolate as a sweet with after-dinner coffee.

Left: The flesh of pink grapefruit can range from rosy pink to deep pink. As a rule of thumb, the pinker the color, the sweeter the grapefruit.

Below: Chocolate-coated grapefruit peel—a delectable sweet treat.

POMELOS

Although they resemble grapefruit, true pomelos are not a hybrid of the grapefruit, but a species in their own right. They are sometimes known as "shaddocks," after the sea captain who brought them from Malaysia to the West Indies. They are much larger than grapefruit, with thick, yellow, dimpled skin, pinkish yellow flesh and a sharp, refreshing flavor, which often needs a little sugar to make it palatable.

Below: Pomelos sold today are a smaller, rounder and smoother-skinned cross between the original pomelo or shaddock and grapefruit.

UGLI FRUIT

Despite its large size, baggy shape and mottled green skin, the Ugli is a hybrid of the grapefruit, orange and tangerine. It may not be the beauty of the citrus family, but the flavor is sweet and delicious—a cross between grapefruit and tangerine. The peel can be candied like grapefruit peel.

LEMONS

Arguably the most useful of all fruit, the distinctively shaped lemon can be very large or quite small, with thick or thin, smooth or knobbly skin. The skin contains aromatic essential oils, and a good lemon will perfume the air with its fragrance. The juicy, pale yellow, acid flesh enhances almost any other food and never fails to awaken and refresh the taste buds.

History

Originally from India or Malaysia, lemons were introduced into Assyria, where they were discovered by the soldiers serving Alexander the Great. They took them back to Greece, where lemons were used as a condiment and for medicinal and cosmetic purposes. The Crusaders brought lemons to the rest of Europe from Palestine, and their cultivation became widespread. Like limes, lemons became invaluable as a protection against scurvy and were carried by sailors on every sea voyage.

Nutrition

Rich in vitamin C and very low in calories, lemons provide only about 22 calories per 3¾ ounce.

Buying and Storing

Choose lemons that are firm and heavy for their size. Smooth-skinned lemons are best for juicing and cooking, while

the knobbly-skinned varieties are easier to grate. Lemons become paler as they ripen and lose some juiciness and acidity, so avoid light yellow fruit; look instead for deep yellow specimens with glossy, unblemished skins. Do not buy lemons with patches of mold or those with hard, shriveled skins.

Lemons have often been treated with diphenyl, an ethylene gas that keeps the skins yellow and fresh-looking. If you are going to use the lemon rind, buy untreated or "unwaxed" fruit.

Lemons do not ripen once picked. They can be kept in a cool room or the refrigerator for at least a week.

Preparing and Cooking

Although few people would choose to eat a lemon raw, these citrus fruits are infinitely versatile. Their high ascorbic acid (vitamin C) content prevents oxidization, so lemon juice is often brushed over cut fruit or white vegetables, such as potatoes, celeriac or artichokes, to stop them from turning brown. Lemons can be distilled into alcoholic drinks, such as *limoncello,* a sweet *digestivo* that is served straight from the freezer.

Every part of the lemon can be used in sweet and savory cooking, from the juice to the zest. Lemon wedges are traditionally served as an accompaniment to fish dishes, particularly fried fish; their acidity counteracts the fattiness of all fried

Left: Smooth-skinned lemons are best for juicing and cooking.

Zesting or grating a lemon
1 Choose an unwaxed lemon. Hold it firmly in one hand.

2 Scrape a zester down the length of the lemon to pare off fine slivers of zest.

3 Chop the pared zest finely with a sharp knife if desired.

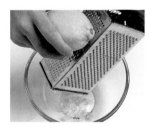

4 For grating, choose a knobbly-skinned lemon if possible. Grate it on the fine side of a grater, taking care to remove only the yellow zest. Work over a bowl, or, if you prefer, work over a piece of foil—this makes it easy to transfer the grated rind to a bowl or pan with the aid of a pastry brush.

foods. Lemon slices are a popular addition to tea and cold drinks, or can be used to garnish any number of sweet or savory dishes. Whole lemons can be preserved in salt and are widely used in North African dishes, such as Moroccan tagines.

Lemons give a wonderful flavor to sweet dishes. They can be used for jellies, jams and lemon curd or cheese and make refreshing mousses, sorbets and ice creams.

Lemon juice Lemon juice can be drunk on its own, with added sugar or as a refreshing tall drink, such as lemonade. It enhances the flavor of most other foods and can be used as a healthy substitute for salt. Use it in dressings, sauces and marinades; marinating fish for a long time in lemon juice will even "cook" the fish without heat, as in the Latin American dish seviche. Lemon

Below: Lemon juice enhances the flavor of most other fruits.

Above: Knobbly-skinned lemons are easy to grate.

juice will also tenderize meat. A few drops added to the cooking water helps poached eggs to coagulate, and a couple of spoonfuls will turn fresh cream into sour cream.

Lemon juice has nonculinary uses too. It acts as a bleach and can be used as a household cleaner or cosmetically, to whiten the skin or lighten blond hair.

Lemons yield more juice if they are warmed before squeezing; roll them between the palms of your hands for a minute or two, cover with boiling water or microwave on High for 30 seconds before squeezing. Do not squeeze lemons too hard, or the juice will become bitter.

Lemon zest and peel

The essential oils in lemon zest have an aromatic flavor that enhances many dishes. The zest can be obtained by grating or peeling it into strips with a zester or channel knife. Use it as a flavoring for butter, sauces, custards, mousses, cakes, cookies and tarts. For a milder lemon flavor, rub a lump of sugar over the surface of a lemon so that it absorbs the oils, then add the sugar cube to a sauce or dessert.

Lemon peel (including the white pith) contains pectin, which helps to set jams and jellies. Strips of peel (minus pith) can be added to casseroles, or candied to serve with coffee or to add to cakes and puddings.

CITRON

A lemon or pear-shaped citrus fruit originally from China, citrons are large fruit, sometimes up to 8 inches long, with thick, knobbly, greenish skin. They give very little juice, but this can be used like lemon juice. Citron flesh is very bitter and unpalatable, but the attractive green peel can be candied and used like candied lemon peel; it develops a lovely translucency. The peel can also be used for marmalade and jams. In Corsica, citrons are used to make a liqueur called *Cédratine*.

Right: Citrons are large fruit with bitter, unpalatable flesh.

LIMES

Limes are the smallest members of the true citrus family. They have thin, fairly smooth, green skins and a highly aromatic, acid flavor. Unlike lemons, limes will grow in tropical regions and are an essential ingredient of Southeast Asian, Mexican, Latin American and Caribbean cooking.

History

Limes originated in India. Attempts were made to grow them in Mediterranean countries, but they proved insufficiently hardy. They do very well in Egypt, however, where they are more plentiful than lemons. They are widely grown in the West Indies, and it was from these islands that supplies came for the British navy, to supplement the sailors' rations and help to prevent scurvy. Limehouse, in London's docklands, takes its name from the warehouses where the fruit was stored.

Varieties

There are two or perhaps three types of true limes:
Persian or Tahitian Large limes, with pale fine-grained pulp and a very acidic flavor.
Bearss are seedless but otherwise almost identical, and are regarded by some as a variety of the Persian or Tahitian lime and not a separate type.
Mexican, Key and West Indian limes are small and oval, with a strong, sharp flavor.

Nutrition

High in vitamin C, limes contain some potassium, calcium and phosphorus, and provide about 20 calories per 3¾ ounces.

Right: Limes have a sharper flavor than lemons.

Buying and Storing

Limes are the most perishable of all citrus fruit and quickly dry out and develop brown patches on their skins. Choose unblemished fruits that feel heavy for their size and avoid those with yellowish skins, as they may have lost some of their tanginess. Store limes in the refrigerator for up to a week.

Preparing and Serving

Limes can be used in the same way as lemons, but will add a sharper flavor, so use fewer of them. Classic seviche is made by marinating chunks of white fish in lime juice until they turn opaque. Freshly squeezed juice is used in rum punches, margaritas and daiquiris, or commercially made into a cordial.

Strips of lime zest can be buried in sugar to add a delicious fragrance. A few drops of lime juice squeezed over tropical fruit, such as papayas, melons and prickly pears, will do wonders for the flavor. In Caribbean and Latin American cooking, limes are cooked with fish, poultry and meat, while in Southeast Asia they are made into pickles and chutneys to serve with curries.

Limes can be made into jams and jellies and add a special zing to marmalade. One of the world's great desserts is Florida Key lime pie, which is similar to a lemon meringue pie. Lime blossoms are dried and made into infusions or used to flavor ice creams and mousses.

Paring and cutting julienne strips of citrus zest
1 Wash and dry the lime, lemon or orange. Using a swivel-blade vegetable peeler, peel downward to remove long strips of zest. Do not include the bitter white pith.
2 With a small sharp knife, square off the strips.
3 Cut them lengthwise into fine julienne strips.

KAFFIR LIMES

These are not true limes, but belong to a subspecies of the citrus family. Pale green and gnarled, the fruits have a haunting, scented citrus bouquet, but unfortunately the flesh is inedible. In Thailand and Indonesia, the finely grated rind is sometimes used in cooking, but it is the leaves that are most useful in culinary terms. When torn or shredded, they impart a distinctive flavor to soups, fish and chicken dishes, and curries.

Right: Kaffir limes are not eaten, but the finely grated rind is used in Southeast Asian cooking.

KUMQUATS

Kumquats are not true citrus fruits, but belong to a similar species, *Fortunella.* Their name comes from the Cantonese *kam kwat,* meaning "golden orange." The small, elongated fruits are about the size and shape of a large olive, with a thin orange rind that is edible. The rind is sweeter than the sour pulp and the two parts eaten together provide a delicious sour-sweet sensation.

Nutrition

Kumquats are a source of vitamins C and A and have some calcium, phosphorus and riboflavin. They provide about 65 calories per 3¾ ounces.

Buying and Storing

Look for unblemished fruit with taut orange rind. Kumquats can be kept in the refrigerator for up to a week.

Preparing and Cooking

Kumquats can be eaten whole, just as they are, or sliced into miniature rings and used in winter salads and fruit salads. They taste superb poached in syrup, and can also be canned with sugar and alcohol and served whole or chopped with ice cream, duck, red meats or cheese. They make delicious marmalade and jam and can be used in cake and cookie mixes. For unusual petits fours, dip whole kumquats into melted bittersweet chocolate.

Kumquats combine well with bitter salad greens like chicory and frisée and make excellent stuffings for poultry.

Limequats

These are, as the name suggests, a cross between limes and kumquats. Limequats are bright green with thin, edible skins, but they are extremely sour, so cannot be eaten raw. They should be cooked or preserved like kumquats and can be served in the same way.

Whole kumquats can be cooked with fish, poultry and white meats, and spiced kumquat preserve is a Christmas treat.

Left: Not true citrus fruits, kumquats can be eaten whole—skin and all.

BERGAMOTS

These small, yellow citrus fruit are seldom found in their natural state. They are best known for the essential oil contained in the rind, which is used in confectionery and perfumery, but most famously as a highly distinctive flavoring for Earl Grey tea. Bergamot oil is used in the barley sugar made in the French town of Nancy. The fruit can also be made into delicious and unusual marmalade.

Right: Seldom used for cooking, bergamots are best known for their essential oil, which gives Earl Grey tea its unusual, aromatic aroma and flavor.

TANGERINES OR MANDARINS

Sometimes known as "easy peelers," tangerines or mandarins are part of a large family of small citrus fruit. They resemble slightly flattened oranges with loose orange skin and have a fragrant aroma, which in Great Britain is inextricably bound up with Christmas. The tangerine family all have aromatic skins, which can easily be detached from the segments (unlike oranges and lemons), and segments that separate easily. The flesh is sweet and perfumed, but often contains a large number of seeds.

History

As the name suggests, tangerines or mandarins almost certainly originated in China and were brought to Italy in Roman times by Arab traders. Like oranges, they were regarded as a symbol of luxury and prosperity. They

Right: Easy to peel, satsumas have a refreshing tart flavor.

Right: These tangerines, grown in Italy, have sweet flesh but often contain a large number of seeds.

are now grown throughout North Africa and the Mediterranean.

Varieties

The names of many types of tangerine are commonly interchanged, so you may find a bewildering variety of fruits that are essentially the same.

Clementine The smallest of the tangerines, with bright orange skin and no seeds. This, and their sweet, aromatic flesh, make clementines the most popular tangerine variety. They are sometimes sold with the leaves still attached, which makes them particularly attractive.

Mandarin Most commonly sold canned, tiny peeled tangerine segments are sold as mandarin oranges, although they are usually satsumas. The deliciously sweet, vibrant segments make an attractive decoration for a dessert.

Satsuma These largish tangerines from Japan have loose skin and a refreshing, rather tart flavor. Satsumas contain very few seeds.

Making tangerine shells

1 Choose attractive, well-shaped fruit. Cut off the top of each to make a lid.

2 Carefully scoop out the segments with a teaspoon, a few at a time. Scrape out any pith or membrane, taking care to avoid breaking the skin. Fill the shells with iced tangerine pulp.

Right: The clementine is the smallest and most popular variety of tangerine.

Ortanique Also known as "honey tangerines" because of their delicious sweetness, ortaniques are a hybrid, which can be found growing on the same trees as tangerines or oranges.

Tangelo These are a cross between a tangerine and a grapefruit, and have the easy-peeling qualities of the former. Tangelos are irregularly shaped and have a refreshing, tart flavor, rather like an orange.

Mineola Another tangerine–grapefruit hybrid, mineolas can be recognized by the distinctive bulge at their stem end. They have bright orange skin and are very easy to peel. The sweet, juicy flesh has no seeds.

Nutrition

All tangerines and their hybrids are extremely good sources of vitamin C and beta-carotene. They provide about 40 calories per 3¾ ounces.

Buying and Storing

Many varieties of tangerine have loose, puffy skins, which are no indication of quality. Choose fruits that feel heavy for their size; they will contain more juice. Avoid fruits with damaged skins and, if you are buying prepacked fruits, check that none is moldy—it will quickly taint all the others.

Tangerines do not keep as long as other citrus fruit, but can be stored in the refrigerator for up to a week.

Canned mandarin oranges are a very useful pantry item. Use them in trifles, chocolate desserts and on cheesecakes. Children love them set in orange or mandarin jelly.

It is also possible to buy canned peeled whole mandarins in syrup— the lazy cook's answer for a simply sensational dessert. Just make a caramel sauce, add the drained fruit and decorate with some fresh orange or mandarin zest. A dash of orange liqueur gilds the lily.

Preparing and Serving

All varieties of tangerine can be used in the same way as oranges. The peel is as useful as the flesh, and the zest can be candied or used to flavor sweet liqueurs. Strips of peel can be dried and used in savory stews or included with herbs to make a bouquet garni.

Tangerine segments can be eaten on their own. Dipped in melted chocolate or crystallized, they make a delicious after-dinner sweet. Tangerine juice adds a distinctive flavor to marinades for pork and poultry; combine it with Asian aromatics like five-spice powder, ginger and soy sauce.

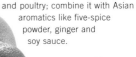

ORANGES

Below: Navel
oranges contain
a tiny embryonic
fruit.

Despite their name,
oranges are not always
orange; they can also be
green, yellow or mottled with
red. The size can vary too—an
orange can be as large as a football or
as small as a cherry—and the flavor can
range from sweet to intensely sour.
Orange trees are beautiful all year round.
Their dark, glossy evergreen leaves give
off a wonderful citrus scent. The
beautiful, waxy white, star-
shaped flowers also have an
intense aroma, which is captured
in orange-flower water. The fruits
turn from green to bright orange
or yellow, making a striking
contrast with the leaves.

Like other citrus peel,
orange rind contains
essential oils that
are used in cooking
and perfumery.

History

Oranges originated in
China. They were
probably known to
the ancient Greeks
and may have been
the mythical Golden
Apples of the
Hesperides. If so,
they would have been
bitter oranges, which
were the only variety

Right: Cointreau—
flavored with the peel
of bitter oranges.

known at the time. Over the
centuries, traders took oranges to
India and Arabia and thence to the
Mediterranean region. When the first
oranges reached Europe, they
were so rare that they became a
symbol of opulence, to be offered
as luxury gifts; the Medici family
adopted five oranges as their coat
of arms. The oranges were too
precious to be eaten raw (in any
case, they would have been too
sour), but were made into
preserves. The first sweet
oranges to arrive in
Europe were brought
from India by traders
in the seventeenth
century. They became
popular throughout
Europe and were
served in theaters as
refreshments—hence
Nell Gwynn's
appearance in the
history books.

Varieties

Oranges fall into two
groups: sweet oranges,
which can be eaten
raw, and bitter oranges,
which cannot.

Sweet oranges

Sweet oranges can be divided into four
main categories, which are available at
different times of the year.
Navel These seedless oranges take
their name from the navellike
protuberance at the end, which
contains a tiny embryonic fruit. They
have thick, pebbly skins and very sweet,
juicy flesh. The skin is particularly good
for making candied peel.
Blond These pale-skinned winter
oranges include **Jaffa** and **Shamouti**.
The large fruit have thick skins that
are easy to peel. The flesh is crisp and
juicy. If you are lucky, you may find
Salustianas oranges, which are full of
juice and contain no seeds.
Blood oranges These small oranges
have red-flushed skins and jewellike
flesh, which can range from golden to
deep ruby red. These are the best
oranges to use for sorbets and desserts,
where color is important. They are an
essential ingredient of sauce Maltaise,

Peeling and segmenting oranges

1 Using a serrated knife, cut a thin slice from each end of the orange to expose the flesh.

2 Cut off the peel in a circular motion, removing the white pith.

3 Hold the fruit over a bowl to catch the juice. Cut each segment between the membranes.

4 Squeeze out all the juice.

Below: Seedless Navel oranges have very sweet, juicy flesh.

an orange-flavored hollandaise that takes its name from the sour but juicy Maltese blood orange.

Late oranges These include **Valencia** oranges, which have smooth, thin skins and contain few or no seeds; they are the world's most popular variety. They have pale flesh and are very juicy, with a sharp flavor. Valencia are the best oranges for juicing.

Bitter oranges

As well as the sweet oranges, there are bitter, or sour oranges.

Seville or **Bigarade** cannot be eaten raw, but are used for making marmalade, jams and jellies. Vast numbers are grown in Seville, but surprisingly, the Spaniards never make marmalade; almost all their oranges are exported to Britain. Seville oranges are used in the classic *sauce bigarade*, which is traditionally served with roast duck. In the south of France, these oranges are crystallized and the blossoms are distilled to make aromatic orange-flower water. The aromatic oils from the peel are used to flavor such liqueurs as Grand Marnier and Cointreau. Bitter oranges have a very short season and are available only in late winter and early spring.

Nutrition

An orange provides twice the adult daily requirement of vitamin C and is high in dietary fiber. The average fruit provides about 50 calories.

Buying and Storing

Choose firm oranges that feel heavy for their size—these will be juicy. Never buy oranges with damaged, shriveled or moldy skin. Oranges keep well; they can be stored at room temperature or in the refrigerator for up to two weeks. The juice and grated zest can be frozen.

Right: Bitter Seville oranges have a very short season—they are available only in January.

Right: Valencia oranges are the world's most popular variety of orange and are the best type for juicing.

Candied orange peel
1 Choose thick-skinned oranges. Wash and dry well. Peel the oranges with a swivel vegetable peeler.

2 Using a sharp knife, cut the peel into thin julienne strips.

3 For each orange, bring to a boil 1 cup water with ½ cup granulated sugar. Add the strips of orange peel, half-cover the pan and simmer until the syrup has reduced by three-quarters. Let cool completely.

4 Sift confectioners' sugar in a thick, even layer over a baking sheet. Roll the candied peel in the sugar. Dry in a cool oven. Store the peel in a jar; it will keep for 2–3 months.

Preparing and Serving

Oranges are best eaten in their natural state, but can be used in an almost infinite variety of desserts, pastries and sweetmeats: fruit salads, mousses, soufflés, ice creams, sorbets and granitas and, perhaps most famous of all, crêpes suzette. They can be squeezed for juice, in which case keep the rind to use in other ways (grated zest can be ground with sugar for sprinkling on breakfast cereals or for use in cakes or custards, for example). The juice can be drunk or used in a marinade for poultry or fish. Fresh sliced oranges combine well with spices like cinnamon, ginger and cardamom, and a sprinkling of distilled orange-flower water enhances their flavor dramatically. Candied orange peel is good in cakes, cookies and Christmas pudding. Crystallized quartered orange slices make an attractive decoration for desserts and cakes.

Oranges go well in savory dishes. Combine them with watercress, beet or chicory and thinly sliced raw red onion for a refreshing salad, or glaze carrots in orange juice and butter. Add orange juice and zest to tomato sauces and soups, or add strips of pared rind to hearty fish soups and

Right: Blood oranges

meat or poultry casseroles. Peeled orange slices are also good with liver and fish (especially trout and salmon).

Duck in bitter orange sauce
The acidity of bitter oranges is the perfect foil for the richness of duck. For *caneton à la bigarade*, pare the rind of a Seville orange, removing only the zest. Cut this into julienne strips. Squeeze the orange and set the juice aside. Roast a duck, then keep it hot. Drain off the fat from the roasting tin, then deglaze the pan with a little white wine. Add 1¼ cups rich chicken stock and the orange juice, reduce until syrupy, then add the orange zest, season and simmer for about 5 minutes. Beat in 2 tablespoons cubed chilled butter. Carve the duck and pour the sauce over. Garnish with peeled orange segments.

CITRUS
FRUIT
RECIPES

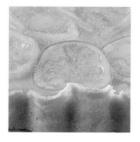

Put the squeeze on citrus for some of the finest
desserts and preserves in the good cook's repertoire.
Lemon Surprise Pudding, Moist Orange and Almond
Cake, Key Lime Pie and Lemon Meringue Pie are
perennially popular, while new delights include
Lemon Coeur à la Crème with Cointreau Oranges.

LEMON COEUR A LA CREME WITH COINTREAU ORANGES

THIS ZESTY DESSERT IS THE IDEAL CHOICE TO FOLLOW A RICH MAIN COURSE, SUCH AS ROAST PORK.

SERVES FOUR

INGREDIENTS

1 cup cottage cheese
generous 1 cup mascarpone
  cheese
¼ cup granulated sugar
grated zest and juice of 1 lemon
spirals of orange zest, to decorate
For the Cointreau oranges
4 oranges
2 teaspoons cornstarch
1 tablespoon confectioners' sugar
4 tablespoons Cointreau

1 Put the cottage cheese in a food processor or blender and process until smooth. Add the mascarpone, granulated sugar, lemon zest and juice and process briefly to mix the ingredients.

2 Line four coeur à la crème molds with cheesecloth, then divide the mixture among them. Level the surface of each, then place the molds on a plate to catch any liquid that drains from the cheese. Cover and chill overnight.

3 Make the Cointreau oranges. Squeeze the juice from two oranges and pour into a measuring cup. Add water, if necessary, to the juice to make 1 cup, then pour into a small saucepan. Blend a little of the juice mixture with the cornstarch and add to the pan with the confectioners' sugar. Heat the sauce, stirring until thickened.

4 Using a sharp knife, peel and segment the remaining oranges. Add the segments to the pan, stir to coat, then set aside. When cool, stir in the Cointreau. Cover and chill overnight.

5 Turn the molds out onto plates and surround with the oranges. Decorate with spirals of orange zest and serve at once.

CLEMENTINE JELLY

GELATIN-BASED DESSERTS AREN'T ONLY FOR CHILDREN: THIS ADULT VERSION HAS A CLEAR FRUIT TASTE AND CAN BE MADE EXTRA SPECIAL BY ADDING A LITTLE WHITE RUM OR COINTREAU.

SERVES FOUR

INGREDIENTS
12 clementines
clear grape juice (see method for amount)
1 tablespoon powdered gelatin
2 tablespoons sugar
whipped cream, to decorate

VARIATION
Use four ruby grapefruit instead of clementines, if you prefer. Squeeze the juice from half of them and segment the rest, discarding any bitter white pith.

1 Squeeze the juice from eight of the clementines and pour it into a measuring cup. Add enough grape juice to make 2½ cups, then strain the juice mixture through a fine strainer.

2 Pour half the juice mixture into a pan. Sprinkle the gelatin on top, set aside for 5 minutes, then heat gently until the gelatin has dissolved. Stir in the sugar, then the remaining juice; set aside.

3 Pare the zest very thinly from the remaining fruit and set it aside. Using a small sharp knife, cut between the membrane and fruit to separate the citrus segments. Discard the membrane and white pith.

4 Place half the segments in four dessert glasses and cover with some of the liquid fruit jelly. Place in the refrigerator and allow to set.

5 When the jellies are set, arrange the remaining fruit segments on top. Carefully pour the remaining liquid jelly over and chill until set. Cut the pared clementine zest into fine shreds. Serve the jellies topped with a generous spoonful of whipped cream scattered with clementine zest shreds.

RUBY ORANGE SHERBET
IN GINGER BASKETS

THIS SUPERB FROZEN DESSERT IS PERFECT FOR PEOPLE WITHOUT ICE CREAM MAKERS WHO CAN'T BE BOTHERED WITH THE FREEZING AND STIRRING THAT HOMEMADE ICES NORMALLY REQUIRE. IT IS ALSO IDEAL FOR SERVING AT A SPECIAL DINNER PARTY, AS BOTH THE SHERBET AND GINGER BASKETS CAN BE MADE IN ADVANCE AND THE DESSERT SIMPLY ASSEMBLED BETWEEN COURSES.

SERVES SIX

INGREDIENTS
   grated zest and juice of
    2 blood oranges
   1½ cups confectioners' sugar
   1¼ cups heavy cream
   scant 1 cup strained plain yogurt
   blood orange segments, to
    decorate (optional)
For the ginger baskets
   2 tablespoons unsalted butter
   1 tablespoon golden syrup or
    light corn syrup
   2 tablespoons sugar
   ¼ teaspoon ground ginger
   1 tablespoon finely chopped mixed
    citrus zest
   1 tablespoon all-purpose flour

2 Beat the heavy cream in a large bowl until the mixture forms soft peaks, then fold in the yogurt.

3 Gently stir in the orange juice mixture, then pour into a freezerproof container. Cover and freeze until firm.

6 Lightly grease two baking sheets. Using about 2 teaspoons of the mixture at a time, drop three portions of the ginger dough onto each baking sheet, spacing them well apart. Spread each one to a 2-inch circle, then bake for 12–14 minutes, or until the cookies are dark golden in color.

1 Place the orange zest and juice in a bowl. Sift the confectioners' sugar over the top and set aside for 30 minutes, then stir until smooth.

4 Make the baskets. Preheat the oven to 350°F. Place the butter, syrup and sugar in a heavy saucepan and heat gently until melted.

5 Add the ground ginger, mixed citrus zest and flour and stir until the mixture is smooth.

7 Remove the cookies from the oven and let stand on the baking sheets for 1 minute to firm slightly. Lift off with a spatula and drape over six greased individual muffin pans or upturned cups; flatten the top (which will become the bottom) and flute the edges to form a basket shape.

8 When cool, lift the baskets off the pan or cups and place on individual dessert plates. Arrange small scoops of the frozen orange sherbet in each basket. Decorate each portion with a few orange segments, if you like.

COOK'S TIP
When making the ginger baskets it is essential to work quickly. Have the greased pans or cups ready before you start. If the cookies cool and firm up before you have time to drape them all, return them to the oven for a few seconds to soften them again.

CHOCOLATE AND MANDARIN TRUFFLE LOAF

CHOCOHOLICS WILL LOVE THIS WICKEDLY RICH DESSERT. THE MANDARINS GIVE IT A DELICIOUS TANG.

SERVES EIGHT

INGREDIENTS
  14 ounces semisweet chocolate
  4 egg yolks
  3 mandarin oranges
  scant 1 cup crème
    fraîche
  2 tablespoons raisins
  chocolate curls, to decorate
For the sauce
  2 tablespoons Cointreau
  ½ cup crème fraîche

1 Grease an 8 x 4 x 2 ½-inch loaf pan and line it with plastic wrap. Break the chocolate into a large heatproof bowl. Place over a pan of hot water until melted.

2 Remove the bowl of chocolate from the heat and beat in the egg yolks.

COOK'S TIP
Chocolate-tipped mandarin slices would also make a superb decoration. Use small segments; pat dry on paper towels, then half-dip them in melted chocolate. Let sit on baking parchment until the chocolate has set.

3 Pare the zest from the mandarins, taking care to leave the pith behind. Cut the zest into slivers.

4 Stir the slivers of mandarin zest into the chocolate with the crème fraîche and raisins. Beat until smooth, then spoon the mixture into the prepared loaf pan and chill for 4 hours.

5 Cut the pith and any remaining zest from the mandarins, then slice thinly.

6 For the sauce, stir the Cointreau into the crème fraîche. Remove the truffle loaf from the pan, peel off the plastic wrap and slice. Serve each slice on a dessert plate with some sauce and mandarin slices, and decorate.

LEMON AND LIME CHEESECAKE

TANGY LEMON CHEESECAKE IS ALWAYS A HIT. THE LIME SYRUP MAKES THIS A CITRUS SENSATION.

2 Make the topping. Place the lemon zest and juice in a small saucepan and sprinkle the gelatin over. Let soften for 5 minutes. Heat gently until the gelatin has melted, then set the mixture aside to cool slightly. Beat the ricotta cheese and sugar in a bowl. Stir in the cream and egg yolks, then beat in the cooled gelatin mixture.

3 Beat the egg whites in a greasefree bowl until they form soft peaks. Fold them into the cheese mixture. Spoon onto the crust, level the surface and chill for 2–3 hours.

MAKES EIGHT SLICES

INGREDIENTS
5 ounces digestive biscuits or graham crackers (1½ cups ground)
3 tablespoons butter
For the topping
grated zest and juice of 2 lemons
2 teaspoons powdered gelatin
generous 1 cup ricotta cheese
⅓ cup sugar
⅔ cup heavy cream
2 eggs, separated
For the lime syrup
finely pared zest and juice of 3 limes
⅓ cup sugar
1 teaspoon arrowroot mixed with 2 tablespoons water

1 Lightly grease an 8-inch round springform pan. Place the biscuits or graham crackers in a food processor or blender and process until they form fine crumbs. Melt the butter in a large saucepan, then stir in the crumbs until well coated. Spoon into the prepared pan, press the crumbs down well in an even layer, then chill.

4 Meanwhile, make the lime syrup. Place the lime zest, juice and sugar in a small saucepan. Bring to a boil, stirring, then boil the syrup for 5 minutes. Stir in the arrowroot mixture and continue to stir until the syrup boils again and thickens slightly. Cool, then chill until required.

5 Spoon the lime syrup over the set cheesecake. Remove from the pan and cut into slices to serve.

LEMON SURPRISE PUDDING

THE SURPRISE IN THIS MUCH-LOVED DESSERT IS THE UNEXPECTED SAUCE CONCEALED BENEATH THE DELECTABLE SPONGE.

SERVES FOUR

INGREDIENTS
   4 tablespoons butter, plus extra
     for greasing
   grated zest and juice of 2 lemons
   ½ cup superfine sugar
   2 eggs, separated
   ½ cup self-rising flour
   1¼ cups milk

1 Preheat the oven to 375°F. Use a little butter to grease a 5-cup baking dish.

2 Beat the lemon zest, 4 tablespoons butter and sugar in a bowl until pale and fluffy. Add the egg yolks and flour and beat together well. Gradually beat in the lemon juice and milk (don't be alarmed if the mixture curdles horribly!). In a greasefree bowl, beat the egg whites until they form stiff peaks.

3 Fold the egg whites lightly into the lemon mixture, then pour into the prepared baking dish.

4 Place the dish in a roasting pan and pour in hot water to come halfway up the side of the dish. Bake for about 45 minutes, until golden. Serve at once.

CREPES SUZETTE

SIMPLY SUPERB—THAT'S THE VERDICT ON THIS PERENNIALLY POPULAR DESSERT. THESE CRÊPES DESERVE NOTHING LESS THAN THE BEST-QUALITY VANILLA ICE CREAM YOU CAN FIND.

SERVES FOUR

INGREDIENTS
   8 crêpes (see Summer Berry Crêpes
     for method)
   2 tablespoons unsalted butter
   ¼ cup sugar
   juice of 2 oranges
   juice of ½ lemon
   ¼ cup Cointreau or other orange
     liqueur
   best-quality vanilla ice cream,
     to serve

COOK'S TIP
Crêpes freeze well and can be reheated by the method described in step 1, or simultaneously thawed and reheated in the microwave. A stack of eight crêpes, interleaved with waxed paper, will take 2–3 minutes on High (100 percent power). Be sure to cover the top crêpe with paper as well.

1 Warm the cooked crêpes between two plates placed over a saucepan of simmering water.

2 Melt the butter in a heavy frying pan. Stir in the sugar and cook over medium heat, tilting the pan occasionally, until the mixture is golden brown. Add the orange and lemon juices and stir until the caramel has completely dissolved.

3 Add a crêpe to the pan. Using kitchen tongs, fold it in half, then in half again. Slide to the side of the pan. Repeat with the remaining crêpes

4 When all the crêpes have been folded in the sauce, pour the Cointreau over and carefully set it alight. Shake the pan until the flames die down. Divide the crêpes and sauce among dessert plates and serve at once with vanilla ice cream.

CITRUS FRUIT FLAMBE
WITH PISTACHIO PRALINE

A FRUIT FLAMBE MAKES A DRAMATIC FINALE FOR A DINNER PARTY. TOPPING THIS REFRESHING CITRUS FRUIT DESSERT WITH CRUNCHY PISTACHIO PRALINE MAKES IT EXTRA SPECIAL.

SERVES FOUR

INGREDIENTS
    4 oranges
    2 ruby grapefruit
    2 limes
    4 tablespoons butter
    ⅓ cup light brown sugar
    3 tablespoons Cointreau
    fresh mint sprigs, to decorate
For the praline
    oil, for greasing
    ½ cup granulated sugar
    ½ cup pistachio nuts

4 Heat the butter and brown sugar together in a heavy frying pan until the sugar has melted and the mixture is golden. Strain the citrus juices into the pan and continue to cook, stirring occasionally, until the juice has reduced and is syrupy.

5 Add the fruit segments and warm through without stirring. Pour the Cointreau over and set it alight. As soon as the flames die down, spoon the fruit flambé into serving dishes. Scatter some praline over each portion and decorate with mint. Serve at once.

1 First, make the pistachio praline. Brush a baking sheet lightly with oil. Place the granulated sugar and nuts in a small, heavy saucepan and cook gently, swirling the pan occasionally, until the sugar has melted.

2 Continue to cook over fairly low heat until the nuts start to pop and the sugar has turned a dark golden color. Pour onto the oiled baking sheet and set aside to cool. Using a sharp knife, chop the praline into rough chunks.

3 Cut off all the zest and pith from the citrus fruit. Holding each fruit in turn over a large bowl, cut between the membranes so that the segments fall into the bowl, with any juice.

COOK'S TIP
If desired, use a rolling pin or toffee hammer to break up the praline.

COLD LEMON SOUFFLE WITH CARAMELIZED ALMOND TOPPING

THIS TERRIFIC-TO-LOOK-AT, REFRESHING DESSERT SOUFFLE IS LIGHT AND LUSCIOUS.

2 Put the lemon zest and egg yolks in a bowl. Add 6 tablespoons of the granulated sugar and whisk until creamy.

3 Place the lemon juice in a small heatproof bowl and sprinkle the gelatin over. Set aside for 5 minutes, then place the bowl in a pan of simmering water. Heat, stirring occasionally, until the gelatin has dissolved. Cool slightly, then stir the gelatin mixture into the egg yolk mixture.

4 In a separate bowl, lightly whip the cream to soft peaks. Fold into the egg yolk mixture and set aside.

5 Beat the egg whites in a greasefree bowl until stiff peaks form. Gradually beat in the remaining sugar until the mixture is stiff and glossy. Quickly and lightly fold the whites into the yolk mixture. Pour into the prepared dish, smooth the surface and chill for 4–5 hours, or until set.

6 Make the decoration. Brush a baking sheet lightly with oil. Preheat the broiler. Scatter the almonds over the sheet and sift the confectioners' sugar over. Broil until the nuts are golden and the sugar has caramelized. Allow to cool, then remove the mixture from the sheet with a spatula and break it into pieces.

7 When the soufflé has set, carefully peel off the paper. Pile the caramelized almonds on top of the soufflé and decorate with the physalis.

SERVES SIX

INGREDIENTS
oil, for greasing
grated zest and juice of
  3 large lemons
5 large eggs, separated
½ cup granulated sugar
1½ tablespoons powdered gelatin
scant 2 cups heavy cream
For the decoration
  ¾ cup sliced almonds
  ¾ cup confectioners' sugar
  3 physalis (cape gooseberries)

COOK'S TIP
When peeling off the soufflé collar, hold the blade of a knife against the set soufflé so that it keeps its shape.

1 Make a soufflé collar. Cut a strip of baking parchment long enough to fit around a 3¾-cup soufflé dish and wide enough to extend 3 inches above the rim. Fit the strip around the dish, tape, then tie it around the top of the dish with string. Brush the inside of the paper lightly with oil.

LEMON ROULADE WITH LEMON CURD CREAM

THIS FEATHERLIGHT ROULADE FILLED WITH A RICH LEMON CURD CREAM MAKES A MARVELOUS DESSERT OR SNACK-TIME TREAT. THE LEMON CURD CAN BE MADE AHEAD AND KEPT IN THE REFRIGERATOR.

MAKES EIGHT SLICES

INGREDIENTS
    4 eggs, separated
    ½ cup granulated sugar
    finely grated zest of 2 lemons
    1 teaspoon pure vanilla extract
    ¼ cup ground almonds
    ⅓ cup all-purpose flour, sifted
    3 tablespoons confectioners' sugar
For the lemon curd cream
    1¼ cups heavy cream
    4 tablespoons fresh lemon curd
    (recipe below right)

1 Preheat the oven to 375°F. Grease a 13 × 9-inch jelly roll pan and line with baking parchment.

3 Beat the egg whites in a greasefree bowl until they form stiff, glossy peaks. Gradually beat in the remaining granulated sugar to form a stiff meringue. Stir half the meringue mixture into the egg yolk mixture and fold in the rest.

6 Sift the confectioners' sugar liberally over a piece of baking parchment. Turn the sponge out onto it. Peel off the lining paper and spread the lemon curd cream over the surface of the sponge, leaving a border around the edge.

2 In a large bowl, beat the egg yolks with half the granulated sugar until light and foamy. Beat in the lemon zest and vanilla extract, then lightly fold in the ground almonds and flour using a large metal spoon or spatula.

4 Pour into the prepared pan, level the surface with a spatula and bake for 10 minutes, or until risen and spongy to the touch. Cover loosely with a sheet of baking parchment and a damp dish towel. Let cool in the pan.

7 Using the paper underneath as a guide, roll up the sponge from one of the long sides. Place on a serving platter with the seam underneath. Cut the roulade into slices to serve.

FRESH LEMON CURD
Put the grated zest and juice of 3 lemons into a pan with ½ cup sugar. Bring to a boil, stirring until the sugar has dissolved. Stir in 1 tablespoon cornstarch mixed to a paste with 1 tablespoon cold water. Off the heat, beat in 2 egg yolks. Return to low heat and beat for about 2 minutes; remove from the heat. Gradually beat in 4 tablespoons butter, at room temperature. Pour into a sterilized jar, cover and seal at once. Let cool, then chill. Use within 2–3 weeks. Makes 1 pound.

COOK'S TIP
Having filled and rolled the roulade, keep it wrapped in the baking parchment and hold it together for about a minute to allow the shape to set before removing the paper and transferring the roulade to a plate.

5 Make the lemon cream. Whip the cream, then lightly fold in the lemon curd.

LEMON MERINGUE PIE

CRISP SHORTCRUST IS FILLED WITH A MOUTHWATERING LEMON CREAM FILLING AND TOPPED WITH SOFT GOLDEN MERINGUE. THIS CLASSIC OPEN TART NEVER FAILS TO PLEASE. POPULAR WITH ADULTS AND CHILDREN, IT IS THE ESSENTIAL SUNDAY LUNCH DESSERT.

2 Meanwhile, make the filling. Place all the ingredients in a bowl, mix lightly and let soak for 1 hour.

3 Preheat the oven to 400°F. Beat the filling until smooth and pour into the chilled pastry shell. Bake for 20 minutes, or until the filling has just set and the pastry is golden. Remove from the oven and cool on a wire rack for 30 minutes, or until a skin has formed on the surface. Lower the oven temperature to 350°F.

SERVES SIX

INGREDIENTS
   1 cup all-purpose flour
   pinch of salt
   4 tablespoons butter
   ¼ cup solid vegetable shortening or lard
   1 tablespoon granulated sugar
   about 1 tablespoon ice water
For the filling
   3 large egg yolks
   2 tablespoons granulated sugar
   grated zest and juice of 1 lemon
   ½ cup fresh white bread crumbs
   1 cup milk
For the topping
   3 large egg whites
   ½ cup superfine sugar

1 Sift the flour and salt into a bowl. Rub in the butter and shortening or lard until the mixture resembles fine bread crumbs. Stir in the sugar and add enough ice water to make a soft dough. Roll out the pastry on a lightly floured surface and use it to line an 8½-inch pie plate or pan. Chill until required.

4 Make the topping. Beat the egg whites in a greasefree bowl until they form stiff peaks. Beat in the superfine sugar to form a glossy meringue. Spoon on top of the set lemon filling and spread over, making sure you spread the meringue right to the rim of the pie shell. Swirl the meringue slightly.

5 Bake the pie for 20–25 minutes, or until the meringue is crisp and golden brown. Allow to cool on a wire rack for 10 minutes before serving.

FRESH LEMON TART

THIS TART SHOULD BE SERVED AT ROOM TEMPERATURE IF THE ZESTY LEMON FLAVOR IS TO BE ENJOYED TO THE UTMOST.

SERVES SIX TO EIGHT

INGREDIENTS
12-ounce package prepared rich
  sweet shortcrust pastry, thawed
  if frozen
For the filling
  3 eggs
  ½ cup sugar
  1 cup ground almonds
  7 tablespoons heavy cream
  grated zest and juice of 2 lemons
For the topping
  2 thin-skinned unwaxed lemons,
    thinly sliced
  scant 1 cup sugar
  7 tablespoons water

COOK'S TIP
If you prefer not to candy the lemons,
dust the tart with confectioners' sugar.

1 Roll out the pastry and use it to line a deep 9-inch fluted tart pan. Prick the bottom and chill for 30 minutes.

2 Preheat the oven to 400°F. Line the pastry with baking parchment and baking beans and bake for 10 minutes. Remove the paper and beans and return the pastry shell to the oven for 5 minutes more.

3 Meanwhile, make the filling. Beat the eggs, sugar, almonds and cream in a bowl until smooth. Beat in the lemon zest and juice. Pour the filling into the pastry shell. Lower the oven temperature to 375°F and bake for 20 minutes, or until the filling has set and the pastry is golden.

4 Make the topping. Place the lemon slices in a pan and pour in water to cover. Simmer for 15–20 minutes, or until the skins are tender, then drain.

5 Place the sugar in a saucepan and stir in the measured water. Heat gently until the sugar has dissolved, stirring constantly, then boil for 2 minutes. Add the lemon slices and cook for 10–15 minutes, until the skins become shiny and candied.

6 Lift out the candied lemon slices and arrange them over the top of the tart. Return the syrup to the heat and boil until reduced to a thick glaze. Brush this over the tart and allow to cool completely before serving.

KEY LIME PIE

THIS IS ONE OF AMERICA'S FAVORITES. AS THE NAME SUGGESTS, IT ORIGINATED IN THE FLORIDA KEYS.

MAKES TEN SLICES

INGREDIENTS
  2 cups all-purpose flour
  8 tablespoons (1 stick) chilled
    butter, diced
  2 tablespoons granulated sugar
  2 egg yolks
  pinch of salt
  2 tablespoons cold water
  thinly pared lime zest and mint
    leaves, to decorate
For the filling
  4 eggs, separated
  14-ounce can condensed milk
  grated zest and juice of 3 limes,
    preferrably Key limes
  2 tablespoons superfine sugar
For the topping
  1¼ cups heavy cream
  2–3 Key limes, thinly sliced

3 Preheat the oven to 400°F. Trim off the excess pastry from around the edge of the pastry shell using a large, sharp knife and line the pastry shell with baking parchment and baking beans.

4 Bake the pastry shell for 10 minutes. Remove the paper and beans and return the pastry shell to the oven for 10 minutes.

6 In a greasefree bowl, beat the egg whites to stiff peaks. Beat in the superfine sugar, then fold into the lime mixture.

7 Lower the oven temperature to 325°F. Pour the lime filling into the pastry shell. Bake for 20–25 minutes, or until it has set and is starting to brown. Cool, then chill.

1 Sift the flour into a mixing bowl and, using your fingertips, rub in the butter until the mixture resembles fresh bread crumbs. Add the granulated sugar, egg yolks, salt and water. Mix to a soft dough.

2 Roll out the pastry on a lightly floured surface and use to line a deep 8½-inch fluted flan pan, allowing the excess pastry to hang over the edge. Prick the pastry bottom and chill for at least 30 minutes.

5 Meanwhile, make the filling. Beat the egg yolks in a large bowl until light and creamy, then beat in the condensed milk, with the lime zest and juice, until well combined. Continue to beat until the mixture is thick.

COOK'S TIP
You can make the pastry in a food processor, but take care not to overprocess the dough. Use the pulse button and process for a few seconds at a time; switch off the motor the moment the dough clumps together.

8 Just before serving, whip the heavy cream for the topping and spoon it around the edge of the pie. Cut the lime slices once from the center to the edge, then twist each slice and arrange between the spoonfuls of cream. Decorate with lime zest and mint leaves.

MOIST ORANGE AND ALMOND CAKE

THE KEY TO THIS RECIPE IS TO COOK THE ORANGE SLOWLY FIRST, SO IT IS FULLY TENDER BEFORE BEING BLENDED. DON'T USE A MICROWAVE TO SPEED THINGS UP—THIS MAKES ORANGE SKIN TOUGH.

SERVES EIGHT

INGREDIENTS
 1 large orange
 3 eggs
 1 cup granulated sugar
 1 teaspoon baking powder
 2 cups ground almonds
 ¼ cup all-purpose flour
 confectioners' sugar, for dusting
 whipped cream and orange slices
  (optional), to serve

1 Wash the orange and pierce it with a skewer. Put it in a deep saucepan and pour in water to cover completely. Bring to a boil, then lower the heat, cover and simmer for 1 hour, or until the skin is very soft. Drain, then cool.

COOK'S TIP
For a treat, serve this with spiced poached kumquats.

2 Preheat the oven to 350°F. Grease an 8-inch round cake pan and line it with baking parchment. Cut the cooled orange in half and discard the seeds. Place the orange, skin and all, in a blender or food processor and purée until smooth and pulpy.

3 In a bowl, beat the eggs and sugar until thick. Fold in the baking powder, almonds and flour, then fold in the purée.

4 Pour into the prepared pan, level the surface and bake for 1 hour, or until a skewer inserted into the middle comes out clean. Cool the cake in the pan for 10 minutes, then turn out onto a wire rack, peel off the lining paper and cool completely. Dust the top liberally with confectioners' sugar and serve with whipped cream. For added color, tuck thick orange slices under the cake just before serving.

LEMON AND LIME SYRUP CAKE

THIS CAKE IS PERFECT FOR BUSY COOKS, AS IT CAN BE MIXED IN MOMENTS AND NEEDS NO ICING.
THE SIMPLE TANGY LIME TOPPING TRANSFORMS IT INTO A FABULOUSLY MOIST CAKE.

SERVES EIGHT

INGREDIENTS
    2 cups self-rising flour
    1 teaspoon baking powder
    1 cup sugar
    ½ pound (2 sticks) butter, softened
    4 eggs, beaten
    grated zest of 2 lemons
    2 tablespoons lemon juice
For the topping
    finely pared zest of 1 lime
    juice of 2 limes
    ⅔ cup sugar

1 Make the cake. Preheat the oven to 325°F. Grease and line an 8-inch round cake pan. Sift the flour and baking powder into a large bowl. Add the sugar, butter and eggs and beat together well until the mixture is smooth, creamy and fluffy.

2 Beat in the lemon zest and juice. Spoon the mixture into the prepared pan, then smooth the surface and make a shallow indentation in the top with the back of a spoon.

3 Bake for 1¼–1½ hours, or until the cake is golden on top and spongy when lightly pressed and a skewer inserted in the center comes out clean.

4 Meanwhile, mix the topping ingredients together. As soon as the cake is done, remove it from the oven and pour the topping over the surface. Allow the cake to cool in the pan.

VARIATION
Use lemon zest and juice instead of lime for the topping if you prefer. You will need only one large lemon.

SPICED POACHED KUMQUATS

KUMQUATS ARE NOT AVAILABLE THROUGHOUT THE YEAR, BUT THEY ARE UNDOUBTEDLY AT THEIR BEST JUST BEFORE THE CHRISTMAS SEASON. THESE FRUITS CAN BE CANNED AND GIVEN AS PRESENTS. THEIR MARVELOUS SPICY-SWEET CITRUS FLAVOR COMPLEMENTS BOTH SWEET AND SAVORY DISHES.

SERVES SIX

INGREDIENTS
  4 cups kumquats
  ½ cup sugar
  ⅔ cup water
  1 small cinnamon stick
  1 star anise
  a citrus leaf, to decorate

1 Cut the kumquats in half and discard the seeds. Place the kumquats in a saucepan with the sugar, water and spices. Cook over gentle heat, stirring until the sugar has dissolved.

2 Increase the heat, cover the pan and boil the mixture for 8–10 minutes, until the kumquats are tender. To can the kumquats, spoon them into warm, sterilized jars, seal and label.

3 If you want to serve the spiced kumquats soon after making them, let the mixture cool, then chill it. Decorate with a citrus leaf, if you like.

COOK'S TIP
Try these delectable treats with baked ham or roast pork. They would also make a perfect accompaniment for moist almond or chocolate cake.

THREE-FRUIT MARMALADE

SEVILLE ORANGES HAVE A FINE FLAVOR AND ARE THE BEST VARIETY FOR MARMALADE. SWEET ORANGES CAN BE USED IN A PINCH, BUT THEY TEND TO MAKE THE MARMALADE CLOUDY.

MAKES 5–5¼ POUNDS

INGREDIENTS
  2 Seville oranges
  2 lemons
  1 grapefruit
  7½ cups water
  6¾ cups sugar
  croissants, to serve (optional)

1 Wash the fruit, halve and squeeze their juice. Pour into a large, heavy saucepan or preserving pan. Place the seeds and pulp in a square of cheesecloth, gather the sides into a bag and tie the neck tightly with string. Tie the bag to the handle of the pan so that it dangles in the citrus juice.

2 Cut the citrus skins into thin wedges; scrape off and discard the membranes and pith. Cut the rinds into slivers and add to the pan with the measured water. Bring to a simmer and cook gently for 2 hours, until the rinds are very tender and the water has reduced by half. Test the rinds for softness by pressing a cooled piece with a finger.

3 Lift out the cheesecloth bag, squeezing out the juice into the pan. Discard the bag. Stir the sugar into the pan and heat very gently, stirring occasionally, until all the sugar has dissolved.

4 Bring the mixture to a boil and boil for 10–15 minutes, or until the marmalade registers 220°F.

5 Alternatively, test the marmalade for setting by pouring a small amount onto a chilled saucer. Chill for 2 minutes, then push the marmalade with your finger; if wrinkles form on the surface, it is ready. Cool for 15 minutes.

6 Stir the marmalade and pour it into warm, sterilized jars. Cover with waxed paper disks. Seal and label when cool. Store in a cool, dark cupboard. Serve with warm croissants, if you like.

COOK'S TIP
Allowing the marmalade to cool slightly before canning lets it set enough to prevent the fruit from sinking. Stir before pouring it into the jars.

EXOTIC
FRUITS

Thanks to modern transportation methods, tropical fruits are no longer merely the stuff of travelers' tales. Rambutans, carambolas, guavas, passion fruit and pomegranates are stocked on greengrocers' shelves, alongside recent rarities, which have now become commonplace, such as mangoes, fresh dates and kiwi fruit. Most supermarkets now label tropical fruits with preparation and serving suggestions, so it is easy to venture into the realms of the exotic.

BANANAS

Bananas are surely the best-known tropical fruit and one of the most healthy and versatile. Neatly packaged in their attractive easy-to-peel skins, hygienically enclosing the sweet, creamy white flesh, bananas are the perfect convenience food.

The banana plant, whose elongated, fanlike leaves can grow to over 4 yards long, is actually an enormous herb. "Hands" of up to 200 bananas point upward through the leaves like fingers.

History

Bananas originated in Southeast Asia and have grown in the tropics since ancient times. There is a theory that the fruit of the Tree of Knowledge in the Garden of Eden was actually a banana; certainly, a banana leaf would have protected Adam's modesty more effectively than a fig leaf. Before man began to cultivate bananas, the fruits contained so many bitter black seeds that they were almost inedible.

Varieties

Hundreds of different varieties of banana flourish in the tropics, from sweet yellow pygmy fruit to large, fibrous plantains and green bananas, which can only be used for cooking.

The most common varieties of sweet banana are the long, curved yellow dessert fruit, which develop a speckled brown skin as they ripen. The most widely available of these is Cavendish, but unless you are an expert it is practically impossible to differentiate between individual varieties.

Finger or **Sugar** These are tiny bananas, often no more than 3 inches long. They have creamy flesh and a very sweet flavor.

Apple These yellow bananas are also very small. They have golden flesh and when very ripe have a faint taste and aroma of apple.

Left: Finger or Sugar bananas are tiny— often no more than the length of a lady's finger!

Above: Bananas, shown here in their unripe state, grow upward in bunches on a huge plant that is actually a giant herb.

Right: Perhaps the best-known tropical fruit, easy-to-peel yellow bananas, which come in a variety of sizes, are the perfect convenience food.

Right: When very ripe, small Apple bananas have a faint taste and aroma of apple.

Red bananas These bananas from Ecuador have brownish red skins and smooth, yellowish pink, sweet flesh with a creamy texture. Their color makes it hard to assess the exact degree of ripeness, so they can sometimes prove rather disappointing. Allow a few blackish patches to develop on the skin before eating.

Green bananas Large green bananas are suitable only for cooking. They have crisp flesh and are often used as a substitute for potatoes, although they have a blander flavor. Fried green banana rings are good in curries.

Plantain These fruits resemble large bananas, but are flatter in shape. They have firm, pinkish flesh, which is less sweet than that of dessert bananas but contains more starch. They are almost always used in savory dishes and can be cooked like potatoes. Very firm plantains can be peeled, then sliced wafer-thin and deep-fried like potato chips. As plantains ripen, their flesh becomes darker and sweeter, and the fruit can be used in desserts.

Right: Small (as here) or large, red bananas have the same sweet, creamy flesh.

Nutrition

Bananas are extremely nutritious, being rich in potassium, riboflavin, niacin and dietary fiber. Bananas also contain vitamins A and C and some calcium and iron. They have a high energy value (99 calories per 3¾ ounces) and are good for growing children and athletes. They are also excellent for low-salt, low-fat and cholesterol-free diets.

Buying and Storing

Bananas are harvested unripe and stored in a humid atmosphere to ripen slowly. Unripe bananas are green all over; these are inedible. Fruit with green-tinged ends are slightly underripe, with a crisp texture and refreshing taste. Perfectly ripe bananas are uniformly yellow; as the fruit continues to ripen, brown speckles appear on the skin until it is covered with brown mottling. By this stage, the flesh is soft and sweet and is best for mashing. Once the skin has become brown all over, the banana is too ripe to eat; the flesh will have collapsed, but it can still be used for cooking.

Do not buy bananas with damaged skins, or those that are too ripe. Unlike other fruit, they will continue to ripen rapidly at home. Never store them in the refrigerator, as the skins will blacken. Kept in a fruit bowl, bananas will hasten the ripening of other fruit.

Dried bananas Drying intensifies the sweetness of bananas. Dried bananas are dark brown, sticky and extremely sweet. They are usually eaten as a highly nutritious but calorific snack, but can also be added to winter fruit salads or savory stews.

Canned bananas Asian food stores sell whole baby bananas, sometimes complete with blossom, canned in heavy syrup. Only for those with a very sweet tooth!

Peeling plantains

1 Using a sharp knife, trim the fruit. Cut in half horizontally.

2 Slit the plantain skin along the natural ridge with a sharp knife. Take care not to cut through the flesh.

3 Ease up the edge of the skin and run your thumb tip underneath to lift up the skin. Lift off and discard the skin.

Right: Plantains are almost always used in savory dishes and can be cooked like potatoes.

Preparing and Cooking

Peel bananas just before using, removing the white threads from the flesh. Slice the bananas and, if not serving immediately, brush with lemon juice to prevent discoloration.

Dessert bananas are delicious eaten raw, but cooking brings out the sweetness and enhances the flavor. Raw bananas can be made into ice cream, milk shakes and trifles. Sliced bananas can be added to fruit salads or used to garnish sweet and savory dishes. In Indonesia and the Far East, they are served as an accompaniment to rice dishes such as *nasi goreng* and curries. They combine well with other tropical ingredients, especially brown sugar, coconut, exotic fruits like pineapple, passion fruit and mango, and rum.

Bananas can be baked in their skins, then split and served with melted butter and lemon juice. Alternatively, cook them over the dying embers of a grill until the skins turn black. Split them, sprinkle with rum and serve with heavy cream. Another rich dessert is banoffi pie, a very sweet concoction of bananas and toffee. A less sweet but equally delicious combination is broiled bananas wrapped in bacon. Banana fritters are always popular; cut the fruit into chunks, coat in batter and deep-fry, or wrap in phyllo pastry, brush with melted butter and

Above: Dried bananas are dark brown, sticky and very sweet.

deep-fry. Mashed bananas make deliciously moist cakes and tea breads.

Green bananas and plantains are starchier than sweet bananas and contain less sugar, so they are served as a vegetable. They can be boiled, baked, mashed, fried or broiled, and are an essential ingredient of many African and West Indian dishes. Banana leaves are often used as a wrapping for savory fillings and add a pleasant aromatic flavor to both chicken and fish.

BABACOS

The babaco is a hybrid of the papaya. Pointed at the stem end and blunt at the other, this large five-sided fruit reveals a soft white core when halved. When unripe, the waxy skin is pale green, maturing to yellow. When ripe, the pale orangey pink flesh is succulent and juicy, with a faint aroma of fresh strawberries, and the flavor resembles that of a rather bland papaya.

History

The babaco is native to Ecuador. European botanists discovered it about seventy years ago, and it is now widely grown in New Zealand and in the Channel Islands.

Nutrition

The fruit contains valuable enzymes that help to digest fat and proteins and can be used to tenderize meat. It is a good source of vitamin C.

Buying and Storing

Babacos keep well. Yellow fruit are ready to eat right away and should be stored in the refrigerator, where they will keep for about five days. Pale green babacos can be kept for a few days at room temperature, until yellow and ripe.

Preparing and Cooking

Babacos can be sliced, skin and all, and eaten raw. The delicate flavor can be livened up with lemon or lime juice and sugar. The flesh can be diced and used raw in salads, or squeezed to make a refreshing juice. Babacos can also be poached in syrup and served as a dessert with cream, custard or vanilla or ginger ice cream, but you will need to flavor the syrup with lime juice and

aromatics. On a savory note, the fruit makes excellent sauces, chutneys and relishes. Stewed babaco can be served as an accompaniment to roast chicken, pork and ham.

Babaco for breakfast

For a deliciously different breakfast experience, try serving your favorite cereal with chilled cooked babaco. Make a syrup by boiling equal quantities of water and sugar with the juice of a lemon or lime and a split vanilla bean, a cinnamon stick or a grating of nutmeg. Dice the babaco (there is no need to peel it) and poach gently in the syrup for about 10 minutes, until tender. Chill well before using.

Right:
Babacos are ripe
when yellow all
over—keep fruits that
are still mottled green
(as here) at room temperature for a few
days, until they are completely yellow.

BREADFRUIT

The fruit of a very tall tree, these large round- to egg-shaped fruits weigh from 11 ounces to 6½ pounds. They have thick, warty, greenish skin and white starchy flesh with a breadlike texture, which sometimes contains up to 200 edible seeds and sometimes none at all. Breadfruit form part of the staple diet in the tropics.

History

Native to the Pacific and East Indies, breadfruit came to fame in the famous 1787 mutiny on the *Bounty*, when, during the voyage to the West Indies, Captain William Bligh gave the last remaining fresh water to his precious cargo of breadfruit in preference to the crew. After being cast adrift, and enduring immense hardship, the overbearing captain arrived in Timor and was again sent out to collect breadfruit, earning himself the name "Breadfruit Bligh."

Nutrition

Breadfruit is very starchy. It is high in fiber and contains small amounts of vitamin C and folic acid.

Below: Breadfruit

Preparing and Cooking

Breadfruit are normally eaten as a vegetable. When really ripe, they can be eaten raw, but they are more usually cooked. They can be peeled and boiled, roasted or fried like potatoes, or baked whole in the oven.

CARAMBOLAS

Native to Indonesia and the Moluccas, carambolas, or star fruit, are now widely available in supermarkets. The uncut yellow or pale amber fruit has a waxy skin and is cylindrical in shape, with concave sides and five ridged edges; it resembles an elongated Chinese lantern. When the fruit is sliced crosswise, the slices are perfect star shapes, which are wonderful for decorative purposes. Although the fruit often tastes less exciting than it looks, it is refreshing and juicy to eat.

History

Carambolas originated in the Malay Archipelago, between Southeast Asia and Australia, but they are now also grown in Africa, Brazil, the West Indies and the United States.

Nutrition

Carambolas are a good source of vitamin C, and contain some potassium, niacin and phosphorus. They provide about 50 calories per 3¾ ounces.

Buying and Storing

Some carambolas have more flavor than others; there is no way of telling before you taste, so they are best used as an attractive decoration or in conjunction with other exotic fruits. Choose firm, undamaged fruits and hope for the best. They will keep in the refrigerator for up to a week.

Preparing and Serving

A good carambola will be sweet and tangy enough to eat on its own, complete with skin. Slice the fruit crosswise and, if you wish, cut out the flat central seeds with a sharp knife. The fruits are generally eaten raw as part of a fruit salad or made into jams, but they can also be poached in a syrup enlivened with lime juice.

Left: Carambolas make a wonderful garnish. When cut crosswise, the slices are perfect star shapes, hence the carambola's other name—star fruit.

CHERIMOYAS, CUSTARD APPLES AND SOURSOPS

Native to South America and the West Indies, cherimoyas are the fruit of shrubs belonging to the annona species. The large heart-shaped or oval fruit is made up of many corpels, or concave sections, with scaly yellowish green or tan skin, rather like a pinecone or a half-prepared globe artichoke. Inside, the fruit has creamy white, custardlike flesh with a sweet-sour flavor (hence its name) reminiscent of pineapples and bananas, and large black seeds.

Varieties

There are many different varieties of cherimoya, of which custard apples and soursops are the most widely available.
Custard apples These are heart-shaped or oval and can weigh up to 1 pound.

Below: Heart-shaped soursops have a tangy, acidic flavor.

They have light tan or greenish quilted skin, which develops brown patches as the fruit ripens; the flesh is particularly mellow and custardlike.
Soursop Also called prickly custard apples or bullock's hearts, soursops are the largest of this group of fruits. They have dark green skins covered in numerous short spines. The white juicy flesh has a tangy, acidic flavor, which gives the fruit its descriptive name. Once ripe, soursops rapidly ferment and become inedible.

Nutrition

Cherimoyas are high in vitamin C and iron, and provide 92 calories per 3¾ ounces.

Buying and Storing

Cherimoyas are fragile, so choose compact fruit with unblemished skin and tightly packed corpels; once these have separated, the fruit is past its best. Press gently to check that the fruit has a slight "give." Cherimoyas should be eaten as soon as possible after buying, but can be kept in the bottom of the refrigerator for a day or two. Unripe fruit should be kept in a brown paper bag at room temperature until they are ready to eat.

Preparation and Serving

All types of cherimoya can be eaten fresh. Simply cut the fruit in half

Above: Custard apples have delicious mellow flesh that is soft, almost like custard (hence their name).

lengthwise and scoop the flesh straight from the shell with a spoon, discarding the inedible seeds. For a special treat, add a dollop of cream.

Cherimoya flesh makes a delicious fruit sauce when blended with bananas and cream, or it can be blended with four times its volume of water to make a refreshing drink; stir in sugar to taste. The fruits can also be made into jams, jellies and sorbets.

CURUBA

Also known as the "banana passion fruit," the curuba is like an elongated passion fruit, with soft yellowish skin. The orange pulp has a sharp flavor and needs a little sugar to make it palatable. The skin can be peeled off in the same way as a banana. Curubas marry well with other tropical fruits and can be used in the same way as you would passion fruit.

Right: Curuba have a sharp flavor and can be used like passion fruit.

DATES

Dates are the fruit of the date palm, which grows in subtropical and desert areas throughout North Africa, the Arab States, California and Australia. The finger-shaped fruit grows in clusters of several dozen at the top of the tall trees, ripening from green to burnished brown. Date palms are prolific; the average annual yield of a single palm is 110 pounds.

Until a few years ago, only dried dates were available outside their native lands, but now fresh dates are exported, although only a few of the many varieties reach the stores.

History

Dates are one of the world's oldest cultivated fruits. It is probable that the Babylonians grew them as long as 8,000 years ago; certainly records show that they have been cultivated for over 5,000 years. In early times, the date palm was regarded as the "tree of life." Every part of it was used; the buds and fruit were eaten or dried and ground into flour, the sap was drunk, the fibers were woven and the date pits were used as fuel or fodder for donkeys and camels. Even today, dates are still known as the "bread of the desert."

Left: Boxed halawi dates.

Above: Date palms grow throughout North Africa, the Arab States, California and Australia.

The ancient Greeks and Romans were also fond of dates and often combined them with meat in their cooking.

Varieties

Of the many varieties of date, only a few are exported, and these are seldom sold by name. The most popular variety is the golden brown *deglet noor* ("date of the light") from North Africa and Israel; you may also find the very sweet *halawi* or the fragrant *khaleseh,* which can be recognized by its orange-brown skin. The finest dates are the large crinkly-skinned *medjool* from Egypt and California, whose flesh is intensely mellow and sweet.

Nutrition

Dates are extremely nutritious. They contain more natural sugar than any other fruit and deliver a substantial amount of dietary fiber and potassium, as well as providing many vitamins and mineral salts. They provide 144 calories per 3¾ ounces.

Buying and Storing

Fresh dates These should be plump and moist, with a smooth skin and a slightly crunchy texture. They are sold loose or in baskets. Dates are ripe when they are burnished brown. Unripe dates are more golden; they can be eaten in this state, but the flesh will be crisp and less honeyed than that of ripe dates. To ripen, keep the dates at room temperature. Fresh dates can be frozen whole, but check that they have not been previously frozen (they almost always have been).

Semi-dried dates These are sold in a cluster on the stem. They have wrinkled skins and a chewy texture.

Dried dates These are the old familiar Christmas favorites, sticky and intensely sweet, and are often sold sitting on a frilly doily inside a long box decorated with palm trees and camels. Since the advent of fresh dates, their popularity has declined. Dried dates are also sold pressed into blocks for use in cooking. Some Asian markets stock tiny, wrinkled red dates and smoky black dates with the flavor of a bonfire, which are only suitable for cooking. Semi-dried and dried dates will keep for months, but do not store them near strong-smelling foods like onions, as they absorb odors.

Below: Dried deglet noor dates in their familiar long box.

Stuffed dates

1 Cut the dates in half and pick out the pits.

2 Fill the cavities of the dates with cream cheese and sandwich the halves together.

3 Alternatively, mold a little marzipan to fill the cavities, roll the date halves in sugar and top each with a walnut half.

Right: Dried dates pressed into a block. For cooking, this type of date may need to be softened in hot water before using.

Above: Crinkly-skinned medjool dates have intensely sweet flesh.

Below: Fresh dates, which are often frozen in their country of origin, then thawed before being sold.

Preparation and Cooking

Fresh dates can be eaten just as they are. If you prefer to peel them, gently pinch the skin at the stem end until the fruit pops out. They can be pitted and filled with plain or colored marzipan or nuts, or rolled in sugar to serve as decorative petits fours.

Fresh dates also make good additions to fruit salads and winter compotes. Surprisingly, they are also good in savory dishes; in North Africa, they are used in tagines (fragrant stews) and curries, or as a sauce or stuffing for fish, meat or poultry.

Above: Dried Chinese dates are only suitable for cooking.

Dates have a particular affinity with cheese. Serve them on a cheese board, or halve and pit them and sandwich together with cream cheese.

Dried dates are good in moist cakes and hot sticky puddings, and combine very well with nuts, particularly walnuts and almonds. For cooking, dried dates should be pitted and chopped, using scissors dipped in hot water.

DRAGON FRUIT

Dragon fruit, or pitihayas, come in both yellow and pink versions. Pink dragon fruit are large, fuschia-pink fruit about 4 inches long, covered with pointed green-tipped scales, rather like the leaves of a globe artichoke. Inside, they are spectacularly beautiful, with translucent pearly white flesh dotted with a mass of edible black seeds, which add an appealing crunch. The flesh is sweet and refreshing, with a slightly acidic melonlike flavor. It has the texture of kiwi fruit.

Yellow dragon fruit look more like prickly pears or mini-pineapples. They taste exactly like the pink variety.

Nutrition

Dragon fruit are rich in vitamin C and dietary fiber.

Buying and Storing

Yellow dragon fruit are ripe when golden all over. Both pink and yellow varieties should yield when gently squeezed in the hand. Best eaten as soon as they are ripe, but the fruits can be kept in the refrigerator for up to three days.

Preparing and Serving

Dragon fruit are best eaten on their own, sprinkled with lemon or lime juice to enhance the flavor. They should be served chilled. Cut them in half lengthwise, then scoop out the flesh from the shell. The shells can be used as unusual serving dishes.

Above: Brightly colored dragon fruit have sweet, refreshing flesh.

DURIANS

The disgusting, all-pervading, sewagelike smell is legendary and has given rise to the alternative name: civet fruit. When ripe, the flavor of the flesh, however, is delicious.

Durians are large fruit that can weigh up to 10 pounds. Round or oval, they have a woody, olive green outer layer covered with stubby, sharp spikes, which turns yellow as they ripen. They consist of three to five segments containing aromatic creamy white flesh with the texture of rich custard; the flavor is sweet, a little like that of strawberries, with a creamy aftertaste. The large brown seeds are edible if cooked.

History

Durians originated in Malaysia or Borneo and from there spread to Southeast Asia in prehistoric times. Despite their unspeakable smell, they have always been considered an aphrodisiac.

Nutrition

Durians are starchy fruits. They contain a small amount of fat and are a good source of potassium and vitamin C.

Buying and Storing

It is essential to eat durians very fresh; don't attempt to store them, however briefly, or your house will smell of blocked sewers. Never buy fruit with damaged skin, or the smell will be

unbearable. Do not buy durians abroad and attempt to bring them home, as they are banned by most airlines! Take care not to drip juice onto clothing or table linen, as it stains indelibly. Despite all these dire warnings, don't be put off from trying this exotic fruit; it really does taste wonderful.

Preparing and Serving

Durians are best eaten raw. Use a large sharp knife to slit the skin at the segment joints, press out the segments and scoop out the flesh and seeds with a spoon. The rich, custardy flesh can be eaten just as it is, or puréed to make ice cream or milk shakes. Durian flesh is also used for making jam and cakes, and is available canned. The richness of the pulp also makes an excellent foil to hot, spicy foods like curries and chile dishes. Durian seeds can be roasted or boiled and eaten like nuts.

Left: The horrible, all-pervading sewage-like smell of durians is legendary. However, when they are ripe, the flavor of the flesh is delicious.

FEIJOAS

Although a distant member of the guava family, feijoas resemble small, slightly pear-shaped passion fruit, with a dark green skin that yellows as the fruit ripens. The thin, tough skin protects a soft jellylike pulp containing tiny, hard seeds, which are edible. Despite its alternative name of "pineapple guava," the feijoa tastes more like an aromatic strawberry. Treat it like guava.

History

Originally from South America, the feijoa takes its name from the Portuguese botanist Dom da Silva Feijoa, who discovered it in Brazil. It is also cultivated in New Zealand.

Nutrition

Feijoas are an excellent source of vitamin C and are rich in iodine. They provide 20 calories per 3¾ ounces.

Right: Feijoas taste a little like aromatic fresh strawberries.

GENIP

The bright green dimpled skin of the genip, or mamoncilla, gives rise to its alternative name of "Spanish lime," but it is related to neither the lime nor the lychee, which it resembles in flavor.

Genips are small, round tropical fruits, about 1¼ inches in diameter, that grow on trees in bunches like grapes. The tough green skin protects a jellylike pink pulp containing a large central seed.

The flesh is juicy and sweet, with a slightly acidic note. Despite its pale color, genip juice stains horribly and if you get it on your clothes or table linen, it will never come out.

GRANADILLAS

Granadillas, or grenadillas, are the largest members of the passion fruit family and can weigh several pounds. In their unripe state, these large specimens are used as vegetables, but they are seldom exported. The granadillas you will find in stores are smooth, round, orange-skinned fruits, with grayish pulp containing small, hard seeds. They look more attractive than passion fruit, but taste less fragrant. Granadillas can be eaten and used in exactly the same way as passion fruit.

Right: Granadillas

GUAVAS

Similar in shape to pears or plums, guavas can be as small as 1 inch or as large as 4 inches in diameter. They have thin, pale green skins, which turn light yellow as they ripen; the flesh varies from white to deep pink or salmon red. It contains a number of flattish, hard but edible seeds. Guavas are highly scented with an aromatic sweet-acid flavor, not unlike that of quinces.

Above: Guavas are delicious eaten raw.

Guavas are available canned in syrup and made into sweet fruit drinks.

Varieties

There are several varieties of guava, the most common being the familiar yellow fruit. Strawberry or cherry guavas are smaller, with reddish purple skins.

Nutrition

Guavas are exceptionally rich in vitamin C and are a good source of niacin, potassium and dietary fiber. They provide 62 calories per 3¾ ounces.

Preparing and Cooking

Ripe guavas are delicious eaten raw. They can be poached in syrup, but must be simmered gently, as the flesh easily disintegrates. The flesh can be puréed to use in ice creams and sorbets, or made into jams and jellies (alone, or with other fruits) or sweet drinks. Like quinces, they have an affinity for apples; a few slices of peeled guava added

Preparing guavas

To eat guavas raw, cut in half and squeeze over a little lime juice. Scoop out the flesh from the skin.

to an apple pie or applesauce impart a special fragrance.

Guavas can also be used in savory dishes and are particularly good in a sauce for duck or game birds. They make an interesting addition to salads, and can be stuffed with cream cheese and served as an appetizer.

JACKFRUIT

Jackfruit are related to breadfruit. The large, irregularly shaped oval fruits can weigh as much as 44 pounds. They have a rough, spiny skin, which ripens from green to brown, and each fruit contains large, white edible seeds. Ripe jackfruit have a pungent, musty odor.

History

Jackfruit come originally from the rain forests of India and Malaysia, and are now grown in Asia, Africa, South America and Australia.

Preparing and Cooking

Ripe jackfruit can be peeled and eaten raw; the pulp is sweet and rather bland. They are better boiled,

roasted or fried, to be served as a vegetable or in a curry. The seeds can be eaten boiled, fried or roasted like chestnuts. Jackfruit is only available canned, in syrup, in the United States.

Below: Jackfruit are huge—they can weigh up to 44 pounds.

JAMAICAN PLUMS

Also known as "hoy" or "hog" plums, golden apple, limbu and mombin, this fruit belongs to the same family as the mango and is grown in the West Indies, Central and South America, Southeast Asia and India. The golden yellow to deep red and purple fruits are small, about 1½ inches long and 1 inch in diameter. They grow several to a branch and, like mangoes, have soft skin and contain a large central pit. The firm, yellow flesh, which is juicy, deliciously fragrant and sweet, is more akin to pineapple or apple than mango. The distinctive flavor has a slightly acidic tang. Unfortunately, these fruits are fragile and do not travel well, but you may find them in Indian markets. Jamaican plums can be eaten raw, sweetened with a little brown sugar or sprinkled with rum or liqueur and served with cream. They combine well with other fruits in a fruit salad, and can also be poached, pickled or made into jams, jellies and sorbets. They make a good addition to curries.

Right: Unripe Jamaican plums

JUJUBES

Also known as Chinese jujubes, apples or dates, these small greeny brown fruits have been cultivated in Northern China for more than 4,000 years and are now grown extensively in India (where they are known as *bec* or *bor*), Asia, Southern Europe and more recently on the West Coast of the U.S. and in Australia. Jujubes, which ripen

Left: Jujubes

in the autumn, can be oblong, egg-shaped or round. They have crisp pearly white flesh enclosing a single pit, with the sweet flavor and texture of an unripe pear. Most fruits are deep brown when ripe, but can be bought while still firm but orange-red with just a hint of brown and left at room temperature for a day or two to ripen. They can be eaten raw, stewed with orange juice, candied or made into jams and jellies.

KIWANOS

This strange-looking fruit is also known as horned melon, horned cucumber and jelly melon. The oval fruits have thick, bright golden orange skin covered in sharp spikes. The skin conceals a bright green, jellylike flesh encasing edible seeds, rather like a passion fruit, with a subtle taste of cucumber, banana and lime.

History

Originally from Africa, kiwanos are now grown commercially in New Zealand, Portugal and the United States.

Preparing and Cooking

Cut the fruit in half, then spoon the pulp straight from the shell. It makes a refreshing drink or it can be added to fruit salads or cocktails. The shells can be used as serving dishes. Blend the pulp with plain yogurt, honey and vanilla ice cream to make an unusual milk shake.

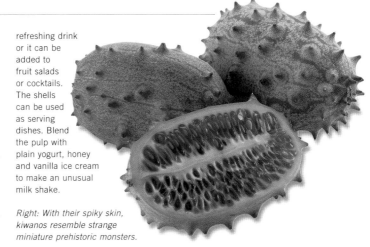

Right: With their spiky skin, kiwanos resemble strange miniature prehistoric monsters.

KIWI FRUIT

These cylindrical fruit, 3–4 inches in length, are covered with a light brown fuzzy skin that looks very dull in comparison with the beautiful bright green interior, with its crown of tiny, edible black seeds arranged around a white core. The flavor is delicate, yet refreshing and tangy.

History

Kiwi fruit were formerly known as Chinese gooseberries, in recognition of the fact that they originated in the Yangtze Valley. They are now extensively grown in New Zealand, Australia, South America and even Italy and France.

Nutrition

A single kiwi fruit contains more than a day's vitamin C requirement for an adult, plus vitamin E, and provides only 50 calories per 3¾ ounces.

Buying and Storing

Choose plump, unwrinkled fruit with unblemished skins. Kiwis are ripe when they yield to gentle pressure like a ripe pear; however, hard, unripe fruit can easily be ripened at home. Store at room temperature, but not in a bowl with other fruits, since the enzymes

Right: Kiwi fruit are delicious eaten raw—scoop out the flesh with a teaspoon.

in kiwi fruit cause them to ripen very quickly. Firm, unripe kiwis will keep for several weeks if stored in a cool place.

Preparing and Serving

The skin of a kiwi fruit is edible but the fuzzy texture is not particularly pleasant, so it is best to peel the fruit with a small sharp knife. For the most attractive effect, slice kiwis horizontally.

When nouvelle cuisine was in its heyday, slices of kiwi fruit appeared as a garnish for almost every dish, however inappropriate. Kiwis are certainly decorative, but they are good eaten as a fruit in their own right. They make an attractive addition to fruit salads, open fruit tarts and meringues, or can be puréed to make a sorbet or coulis. They go well with

white meats, prosciutto, poultry and fish, especially salmon and shellfish.

Kiwi fruit contain enzymes that make an excellent meat tenderizer. Rub the peeled skin or slices of kiwi into both sides of a cheaper cut of meat and leave for 20 minutes; the meat will become tender enough to broil.

The same enzymes, however, will prevent gelatin from setting and will curdle milk products, so do not attempt to make ice cream with raw kiwi. Cooking destroys the enzymes, but also the delicate flavor and texture.

KUBOS

Looking rather like wine red guavas, kubos are pear-shaped fruit with thick bitter skin and refreshingly sweet, slightly tangy, creamy white flesh

spattered with tiny, edible, crunchy black seeds. The texture is a little like that of an unripe pear. To eat, cut the fruit in half lengthwise and scoop out

the pulp with a spoon, or spoon the pulp over ice cream. The flesh can be combined with other fruits and makes a good addition to fruit salads.

LONGANS

Distant relatives of the lychee, longans are small, round, undistinguished-looking fruit. The brittle light brown skin encloses translucent, jellylike flesh around a single large inedible pit. They

taste similar to lychees but have a pleasant peppery tang. Longans are grown throughout Southeast Asia and China, where they are particularly popular; the Chinese name means

"dragon's eye." Fresh longans can be peeled and eaten like lychees, on their own or in fruit salads, sweet-and-sour dishes and stir-fries. Asian food stores sell longans canned in syrup.

LOQUATS

Native to China and South Japan, the loquat is one of the few subtropical fruits that belongs to the apple and pear family; it is sometimes known as a Japanese medlar. The name comes from the Cantonese *luk-kwyit*, meaning "rush orange," which describes the color of the loquat's flesh. The fruits are small and plum-shaped, with apricot-colored skin and white or yellowy orange flesh surrounding inedible brown pits. They have a sweet scent and a delicate mangolike flavor that is greatly enhanced by a squeeze of lime or lemon juice.

Buying and Storing

Ripe loquats are speckled with brown patches; perfect, apricotlike fruit are

Right: Loquats are one of the few sub-tropical fruits that belong to the apple and pear family.

still unripe. These can be ripened at home by being kept in a fruit bowl for a few days.

Preparing and Serving

Loquats can be eaten raw, complete with skin, or poached in a light syrup. They go well with other fruits, like

apples, pears and peaches, and make a wonderful ice cream to accompany these fruits. Loquats make good jams, jellies and chutneys (leave in a few of the seeds to impart a bitter almond flavor); they can also be cooked with brown sugar and wine vinegar to make a sauce for poultry.

LYCHEES

The leathery, scaly, reddish skin or "shell" of the lychee encloses pearly white translucent flesh that is firm and jellylike. This sweet, fragrant flesh is wrapped around a large, shiny, inedible brown seed. Canned lychees are

Left: Lychees

available in stores—and are often served as a dessert in Chinese restaurants—but they have none of the fragrance and subtlety of the fresh fruit.

History

Lychees have been cultivated in China for thousands of years. They have been considered a symbol of romance ever since a concubine of one of the Chinese emperors insisted on having teams of horses carry lychees hundreds of miles across country for her pleasure.

Nutrition

Lychees are rich in vitamin C. They provide about 65 calories per 3³⁄4 ounces.

Buying and Storing

Choose lychees whose shells are as pink or red as possible. Greenish fruits are underripe, while brown fruit are past

their prime. Although the shells act as protection, lychees quickly dry out, so do not buy too many at a time, and eat them as soon as possible after purchase. They will keep in the refrigerator for up to a week.

Preparing and Serving

Fresh lychees are best eaten raw as a refreshing end to a meal. Diners simply remove the shells, then nibble or suck the flesh off the pits.

Lychees can also be pitted and added to fruit salads, or poached in lemon-scented syrup and served chilled, alone or with ice cream or other poached fruits. For an unusual appetizer, serve pitted fresh lychees stuffed with cream cheese and nuts.

Use these succulent fruits in savory dishes too—they are good in Chinese sweet-and-sour dishes and also in salads (particularly when combined with avocado). They also make an interesting accompaniment to cold meats like pork and duck.

MANGOES

Among the most delicious and luxurious of all tropical fruits, different varieties of mangoes are grown throughout the tropics, from the Caribbean to Africa, Southeast Asia, Australia and India. Although they come in many different shapes, sizes and colors, mangoes are typically curved oblong fruits with green, pinkish gold or red skin and glorious orange, highly perfumed flesh surrounding a very large, hairy, inedible flat pit. The meltingly soft flesh is always juicy and sweet, although it sometimes has an acid overtone. Some mangoes have fibrous flesh; others are succulent and buttery. Certain varieties are said to have a flavor of mint, lemon, banana or pineapple, but in reality mangoes have their own distinctive taste, unlike any other fruit.

History

The history of the mango goes back over 6,000 years and is closely connected with Hinduism. Buddha was said to have been presented with a mango grove so that he could rest in its shade. Mangoes are native to Malaysia and India, and they form part of the local legend and folklore. The name comes from the Tamil *man-key* ("fruit of the tree"). Nineteenth-century traders introduced the fruit to the West Indies, Africa and South America.

Varieties

There are over 2,500 varieties of mango. They can be round-, oval-, heart- or kidney-shaped and can weigh between 5 ounces and 1½ pounds. All mangoes are green when unripe, but some remain green when they ripen, while others turn golden or bright red, or a combination of these colors.

Popular varieties include the **Alphonso** or **Alphonsine** from India, which has supple, buttery flesh and a heady, sweet flavor. West Indian varieties include the small **Julie** and the round, juicy **Bombay**. Cultivated varieties like **Parvin, Kent** and **Tommy Atkins** have thinner skins than wild mangoes and are less fibrous. **Ruby mangoes**, from the Gambia, have an excellent flavor but are rather fibrous. To eat one of these glowing red fruit, squeeze it gently between your hands, then pierce the skin and suck out the juice.

Nutrition

Ripe mangoes are rich in vitamins, especially A and C, and are a good source of beta-carotene. They provide about 59 calories per 3¾ ounces.

Below: Mangoes have meltingly soft flesh that is juicy and sweet.

Buying and Storing

Color is not necessarily an indication of ripeness in a mango; some remain solidly green when ripe. Buy unblemished fruit with no black blotches on the skin, as these indicate that the fruit is overripe and will have mushy flesh. The best test of a mango is its aroma, which should be highly perfumed. The fruit should be just yielding when gently pressed.

Mangoes will ripen at home if left in a warm place. To hasten ripening, place them in a brown paper bag with a banana or kiwi fruit. Eat the mangoes as soon as they are ripe.

Canned mangoes Mango slices are available canned in syrup. These are extremely sweet and are best drained before eating. They can be puréed to make a coulis or ice cream.

Above: Parvin

Preparing a mango

1 Place the mango narrow side down on a chopping board. Cut off a thick lengthwise slice, keeping the knife as close to the pit as possible. Turn the mango around and repeat on the other side. Cut off the flesh adhering to the pit and scoop out the flesh from the mango slices.

2 To make a "hedgehog," prepare the mango as above and score the flesh on each thick slice with crisscross lines at 1/2-inch intervals, taking care not to cut through the skin.

3 Fold the mango halves inside out and serve.

Right: Thin-skinned Tommy Atkins mangoes.

Dried mangoes

These can be added to chutneys and relishes, or mixed with other dried fruits in cake and tea bread recipes.

Preparing and Serving

Mangoes are so delicious that they are best savored in their raw state, perhaps with a squeeze of lime or lemon. The main disadvantage of this is that they are extremely difficult to eat elegantly. Indeed, it is said that the only way to eat them is in the bath. The secret of retaining a modicum of dignity is to remove the pit before attempting to eat the juicy flesh.

Whichever way you cut a mango, some flesh will always be left clinging to the pit. On no account waste this—wait until no one can see you, then cut off the skin and suck the aromatic pulp off the pit for a real treat!

Mangoes make an exotic addition to fruit salads and can be puréed to make sorbets and ice creams. They go well with other tropical flavors, like passion fruit and rum. They are excellent served with cured meats like prosciutto or smoked chicken, and make a refreshing accompaniment to spicy dishes and curries. Shrimp or other shellfish combine well with mango.

Ripe mangoes can be mixed with chiles to make a delicious salsa, while unripe green fruit are traditionally used to make mango chutney and pickles, which go well with cold meats and curries. In the West Indies and Asia, unripe mangoes are used as a vegetable and are baked or stewed with chicken and meat dishes.

Right: Kent, another of the 2,500 varieties of mango.

MANGOSTEENS

Despite their name, mangosteens have nothing to do with mangoes. Nor are they related to lychees, although their pearly white flesh looks very similar.

Mangosteens are apple-shaped with rather leathery, reddish brown skin that is deep purple when ripe. The flesh is divided into five segments, each containing a large seed. The segments are enclosed in dark pink pith, which should be removed before eating. Mangosteens have a sweet, refreshing flavor, rather like that of a plum, but more highly perfumed.

History

Mangosteens are indigenous to Southeast Asia. The trees are slow to grow; it is fifteen years before they bear fruit. They are now grown commercially in parts of Thailand, Central America and Australia.

Preparing and Serving

The flavor of mangosteens is too fragrant and delicate to be impaired by cooking. Eat them just as they are, or add to fruit salad. Peeled mangosteens look spectacular surrounded by a ribbon of strawberry or raspberry coulis.

Above: Mangosteens have a highly perfumed flavor. Eat the pearly white fruit segments just as they are, or add them to fruit salad.

Serving a mangosteen

1 Using a small, sharp knife, cut the skin around the equator of the shell, then lift off the top half of the shell and spoon out the flesh.

2 Alternatively, cut the mangosteens in half and scoop out the flesh with a spoon.

MARACOYAS

Also known as yellow passion fruit, maracoya is a largish fruit with vibrant green, thick, shiny skin that turns yellow as it ripens. Inside is a mass of translucent orange pulp enclosing hard gray seeds, just like a passion fruit, but sharper and less aromatic. Use in exactly the same way as passion fruit, adding plenty of sugar.

Right: Maracoyas

PASSION FRUIT

Passion fruit takes its name from its exotic flower, which is said to symbolize the Passion of Christ. Native to the Americas, these round or oval fruits have a leathery purplish brown skin (some, like those from Brazil, are yellow in color), which wrinkles when the fruits are fully ripe. Inside, the edible seeds are surrounded by intensely fragrant, translucent greenish orange pulp with a distinctive sour-sweet flavor and a wonderful scent. The fruits can be as small as a cherry or as large as an orange, but the ones most commonly available in stores are about 3 inches long.

Left: Passion fruit

Nutrition

The fruits contain vitamins A and C and are a good source of dietary fiber. They contain 34 calories per 3¾ ounces.

Buying and Storing

Choose fruit that feel heavy for their size, with firm, slightly wrinkled skins. Very wrinkly passion fruit with extremely dark skins will have dried out. Passion fruit can be ripened at room temperature; do not keep them in the refrigerator. The pulp can be frozen in ice cube trays, then packed into plastic bags. The juice is sold in cartons.

Preparing and Serving

The simplest way to eat passion fruit is on its own; cut the fruit in half and scoop out the pulp and seeds with a spoon. Both are edible, but the pulp can be strained to make a smooth coulis or refreshing drink. Passion fruit enhances the flavor of all other fruits and makes a delicious topping for a meringue or cheesecake.

Strained pulp can be made into ice creams and sorbets, or added to yogurt. Passion fruit jelly goes well with roast meats, or it can be spread on bread or toast. The juice makes an excellent marinade for rich meats like venison and game birds.

PAPAYAS

The papaya is native to North America, but it is now grown in most tropical or subtropical regions of the world. The large, pear-shaped fruits grow to about 8 inches in length. Some varieties remain green when ripe, but most turn deep yellow or orange. Papayas have beautiful, deep salmon pink flesh, with an abundance of edible gray-black seeds in the central cavity. The soft, juicy, sweet flesh tastes like a cross between melons and peaches.

Right: Papayas

Nutrition

Papayas are rich in vitamin A and calcium and contain large quantities of the enzyme papain, which breaks down protein and can be used to tenderize meat. Papain also makes papayas very easy to digest. They provide about 45 calories per 3¾ ounces.

Buying and Storing

Choose uniformly yellow fruit. Sniff them; they should have a delicate scent. Papayas bruise easily, so do not buy any with damaged or shriveled skins. If the fruit is not ripe, check the skin around the stem end; it should be yellow, otherwise the papaya will never ripen. Ripe papayas should be eaten immediately. Fruit that is not quite ripe should be left at room temperature until soft and yellow. The flesh can be cubed or puréed and frozen.

Preparing and Serving

Simply cut the papaya in half lengthwise and scoop out the seeds from the cavity. You can eat them (they have a peppery flavor), but they are not particularly pleasant. Squeeze a little lime or lemon juice on the flesh before serving.

Papayas can be used in the same way as melons, served solo with a good squeeze of lime, or sprinkled with ground ginger and served with cured meats like prosciutto or smoked chicken. The cubed flesh can be added to fruit salads, piled on top of meringues, made into ice creams and sorbets, or served with yogurt and preserved ginger. It also goes well with savory dishes like seafood and chicken curries. Finely chopped papaya is perfect with chiles in a fresh salsa. The skins can be used to tenderize cheaper cuts of meat. The papain, however, prevents gelatin from setting, so do not attempt to make a fruit jelly, cold soufflé or mousse with papaya.

Slightly unripe papayas can be used in salads, while fruit that is still hard is ideal for relishes and chutneys. Large fruit can be stuffed like zucchini and baked as a vegetable dish.

PERSIMMONS

Persimmons, also known as "kaki" or "date" plums, arouse strong feelings. People either love them or loathe them. When fully ripe these fruits, which originated in Japan, are exceptionally beautiful; the name means "food of the gods." They resemble large orange tomatoes, but have a wide, pale brown calyx and translucent, inedible skin. At their best, they have very sweet, honeyed flesh; unripe persimmons, however, are almost inedible, horribly sour and astringent.

Nutrition

Persimmons, rich in vitamin A, yield potassium, calcium and iron. They contain about 30 calories per 3¾ ounces.

To dry persimmons

Peel the fruit, leaving the calyxes and stems intact. Arrange on a rack over a baking sheet and dry in a very low oven. The sugar that is naturally present in the persimmons will crystallize on the outside. Dried persimmons taste like a mixture of dried figs, prunes and dates. They can be used in place of these fruits and added to cakes and puddings.

Above: Persimmon

Buying and Storing

Persimmons should be plump and extremely soft and pulpy, with undamaged skins. A perfect specimen will look as though it is about to burst, but this is exactly as it should be. Handle with great care and eat immediately, or store briefly in the bottom of the refrigerator. To ripen, place in a brown paper bag with a banana.

Preparing and Cooking

The fruit are best eaten raw; slice off the top and spoon out the flesh. Serve with cream or yogurt, use to make mousses, custards and ice creams or purée the flesh to make a sauce for ham, pork and game. Slightly unripe fruit can be poached in syrup or peeled and cooked like applesauce.

Sharon fruit

Developed in the Sharon Valley in Israel, this nonastringent variety of persimmon can be eaten while still firm and does not require peeling. Sharon fruit are less highly flavored than persimmons, and benefit from a squeeze of lemon or lime juice, but are treated in much the same way. They can be added to salads and make an attractive garnish for avocado vinaigrette.

PEPINOS

This beautiful fruit, with its smooth golden skin heavily streaked with purple, is sometimes called a "tree melon." Native to Peru, the pepino is a relative of the tomato, potato and eggplant family (*Solanacae*), but looks rather like a melon. The pale yellow flesh is quite tart, with a flavor suggestive of lemon, pineapple and melon. The sweet seeds of this fruit are edible.

Nutrition

Pepino fruits are rich in vitamin C, and also yield some vitamin A. They contain about 25 calories per 3¾ ounces.

Preparing and Serving

Pepinos can be peeled and eaten raw, but they are best poached with sugar or honey to counteract their acidity. Serve the fruit like melon, add pepino cubes to fruit salad or serve with vanilla ice cream.

Right: Pepinos

PHYSALIS

Also known as "cape gooseberries," "ground cherries," and "golden berries," physalis are distantly related to tomatoes, peppers, eggplant and potatoes, although you would never guess this by looking at them. The small, orange-gold berries are encased in a papery beige husk, similar to a Chinese lantern. They have a rather tart, mildly scented flavor reminiscent of a ripe dessert gooseberry with a hint of strawberry.

History

Although physalis are native to South America, the fruits seem to have been known to the Greeks as early as the third century AD. Physalis were introduced to England in the eighteenth century, but did not become popular until two centuries later. The early settlers in South Africa cultivated physalis in the Cape of Good Hope, which gave rise to their common name, cape gooseberries.

Preparing and Serving

Physalis are delicious eaten raw; the inedible papery husk is simply peeled back and used as a "handle," leaving the luscious berries free to be devoured as they are or dipped in fondant icing or melted chocolate. As such, they are very popular as petits fours and make attractive decorations for cheesecakes, meringues and pastries.

Physalis can also be cooked—they make the most delicious jams and jellies.

Above: Physalis

Dipping physalis in fondant icing

1 Peel back the papery husk like petals and fold into "wings."

2 Holding each physalis by the husk, dip into warm fondant icing.

3 Transfer to a plate lined with baking parchment and let cool.

PINEAPPLES

Pineapples are probably the most recognizable of all fruit. In fact, they are multiple fruits consisting of dozens of lozenge-shaped protuberances, each one being the fruit of a single flower, which together make up a single pineapple. Resembling a large pinecone topped with a spiky gray-green plume of leaves, a whole pineapple makes a spectacular addition to a fruit platter.

Above: Crystallized pineapple

The warm, distinctive aroma of the fruit is also very pleasing.

Pineapples are very versatile fruit, their sweet, acidic taste lending itself to sweet and savory dishes.

History

Native to South and Central America, pineapples had been cultivated for centuries before Christopher Columbus discovered them on his voyage to the West Indies in 1493. Astonished by the extraordinary appearance and flavor of the fruit, he brought some back to Europe, where they were regarded with wonder and awe. Due to their rarity and high cost, they became a symbol of hospitality, and stone pineapples often featured on the gateposts of houses to welcome guests.

The first pineapples, ripened in greenhouses, were presented to Louis XV of France, whose passion for the fruit made them even more highly prized. Pineapples are now grown in every tropical region of the world.

Varieties

There are hundreds of pineapple varieties, ranging from very large to miniature fruits. They are seldom sold by name, although **Golden Pineapple** is becoming familiar in some stores and markets. The color of the skin varies from orange to greenish yellow, while the degree of juiciness and sweetness depends upon the season.

Nutrition

Pineapples, rich in vitamin C and dietary fiber, provide about 46 calories per 3¾ ounces. They contain bromelain, an enzyme that aids digestion, so are the perfect

Left: Large, small and baby pineapples

Making pineapple wedges with plumes

1 Place the fruit upright, hold it firmly and slice it in half vertically with a sharp serrated knife, cutting down through the plume into the flesh. Cut each piece in half again to make four wedges.
2 Run a small, sharp knife between the rind and flesh. Slice off the core on each wedge, then slice the fruit into neat pieces, leaving these in place.

fruit to finish a rich meal. The enzyme breaks down protein, and so can be used to tenderize meat, but it will prevent gelatin from setting.

Buying and Storing

Choose a plump pineapple that feels heavy for its size, with a fresh, stiff plume. To test for ripeness, gently pull out one of the bottom leaves; it should come out easily. Avoid lifeless-looking, bruised or withered fruit with browning leaves. Use the fruit as soon as possible after purchase. Do not store whole pineapples in the refrigerator, although peeled, sliced or cubed pineapple can be chilled in an airtight container for up to three days. Fresh, peeled and sliced pineapple is available and should also be kept chilled.
Dried and crystallized pineapple Both can be eaten as a snack or used to make cakes and desserts.
Canned pineapple Chunks and rings are available in syrup or juice. They are useful pantry items, but lack the aromatic flavor of fresh pineapple. Crushed pineapple is also available.

Preparing and Cooking

Pineapples are delicious on their own, served in wedges or rings. Some people like to add a splash of kirsch, but a good pineapple should need no enhancement (although, surprisingly, a grinding of black pepper does wonders for the flavor). They go very well with other fruits; a hollowed-out pineapple shell complete with plume makes a spectacular container for fruit salad or tropical fruit sorbets.

Sliced pineapple can be made into a variety of hot desserts. Sauté in butter and brown sugar, make crisp fritters or combine with other fruits on skewers to make grilled fruit kebabs.

Tropical flavors, such as ginger, vanilla, cinnamon, allspice, coconut and rum, go extremely well with pineapple. Perhaps the most famous combination of pineapple, coconut and rum is the piña colada cocktail.

Pineapples' refreshing sweet-sour flavor makes them perfect for savory dishes, and they are often used in Chinese cooking. Traditionally, pineapple is cooked with ham and pork, but it also goes well with lamb, poultry and fish, particularly in spicy dishes and curries.

Below: Dried pineapple can be eaten as a snack or chopped to use in cake and other dessert recipes.

Peeling a pineapple

1 Cut the pineapple across into slices of the desired width.

2 Use a small, sharp knife to cut off the rind.

3 Hold each slice upright and cut out the "eyes."

4 Remove the central core of each slice with an apple corer.

POMEGRANATES

This attractive, apple-shaped fruit has leathery reddish gold skin and a large calyx or crown. Inside is a mass of creamy white edible seeds, each encased in a translucent sac of deep pink or crimson pulp and held together by segments of bitter, inedible yellow membrane that extend outward to the skin. These seeds gave the fruit its name, which means "grain apple." Eating a pomegranate is hard work, as each fleshy seed must be picked out individually, but their delicate, slightly tart flavor and refreshing, juicy texture make the effort worthwhile. Be warned, however, that pomegranate juice stains indelibly.

History

Originally from Persia, pomegranates have been linked with many cultures and religions for centuries and have been a symbol of fertility since ancient times because of their numerous seeds. Venus, the goddess of love, was said to have given pomegranates as presents to her favorites.

Until the Renaissance, pomegranates were used mainly for medicinal purposes in Europe, although they have always featured in the cooking of Middle Eastern countries. Nowadays, they are widely cultivated, from France, Spain and Israel to America and all over Asia.

Nutrition

Pomegranate seeds are rich in vitamin C and are a good source of dietary fiber. They provide about 72 calories per 3¾ ounces.

Buying and Storing

A pomegranate that feels heavy for its size is likely to be full of juice. Choose glossy fruit and avoid those whose skin looks hard and dry. They will keep in the refrigerator for up to a week. Dried pomegranate seeds are used in Middle Eastern cooking.

Preparing and Serving

If you have the patience, pomegranates are fun to eat raw; cut them open and pick out the seeds with a pin. Either suck out the juice and discard the

Below: Inside pomegranates is a mass of seeds, each encased in deep pink pulp.

Preparing a pomegranate

1 Cut off a thin slice from one end.

2 Stand the fruit upright. Cut downward through the skin at intervals, using a small, sharp knife.

3 Bend back the segments and use your fingers to push the seeds into a bowl.

4 Remove all the bitter pith and membrane.

seeds or eat the jellylike cells, seeds
and all. The seeds make a decorative
addition to fruit salads and can be used
as a pretty topping for creamy desserts,
ice cream or cheesecake. They have a
particular affinity with almonds and
make a jewellike garnish for couscous.
In India and Pakistan, the seeds are
used in meat dishes.
Pomegranate juice Extract the juice
very gently, using a handheld lemon
squeezer; electric or mechanical juicers
will crush the seeds and make the juice
bitter. The juice is delicious in

refreshing tall drinks, such as
pomegranate-flavored lemonade,
or it can be used to make a syrup to
color and flavor alcoholic drinks and
cocktails. Commercially produced
pomegranate syrup is called grenadine.
    The juice can also be used for
sorbets and sauces, and makes a
delicious pink jelly for savory dishes,
particularly those from the Middle East.
Use it to marinate pheasant, turkey or
chicken, or to make a sauce for chicken
or turkey, which can then be garnished
with pomegranate seeds.

PRICKLY PEARS

Also known as "cactus pears" and
"Indian figs," prickly pears are the fruit
of a cactus. They certainly live up to
their name, the skin being covered in
tiny, painful prickles. Prickly pears are
generally 3 inches long, with greenish
orange skin and orangey pink flesh with
a melonlike texture. The flavor is sweet
and aromatic. The small seeds can be
eaten raw, but become hard when they
are cooked.

Buying and Storing

Prickly pears are orangey yellow when
ripe. Choose unblemished fruit and
ripen it at room
temperature if
necessary.

Preparing and Cooking

Prickly pears are usually peeled and
eaten raw with a squeeze of lime or
lemon and perhaps a little cream.
    Prickly pears go well with other fruit
and are good in fruit salads. They can
be made into jams or mixed with oranges
to make an unusual marmalade. Mix raw
strained pulp with ginger to make a
sauce for cooked ham, or serve slices of
prickly pear instead of melon with cured
meats like prosciutto. Try adding stewed
prickly pear segments to a fruit
compote, or make a sauce or ice cream
with the strained purée. Candied or
crystallized slices of prickly pear can be
used to decorate cakes and desserts.

*Right: Prickly pears have a sweet and
aromatic flavor.*

RAMBUTANS

Rambutans are related to lychees and are sometimes known as "hairy lychees." Originally from Malaysia but now grown in tropical Central America and Southeast Asia, they are larger than lychees (about 2 inches in diameter) and look quite different, but have a similar texture. The taste is similar too, but slightly sharper. Rambutans resemble small, hairy animals, their reddish brown leathery skins being covered with soft, curly spines or hairs.

Preparing and Serving

Rambutans can be used in exactly the same way as lychees. To prepare, cut around the equator of the rambutan with a sharp knife, penetrating the skin only. Lift off the top half of the skin, leaving the fruit on the half shell, like an egg in a (rather hairy) egg cup. They can be added to fruit salads, served with ice cream (coffee ice cream is particularly compatible) or made into

jams or jellies, but are best eaten on their own. For an unusual appetizer, wrap peeled and pitted rambutans in prosciutto and serve speared on

Above: Rambutans

toothpicks. Rambutans are also available canned in syrup.

SAPODILLAS

The unprepossessing appearance of this drab oval fruit from Central America belies its delicious taste, which resembles that of vanilla-flavored banana custard. Inside the rough, light brown skin of the ripe fruit, the honey-colored flesh is sweet and luscious, with a core containing inedible, hard black seeds.

Right: Sapodillas are sweet and luscious—like vanilla-flavored banana custard.

Buying and Storing

Ripe sapodillas should have wrinkled brown skins and "give" slightly when pressed. Unripe fruit has smooth skin with a greenish tinge. Avoid this— unripe fruit is full of tannin and the flesh is unpleasantly grainy and mouth-puckeringly unpalatable. Instead, let the fruit ripen for up to a week in a fruit bowl. Ripe sapodillas can be kept in the refrigerator for up to a month.

Preparing and Serving

Sapodillas can be eaten just as they are—simply cut them in half, scoop out the flesh and discard the seeds. A squeeze of lime or lemon enhances the flavor. The flesh can be mashed and stirred into cream or custard, or made into ice creams, fools and mousses. It can be added to cakes and tea breads

and makes an unusual pancake filling.Mix puréed sapodilla flesh with homemade mayonnaise or lime vinaigrette to make a sauce or dressing to be served with cold fish or chicken.

The milky sap of the sapodilla tree is used to make chicle gum, the main component of chewing gum.

SNAKE FRUIT

Also known as salak, this large member of the lychee family acquired its nickname from its beautifully patterned scaly brown snakelike skin. The creamy flesh is divided into four segments, each enclosing a very large inedible brown pit. The flesh is denser and less juicy than a lychee's and has a distinctive apple flavor. Although the hard shells protect the fruit, the flesh quickly dries out, so eat them as soon as possible after purchase.

Snake fruit can be peeled and eaten just as they are, or added to fruit salads. They are delicious poached in a light lemon- or vanilla-scented syrup and served chilled, alone or with vanilla ice cream or sorbet as a refreshing end to a meal.

Right: Snake fruit—so named because the patterned, scaly brown shell resembles snake skin.

TAMARILLOS

Also known as "tree tomatoes," tamarillos look like large egg-shaped tomatoes with thick, smooth, wine red skins. Each fruit has two lobes containing a multitude of black seeds.

Buying and Storing

Tamarillos with a greenish tinge will be unripe. Ripe fruit is bright purplish or orangey red and is soft to the touch. The fruit will keep in the refrigerator for several days.

Preparing and Cooking

Tamarillos can only be eaten raw when they are completely ripe. At this stage the flavor is tangy, sweet and sour, while unripe fruit has a quite unpleasant tannin taste.

To enjoy tamarillos at their best, cut them in half, sprinkle with a little sugar and leave overnight in the refrigerator. The next day, scoop out the chilled pulp with a spoon. Do not attempt to eat the

skin, which is horribly bitter. Remove it by plunging the fruit into boiling water for about a minute, then slipping it off, or peel the fruit with a sharp vegetable peeler or knife.

Raw tamarillos can be used in fruit salads or puréed and made into jam and ice cream. They can be stewed or dredged in brown sugar and broiled. They make excellent chutney and a delicious sweet-sour sauce to go with fish or poultry.

Above: Tamarillos are members of the same family as tomatoes, eggplant and potatoes.

EXOTIC
FRUIT
RECIPES

Who can resist the colors, textures and flavors of
exotic fruits? Now that many varieties are widely
available all year, there's every excuse for taking the
taste trip and trying such delights as Lychee and
Elderflower Sorbet, Passion Fruit Crème Caramels
with Dipped Physalis or Exotic Fruit Sushi.

COLD MANGO SOUFFLES TOPPED WITH TOASTED COCONUT

FRAGRANT, FRESH MANGO IS ONE OF THE MOST DELICIOUS EXOTIC FRUITS AROUND, WHETHER IT IS SIMPLY SERVED IN SLICES OR USED AS THE BASIS FOR AN ICE CREAM OR SOUFFLÉ.

MAKES FOUR

INGREDIENTS
    4 small mangoes, peeled, pitted
      and chopped
    2 tablespoons water
    1 tablespoon powdered gelatin
    2 egg yolks
    ½ cup sugar
    ½ cup milk
    grated zest of 1 orange
    1¼ cups heavy cream
    toasted flaked or coarsely shredded
      coconut, to decorate

COOK'S TIP
Cool and creamy, these are great after a curry. Add some juicy pieces of fresh mango on the side, if you like.

1 Place a few pieces of mango in the bottom of each of four ⅔-cup ramekins. Wrap a greased collar of baking parchment around the outside of each dish, extending well above the rim. Secure with tape, then tie tightly with string.

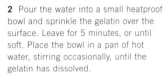

2 Pour the water into a small heatproof bowl and sprinkle the gelatin over the surface. Leave for 5 minutes, or until soft. Place the bowl in a pan of hot water, stirring occasionally, until the gelatin has dissolved.

3 Meanwhile, beat the egg yolks with the sugar and milk in another heatproof bowl. Place the bowl over a saucepan of simmering water and continue to beat until the mixture is thick and frothy. Remove from the heat and continue beating until the mixture cools. Beat in the liquid gelatin.

4 Purée the remaining mango pieces in a food processor or blender, then fold the purée into the egg yolk mixture with the orange zest. Set the mixture aside until it starts to thicken.

5 Whip the heavy cream to soft peaks. Reserve 4 tablespoons and fold the rest into the mango mixture. Spoon into the ramekins until the mixture is 1 inch above the rim of each dish. Chill for 3–4 hours, or until set.

6 Carefully remove the paper collars from the soufflés. Spoon a little of the reserved cream on top of each soufflé and decorate with some toasted flaked or coarsely shredded coconut.

PASSION FRUIT CREME CARAMELS
WITH DIPPED PHYSALIS

PASSION FRUIT HAS AN AROMATIC FLAVOR THAT REALLY PERMEATES THESE CRÈME CARAMELS.
USE SOME OF THE CARAMEL TO DIP PHYSALIS TO CREATE A UNIQUE DECORATION.

MAKES FOUR

INGREDIENTS
 generous ¾ cup sugar
 5 tablespoons water
 4 passion fruit
 4 physalis (cape gooseberries)
 3 eggs plus 1 egg yolk
 ⅔ cup heavy cream
 ⅔ cup whole milk or half-and-half

1 Place ⅔ cup of the sugar in a heavy saucepan. Add the water and heat the mixture gently until the sugar has dissolved. Increase the heat and boil until the syrup turns a dark golden color.

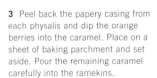

2 Meanwhile, cut each passion fruit in half. Scoop out the seeds from the passion fruit into a strainer set over a bowl. Press the seeds against the strainer to extract all their juice. Spoon a few of the seeds into each of four ⅔-cup ramekins. Set the juice aside.

3 Peel back the papery casing from each physalis and dip the orange berries into the caramel. Place on a sheet of baking parchment and set aside. Pour the remaining caramel carefully into the ramekins.

4 Preheat the oven to 300°F. Beat the eggs, egg yolk and remaining sugar in a bowl. Beat in the cream and milk, then the passion fruit juice. Strain through a strainer into each ramekin, then place the ramekins in a baking pan. Pour in hot water to come halfway up the sides of the dishes; bake for 40–45 minutes, or until just set.

5 Remove the custards from the pan and let cool, then cover and chill them for 4 hours before serving. Run a knife between the edge of each ramekin and the custard and invert each in turn onto a dessert plate. Shake the ramekins firmly to release the custards. Decorate each with a dipped physalis.

L Y C H E E <u>AND</u> E L D E R F L O W E R   S O R B E T

THE FLAVOR OF ELDERFLOWERS IS FAMOUS FOR BRINGING OUT THE ESSENCE OF GOOSEBERRIES, BUT WHAT IS LESS WELL KNOWN IS HOW WONDERFULLY IT COMPLEMENTS LYCHEES.

SERVES FOUR

INGREDIENTS
 ¾ cup sugar
 1⅔ cups water
 1¼ pounds fresh lychees, peeled
  and pitted
 1 tablespoon elderflower cordial
 dessert cookies, to serve

COOK'S TIP
Switch the freezer to the coldest setting
before making the sorbet—the faster the
mixture freezes, the smaller the ice
crystals that form and the better the final
texture will be. To ensure rapid freezing,
use a metal freezerproof container and
place it directly on the freezer shelf.

1 Place the sugar and water in a
saucepan and heat gently until the
sugar has dissolved. Increase the heat
and boil for 5 minutes, then add the
lychees. Lower the heat and simmer for
7 minutes. Remove from the heat and
set aside to cool.

2 Purée the fruit and syrup in a
blender or food processor. Place a
strainer over a bowl and pour the purée
into it. Press through as much of the
purée as possible with a spoon.

3 Stir the elderflower cordial into the
strained purée, then pour the mixture
into a freezerproof container. Freeze
for 2 hours, until ice crystals start to
form around the edges.

4 Remove the sorbet from the freezer
and process briefly in a food processor
or blender to break up the crystals.
Repeat this process twice more, then
freeze until firm. Transfer to the
refrigerator for 10 minutes to soften
before serving in scoops, with cookies.

EXOTIC FRUIT SUSHI

THIS IDEA CAN BE ADAPTED TO INCORPORATE A WIDE VARIETY OF FRUITS, BUT TO KEEP TO THE EXOTIC THEME TAKE YOUR INSPIRATION FROM THE TROPICS. THE SUSHI NEEDS TO CHILL OVERNIGHT TO ENSURE THAT THE RICE MIXTURE FIRMS PROPERLY, SO BE SURE YOU START THIS IN GOOD TIME.

SERVES FOUR

INGREDIENTS
⅔ cup short-grain rice
1½ cups water
1⅔ cups coconut milk
⅓ cup sugar
a selection of exotic fruit, such as
  1 mango, 1 kiwi fruit, 2 figs and
  1 star fruit, thinly sliced
2 tablespoons apricot jam, strained
For the raspberry sauce
  2 cups raspberries
  ¼ cup confectioners' sugar

COOK'S TIP
To cut the rice mixture into bars, turn out of the pan, cut in half lengthwise, then make 7 crosswise cuts for 16 bars. Shape into ovals with damp hands.

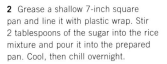

1 Rinse the rice well under cold running water, drain and place in a saucepan with 1¼ cups of the water. Pour in ¾ cup of the coconut milk. Cook over very low heat for 25 minutes, stirring often and gradually adding the remaining coconut milk, until the rice has absorbed all the liquid and is tender.

2 Grease a shallow 7-inch square pan and line it with plastic wrap. Stir 2 tablespoons of the sugar into the rice mixture and pour it into the prepared pan. Cool, then chill overnight.

3 Cut the rice mixture into 16 small bars, shape into ovals and flatten the tops. Place on a baking sheet lined with baking parchment. Arrange the sliced fruit on top, using one type of fruit only for each piece of sushi.

4 Place the remaining sugar in a small pan with the remaining ¼ cup water. Bring to a boil, then lower the heat and simmer until thick and syrupy. Stir in the jam and cool slightly.

5 To make the sauce, purée the raspberries with the confectioners' sugar in a food processor or blender. Press through a strainer, then divide among four small bowls. Arrange a few different fruit sushi on each plate and spoon a little of the cool apricot syrup over. Serve with the sauce.

LEMONGRASS SKEWERS WITH LIME CHEESE

GRILLED FRUITS MAKE A FINE FINALE TO A BARBECUE, WHETHER THEY ARE COOKED OVER THE COALS OR UNDER A HOT BROILER. THE LEMONGRASS SKEWERS GIVE THE FRUIT A SUBTLE CITRUS TANG. THE FRUITS USED HERE MAKE AN IDEAL EXOTIC MIX, BUT ALMOST ANY SOFT FRUIT CAN BE SUBSTITUTED.

SERVES FOUR

INGREDIENTS
    4 long fresh lemongrass stalks
    1 mango, peeled, pitted and cut
    into chunks
    1 papaya, peeled, seeded and cut
    into chunks
    1 star fruit, cut into thick slices
    and halved
    8 fresh bay leaves
    a nutmeg
    ¼ cup maple syrup
    ⅓ cup demerara sugar
For the lime cheese
    ⅔ cup cottage cheese or low-fat
    cream cheese
    ½ cup heavy cream
    grated zest and juice of ½ lime
    2 tablespoons confectioners' sugar

1 Prepare the grill or preheat the broiler. Cut the top of each lemongrass stalk into a point with a sharp knife. Discard the outer leaves, then use the back of the knife to bruise the length of each stalk to release the aromatic oils. Thread each stalk, skewer-style, with the fruit pieces and bay leaves.

2 Support a piece of foil on a baking sheet and roll up the edges to make a rim. Grease the foil, lay the kebabs on top and grate a little nutmeg over each. Drizzle the maple syrup over and dust liberally with the demerara sugar. Grill for 5 minutes, until lightly charred.

3 Meanwhile, make the lime cheese. Mix together the cheese, cream, grated lime zest and juice and confectioners' sugar in a bowl. Serve at once with the lightly charred fruit kebabs.

COOK'S TIP
Only fresh lemongrass will work as skewers for this recipe.

COCONUT JELLY WITH STAR ANISE FRUITS

SERVE THIS DESSERT AFTER ANY ASIAN-STYLE MEAL WITH PLENTY OF REFRESHING EXOTIC FRUIT.

SERVES FOUR

INGREDIENTS
    1 cup cold water
    ⅓ cup sugar
    1 tablespoon powdered gelatin
    1⅔ cups canned coconut milk
For the syrup and fruit
    1 cup water
    3 star anise
    ¼ cup sugar
    1 star fruit, sliced
    12 lychees, peeled and pitted
    1 cup blackberries

1 Pour the water into a saucepan and add the sugar. Heat gently until the sugar has dissolved. Sprinkle the gelatin over and continue to heat the mixture gently, stirring occasionally, until the gelatin has dissolved. Stir in the coconut milk, remove from the heat and set aside to cool.

2 Grease a 7-inch square cake pan. Line with plastic wrap. Pour in the coconut milk mixture and chill until set.

3 To make the syrup, combine the water, star anise and sugar in a pan. bring to a boil, stirring, then lower the heat and simmer for 10–12 minutes, until syrupy. Place the fruit in a heatproof bowl and pour the hot syrup over it. Cool, then chill.

4 To serve, cut the coconut jelly into diamonds and remove from the pan. Arrange the coconut jelly on individual plates, adding a few of the fruits and their syrup to each portion.

PAPAYA BAKED <u>WITH</u> GINGER

GINGER ENHANCES THE FLAVOR OF PAPAYA IN THIS RECIPE, WHICH TAKES NO MORE THAN TEN MINUTES TO PREPARE! DON'T OVERCOOK PAPAYA, OR THE FLESH WILL BECOME VERY WATERY.

SERVES FOUR

INGREDIENTS

2 ripe papayas
2 pieces preserved ginger in syrup,
    drained, plus 1 tablespoon syrup
    from the jar
8 amaretti or other dessert cookies,
    coarsely crushed
3 tablespoons raisins
shredded, finely pared zest and juice
    of 1 lime
¼ cup pistachio nuts, chopped
1 tablespoon light brown sugar
¼ cup crème fraîche, plus
    extra to serve

VARIATION
Use strained plain yogurt and almonds
instead of crème fraîche and pistachios.

1 Preheat the oven to 400°F. Cut the papayas in half and scoop out their seeds. Place the halves in a baking dish and set aside. Cut the preserved ginger into fine matchsticks.

2 Make the filling. Place the crushed amaretti cookies, ginger matchsticks and raisins in a bowl.

3 Stir in the lime zest and juice and two-thirds of the nuts, then add the sugar and the crème fraîche. Mix well.

4 Fill the papaya halves and drizzle with the ginger syrup. Sprinkle with the remaining nuts. Bake for about 25 minutes, or until tender. Serve with extra crème fraîche.

EXOTIC FRUIT SALAD <u>WITH</u> PASSION FRUIT DRESSING

PASSION FRUIT MAKES A SUPERB DRESSING FOR ANY FRUIT, BUT REALLY BRINGS OUT THE FLAVOR OF EXOTIC VARIETIES. YOU CAN EASILY DOUBLE THE RECIPE, THEN SERVE THE REST FOR BREAKFAST.

SERVES SIX

INGREDIENTS
    1 mango
    1 papaya
    2 kiwi fruit
    coconut or vanilla ice cream, to serve
For the dressing
    3 passion fruit
    thinly pared zest and juice of 1 lime
    1 teaspoon hazelnut or walnut oil
    1 tablespoon honey

COOK'S TIP
A clear golden honey scented with orange blossom or acacia blossom would be perfect for the dressing.

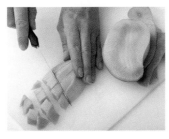

1 Peel the mango, cut it into three slices, then cut the flesh into chunks and place it in a large bowl. Peel the papaya and cut it in half. Scoop out the seeds, then chop the flesh.

2 Cut both ends off each kiwi fruit, then stand them on a board. Using a small, sharp knife, cut off the skin from top to bottom. Cut each kiwi fruit in half lengthwise, then cut into thick slices. Combine all the fruit in a large bowl.

3 Make the dressing. Cut each passion fruit in half and scoop the seeds out into a strainer set over a small bowl. Press the seeds well to extract all their juices. Lightly beat the remaining dressing ingredients into the passion fruit juice, then pour the dressing over the fruit. Mix gently to combine. Let chill for 1 hour before serving with scoops of coconut or vanilla ice cream.

TROPICAL FRUIT GRATIN

*THIS OUT-OF-THE-ORDINARY GRATIN IS STRICTLY FOR GROWN-UPS. A COLORFUL COMBINATION
OF FRUIT IS TOPPED WITH A SIMPLE SABAYON BEFORE BEING FLASHED UNDER THE BROILER.*

SERVES FOUR

INGREDIENTS
2 tamarillos
½ sweet pineapple
1 ripe mango
1½ cups blackberries
½ cup sparkling white wine
½ cup sugar
6 egg yolks

VARIATION
Although boiling drives off the alcohol
in the wine, children do not always
appreciate the flavor, so substitute
orange juice if making the gratin for
them. White grape juice or pineapple
juice would also work well.

1 Cut each tamarillo in half lengthwise
and then into thick slices. Cut the zest
and core from the pineapple and take
spiral slices off the outside to remove
the eyes. Cut the flesh into chunks.
Peel the mango, cut it in half and cut
the flesh from the pit in slices.

2 Divide all the fruit, including the
blackberries, among four 5½-inch gratin
dishes set on a baking sheet and set
aside. Heat the wine and sugar in a
saucepan until the sugar has dissolved.
Bring to a boil and cook for 5 minutes.

3 Put the egg yolks in a large heatproof
bowl. Place the bowl over a pan of
simmering water and beat until pale.
Slowly pour in the hot sugar syrup,
beating all the time, until the mixture
thickens. Preheat the broiler.

4 Spoon the mixture over the fruit.
Place the baking sheet holding the
dishes on a low shelf under the hot
broiler until the topping is golden.
Serve hot.

GRILLED PINEAPPLE WITH PAPAYA SAUCE

*PINEAPPLE COOKED THIS WAY TAKES ON A SUPERB FLAVOR AND IS SENSATIONAL WHEN SERVED WITH
THE PAPAYA SAUCE.*

SERVES SIX

INGREDIENTS
1 sweet pineapple
melted butter, for greasing
and brushing
2 pieces drained preserved ginger in
syrup, cut into fine matchsticks,
plus 2 tablespoons of the syrup
from the jar
2 tablespoons demerara sugar
pinch of ground cinnamon
fresh mint sprigs, to decorate
For the sauce
1 ripe papaya, peeled and seeded
¾ cup apple juice

1 Peel the pineapple and take spiral
slices off the outside to remove the
eyes. Cut it crosswise into six slices,
each 1 inch thick. Line a baking sheet
with a sheet of foil, rolling up the sides
to make a rim. Grease the foil with
melted butter. Preheat the broiler.

2 Arrange the pineapple slices on the
lined baking sheet. Brush with butter,
then top with the ginger matchsticks,
sugar and cinnamon. Drizzle the ginger
syrup over. Broil for 5–7 minutes, or
until the slices are golden and lightly
charred on top.

3 Meanwhile, make the sauce. Cut a
few slices from the papaya and set aside,
then purée the rest with the apple juice
in a blender or food processor.

4 Press the purée through a strainer
placed over a bowl, then stir in any
juices from cooking the pineapple.
Serve the pineapple slices with a little
sauce drizzled around each plate.
Decorate with the reserved papaya
slices and the mint sprigs.

COOK'S TIP
Try the papaya sauce with savory dishes
too. It tastes great with grilled chicken
and game birds as well as pork and lamb.

JAMAICAN FRUIT TRIFLE

THIS TRIFLE IS ACTUALLY BASED ON A CARIBBEAN FOOL THAT CONSISTS OF FRUIT STIRRED INTO THICK VANILLA-FLAVORED CREAM. THIS VERSION IS MUCH LESS RICH, REDRESSING THE BALANCE WITH PLENTY OF FRUIT, AND WITH CREME FRAICHE REPLACING SOME OF THE CREAM.

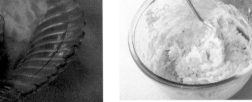

2 Whip the heavy cream to very soft peaks, then lightly but thoroughly fold in the crème fraîche, sifted confectioners' sugar, vanilla extract and rum.

3 Fold the drained chopped pineapple into the cream mixture. Place the chopped papayas and mangoes in a large bowl and pour the lime juice over. Gently stir the fruit mixture to combine. Shred the pared lime zest.

4 Divide the fruit mixture and the pineapple cream among eight dessert plates. Decorate with the lime shreds, toasted coconut and a few small pineapple leaves, if you like, and serve at once.

SERVES EIGHT

INGREDIENTS

  1 large sweet pineapple, peeled and
    cored, about 12 ounces
  1¼ cups heavy cream
  scant 1 cup crème fraîche
  ¼ cup confectioners' sugar, sifted
  2 teaspoons pure vanilla extract
  2 tablespoons white or coconut rum
  3 papayas, peeled, seeded
    and chopped
  3 mangoes, peeled, pitted
    and chopped
  thinly pared zest and juice of 1 lime
  ⅓ cup coarsely shredded or flaked
    coconut, toasted

1 Cut the pineapple into large chunks, place in a food processor or blender and process briefly until chopped. Pour into a strainer placed over a bowl and leave for 5 minutes, so that most of the juice drains from the fruit.

COOK'S TIP
It is important to let the pineapple purée drain thoroughly, otherwise the pineapple cream will be watery. Don't throw away the drained pineapple juice—mix it with sparkling mineral water for a refreshing drink.

POMEGRANATE JEWELED CHEESECAKE

THIS LIGHT CHEESECAKE IS FLAVORED WITH COCONUT AND HAS A STUNNING POMEGRANATE GLAZE.

SERVES EIGHT

INGREDIENTS
8 ounces oat biscuits or graham
   crackers (1½ cups crumbed)
6 tablespoons unsalted butter, melted
For the filling
3 tablespoons orange juice
1 tablespoon powdered gelatin
generous 1 cup mascarpone
   cheese
scant 1 cup full-fat cream cheese
¾ cup confectioners' sugar, sifted
scant 1 cup coconut cream
2 egg whites
For the topping
2 pomegranates, peeled and
   seeds separated
grated zest and juice of 1 orange
2 tablespoons granulated sugar
1 tablespoon arrowroot, mixed to a
   paste with 2 tablespoons kirsch

2 For the filling, pour the orange juice into a heatproof bowl, sprinkle the gelatin on top and set aside for 5 minutes, until softened. Place the bowl in a pan of hot water and stir until the gelatin has dissolved.

3 In a bowl, beat together both cheeses and the confectioners' sugar, then beat in the coconut cream. Beat the egg whites in a greasefree bowl to soft peaks. Quickly stir the melted gelatin into the coconut mixture and fold into the egg whites. Pour over the crust in the pan, level and chill until set.

4 Make the cheesecake topping. Place the pomegranate seeds in a saucepan and add the orange zest and juice and granulated sugar. Bring to a boil, then lower the heat, cover and simmer for 5 minutes. Add the arrowroot paste and heat, stirring constantly, until thickened. Allow to cool, stirring occasionally.

5 Pour the glaze over the top of the set cheesecake, then chill. To serve, run a knife between the edge of the pan and the cheesecake, then remove the side of the pan.

1 Grease a 9-inch springform pan. Crumb the biscuits or graham crackers in a food processor or blender. Add the melted butter and process briefly to combine. Spoon into the prepared pan, press the mixture in well, then chill.

COOK'S TIP
If you do not have a blender or food processor, crumb the biscuits or graham crackers by placing them in a large, strong plastic bag and crushing them with a rolling pin. For the best results, crush the crumbs as finely as possible.

BANANA AND MASCARPONE CREAMS

IF YOU ARE A FAN OF BANANA PUDDING, YOU'LL LOVE THIS RECIPE. IT IS A GROWN-UP VERSION OF AN OLD FAVORITE. NO ONE WILL GUESS THAT THE SECRET IS PREPARED CUSTARD SAUCE.

SERVES FOUR TO SIX

INGREDIENTS
generous 1 cup mascarpone
    cheese
1¼ cups custard sauce (créme
anglaise), prepared in advance
    ⅔ cup plain strained yogurt
    4 bananas
    juice of 1 lime
    ½ cup pecans,
        coarsely chopped
    ½ cup maple syrup

VARIATION
Use honey instead of maple syrup and
walnuts instead of pecans, if you like.
Also, try layering in some crumbled
cookies, such as amaretti or ratafia
(almond paste), shortbread crumbs or
crushed meringues. Or add a handful of
finely grated dark or white chocolate.

1 Combine the mascarpone, custard sauce and yogurt in a large bowl and beat together until smooth. Make this mixture up to several hours ahead, if you like. Cover and chill, then stir before using.

2 Slice the bananas diagonally and place in a separate bowl. Pour the lime juice over and toss together until the bananas are coated in the juice.

3 Divide half the custard mixture among four or six dessert glasses and top each portion with a generous spoonful of the banana mixture.

4 Spoon the remaining custard mixture into the glasses and top with the rest of the bananas. Scatter the nuts over the top. Drizzle maple syrup over each dessert and chill for 30 minutes before serving.

BANANAS WITH LIME AND CARDAMOM SAUCE

SERVE THESE BANANAS WITH VANILLA ICE CREAM, OR SPOON THEM OVER FOLDED CRÊPES.

SERVES FOUR

INGREDIENTS
    6 small bananas
    4 tablespoons butter
    seeds from 4 cardamom
        pods, crushed
    ½ cup sliced almonds
    thinly pared zest and juice
        of 2 limes
    ⅓ cup light brown sugar
    2 tablespoons dark rum
    vanilla ice cream, to serve

VARIATION
If you prefer not to use alcohol in your
cooking, replace the rum with orange
juice or even pineapple juice.

1 Peel the bananas and cut them in half lengthwise. Heat half the butter in a large frying pan. Add half the bananas and cook until the undersides are golden. Turn carefully, using a spatula. Cook until golden.

2 As they cook, transfer the bananas to a heatproof serving dish. Cook the remaining bananas in the same way.

3 Melt the remaining butter, then add the cardamom seeds and almonds. Cook, stirring, until golden.

4 Stir in the lime zest and juice, then the sugar. Cook, stirring, until the mixture is smooth, bubbling and slightly reduced. Stir in the rum. Pour the sauce over the bananas and serve immediately, with vanilla ice cream.

TOFFEE BANANAS

ALTHOUGH THE METHOD FOR THIS RECIPE SOUNDS SIMPLE, IT CAN BE A BIT TRICKY TO MASTER.
YOU NEED TO WORK FAST, ESPECIALLY WHEN DIPPING THE FRUIT IN THE CARAMEL, AS IT WILL COOL
AND SET QUITE QUICKLY. THE LUSCIOUS RESULTS, HOWEVER, ARE WORTH THE EFFORT.

2 Heat the peanut, sunflower or corn oil in a deep pan until it registers 350ºF, or until a cube of bread added to the oil turns pale brown in 45 seconds.

3 Using a fork, remove a piece of banana from the batter, allowing the excess batter to drain back into the bowl. Gently lower the piece of banana into the hot oil. Add more pieces in the same way; do not overcrowd the pan. Fry for about 2 minutes, or until the coating is golden.

4 As they are cooked, remove the banana fritters from the oil with a slotted spoon and place on paper towels to drain. Cook the rest of the battered bananas in the same way.

SERVES FOUR

INGREDIENTS
    4 firm bananas
    ¾ cup all-purpose flour
    ½ cup cornstarch
    2 teaspoons baking powder
    ¾ cup water
    1 teaspoon sesame oil
    peanut, sunflower or corn oil, for
        deep-frying
For the caramel
    1 cup sugar
    2 tablespoons sesame seeds
    ¼ cup water

1 Peel the bananas, then cut them diagonally into thick slices. Sift the flour, cornstarch and baking powder into a large bowl. Quickly beat in the water and sesame oil, taking care not to overmix. Stir in the bananas until coated.

5 When all the banana pieces have been fried, make the caramel. Mix the sugar, sesame seeds and water in a pan. Heat gently, stirring occasionally, until the sugar has dissolved. Raise the heat slightly and continue cooking, without stirring, until the syrup becomes a light caramel. Remove from the heat.

6 Have ready a bowl of ice water. Working quickly, drop one fritter at a time into the hot caramel. Flip over with a fork, remove immediately and plunge the piece into the ice water. Remove from the water quickly (using your fingers for speed, but taking care) and drain on a wire rack while coating the rest. Serve immediately.

HOT DATE PUDDINGS WITH TOFFEE SAUCE

FRESH DATES MAKE THIS PUDDING LESS RICH THAN THE CONVENTIONAL DRIED DATE VERSION, BUT IT IS STILL A BIT OF AN INDULGENCE! IT IS PREFERABLE TO PEEL THE DATES, AS THEY CAN BE RATHER TOUGH: SIMPLY SQUEEZE THEM BETWEEN YOUR THUMB AND FOREFINGER AND THE SKINS WILL POP OFF.

SERVES SIX

INGREDIENTS
  4 tablespoons butter, softened
  ½ cup light brown sugar
  2 eggs, beaten
  1 cup self-rising flour
  ½ teaspoon baking soda
  1 cup fresh dates, peeled, pitted
    and chopped
  5 tablespoons boiling water
  2 teaspoons very strong black coffee
For the toffee sauce
  ½ cup light brown sugar
  ¼ cup butter
  ¼ cup heavy cream
  2 tablespoons brandy

1 Preheat the oven to 350°F. Place a baking sheet in the oven to heat up. Grease six individual pudding molds or pans. Cream the butter and sugar in a mixing bowl until pale and fluffy. Gradually add the eggs, beating well after each addition.

2 Sift the flour and baking soda together and fold into the creamed mixture. Put the dates in a heatproof bowl, pour the boiling water over and mash with a potato masher. Add the coffee, then stir the paste into the creamed mixture.

3 Spoon the mixture into the prepared molds or pans. Place on the hot baking sheet and bake for 20 minutes.

4 Meanwhile, make the toffee sauce. Put all the ingredients in a pan and heat very gently, stirring occasionally, until the mixture is smooth. Increase the heat and boil for 1 minute.

5 Turn the warm puddings out onto individual dessert plates. Spoon a generous amount of sauce over each portion and serve at once.

COOK'S TIP
The sauce is a great standby. Try it on poached apple or pear slices, over ice cream or with a steamed pudding.

RUM AND BANANA WAFFLES

TO SAVE TIME, THESE SCRUMPTIOUS DESSERT WAFFLES CAN BE MADE IN ADVANCE, WRAPPED TIGHTLY, FROZEN, AND THEN WARMED THROUGH IN THE OVEN JUST BEFORE SERVING.

SERVES FOUR

INGREDIENTS
  2 cups all-purpose flour
  2 teaspoons baking powder
  1 teaspoon baking soda
  1 tablespoon granulated sugar
  2 eggs
  4 tablespoons butter, melted
  ¾ cup milk, plus additional
    if needed
  1¼ cups buttermilk
  1 teaspoon pure vanilla extract
  light cream, to serve
For the bananas
  6 bananas, thickly sliced
  1 cup pecans, broken
    into pieces
  ⅓ cup demerara sugar
  5 tablespoons maple syrup
  3 tablespoons dark rum

1 Sift the dry ingredients into a large mixing bowl. Make a well in the center. Add the eggs, melted butter and milk. Beat together, gradually incorporating the flour mixture, until smooth.

2 Add the buttermilk and vanilla to the batter and mix well. Cover and let stand for 30 minutes. Preheat the oven to 300°F.

3 Heat a handheld waffle iron over the heat. Stir the batter and add more milk if required (the consistency should be quite thick). Open the waffle iron and pour some batter over two-thirds of the surface. Close it and wipe off any excess batter.

4 Cook for 3–4 minutes, carefully turning the waffle iron over once during cooking. If using an electric waffle maker, follow the manufacturer's instructions for cooking.

5 When the batter stops steaming, open the iron and lift out the waffle with a fork. Put it on a heatproof plate and keep it hot in the oven. Repeat with the remaining batter to make eight waffles in all. Preheat the broiler.

6 Cook the bananas. Spread them out on a large shallow baking tin and top with the pecans. Scatter the demerara sugar over. Mix the maple syrup and rum together and spoon over.

7 Broil for 3–4 minutes, or until the sugar begins to bubble. Serve on top of the waffles with light cream.

COOK'S TIP
If you don't own a waffle iron, prepare the batter as directed, but make small pancakes in a heavy frying pan. Alternatively, use frozen waffles, and reheat as directed on the package before serving with the hot banana topping.

VARIATIONS
Use other fruits for the waffle topping, if you like. Small chunks of fresh or drained canned pineapple, thin wedges of peaches or nectarines, or even orange slices would be delicious alternatives to the banana.

MANGO <u>AND</u> TAMARILLO PASTRIES

THESE LITTLE FRUIT-TOPPED PASTRIES GO VERY WELL WITH A CUP OF AFTERNOON TEA.

MAKES EIGHT

INGREDIENTS
  8 ounces prepared puff pastry
  (12 × 10-inch rectangle)
  1 egg yolk, lightly beaten
  ½ cup white marzipan
  8 teaspoons ginger or apricot conserve
  1 mango, peeled and thinly sliced off
  the pit
  2 tamarillos, halved and sliced
  sugar, for sprinkling

1 Preheat the oven to 400°F. Cut the
pastry into 8 rectangles. Place on
baking sheets.

VARIATION
Use apricot slices instead of tamarillos,
or a mixture of plums and peaches.

2 Using a sharp knife, score the
surface of each piece of pastry into a
diamond pattern, then brush with the
egg yolk to glaze. Cut eight thin slices
of marzipan and lay one slice on each
pastry rectangle. Top each with a
teaspoon of the ginger or apricot
conserve and spread over evenly.

3 Top the pastry rectangles with
alternate slices of mango and tamarillo.
Sprinkle with some of the sugar, then
bake for 15–20 minutes, until the pastry
is well puffed up and golden. Remove
the pastries to a wire rack to cool.
Sprinkle with more sugar before serving.

EXOTIC FRUIT TART

THIS IS A GOOD WAY TO MAKE THE MOST OF A SMALL SELECTION OF EXOTIC FRUIT.

SERVES EIGHT

INGREDIENTS

1½ cups all-purpose flour
4 tablespoons unsalted butter
2 tablespoons solid vegetable
   shortening
¼ cup granulated sugar
2 egg yolks
about 1 tablespoon cold water
scant ½ cup apricot conserve,
   strained and warmed

For the filling

⅔ cup heavy cream, plus extra to serve
generous 1 cup mascarpone cheese
¼ cup confectioners' sugar, sifted
grated zest of 1 orange
3 cups mixed prepared fruits, such
   as mango, papaya, star fruit, kiwi
   fruit and blackberries
6 tablespoons apricot conserve,
   strained
1 tablespoon white or coconut rum

1 Sift the flour into a bowl and rub in the butter and solid vegetable shortening until the mixture resembles fine bread crumbs. Stir in the granulated sugar. Add the egg yolks and enough cold water to make a soft dough. Thinly roll out the pastry between two sheets of plastic wrap and use the pastry to line a 14 × 4½-inch fluted tart pan. Allow the excess pastry to hang over the edge of the pan and chill for 30 minutes.

2 Preheat the oven to 400°F. Prick the base of the pastry shell and line with baking parchment and baking beans. Bake for 10–12 minutes. Lift out the paper and beans and return the pastry shell to the oven for 5 minutes. Trim off the excess pastry and brush the inside of the shell with the warmed apricot conserve to form a seal. Let cool on a wire rack.

3 Make the filling. Whip the cream to soft peaks, then stir it into the mascarpone with the confectioners' sugar and orange zest. Spread in the cooled pastry shell and top with the prepared fruits. Warm the apricot conserve with the rum and drizzle or brush over the fruits to make a glaze. Serve with extra cream.

COOK'S TIP

You can also use a 9-inch round tart pan for this recipe.

MANGO PIE

THIS RECIPE COMES STRAIGHT FROM THE CARIBBEAN AND CAPTURES ALL THE SUNSHINE FLAVORS OF THAT EXOTIC SETTING. FOR THE TASTIEST PIE, BE SURE THE MANGOES ARE RIPE.

SERVES SIX

INGREDIENTS

1½ cups all-purpose flour
pinch of salt
6 tablespoons unsalted butter,
   chilled and diced
2 tablespoons solid vegetable
   shortening, chilled and diced
1 tablespoon sugar, plus extra
   for sprinkling
about 3 tablespoons cold water
beaten egg, to glaze
vanilla ice cream, to serve
For the filling
2 ripe mangoes
3 tablespoons fresh lime juice
½ cup sugar
1 tablespoon arrowroot mixed to a
   paste with 1 tablespoon water

1 Sift the flour and salt into a large mixing bowl. Rub in the butter and solid vegetable shortening with your fingertips until the mixture resembles fine bread crumbs, then stir in the sugar. Add just enough of the cold water to make a dough.

VARIATIONS

Make the pie using one mango and one papaya, peeled, seeded and sliced. Add a little ground cinnamon and some freshly grated nutmeg to the filling for a sweet spice flavor.

COOK'S TIP

If the top of the pie begins to brown too much during baking, simply cover it loosely with a piece of foil.

2 Knead lightly, then roll out two-thirds of the pastry and use it to line a 7-inch pie dish. Wrap the remaining pastry in plastic wrap and chill both the pastry and the pastry shell for 30 minutes.

3 Meanwhile, make the filling. Peel the mangoes and slice the flesh off the pit. Reserve half the sliced mango and coarsely chop the rest.

4 Place the chopped mango in a saucepan with the lime juice and sugar. Cover and cook for 10 minutes, or until soft. Pour in the arrowroot paste and cook, stirring all the time, until thickened. Set the filling aside to cool.

5 Preheat the oven to 375°F. Pour the cooled mango filling into the chilled pastry shell and top with the reserved mango slices. Roll out the remaining pastry to make a top crust.

6 Dampen the rim of the pastry shell and add the top crust. Crimp the edges to seal, then cut a cross in the center to allow the steam to escape.

7 Glaze the pastry with the beaten egg and sprinkle lightly with sugar. Bake for 35–40 minutes, until the pastry is golden brown. Cool slightly on a wire rack. Serve warm with vanilla ice cream.

B A N A N A <u>AND</u> P E C A N   B R E A D

BANANAS AND PECANS JUST SEEM TO BELONG TOGETHER. THIS IS A MOIST AND DELICIOUS TEA BREAD.
SPREAD IT WITH CREAM CHEESE OR JAM, OR SERVE AS A DESSERT WITH WHIPPED CREAM.

MAKES A 2-POUND LOAF

INGREDIENTS
   8 tablespoons (1 stick) butter,
      softened
   1 cup light brown sugar
   2 large eggs, beaten
   3 ripe bananas
   ¾ cup pecans, coarsely chopped
   2 cups self-rising flour
   ½ teaspoon ground apple pie spice

1 Preheat the oven to 350°F.
Generously grease a 9 x 5 x 3-inch loaf
pan and line it with baking parchment.
Cream the butter and brown sugar in a
large mixing bowl until the mixture is
light and fluffy. Gradually add the
eggs, beating after each addition, until
well combined.

2 Peel and then mash the bananas
with a fork. Add them to the creamed
mixture with the chopped pecans. Beat
until well combined.

COOK'S TIP
If the mixture shows signs of curdling
when you add the eggs, stir in a little
of the flour to stabilize it.

3 Sift the flour and apple pie spice
together and fold into the banana
mixture. Spoon into the pan, level the
surface and bake for 1–1¼ hours, or
until a skewer inserted into the middle
of the loaf comes out clean. Cool for
10 minutes in the pan, then invert the
pan on a wire rack. Lift off the pan, peel
off the lining paper and cool completely.

D A T E   <u>AND</u>   W A L N U T   B R O W N I E S

THESE RICH BROWNIES ARE GREAT FOR AN AFTERNOON SNACK, BUT THEY ALSO MAKE A FANTASTIC
DESSERT. REHEAT SLICES BRIEFLY IN THE MICROWAVE OVEN AND SERVE WITH CREME FRAICHE.

MAKES TWELVE

INGREDIENTS
   12 ounces semisweet chocolate,
      broken into squares
   ½ pound (2 sticks) butter, diced
   3 large eggs
   ½ cup granulated sugar
   1 teaspoon pure vanilla extract
   ¾ cup all-purpose flour, sifted
   1½ cups fresh dates, peeled, pitted
      and chopped
   1¾ cups walnut pieces
   confectioners' sugar, for dusting

COOK'S TIP
When melting the chocolate and butter,
keep the water in the pan beneath hot,
but do not let it approach boiling point.
Chocolate is notoriously sensitive to heat;
it is vital not to let it get too hot or it
may stiffen into an unmanageable mass.

1 Preheat the oven to 375°F.
Generously grease a 12 × 8-inch
baking pan and line with baking
parchment.

2 Put the chocolate and butter in a
large heatproof bowl. Place the bowl
over a pan of hot water and leave until
both have melted. Stir until smooth,
then lift the bowl out and cool slightly.

3 In a separate bowl, beat the eggs,
granulated sugar and vanilla. Beat into
the chocolate mixture, then fold in the
flour, dates and nuts. Pour into the pan.

4 Bake for 30–40 minutes, until firm
and the mixture comes away from the
sides of the pan. Cool in the pan, then
turn out, remove the paper and dust
with confectioners' sugar.

MANGO CHUTNEY

THIS CLASSIC CHUTNEY IS CONVENTIONALLY SERVED WITH CURRIES AND INDIAN PAPPADAMS, BUT IT IS ALSO DELICIOUS WITH BAKED HAM OR A TRADITIONAL ENGLISH CHEESE PLOUGHMAN'S LUNCH.

2 Place the mango pieces in a large saucepan, add the vinegar and cover. Cook over low heat for 10 minutes.

3 Stir in the brown sugar, chile, ginger, garlic, bruised cardamoms and coriander. Add the bay leaf and salt. Bring to a boil slowly, stirring often.

4 Lower the heat and simmer, uncovered, for 30 minutes, or until the mixture is thick and syrupy.

MAKES 1 POUND

INGREDIENTS
    3 firm green mangoes
    ⅔ cup cider vinegar
    ⅔ cup light brown sugar
    1 small red finger chile or jalapeño,
      split
    1-inch piece of fresh ginger root,
      peeled and finely chopped
    1 garlic clove, finely chopped
    5 cardamom pods, bruised
    ½ teaspoon coriander seeds, crushed
    1 bay leaf
    ½ teaspoon salt

1 Peel the mangoes and cut the flesh off the pit. Slice the mangoes lengthwise, then cut across into small chunks or thin wedges.

5 Ladle into hot sterilized jars, seal and label. Store for 1 week before eating. Keep chilled after opening.

PAPAYA AND LEMON RELISH

THIS CHUNKY RELISH IS BEST MADE WITH A FIRM, UNRIPE PAPAYA. IT SHOULD BE LEFT FOR A WEEK BEFORE EATING TO ALLOW ALL THE FLAVORS TO MELLOW. STORE THE UNOPENED JARS IN A COOL PLACE, AWAY FROM SUNLIGHT. SERVE WITH ROAST MEATS OR WITH A ROBUST CHEESE AND CRACKERS.

MAKES 1 POUND

INGREDIENTS
    1 large unripe papaya
    1 onion, thinly sliced
    ⅓ cup raisins
    1 cup red wine vinegar
    juice of 2 lemons
    ⅔ cup elderflower
      cordial
    ¾ cup turbinado sugar
    1 cinnamon stick
    1 fresh bay leaf
    ½ teaspoon hot paprika
    ½ teaspoon salt

1 Peel the papaya and cut it in half lengthwise. Remove the seeds with a small teaspoon. Cut the flesh into small chunks and place them in a large saucepan.

2 Add the onion slices and raisins to the papaya chunks, then stir in the vinegar. Bring to a boil, lower the heat and simmer for 10 minutes.

3 Add all the remaining ingredients and bring to a boil, stirring all the time. Check that all the sugar has dissolved, then lower the heat and simmer for 50–60 minutes, or until the relish is thick and syrupy.

4 Ladle into hot sterilized jars. Seal, label and store for 1 week before using. Keep chilled after opening.

MELONS, GRAPES, FIGS AND RHUBARB

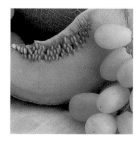

Some fruits are in a class of their own. Melons, grapes and figs

have little in common, apart from the fact that they are all

fruits, and rhubarb cannot even lay claim to that characteristic:

It is technically a vegetable. Without these treasures, however, the

food world would be a poorer place. Melons are the cool fruits,

grapes the sybarites' choice, figs the sweetest treats and rhubarb

the perfect springtime treat!

MELONS

Sweet melons are members of a large family of fruits and vegetables that grow on trailing vines and include cucumbers, and squashes. They come in a huge number of varieties (possibly thousands) and range in size from a single portion to melons that are large enough to provide a dozen servings. They have a hard, often beautifully patterned rind and very juicy, refreshing flesh enclosing a central cavity filled with a large number of pale, pointed, edible seeds.

History

Melons originated in Africa or Asia and have been known in China for at least 3,000 years. These early melons were bitter, rather like cucumbers, and could not be eaten raw. Hybridization resulted in sweeter fruits, which the Moors brought to Spain from Persia or Africa. They were taken to Italy, and by the fifteenth century reached France, where they were propagated

enthusiastically by the Avignon popes. Christopher Columbus took melons to the New World; when his men had eaten the fruit, they discarded the seeds, which produced large melon crops. These popular fruits are now grown in most warm parts of the world.

Varieties

Melons fall into two main categories—summer fruit, which includes all those varieties with crosshatched skin that looks like brown netting, and winter melons, which have smooth or finely ridged pale or bright yellow rind and delicate, pale flesh, which can be rather lacking in taste.

Summer melons

Cantaloupe This summer melon takes its name from the Italian town of Cantalupo near Rome, where the fruits were grown in profusion on the papal estate. Most cantaloupes are slightly elongated, with craggy pale green or golden rinds, marked into segments, and have aromatic orangey yellow flesh.

Charentais Charentais have smooth, gray-green rinds and very fragrant orange flesh. A ripe Charentais gives off a heady, delicious aroma. Most Charentais melons are grown around Cavaillon in France, and are sometimes sold under this name. The French writer Alexandre Dumas so loved these melons that he offered the municipality of Cavaillon all his published and future works in exchange for a lifetime annuity of twelve melons a year.

Galia A relative of the Ogen, Galia is a round melon with a raised pattern of fine netting on the skin. The skin turns from green to golden as it ripens, and the fragrant flesh is green and juicy.

Muskmelons These summer melons, also known as "nutmeg" melons, are round or oval, with a raised pattern of lacy netting on the rind. The skins can be green or orange, and the sweet, highly aromatic flesh ranges from orangey pink to pale green. They take their name from the Romans' habit of sprinkling the fruit with powdered musk to accentuate the flavor. Muskmelons are often hothouse-grown.

Ogen A hybrid developed in Israel, this cantaloupe melon has a smooth, pale green skin, marked with green or orange lines, which turns golden when the fruit is ripe. The juicy flesh is sweet and aromatic.

Pineapple or **khoob melons** These large oval melons have orangey yellow netted skin and beautiful, juicy orange flesh, which has the aroma and faint flavor of pineapple.

Above: Ein d'Or, one of the winter melons, has golden skin and delicately flavored flesh.

Winter melons

In addition to the winter melons listed below, there are the golden **Ein d'Or** and the **Piel de Sapo,** with rough-ridged, dark green skin and green-to-orange flesh. Its name means "toad's skin."

Casaba is a walnut-shaped melon with ridged, deep yellow skin and pale creamy flesh.

Crenshaws are pointed at the stem end and have smooth golden skins. They have the best flavor of all winter melons, with sweet juicy salmon pink flesh and a pleasant aroma.

Honeydew is the most common winter melon. Sadly, its name is often more flavorful than its taste.

Watermelons *See separate entry below.*

Nutrition

Melons have a very high water content, so are low in calories (30 calories per 3¾ ounces). The more orange the flesh, the more beneficial carotenes it contains.

Left: The aromatic orangey yellow flesh of cantaloupes is delicious served with cured meats.

Buying and Storing

Melons should feel heavy for their size and give off a pleasant, sweet aroma; they should not smell too musky, as this is a sign that they are overripe. Gently press the stalk end with your thumb; it should "give" slightly, but check that the fruit has not started to rot. The rind should be thick and unblemished with a good color for its type.

To ripen a melon, keep it at room temperature. Ripe melons are best kept in a cool, airy place. The refrigerator is fine, but wrap the melon in plastic wrap or a plastic bag first, or the smell will permeate other foods. Melon balls or cubes can be frozen in rigid containers for up to three months, either as they are or in a light syrup.

Preparing and Serving

Aromatic ripe melons are best eaten raw, on their own, in a fruit salad (use the melon shell as a container) or as an hors d'oeuvre with prosciutto or salami. Melons can be served in long slices, balls or cubes. They should always be chilled. A sprinkling of salt and pepper or ground ginger enhances the flavor. Small, round varieties can be halved horizontally, seeded and served as they are or with a filling such as raspberry coulis or ice cream. They can also be filled with port, although purists frown on this practice. For single-portion melons, cut off a lid and scoop out the seeds. Always scoop out melons into a strainer set over a bowl to catch all the juice. The seeds can be dried and roasted in the oven to make a delicious snack.

Melon goes well with sweet or savory ingredients. It makes a refreshing salad if mixed with cucumber and tossed in lemon juice, a light cream cheese or yogurt dressing, or a vinaigrette made

Above: Piel de Sapo—its name means "toad's skin."

Left: Galia melons are fragrant and juicy.

with lemon juice. Add cubes of blue cheese, such as Cambozola or Gorgonzola dolce. Melon cubes also enhance cold chicken, shrimp and other seafood bound in a light mayonnaise.

For the simplest and prettiest of desserts, scoop out balls of different-colored melon flesh (white, yellow, orange—perhaps even red watermelon), pile into a glass bowl and serve chilled, with a sprinkling of sugar if needed, and

a decoration of mint sprigs or nasturtium flowers. Melons make very refreshing sorbets, fools, mousses and ice creams. Spiced with pieces of preserved ginger, they also make excellent jams.

Chunks of melon can be made into a cool pickle that goes well with hot and cold meats or cold ham and poultry. The rind can also be pickled; remove the hard, colored, outer layer of rind, leaving the white inner rind.

Preparing melons for serving

1 If the melons are small, either cut off the lids or cut the melons in half, then scoop out the seeds into a strainer set over a bowl. Pour any juice from the bowl back into the melons; serve them plain or with a filling of other fruit like strawberries and raspberries.

2 For a prettier effect, "vandyke" the melon. Make a 1-inch diagonal cut where you want the lid to be. Turn the knife and cut down on the opposite diagonal to make an inverted V. Continue to cut zigzags all around the fruit in this way, then lift off the lid. Remove the seeds.

3 For melon slices, cut a large melon in half lengthwise. Scoop out the seeds and cut the melon into long wedges.

4 To make melon "boats," slice the melon as in step 3. Run a flexible knife between the melon rind and flesh to release the flesh. Slice the flesh on the rind into 3/4-inch chunks. Push alternate chunks in opposite directions to give a staggered effect.

Above: Honeydew melons

WATERMELONS

Watermelons are huge round or oval fruits that weigh up to 26½ pounds—much larger than sweet melons. They have solid dark green or paler striped skins, and vibrant pink or red flesh studded with large, flat, black, edible seeds. The flesh is very watery, and can taste rather insipid, but a slice of chilled watermelon is one of the most refreshing experiences imaginable.

History

Watermelons are thought to have originated in India, but may have come from tropical Africa. They were enjoyed by the ancient Egyptians, but were unknown in Europe until the thirteenth century. They became a symbol of the martyrdom of San Lorenzo in Italy; every year on August 10 in Florence, the patron saint of cooks is celebrated with an orgy of watermelon eating.

Varieties

Smaller varieties of watermelon are now available, weighing from 5½–10 pounds. These include **Sugar Baby,** a particularly sweet, round variety with very dark green skin and red flesh. **Tiger** has a paler green skin, striped with yellow or green, as its name suggests. **Golden watermelons** have bright yellow flesh and a more delicate (or dull) flavor than the red-fleshed varieties. They do, however, look very pretty when mixed with red watermelons.

Nutrition

The high water content of watermelons means that they are low in calories; only 30 calories per 3¾ ounces. They contain some vitamins B and C.

Buying and Storing

Watermelons should be firm and evenly colored and feel heavy. Tap them with your knuckles; they should not sound hollow. The side where the melon has rested should be yellowish, not white or green. Watermelons are usually sold cut into wedges. Do not buy those with faded flesh, or with white seeds; these are unripe. Whole and cut watermelons can be wrapped in plastic wrap and kept in the refrigerator for at least a week.

Preparing and Serving

Watermelons are generally cut into wedges and eaten on their own as a thirst quencher. Cubes or balls make an attractive addition to fruit salads and melon medleys, and they can be made into sorbets (add plenty of lemon for flavor). In some African countries, unripe watermelons are prepared like squashes as a vegetable dish. The rind can be pickled, and is sometimes candied. The seeds can be toasted and eaten (discard the outer shell).

Left: Tiger watermelons are—as the name suggests—striped.

GRAPES

These best known of all vine fruits grow in pendulous bunches on a stalk. The skins can be green, pale yellow, purple, bluish or red; in England, green grapes are known as "white" and purple as "black." Some grapes have a bloom; others have almost waxy skins. Inside, the pulp is translucent and usually contains a few seeds, although there are several varieties of seedless grapes.

Some varieties are grown as dessert or table grapes; others are cultivated exclusively for wine making. Some varieties are also grown for drying into raisins, golden raisins (sultanas) and currants. Generally speaking, table grapes are not used for wine making and vice versa, but there are one or two dual-purpose varieties.

History

Grapes are among the oldest cultivated fruits and were known to man long before Noah planted his vineyard on Mount Ararat. Wild grapes were already established in the Caucasus in the Stone Age, and it was not long before man discovered

Right: Alphonse Lavalle grapes are firm and crisp to eat.

how to ferment them into wine. It is certain that the ancient Egyptians made wine, although they used it for temple rituals rather than social drinking. The ancient Greeks and Romans, however, were enthusiastic consumers of wine and grapes and planted a huge number of vineyards. They also learned the technique of drying the fruit.

It was the Gauls who first put wine into wooden casks, and later, medieval monks became expert wine makers. They also pressed grapes into *verjus,* a sour liquid resembling vinegar. In nineteenth-century England, the Victorians were hugely enthusiastic about grapes and cultivated magnificent specimens in hothouses. At the same time, in France, a *uvarium,* or grape spa, offered medicinal and weight loss cures consisting entirely of grapes.

Varieties

A wide variety of table grapes is available, both seedless and seeded,

Left: Red and white grape juice is refreshing to drink on its own or mixed with sparkling mineral water.

the finest by far being **Muscat.** Seedless grapes contain less tannin than the seeded fruit and are easier to eat. The main varieties are listed below.

GREEN GRAPES

Italia The nearest inexpensive alternative to Muscat grapes, Italia are very large, roundish, seeded fruit with greenish yellow skins and a luscious, musky flavor.

Perlette Small, seedless, thin-skinned grapes with a rather tart flavor.

Sultana These small, elongated grapes with thin, greenish gold, bloomy skins and sweet, juicy pulp grow in compact, conical bunches. The varieties Perlette and Thompson are both hybrids of Sultana.

Thompson Seedless Medium-size elongated fruit with thin, bloomy skins and very sweet, juicy pulp.

RED GRAPES

Alphonse Lavalle These large, round, seeded grapes grow in a compact bunch. They have thick, purplish black skin, with firm, crisp pulp.

Cardinal Large oval fruit with reddish purple skin and firm, fleshy pulp, which can sometimes lack flavor. They grow in large, unevenly shaped bunches.

Flame Seedless A smallish grape with thin, wine red skin and very sweet, juicy pulp. These are mostly grown in Chile.

Napoleon The thick, dark purple skin on these large grapes has a heavy white bloom. The flesh is particularly sweet, although not very juicy.

MUSCAT GRAPES

Without doubt, these are the king of grapes, with a wonderful perfumed flavor almost like nectar. The very best are hothouse-grown and are displayed in shops cocooned in padded paper to preserve their beautiful bloom. All Muscats are large; the green varieties are pale green or golden, while red Muscats can be either red or black. The best Muscat grape of all is the **Chasselas,** whose skin turns almost bronze when ripe.

Muscat grapes are used for making sweet Muscat dessert wines, which encapsulate the honeyed flavor of the grapes.

Nutrition

Grapes are highly nutritious, containing natural sugars, potassium, iron and dietary fiber. They provide about 80 calories per 3¾ ounces.

Buying and Storing

Now that grapes are available all year round, many are sold underripe. The best way to judge a bunch of grapes is to taste a stray fruit; there is nearly always one that has fallen off the bunch. A perfect bunch of grapes should be of equal size and shape, with the bloom still on. Green grapes should have a golden or amber tinge; avoid any

Right: Red Muscat grapes can either be black (as here) or red.

Below: Wonderfully perfumed, Green Muscat are the king of grapes.

Left: Italia grapes, which can be green (as here) or black, have a luscious musky flavor and are the closest inexpensive alternative to Muscat grapes.

Peeling and seeding grapes

1 Put the grapes in a heatproof bowl and pour enough boiling water over to cover. Leave for about 20 seconds.

2 Drain off the hot water, rinse the grapes in cold water, then peel off the skins with your fingers.

3 Cut each grape in half and pick out the seeds with the tip of a sharp knife.

Right: Grown mostly in Chile, rich-colored Flame seedless grapes are sweet and juicy, with thin, easy-to-eat skins.

Above: Immensely popular, Thompson seedless grapes are very sweet, with thin bloomy skins.

that are uniformly vivid green. Red varieties should not be tinged with green. It is easier to spot overripe grapes, as they will fall off the bunch and often show traces of browning or mold. Do not buy wrinkled grapes, or bunches with tiny specimens attached; these will be very sour.

Store grapes in a bowl in a cool, dry place; they will keep for at least a week. To store them for longer, place in a sealed plastic bag and keep in the salad drawer of the fridge for up to two weeks. Remove the grapes from the refrigerator and keep at room temperature for at least an hour before serving so that the flavor can develop fully.

Grape juice Naturally sweet, clear red and white grape juice, from crushed grapes, is delicious served chilled on its own or mixed with sparkling mineral water.

Grapeseed oil Grape seeds are pressed into a very pale oil with a delicate, almost neutral flavor. This healthy oil is extremely rich in polyunsaturated fats. It can be used for cooking, but is best used in its natural state, in salad dressings, for example. It is the perfect oil to choose for making mayonnaise because it has such a mild flavor and it never separates.

Above: Large, golden muscatel raisins from Muscat grapes are often dried and sold on their stems.

DRIED GRAPES

The best of these are sun-dried, without undergoing any chemical processes. Dried grapes—raisins, currants and sultanas—sometimes contain bits of stem and the occasional seed, so pick them over carefully before using.

Artificially dried grapes are usually cleaner, but may need to be plumped up in boiling water for a few seconds before being added to cake mixtures.

Raisins The best raisins are made from Muscat grapes and come from California and Spain. These large, deep amber fruit are tender and sweet and can be eaten on their own, with cheese and nuts, or used in rice and couscous dishes. Smaller, black raisins are used for making cakes and puddings, muesli and mincemeat. All raisins benefit from being plumped up in brandy before cooking.

Golden Raisins or Sultanas These small, golden, dried fruits are made from seedless white grapes. They are deliciously moist, with a tender texture and delicate flavor.

Currants These small dried fruits are made from Turkish and Greek seedless red grapes.

Serving and Cooking

Grapes are best eaten on their own as a snack or dessert, or at the end of a meal with cheese or nuts. For an unusual sandwich, try Brie with halved grapes. They make a good addition to fruit salad and savory salads, combined with crunchy vegetables and walnuts. Green and red grapes make attractive garnishes, particularly in small clusters frosted with egg white and sugar. They can be used to make jams and jellies; a few small grapes look beautiful suspended in a clear jelly.

Their slight acidity makes grapes a good foil for rich meats like foie gras and calf's liver. They can also be used to stuff quail, chicken or guinea fowl, or to make a sauce for

Above: Clockwise from top left, golden raisins (sultanas), currants and raisins.

poultry or ham. A classic French dish is sole Véronique: rolled fillets of sole poached in white wine and garnished with green grapes. It is best to peel and seed grapes before cooking and to poach them lightly in wine or syrup so that they keep their shape. For savory dishes, they can be sautéed in butter.

Caramelizing grapes

1 Combine scant 1 cup sugar and ¼ cup water in a small, heavy saucepan. Stir over low heat until the sugar has dissolved. Bring to a boil, add 1 teaspoon lemon juice and boil until the syrup turns a deep golden brown.
2 Carefully add 1 tablespoon hot water (protecting your hand with an oven mitt, as the mixture will "spit") and shake the pan to mix. Spear a pair of grapes on a fork by the stem and dip them into the caramel to coat. Slide the caramelized grapes off the fork and leave on an oiled baking sheet for about 10 minutes, until the caramel cools and hardens.

FIGS

These oval or pear-shaped fruits are among the most luscious of all and can be eaten fresh or dried. They are not juicy in the conventional sense, nor do they have a particularly strong flavor, but they are succulent and sweet, conjuring up images of sunny Mediterranean gardens.

Figs come in three main varieties—green, black and red—and range in color from palest green to dark gold, burnished brown or deep purple. The entire fig is edible (although some people prefer to peel them), from the soft, thin skin to the sweet, succulent red or purplish flesh and the myriad tiny seeds. Skin color makes little difference to the taste of a fig. Their high natural sugar content makes them the sweetest of all fruits. The flavor varies, depending on where they were grown and how ripe they are.

History

Figs were said to grow in the Garden of Eden and their leaves, it is alleged, were used to cover the nakedness of Adam and Eve. Over the centuries, prudes have delighted in defacing works of art depicting naked bodies with carefully placed fig leaves.

Below: Although green in color, in England these figs are classified as white.

Figs probably originated in Asia Minor and were one of the first fruits to be cultivated. They were known to the ancient Egyptians at the time of the pharaohs and were brought to the Mediterranean long before the arrival of the ancient Greeks and Romans, rapidly becoming an important part of the Mediterranean diet. The world's oldest known living fig tree is said to be growing in a Sicilian garden.

Figs are now widely cultivated and exported from France, Greece, Turkey, Brazil and the United States.

Above:
Turkish purple figs

Varieties

You will seldom find figs in stores or markets labeled according to their variety; instead, they are classified by color—green, black and red. In reality, they range from palest green to dark gold, burnished brown or deep purple. In Italy, you are most likely to find the green **Kadota,** while in France you may come across **Buissone, Barbillone** and **Dauphine Violette.** Imported figs from Turkey are generally purple with deep red flesh.

Nutrition

Figs consist of 83 percent natural sugars. They are a good source of calcium, are high in fibre and contain vitamins A, B and C. They are well known for their laxative and digestive properties. A single fig provides about 30 calories.

Buying and Storing

Ripe figs are very delicate and do not travel well, so it is often difficult to find imported fruit at a perfect stage of maturity. Look for unblemished fruit that is soft and yielding when gently squeezed but still holds its shape. Figs should have a faint, delicate aroma; if they smell sour, they are overripe and will taste sour too. If you are buying figs in their country of origin, you may find some with split skins. Provided you are going to eat them immediately, this does not matter. Be careful not to squash the figs on the way home, or you will end up with a squishy inedible pulp.

Ripe figs should ideally be eaten on the day they are bought, but can be stored in the salad drawer of the refrigerator for up to three days. Remove them well before serving, as chilling spoils the delicate flavor. Underripe fruit can be kept at room temperature for a day or two until the skin softens, but they will never develop the wonderful flavor of figs that have ripened in the sun naturally on the tree.

Right: Dried figs are sometimes sold strung together in a ring.

DRIED FIGS

Dried figs are made from very ripe autumn fruits, usually golden Smyrna figs from Turkey or deep purple Mission figs from California. They are spread out to dry in the sun and must be turned several times before they are dried completely. This process flattens the figs into the familiar cushion shape. Dried figs contain large amounts of sugar and are highly nutritious. The best have a soft texture and are sold loosely packed so that they remain plump. Less high quality figs are commonly sold in blocks or strung together like a necklace. Store them in a cool, dry place.

Eat dried figs as they are, or stuff them with marzipan, nuts or cream cheese. They are used in compotes, poached in wine or served with creamy custard puddings. They can be baked in cakes, steamed puddings and tea breads. They are extensively used in Middle Eastern cooking and go especially well with poultry and game. Dried figs can be substituted for prunes in chicken, pork and rabbit recipes, such as terrines, stews and casseroles. Soak them—preferably in red wine—for several hours before cooking.

Dried figs are also used to make popular, delicious bar cookies, sold commercially and in old-fashioned bake shops.

CANNED OR PRESERVED FIGS

These are usually green Kadota figs preserved in heavy syrup. Canned figs are very sweet and are best served in a fruit compote. A dollop of whipped cream or strained, plain (Mediterranean-style or Greek) yogurt will temper the sweetness.

Preparing and Cooking

The best way to enjoy a fig is to pick a perfectly sun-ripened fruit straight off the tree. Wash it briefly and pat it dry very gently. Always serve figs at room temperature, never chilled. They look particularly attractive on a bed of fig leaves, especially if each fruit is slit into four pieces and opened out to resemble a flower. The centers can be

Left: Dried figs—the best, soft-textured fruits are sold loosely packed.

or ice cream. They also go well with savory dishes like duck and lamb. To poach figs, put them in a saucepan and cover with syrup, red or white wine or port. Add your chosen flavorings—honey, cinnamon, vanilla and lemon are all suitable. Bring to a boil, lower the heat, cover and simmer gently for about 15 minutes, until the figs are tender. Using a slotted spoon, transfer the figs to a serving dish, then boil the poaching liquid until it is thick and syrupy before pouring it over the fruit.

To cook figs in butter, cut them in half vertically, then arrange them cut side up in a heatproof dish. Put a pat of butter on each fig half. Sprinkle with port or Marsala and a pinch of cinnamon or nutmeg, and broil until lightly browned. Serve with meat or poultry, or brush with honey before broiling and serve as a dessert.

To caramelize figs, dip the fruit in water, then roll in granulated or vanilla sugar until completely coated. Place in a shallow baking dish and bake in a preheated oven at 425°F for about 15 minutes, or until the sugar has caramelized. Let cool, then chill before serving.

Above: Dried figs dusted with cornstarch to keep the fruits separate.

stuffed, if you like. Cream cheese mixed with honey and chopped nuts, fresh raspberries or raspberry mousse make delicious fillings.

Fresh figs are usually eaten raw as a dessert fruit, or as an hors d'oeuvre with prosciutto or salami. They have an affinity for nuts such as walnuts, pistachios and almonds and make an excellent addition to a cheese platter with grapes and nuts.

They can be stuffed with sweet or savory fillings like cream or blue cheese, celery and walnuts or marzipan, and are especially delicious filled with mascarpone and berries. Figs can also be successfully cooked in compotes, preserves and jams. For desserts, they can be poached in wine, honey or syrup; they can also be caramelized or made into tarts

Above: Almost too sweet on their own, green preserved figs are best served with cream or plain yogurt.

Making fig flowers

Cut each fig downward into quarters, starting from the stem end and leaving the quarters attached at the base. Gently pull the sections apart to open them out like the petals of a flower. Serve the figs plain or with your chosen creamy filling.

RHUBARB

Strictly speaking, rhubarb is not a fruit, but a vegetable; it is the fleshy stalk of the rhubarb plant, a relative of sorrel and dock. The stems are succulent, but too sour to eat raw, and the leaves contain oxalic acid, which makes them highly poisonous. The normal growing season is late spring to late summer, but early forced rhubarb, grown under covered pots, is available throughout the spring months. Main crop rhubarb stalks vary from green to purplish pink; the forced variety has spindly, tender bright pink or red stems, crowned with yellow leaves, and tastes much better.

History

Rhubarb originated in Northern Asia and Siberia. It has been cultivated for centuries, but was originally used as a medicinal and ornamental plant. It was not until the eighteenth century that British gardeners began to grow rhubarb for cooking.

Preparing rhubarb

1 Using a large knife, cut off and discard the leaves and the root end of the stalk. Peel off any stringy fibers with a swivel-blade vegetable peeler.

2 Cut the rhubarb into pieces.

Nutrition

Rhubarb is one of the lowest calorie foods, providing only 7 calories per 3¾ ounces. It contains significant amounts of calcium, potassium and thiamine (vitamin B1) and has natural laxative properties.

Buying and Storing

Choose crisp, firm stalks that look bright and release sap when you snap them. Rhubarb can be stored for a few days in the bottom of the refrigerator, but wilts quickly. It freezes well: Cut the stalks into short lengths, blanch briefly in boiling water, refresh in ice water and freeze in freezer bags.

Preparing and Cooking

All rhubarb needs to be sweetened when it is cooked, usually with sugar. This can be added at the outset, or when it has been cooked until tender. Use a stainless steel pan and only a spoonful or two of water. Poach gently until the fruit is tender. Rhubarb makes a wonderful pie or tart filling, and a delicious crumble, especially when mixed with banana.

Puréed rhubarb can be made into ice cream, sorbets, mousses and fools. Citrus fruits and spices, particularly ginger, vanilla and cinnamon, complement the flavor of rhubarb. Rhubarb can be combined with any of these to make excellent jams and chutneys. Because it is a vegetable, rhubarb goes well with savory dishes like scrambled eggs, but you will still need to add sugar. It adds piquancy to rich casseroles, particularly pork, lamb and duck. Its sharp acidity makes it a good substitute for sorrel in sauces, especially to serve with oily fish, such as mackerel.

Above: Early forced rhubarb, grown under covered pots, is pink and tender.

Below: Tougher, main-crop rhubarb is grown outdoors.

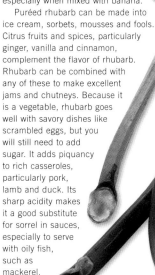

MELON, GRAPE, FIG AND RHUBARB RECIPES

Whether alone or with other fruits, melons, rhubarb,
figs and grapes make wonderful desserts, pies, cakes
and preserves. Don't miss Red Grape and Cheese
Tartlets, One-Crust Rhubarb Pie or
Yogurt and Fig Cake.

MELON TRIO <u>WITH</u> GINGER COOKIES

THE EYE-CATCHING COLORS OF THESE THREE DIFFERENT MELONS REALLY MAKE THIS DESSERT,
WHILE THE CRISP COOKIES PROVIDE A PERFECT CONTRAST IN TEXTURE.

SERVES FOUR

INGREDIENTS
¼ watermelon
½ honeydew melon
½ charentais melon
¼ cup preserved ginger syrup
For the cookies
2 tablespoons unsalted butter
2 tablespoons sugar
1 teaspoon honey
¼ cup all-purpose flour
¼ cup deluxe glacé
   mixed fruit, finely chopped
1 piece of preserved ginger in syrup,
   drained and finely chopped
2 tablespoons sliced almonds

1 Remove the seeds from the melons, cut them into wedges, then slice off the zest. Cut all the flesh into chunks and mix in a bowl. Stir in the ginger syrup, cover and chill until ready to serve.

2 Meanwhile, make the cookies. Preheat the oven to 350°F. Melt the butter, sugar and honey in a saucepan. Remove from the heat and stir in the remaining ingredients.

3 Line a baking sheet with baking parchment. Space four spoonfuls of the mixture on the paper at regular intervals, leaving plenty of room for spreading. Flatten the mixture slightly into rounds and bake for 15 minutes, or until the tops are golden.

4 Let the cookies cool on the baking sheet for 1 minute, then lift each one in turn, using a metal spatula, and drape over a rolling pin to cool and harden. Repeat with the remaining mixture to make eight cookies in all.

5 Serve the melon chunks with some of the syrup and the ginger cookies.

COOK'S TIP
For an even prettier effect, scoop the melon flesh into balls with the large end of a melon baller.

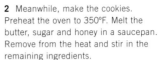

PORT-STEWED RHUBARB
WITH VANILLA DESSERTS

RHUBARB IS ONE OF THOSE FRUITS THAT SELDOM REALIZES ITS FULL POTENTIAL. IT HAS QUITE A SHORT SEASON, SO IF YOU CAN REMEMBER, IT IS WORTH FREEZING SOME FOR USE LATER IN THE YEAR.

2 Meanwhile, pour the water into a ramekin and sprinkle the gelatin over the surface. Set aside to soften for 5 minutes. Place the ramekin in a pan of hot water and set aside until the gelatin is dissolved, stirring occasionally.

3 Add the gelatin mixture to the hot milk mixture and stir until dissolved. Remove the vanilla bean and pour the mixture into the molds or pans. Cool, then chill overnight, or until set.

4 Put the sugar in a pan and add the water, orange zest and juice and cinnamon stick. Bring to a boil over low heat, stirring occasionally until the sugar has dissolved. Increase the heat and boil for 1 minute.

5 Add the port, let the syrup return to a boil, then lower the heat and simmer for 15 minutes, or until it has reduced and thickened. Remove the orange zest and cinnamon stick, add the rhubarb, cover and simmer gently for 2–3 minutes without stirring. Cool.

6 To serve, run a knife around the edge of each vanilla dessert to loosen it, then unmold on to a dessert plate. Serve each dessert with a spoonful or two of the rhubarb with its syrup.

COOK'S TIP
Rhubarb yields a lot of juice when cooked, so make sure the syrup has reduced well before adding the fruit.

SERVES FOUR

INGREDIENTS
½ cup sugar
⅔ cup water
pared zest and juice of 1 orange
1 cinnamon stick
1¼ cups ruby port
10 ounces rhubarb, cut into 1-inch pieces (2 cups)
For the vanilla desserts
¾ vanilla pod
¾ cup heavy cream
¾ cup whole milk or half-and-half
3 tablespoons sugar
2 tablespoons water
1½ teaspoons powdered gelatin

1 Start by making the vanilla desserts. Grease four individual pudding molds or pans. Split the vanilla pod and scrape the seeds into a saucepan. Add the bean, cream, milk and sugar. Simmer gently, stirring, for 5 minutes.

FIG AND WALNUT TORTE

THIS RECIPE IS BASED ON THE TRADITIONAL MIDDLE EASTERN SPECIALITY BAKLAVA. IT IS SWEET, STICKY AND DELICIOUS, AND THE FIGS ADD A REFRESHING TOUCH. SINCE IT IS QUITE RICH, PLAN ON CUTTING THE TORTE INTO FAIRLY SMALL DIAMONDS—GREAT WITH A CUP OF STRONG BLACK COFFEE.

MAKES 20–25 PIECES

INGREDIENTS
6 tablespoons butter, melted,
  plus extra for greasing
1½ cups walnuts,
  finely chopped
1 cup ground almonds
⅓ cup sugar
2 teaspoons ground cinnamon
9 large sheets of phyllo pastry,
  thawed if frozen, each cut into two
  12 × 8-inch rectangles
4 fresh figs, sliced
strained plain yogurt, to serve
For the syrup
1½ cups sugar
4 whole cloves
1 cinnamon stick
2 strips of lemon zest

1 Preheat the oven to 325°F. Generously grease a 12 × 8-inch shallow baking pan with melted butter. Mix together the walnuts, ground almonds, sugar and cinnamon in a bowl and set aside.

2 Fit a sheet of phyllo pastry in the bottom of the baking pan. Brush with some of the melted butter and place another sheet of phyllo on top. Repeat until you have layered eight sheets.

COOK'S TIP
Paper-thin phyllo pastry is delicate and dries out quickly. Work with one sheet at a time, and keep the other sheets covered, or they will dry out.

3 Spoon half the nut mixture evenly over the phyllo pastry, right to the edges, and top with the fig slices.

4 Place two phyllo sheets on top of the figs, brushing each with more melted butter as before, then evenly spoon the remaining nut mixture over.

5 Layer the remaining phyllo sheets on top, buttering each one. Brush any remaining melted butter over the top of the torte, then score the surface with a sharp knife to give a diamond pattern. Bake for 1 hour, until golden.

6 Meanwhile, make the syrup. Place all the ingredients in a saucepan and mix well. Heat, stirring, until the sugar has dissolved. Bring to a boil, lower the heat and simmer, stirring occasionally, for 10 minutes, until syrupy.

7 Allow the syrup to cool for about 15 minutes, then strain it evenly over the hot torte.

8 Allow to cool and soak for 2–3 hours, then cut the torte into diamonds or squares and serve with the yogurt. Store the torte in an airtight container for up to 3 days.

VARIATION
If you like, replace the chopped walnuts with coarsely chopped pistachio nuts, or use finely chopped cashews for an ultra-rich flavor.

RED GRAPE AND CHEESE TARTLETS

FRUIT AND CHEESE IS A NATURAL COMBINATION IN THIS SIMPLE RECIPE. LOOK FOR THE PALE, MAUVE-COLORED OR RED GRAPES THAT TEND TO BE SLIGHTLY SMALLER THAN BLACK GRAPES. THESE ARE OFTEN SEEDLESS AND HAVE THE ADDED ADVANTAGE OF BEING SWEETER.

MAKES SIX

INGREDIENTS
    12 ounces sweet shortcrust pastry,
        thawed if frozen
    1 cup cottage cheese
    ⅔ cup heavy cream
    ½ teaspoon pure vanilla extract
    2 tablespoons confectioners' sugar
    2 cups red grapes, halved, seeded if
        necessary
    ¼ cup apricot conserve
    1 tablespoon water

VARIATIONS

Use cranberry jelly or red currant jelly for the glaze. There will be no need to strain either of these. Also vary the fruit topping, if you like. Try blackberries, blueberries, raspberries, sliced strawberries, kiwi fruit slices, banana slices or well-drained pineapple slices.

1 Preheat the oven to 400°F. Roll out the pastry and line six deep 3½-inch fluted individual tartlet pans. Prick the bottoms and line with baking parchment and baking beans. Bake for 10 minutes, remove the paper and beans, then return the shells to the oven for 5 minutes, until golden and fully cooked. Remove the pastry shells from the pans and cool on a wire rack.

2 Meanwhile, beat the cottage cheese, heavy cream, vanilla and confectioners' sugar in a bowl. Divide the mixture among the pastry shells. Smooth the surface and arrange the halved grapes on top.

3 Strain the apricot conserve into a pan. Add the water and heat, stirring, until smooth. Spoon over the grapes. Cool, then chill before serving.

ONE-CRUST RHUBARB PIE

THIS METHOD CAN BE USED FOR ALL SORTS OF FRUIT AND IS REALLY FOOLPROOF. IT DOESN'T MATTER HOW ROUGH THE PIE LOOKS WHEN IT GOES INTO THE OVEN; IT COMES OUT LOOKING FANTASTIC!

SERVES SIX

INGREDIENTS

12 ounces shortcrust pastry, thawed
 if frozen
1 egg yolk, beaten
3 tablespoons semolina
¼ cup coarsely chopped hazelnuts
2 tablespoons turbinado sugar
For the filling
1 pound rhubarb, cut into
 1-inch pieces
⅓ cup granulated sugar
1–2 pieces preserved ginger in syrup,
 drained and finely chopped

COOK'S TIP
Egg yolk glaze brushed onto pastry gives it a nice golden sheen. However, be careful not to drip the glaze on the baking sheet, or it will burn and be difficult to remove.

1 Preheat the oven to 400°F. Roll out the pastry to a circle 14 inches in diameter. Lay it over the rolling pin and transfer it to a large baking sheet. Brush a little egg yolk over the pastry. Scatter the semolina over the center, leaving a wide rim all around.

2 Make the filling. Place the rhubarb pieces, granulated sugar and chopped ginger in a large bowl and mix well.

3 Pile the rhubarb mixture into the middle of the pastry. Fold the rim roughly over the filling so that it almost covers it. Some of the fruit will remain visible in the center.

4 Glaze the pastry rim with any remaining egg yolk and scatter the hazelnuts and turbinado sugar over. Bake for 30–35 minutes, or until the pastry is golden brown. Serve warm.

FRESH FIG FILO TART

FIGS COOK WONDERFULLY WELL AND TASTE SUPERB IN THIS TART—THE RIPER THE FIGS, THE BETTER.

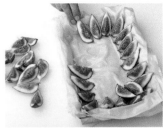

2 Using scissors, cut off any excess pastry, leaving a little overhanging the edge. Arrange the figs in the filo shell.

3 Sift the flour into a bowl and stir in the sugar. Add the eggs and a little of the milk and beat until smooth. Gradually beat in the remaining milk and the almond extract. Pour the mixture over the figs; bake for 1 hour, or until the batter has set and is golden.

SERVES SIX TO EIGHT

INGREDIENTS
  five 14 × 10-inch sheets filo pastry,
    thawed if frozen
  2 tablespoons butter, melted, plus
    extra for greasing
  6 fresh figs, cut into wedges
  ¾ cup all-purpose flour
  ⅓ cup sugar
  4 eggs
  1¾ cups whole milk or half-and-half
  ½ teaspoon pure almond extract
  1 tablespoon confectioners' sugar
  whipped cream or strained plain
    yogurt, to serve

1 Preheat the oven to 375°F. Grease a 10 × 6¼-inch baking pan with butter. Brush each filo sheet in turn with melted butter and use to line the prepared pan.

4 Remove the tart from the oven and allow it to cool in the pan on a wire rack for 10 minutes. Dust with the confectioners' sugar and serve with whipped cream or yogurt.

CREAMY YOGURT AND FIG CAKE

BAKED FRESH FIGS, THICKLY SLICED, MAKE A DELECTABLE BASE FOR A FEATHERLIGHT SPONGE.
FIGS THAT ARE A BIT ON THE FIRM SIDE WORK BEST FOR THIS RECIPE.

SERVES SIX TO EIGHT

INGREDIENTS

6 firm fresh figs, thickly sliced
3 tablespoons honey, plus extra for
  glazing cooked figs
14 tablespoons butter,
  softened
¾ cup sugar
grated zest of 1 lemon
grated zest of 1 orange
4 eggs, separated
2 cups all-purpose flour
1 teaspoon baking powder
1 teaspoon baking soda
1 cup strained plain yogurt

1 Preheat the oven to 350°F. Grease a 9-inch cake pan and line the bottom with baking parchment. Arrange the figs over the bottom of the pan and drizzle the honey over.

2 In a large mixing bowl, cream the butter and sugar with the lemon and orange zests until the mixture is pale and fluffy, then gradually beat in the egg yolks.

3 Sift the dry ingredients together. Add a little to the creamed mixture, beat well, then beat in a spoonful of yogurt. Repeat this process until all the dry ingredients and yogurt have been incorporated.

4 Beat the egg whites in a greasefree bowl until they form stiff peaks. Stir half the whites into the cake mixture to lighten it slightly, then fold in the rest. Pour the mixture over the figs in the pan, then bake for 1¼ hours, or until golden and a skewer inserted in the center of the cake comes out clean.

5 Turn the cake out onto a wire rack, peel off the lining paper and let cool. Drizzle the figs with extra honey before serving.

MELON AND STAR ANISE JAM

MELON AND GINGER ARE CLASSIC COMPANIONS. THE ADDITION OF STAR ANISE IMPARTS A WONDERFUL ASIAN FLAVOR TO THE JAM. IT'S SPLENDID ON TOASTED FRUIT-AND-SPICE MUFFINS.

MAKES 1 POUND

INGREDIENTS
  2 charentais or cantaloupe melons,
    peeled and seeded
  2 cups sugar
  2 star anise
  4 pieces preserved ginger in syrup,
    drained and finely chopped
  finely grated zest and juice of
    2 lemons

COOK'S TIPS
Use this jam in savory dishes instead
of honey to add a spicy, noncloying
sweetness. Jams require a large amount of
sugar for proper jelling—don't cut back.

1 Cut the melons into small cubes and
layer with the sugar in a large
nonreactive bowl. Cover with plastic
wrap and refrigerate overnight, so the
melons can release their juices.

2 Pour the melons and juice into a
large saucepan and add the star anise,
ginger and lemon zest and juice.

3 Bring to a boil, then lower the heat.
Simmer for 25 minutes, or until the
melon has become translucent and the
setting point has been reached. Test for
this by spooning a small amount of the
juice onto a chilled plate. If it wrinkles
when you push a finger through the
cooled liquid, it is ready to be canned.

4 Spoon the jam into hot sterilized jars.
Seal, label and store in a cool, dry
place. Once a jar has been opened,
keep it in the refrigerator.

FIG AND DATE CHUTNEY

THIS CHUTNEY IS USUALLY MADE WITH DRIED FIGS AND DATES, BUT IT WORKS PERFECTLY WELL WITH FRESH FRUIT AND HAS A SUPERB FLAVOR. TRY IT WITH CREAM CHEESE ON BROWN BREAD.

MAKES 1 POUND

INGREDIENTS

1 orange
5 large fresh figs, coarsely chopped
12 ounces fresh dates, peeled, pitted and chopped (2½ cups)
2 onions, chopped
2-inch piece of fresh ginger root, peeled and finely grated
1 teaspoon dried crushed chiles
1½ cups turbinado sugar
1¼ cups cider vinegar
½ teaspoon salt

1 Finely grate the zest of the orange, then cut off the remaining pith and segment the orange.

2 Place the orange segments in a large, heavy saucepan with the chopped figs and dates. Add the zest, then stir in the onions, grated ginger, dried chiles, turbinado sugar, cider vinegar and salt. Bring to a boil, stirring gently until all the sugar has dissolved.

3 Lower the heat and simmer gently for 1 hour, or until the mixture has thickened and become pulpy, stirring often to prevent the mixture from sticking to the bottom of the pan.

4 Spoon the chutney into hot, sterilized jars. Seal while still hot and label once the jars are cool. Store for 1 week before using. Once a jar has been opened, keep it in the refrigerator.

VARIATION
If you would rather use dried figs and dates to make the chutney, you will need to increase the amount of cider vinegar by ⅔ cup to a scant 2 cups. Pit the dates and coarsely chop the figs and dates.

VEGETABLES

DISCOVERING VEGETABLES

AS A CHILD, there were two basic types of vegetables for me: the ones my mother cooked and the ones given to us at school. My mother only ever bought fresh vegetables and she knew how to cook them, so they were simple but good. Vegetables at school were overcooked and invariably tasteless. Travel then broadened my outlook.

From my first teenage sojourns around Europe, I recall, even now, the vegetable stalls in a Barcelona market, piled high with tomatoes, peppers and eggplants. The exotic-looking produce of the Orient, Asia and Caribbean countries cannot fail to spark off an inquisitive and creative enthusiasm in those who are unfamiliar with them and even basic ingredients – potatoes, onions and carrots – do not look like sorry, everyday necessities when they are displayed with pride.

History

Vegetables, whether the root, stems, seeds or fruit, have been an essential part of our diet since the early existence of mankind, and many of our familiar vegetables were cultivated in prehistoric times. The Egyptians grew onions, garlic, radishes, lettuce and fava beans; and later the Greeks and Romans grew artichokes and fennel. By the Middle Ages a wealth of vegetables was

Right: Green, red, orange and yellow peppers

available, with recipes for them recorded in the first cookbooks.

Early explorers returned with exotic ingredients, the spoils of their travels, to their native countries and created a huge appetite for new tastes among the wealthy classes of Europe. Marco Polo traveled to China and carried aromatic spices on his return to Europe. Christopher Columbus and subsequent explorers found potatoes, tomatoes, peppers, squashes and corn. Today we have the option of buying exactly what we want, when we want it. It's a luxury we pay for but one that means you are never stuck for an ingredient whatever the time of year. On the other hand there's much to be said for enjoying vegetables in their season. Vegetables from local growers will be the freshest you can buy and gardeners love the way their produce traces the seasons, never

Above: Roast Asparagus Crêpes with a cheese sauce

Right: Arugula

minding that it means gluts at some times of the year and only cabbages and roots at other times.

Nutrition

Vegetables are really good for you – all nutritionists agree. Vegetables protect against disease, they are an important source of many vitamins and minerals, and we should eat more. The nutritional value of vegetables varies according to type, freshness, preparation and cooking method. In general it can be said that along with fruit they are the main source of vitamin C. Some of the B-group vitamins are also found in vegetables, particularly in green vegetables, peas and beans. Carrots and the dark green vegetables also include carotene which is used by the body to manufacture vitamin A. Vegetable oils are a useful source of vitamin E.

Vegetables can also contain calcium, iron, potassium and magnesium, as well as some trace elements which are also required in small quantities.

Starchy vegetables are an important source of energy-giving carbohydrate and they may include useful quantities of fiber.

Freshly picked vegetables have the highest nutritional content, but this diminishes with staleness and exposure to sunlight. Use fresh vegetables as soon as possible after purchase and always avoid stale limp specimens. The peel and the layer directly beneath it contain the highest concentration of nutrients, so it is best to avoid peeling your vegetables or to remove the thinnest layer for maximum nutrient retention.

Minerals and vitamins C and B are water soluble and they are lost by seepage into cooking water or the liquid over which vegetables are steamed. To minimize loss of nutrients, do not cut up vegetables finely as this creates a greater surface area for seepage. Vitamin C is also destroyed by long cooking and by exposure to alkalines.

Raw and lightly cooked vegetables provide the best nutritional value and source of fiber. Any cooking liquid should, whenever possible, be used in stocks, gravies or sauces.

Vegetables can play a starring role in a recipe or they may be combined with other ingredients in a harmony of flavors. Over the following pages you will find an eclectic mix of classic dishes from around the world, some family favorites that have stood the test of time and others that I have devised over years of cooking. All the recipes make the most of each vegetable, so that their particular virtues can be appreciated to the full. The recipes are not designed for vegetarians although there are plenty of recipes which are vegetarian. In many instances, simply substituting vegetable stock for chicken stock will ensure that the recipe is acceptable. The great thing about cooking with vegetables is, however, that once you have got the hang of using them, a recipe really becomes unnecessary. You will discover how you most enjoy carrots, asparagus or less-common vegetables and this in turn will inspire you to experiment with vegetables you have not used before.

Above: Cherry tomatoes

Below: Tomato and Basil Tart

Right: Chard is striking to look at as well as being delicious to eat.

EQUIPMENT

There is almost no limit to the amount of equipment you could purchase for preparing and cooking vegetables – the only limit will be the depth of your pocket and the size of your kitchen. The most important tool, inevitably, is a good kitchen knife, and for cooking you'll need two or three different sized saucepans and a good sieve. Good equipment not only makes the cook's job easier, but also more of a pleasure, so take stock of the tools you have at the moment and then gradually buy additional pieces. You don't need to buy everything immediately – it's always preferable to buy the more pricey but better made appliances, whether it's food processors, saucepans, knives or a potato peeler.

Peeling and Slicing

Knives

There are dozens of different knives, designed for a variety of tasks. For preparing and chopping vegetables, you ideally should have two types of knife, a general-purpose knife for cutting or chopping hard vegetables, such as potatoes and cabbage, and a smaller paring knife for peeling vegetables and slicing or chopping smaller ones like courgettes and onions. A serrated knife is useful for tomatoes, cucumbers and peppers with tough or slippery skins.

Potato Peeler

Peeling potatoes with a knife means that much of the goodness from the potato, contained just under the skin, is lost along with the peel, and a good potato peeler not only makes the job easier, but means you don't waste this valuable part of the potato.

Swivel-bladed peelers are probably the most effective peelers and, once you have the hang of them, are also very quick and efficient. Make sure to buy one that feels comfortable to hold, or buy a fixed-blade peeler. Left-handed people will need to buy the left-handed version.

Slicing and Grating

Grater

If you don't own a food processor, you'll need a good quality grater for grating carrots, celery root and other hard vegetables. Although most vegetables are grated coarsely, choose a type, such as the box grater, that has a variety of grating surfaces so that it can be used for grating Parmesan or nutmeg, or for zesting lemons.

Mandoline

Professional cooks often prefer the mandoline for slicing firm foods like potatoes, celery root and carrots, as the result is much finer. The best and most expensive are in stainless steel and have

Left: A variety of kitchen knives

Left: Mandoline

several blades for a variety of thicknesses and shapes. More commonly available though are the wooden ones, which generally have two adjustable blades.

Mashers

Potato masher

Essential for mashing potatoes and other root vegetables that can't be puréed any other way. Strong stainless-steel mashers are the most efficient, but if you use non-stick pans, buy a strong plastic masher instead or you will damage the pans.

Garlic Press

This is another simple but useful labor-saving device. Cheaper aluminum garlic presses are usually just as efficient as the more expensive varieties made of stainless steel with comfortable rubber handles. However, more expensive ones normally have self-cleaning devices, which saves you the bother of picking out bits of garlic.

Below: Stainless steel steamer

Right: Pans

Saucepans and Sieves

Your saucepans are the single most important items when it comes to vegetable cooking, and if you're starting from scratch, it is worth investing in good quality pans. Among the best are stainless-steel pans with strong insulated handles and a heavy bottom. A heavy base is essential, as it ensures the heat is properly distributed, and food doesn't scorch or cook unevenly. A set of three saucepans, with lids, will normally be sufficient for general cooking, but in addition a large pan with two handles can be tremendously useful for making soups and stocks.

Colanders and Sieves

A good quality colander or sieve is almost as essential as a good saucepan. A colander is probably best as it can stand alone and has two handles.

Frying pan

A cast-iron frying pan is probably the most versatile for vegetable recipes, as these are the traditional pans used for sautéing. Stainless-steel and non-stick pans, however, are both useful.

Cast-iron/flameproof casserole

These are tremendously useful for any recipe that needs sautéing on the stove before going into the oven. They are by definition extremely heavy, so make sure to buy only those with two handles.

Wok

Though not essential for stir-frying, woks are by far the best option for this type of cooking. Make sure you buy the appropriate wok for your cooker – round-bottomed for gas hobs and flat-bottomed for an electric stove top.

Steamers

If you intend to steam your vegetables regularly, invest in a steamer set, which contains two or three compartments that stack on top of each other. Alternatively, Chinese bamboo steamers can be stacked over a medium-size saucepan.

Electrical Appliances

Food processor

The food processor has become an almost essential piece of kitchen equipment, and is hugely versatile. Ideally choose a heavy-duty model with a pulse button. Most now come complete with grating and slicing blades, but if not, make sure you purchase them as well; they take the effort out of some of the most laborious tasks in the kitchen.

Hand blender

Useful for making vegetable purées, sauces, vegetable pâtés and soups.

Right: Food processor

Blender/liquidizer

These are even better than food processors for making soups and purées. Choose a model where the blades are set as low as possible as these are useful for baby foods, and also for making mayonnaise where you start with just one or two egg yolks.

PURCHASING, PREPARING AND COOKING

BUYING VEGETABLES

The single golden rule for buying vegetables is "use your instinct". All vegetables should be firm and blemish free, without any soft spots or mold. Most vegetables are available all the year round, but even with modern air transportation, the best vegetables are those that are recently picked which is why local seasonal vegetables are always going to have the finest flavor. This is especially true of tomatoes, beans, peas, corn and tomatoes. Farm stores, or better still, pick-your-own farms mean you can buy many seasonal vegetables in their prime. If this is not an option, large supermarkets with a fast turnover tend to sell better quality vegetables simply because they have daily deliveries and they also have a commercial interest in making sure that their produce is of top quality.

STORING VEGETABLES

This depends entirely on the particular vegetable and while onions and potatoes can be successfully stored for months, more tender vegetables, like mushrooms or tomatoes are best eaten as soon as possible. The following are a few basic rules and guidelines:

• If possible, buy vegetables as you need them. If buying for the week, plan your meals so that the more tender vegetables, such as zucchini and peas, are eaten sooner rather than later.
• Whenever storing vegetables, always remove them from any plastic bags or plastic wrap.
• Unless stated otherwise, store vegetables in the salad drawer of the fridge and eat as soon as possible or within 2–3 days.
• Always store potatoes in a dark, cool and dry place. If potatoes are exposed to the light, they will develop green patches which can be poisonous.
• Don't store onions in the fridge as they will go soft: store in a cool, dry place, like a pantry or outhouse.
• Keep garlic in a cool, dry place. If the temperature is too warm, the cloves will turn to a grey powder and if the air is damp, the garlic will sprout.

• If celery has become limp, revive it by wrapping in absorbent kitchen paper and standing in a jar of water.
• Ripen avocados at room temperature. If ripe already, keep in the fridge for up to 2 days.
• Dried beans should always be kept in labeled jars in a dry place. They will keep for about 12 months but after that tend to become tough, lose their flavor and take longer to cook, so throw away beans that are more than a year old.

PREPARING VEGETABLES

Preparation depends largely on the vegetable concerned, the type of recipe and your own preference. Potatoes for mashing, chipping, salads, sautéing and roasting usually need peeling, but new potatoes or potatoes for baking need only be scrubbed. Similarly, many recipes call for fresh tomatoes that are peeled, cored and seeded, and yet for hors d'oeuvres, tomatoes need no preparation at all, save to be sliced – and cherry tomatoes don't even need that! Chilies are the only vegetable for which there is a preparation rule – always wear gloves or wash your hands thoroughly, as the capsaicin contained within them can irritate the skin, especially the eyes.

Washing Vegetables

Because the skin of many vegetables, is full of vitamins it is always preferable to wash your vegetables under cold running water, rather than peel them.

Young root vegetables

Rinse new potatoes, baby carrots or turnips under cold running water. Use a sponge or a scrubbing brush, to remove any stubborn areas of dirt.

Main crop potatoes

Older potatoes need more vigorous scrubbing in order to dislodge lumps of mud. Remove eyes and any blemishes with a knife or the tip of a potato peeler.

Mushrooms

Wipe mushrooms with a damp cloth, as washing makes them soggy.

Leeks

Leeks notoriously contain grit and earth between their layers, so need very careful rinsing.

1 Trim the roots and cut away the dark green leaves. Remove and discard the outer layer of leek and then cut a slit along its length.

2 Wash under running water, pulling the sections apart so that the water washes out all the earth.

Washing Salads

Almost all salad leaves that have not specifically been bought labeled as ready to eat, should be washed, since they may well harbor earth, grit or small insects. This is particularly the case with lettuce from the garden and to a lesser extent organic produce, where nature has been allowed to follow her natural course.

Preparing salad leaves

1 Remove any discolored or damaged leaves, then separate the leaves.

2 Swirl the salad leaves gently in a bowl of cold water to make sure any earth or insects are dislodged. If the leaves are robust enough you could then use a salad spinner to dry them, otherwise pat them dry in a soft dish towel. Make sure that there is no moisture left on them before adding to the salad.

3 All salad leaves should be washed this way, but spinach can often be gritty and so needs particular attention, as does lollo rosso, and it is often recommended to rinse in several bowls of cold water to make sure any earth clinging to the leaves is removed. It is also wise to remove the centre stalk from the larger leaves.

Peeling Vegetables

Almost all root vegetables may need peeling at some time. Potatoes, carrots and turnips only need peeling if old, but sweet potatoes, yams and taros nearly always need to be peeled, either before or after cooking. Other vegetables, such as zucchini and cucumbers, can be peeled for effect, but marrows and other large squash will always require peeling.

A swivel-bladed or a fixed-blade peeler can be used for peeling potatoes, carrots, parsnips, turnips and other root vegetables.

As peeling only shaves away a thin layer of skin you keep most of the valuable nutrients that lie in or just below the skin. Vegetables such as celery and asparagus may need their tough, woody ends peeling.

Potatoes can be peeled after boiling. Once they are cool enough to handle, peel off the skin using a small knife.

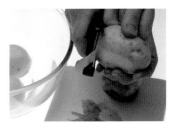

Sweet potatoes, salsify and celery root are among the vegetables that oxidize and turn brown if exposed to air. To prevent this from happening, place the peeled vegetables in a bowl of cold water to which 1 tablespoon lemon juice has been added.

Cucumbers don't need to be peeled, but some producers use a wax coating to give a shine to the vegetable and if you haven't washed the cucumber you may wish to remove this by peeling. If you're handy with a potato peeler or canelle knife it's possible to remove thin strips of peel to give an attractive striped effect. The same technique can be used on zucchini and fruit.

Skinning Tomatoes and Peppers

It is worth the effort of skinning tomatoes for sauces and other cooked tomato dishes, where bits of tomato skin would spoil the effect. Cut a cross in the top of the tomato, and then plunge into boiling water. Leave for 30–60 seconds (it will depend on the ripeness of the fruit) and then remove and peel away the skin, using a knife. If using cold, in a salad or gazpacho, plunge into cold water, to prevent the tomato cooking any further.

Place the peppers under a hot broiler until the skin blisters and blackens. You can cut them into quarters if necessary. Either wrap the pieces in plastic wrap or put them into a plastic bag and tie the end. Leave for about 20 minutes or until the peppers are cool enough to handle. The skin should peel off easily and the seeds can be scraped out.

Chopping Vegetables

Most vegetables need to be chopped to various degrees of fineness before cooking and eating. Vegetables will taste the same however you chop them, but remember that although the smaller you chop your vegetables, the quicker they will cook, it will also be easier to overcook them!

Fine chopping

Finely chopping onion can be fiddly, but not if you follow this simple technique.

1 Peel the onion, leaving on the root end, and cut it in half, straight through the root. Place the onion flat down on a chopping board and make a series of horizontal cuts to the root, but not through it.

2 Make vertical lengthwise cuts in the onion half, again not cutting to the root. Then cut across the onion to produce finely chopped pieces.

Carrot julienne

Julienne is a French term meaning very thin strips. Cut a carrot lengthwise into 2-inch lengths, then cut each of those into ¼-inch slices. Stack the slices and cut into matchsticks to form julienne.

Shredding vegetable leaves

Individual leaves of cabbage, lettuce and spinach can be cut into neat shreds with this method.

1 Stack the leaves, six to eight at a time, and then roll them up tightly parallel with the central rib.

2 With a sharp knife slice the leaves to make shreds of the required thickness.

COOKING VEGETABLES

Some vegetables can be cooked many different ways; others are less versatile, although no less delicious for that.

Boiling

Boiling is one of the most popular techniques for cooking vegetables. Take care not to overcook though, as then all the nutrients will be lost in the water.

Blanching and Refreshing

Vegetables are blanched either when they need further cooking, such as stir-frying, roasting, or reheating in butter, or if they are to be used in salad. After blanching, vegetables are "refreshed" to stop them cooking any further.

1 Immerse the vegetables in a large pan of boiling water. Bring the water back to the boil for 1–2 minutes, then drain immediately.

2 Refresh the vegetables by quickly immersing them in iced water for a few seconds. Drain well.

Sweating

Sweating is a common preliminary step in vegetable cooking, particularly for onions and leeks. It is important to cook the vegetables extremely gently.

Steaming

Tender vegetables, such as baby carrots, pumpkin and snow peas are best cooked by the steaming method.

Set the vegetables in a steamer over a pan of rapidly simmering water. Cover, and cook until tender.

Shallow Frying and Sautéing

The oil and/or butter used in frying adds another dimension to the dish.

Add the sliced or chopped vegetables to the pan once the oil is hot or the butter has melted and stir regularly.

Stir-frying

Stir-frying is a quick and healthy method of cooking. Make sure that vegetables are cut to an appropriate size so that they cook evenly.

Deep-frying

Potatoes are among the favorite vegetables for deep-frying, as French fries, but other vegetables can be deep-fried too. Try deep-frying thinly sliced spring greens to make Chinese style "seaweed", or other root vegetables, such as yams and sweet potatoes.

Heat oil for deep-frying to 360°F or until a cube of bread sizzles when added to the pan. It is best to use an appropriate pan with a wire basket so that the vegetables can be removed quickly and easily. Potato or sweet potato French fries should be soaked in cold water and then drained and patted dry before adding to the pan. Fry until soft, drain for a few minutes and then plunge again into the hot oil until crisp and golden.

Fritters and Tempura

Batter, made from flour, eggs, milk, beer or water, often combined with bread crumbs or another dry coating, helps protect more tender vegetables when deep-frying.

Cut the vegetables into even-sized shapes and coat with the batter then the bread crumbs, if using. Lower gently into the pan. Cook in small batches, so that the fritters don't stick together.

ONIONS AND LEEKS

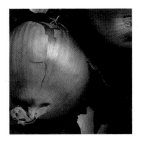

Where would we be without the onion family?
Whether it's the merest hint of chives in a dressing, leeks in a
sauce, garlic adding its unmistakable tang or full-bodied onion
soup, this is the vegetable family that gives so much flavor to
our savory dishes.

ONIONS

There are bound to be vegetables you like better than others but a cook would be lost without onions. There are many classic recipes specifically for onion dishes so they can be appreciated in their own right. Onion tarts or French onion soup, for instance, have a sublime flavor, and only onions are appropriate. But also, there is hardly a recipe where onions, or their cousins – garlic, leeks or shallots – are not used. Gently fried until soft, or fried more fiercely until golden brown, they add a unique, savory flavor to dishes.

History

Onions, along with shallots, leeks, chives and garlic, belong to the *Allium* family which, including wild varieties, has some 325 members. All have the characteristic onion smell which is caused by volatile acids beneath the skin.

Archaeological and historical records show that onions have been eaten for thousands of years. They are believed to have originally come from the Middle East and their easy cultivation suggests that their use spread quickly. There are references to the onion in the Bible and it was widely eaten in Egypt. There was, we are told, an inscription on the Great Pyramid stating that the slaves who built the tomb ate their way through 1,600 talents worth of onions, radishes and garlic – presumably a lot, given that the Great Pyramid was made using more than two million 2^1/$_2$-ton blocks of stone.

By the Middle Ages, onions were a common vegetable throughout Europe and would have been used in soups, stews and sauces when strong flavoring was preferred.

Varieties

As they keep well in a cool place, most people keep a handy stock of onions, usually a general purpose type that can be sautéed or browned. However, onions come in a variety of different colors and strengths, and for certain recipes particular onions are needed.

Right: Spanish onions
Far right top: Yellow onions
Far right below: Red onions

Spanish Onions: Onions raised in warm areas are milder in taste than onions from cooler regions, and Spanish onions are among the mildest cultivated onions. They are a beautiful pale copper color and are noticeably larger than yellow onions. They have a delicate, sweet flavor which makes them ideal for serving raw in salads, thinly sliced, while their size makes them suitable for stuffing and baking whole.

Yellow Onions: These are the widely available onions you find everywhere and, though called yellow onions, their skins are more golden brown. They are the most pungent of all the onions and are a good, all-purpose variety. The smallest ones, referred to as baby, button or pickling onions, are excellent for pickling but can also be added whole to a casserole or sautéed in butter to make a delicious vegetable accompaniment.

Red Onions: Sometimes called Italian onions, these mild onions have an attractive appearance and are now widely available from most good grocers and supermarkets. Below their ruby red skins the flesh is blushed with red. They have a mild, sweet flavor and are excellent thinly sliced and used raw in salads and *antipasti* dishes.

White Onions: These come in all sorts of interesting shapes and sizes – squat, round and oval, big and small. The very small white onions, with shimmery silver skins, are mild and best added whole to stews or served in a creamy sauce. Larger white onions can be mild or strong – there is no way of telling. Like yellow onions, white onions are extremely versatile whether used raw or cooked. The very small white onions, called Paris Silverskin, are the ones used for dry martinis and for commercial pickling.

Vidalia Onions: These popular American onions are a specialty of and named after a town in Georgia. They are a large, pale yellow onion and are deliciously sweet and juicy. Used in salads, or roasted with meat or with other vegetables, they are superb.

Bermuda Onions: These are similar in size to Spanish onions but are more squat. They have a mild flavor and are good thinly sliced, fried until golden and served with steaks or burgers.

remove the next layer of onion, as it is often dry or damaged. Unless slicing onions for stir-fries, for which it is customary to slice the onion into wedges, always slice the onion through the rings, widthwise. Make whole rings, or for half-rings, cut in half lengthwise through the root before slicing (*below*). For finely chopped onion, slice again lengthwise.

Scallions or Spring Onions: These are also true onions but harvested very young while their shoots are still green and fresh. They have a mild, delicate taste and both the small white bulb and the green tops can be used in salads, omelets and stir-fries, or indeed any dish which requires a mild onion flavor.

Nutrition

As well as tasting good, onions are good for you. They contain vitamins B and C together with calcium, iron and potassium. Like garlic, they also contain cycloallin, an anticoagulant which helps protect against heart disease.

Buying and Storing

It used to be a common sight in Europe to see an onion seller traveling around the streets on a bicycle with strings of onions hanging from every available support, including his own neck.

Strings of onions are hard to come by although, if you do find them in stores, they are a good way of buying and storing the vegetable.

Onions, more than almost any other vegetable, keep well provided they are stored in a cool, dry place, such as a larder or an outhouse. Do not store them in the fridge as they will go soft, and never keep cut onions in the fridge – or anywhere else – unless you want onion-flavored milk and an onion-scented home. Onions do not keep well once cut and it is worth buying onions in assorted sizes so that you do not end up having bits left over. Unused bits of onion can be added to stocks; otherwise throw them away.

Preparing

Onions contain a substance which is released when they are cut and causes the eyes to water, quite painfully sometimes. There are all sorts of ways which are supposed to prevent this, including cutting onions under running water, holding a piece of bread between your teeth or wearing goggles!

As well as the outer brown leaves,

Cooking

The volatile acids in onions are driven off during cooking, which is why cooked onion is never as strong as raw onion. The method of cooking, even the way of frying an onion, affects its eventual taste. Boiled onion or chopped onion added neat to soups or casseroles has a stronger, more raw taste. Frying or sautéing briefly, or sweating (frying in a little fat with the lid on) until soft and translucent gives a mild flavor. When fried until golden brown, onions develop a distinct flavor, both sweet and savory, that is superb with grilled meats and is essential for French onion soup.

Above far left: Vidalia onions
Left: White onions
Above left: Large and small scallions

SHALLOTS

Shallots are not baby onions but a separate member of the onion family. They have a delicate flavor, less intense than most onions and they also dissolve easily into liquids, which is why they are favored for sauces. Shallots grow in small, tight clusters so that when you break one open there may be two or three bunched together at the root.

Their size makes them convenient for a recipe where only a little onion is required. Use shallots when only a small amount of onion is needed or when only a fine onion flavor is required. Shallots are a pleasant, if maybe extravagant, alternative to onions, but where recipes specify shallots (especially sauce recipes), they should be used if possible.

Although classic cooking frequently calls for particular ingredients, the art of improvisation should not be ignored. For instance, Coq au Vin is traditionally made with walnut-size white onions, but when substituted with shallots, the result is delightful.

History

Shallots are probably as ancient as onions. Roman commentators wrote eloquently about the excellence of shallots in sauces.

Varieties

Shallots are small slender onions with long necks and golden, copper-colored skins. There are a number of varieties, although there is unlikely to be a choice in the supermarkets. In any case, differences are more in size and color of skin than in flavor.

Buying and Storing

Like onions, shallots should be firm without any green shoots. They will keep well for several months in a cool dry place.

Preparing and Cooking

Skin shallots in the same way as onions, i.e. top and tail them and then peel off the outer skin. Pull apart the bulbs. Slice them carefully and thinly using a sharp knife – shallots are so small, it is easy to slip and cut yourself. When cooking them whole, fry over very low heat without browning too much.

CHIVES

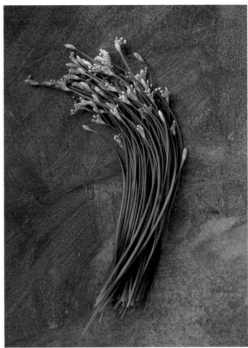

Chives: In culinary terms, chives are really classed as a herb, but as members of the onion family they are worth mentioning here. As anyone who has grown them knows, chives are tufts of aromatic grass with pretty pale lilac flowers, which are also edible.

Preparing and Serving

Chives are often snipped with scissors and added to egg dishes, or used as a garnish for salads and soups, adding a pleasant but faint onion flavor. Along with parsley, tarragon and chervil, they are an essential ingredient of *fines herbes.*

Chives are also a delicious addition to soft cheeses – far nicer than commercially bought cheeses, where the flavor of chives virtually disappears. Stir also into soft butter for an alternative to garlic butter. This can then be spread onto bread and baked like garlic bread.

If adding to cooked dishes, cook only very briefly, otherwise their flavor will be lost.

Garlic Chives: Garlic chives, sometimes called Chinese chives, have a delicate garlic flavor, and if you see them for sale in your local Chinese supermarket, they are worth buying as they add a delicate onion flavor to stir-fries and other oriental dishes.

Preparing and Serving

Use them as you would chives – both the green and white parts are edible. They are also delicious served on their own as a vegetable accompaniment.

Buying and Storing

For both types of chives, look for plump, uniformly green specimens with no brown spots or signs of wilting. They can be stored for up to a week in the fridge. Unopened flowers on garlic chives are an indication that the plant is young and therefore more tender than one with fully opened flowers.

Above left: Chives
Above right: Garlic chives

GARLIC

Garlic is an ingredient that almost any-one who does any cooking at all, and absolutely everyone who enjoys cooking, would not be without.

History

Garlic is known to have been first grown in around 3200 BC. Inscriptions and models of garlic found in the pyramids of ancient Egypt testify to the fact that garlic was not only an important foodstuff but that it had ceremonial significance as well. The Greeks and Romans likewise believed garlic to have magical qualities. Warriors would eat it for strength before going into battle, gods were appeased with gifts of garlic, and cloves of garlic were fastened round the necks of babies to ward off evil. Hence, vampire myth-ology has ancient precedents.

The Greeks and Romans also used garlic for its therapeutic qualities. Not only was it thought to be an aphrodisiac but also it was believed to be good for eczema, toothache and snake bites.

Although garlic found its way all over Europe – vats of butter, strongly flavored with garlic, have been found by archaeologists working in Ireland which date back 200-300 years – fundamen-tally, its popularity today derives from our liking for Mediterranean, Indian and Asian food, in which garlic plays a very important part.

Nutrition

As is often the case, what was once dismissed as an old wives' tale is, after thorough scientific inquiry, found to be true. Garlic is a case in point; most authorities accept that it has many therapeutic properties. The most significant of these is that it lowers blood cholesterol, thus helping prevent heart disease. Also, raw garlic contains a powerful antibiotic and there is evidence that it has a beneficial effect against cancer and strokes, and increases the absorption of vitamins. Many garlic enthusiasts take their garlic in tablet form, but true devotees prefer to take it as it comes.

Right: A string of pink-skinned garlic

Varieties

There are numerous varieties of garlic, from the large "elephant" garlic, to small tight bulbs. Their papery skin can be white, pink or purple. Color makes no difference to taste but the particular attraction of the large purple bulbs is that they make a beautiful display in the kitchen.

As a general rule, the smaller the garlic bulb, the stronger it is likely to be. However, most garlic sold in stores is not classified in either shape or form (unless it is elephant garlic) and in practice you will simply pick up whatever you need, either loose, in bunches or on strings.

Garlic grown in a hot climate is likely to be the most pungent, and fresh new season's garlic has a subtle, mild flavor that is particularly good if it is to be used raw, for example, in salads and for dressings.

Above: Elephant garlic beside normal-size bulbs

Buying and Storing

Garlic bulbs should be firm and round with clear, papery skins. Avoid any that are beginning to sprout. Garlic bulbs keep well stored in a cool, dry place; if the air is damp they will sprout and if it is too warm the cloves will eventually turn to gray powder.

Preparing and Cooking

First break the garlic bulb into cloves and then remove the papery skin. You can blanch this off with hot water but using a fingernail or knife is just as effective. When a garlic clove is split lengthwise a shoot is revealed in the center, which is occasionally green, and some people remove this whatever the color.

Cloves are the little segments which make up the bulb and most recipes call for one or more cloves of garlic. (Don't use a bulb when you just need a clove!)

Crush cloves either with the blade of a knife or use a garlic crusher. Crushed garlic cooks more evenly and distributes its flavor in food better than when it is used sliced or finely chopped (stir-fries are the exception). Prepare garlic according to the strength of flavor required: thinly sliced garlic is milder than chopped, which in turn is milder than crushed garlic and, of course, cooking mutes the pungency.

Garlic Breath

The taste and smell of garlic tends to linger on the breath and can be a problem to get rid of. Chewing parsley is a well-known remedy but is only moderately successful. Chewing the seeds of cardamom pods is also said to work but is rather unplea-sant. The best suggestion is to eat garlic with your friends so that nobody notices!

LEEKS

Leeks are very versatile, having their own distinct, subtle flavor. They are excellent in pies and casseroles with other ingredients, braised in cream and served by themselves, or simmered in butter as an accompanying vegetable.

Leeks are also wonderful in soups and broths and have rightly earned the title, "king of the soup onions." Cock-a-leekie from Scotland and *Crème Vichyssoise*, invented by the chef of New York's Ritz-Carlton, are two classic leek soups, but many other soups call for leeks.

History

Leeks, like onions and garlic, have a long history. They were grown widely in ancient Egypt and were also eaten and enjoyed throughout the Greek and Roman period. In England, there is evidence that leeks were enjoyed during the Dark Ages. There is little mention of them during the Middle Ages, and history suggests that between the sixteenth and eighteenth centuries eating leeks was not considered fashionable.

However, while they may not have enjoyed a good reputation among the notoriously fickle aristocracy, the rural communities probably continued to eat leeks. They grow in all sorts of climates and are substantial enough to make a reasonable meal for a poor family. It was probably during this time that they were dubbed "poor man's asparagus" – a name which says more about people's snobbishness about food than it does about leeks.

Many place names in England, such as Leckhampstead and Leighton Buzzard, are derived from the word leek and, of course, the leek has been a national emblem of Wales for hundreds of years.

Varieties

There are many different varieties of leeks but among them there is little difference in flavor. Commercially grown leeks tend to be about 10 inches long and about 3/4 inch in diameter. Leeks nurtured in home gardens can be left to grow to an enormous size, but these may develop a woody center.

the first layer of white; then cut a slit from one end to the other through to the center of the leek *(below)*. Wash under cold running water, pulling the sections apart so that the water rinses out any stubborn pieces of earth. If you slice the leeks – either slice thickly or thinly – place them in a colander and rinse thoroughly under cold water.

RAMP

Among the many wild onions and leeks, the Canadian ramp is perhaps the best known. Also called the wild leek, it looks a little like a scallion, but has a stronger and more assertive garlic-onion flavor. Choose unblemished, clear white specimens with bright, fresh leaves and keep in a cool place, wrapped in a plastic bag to store.

Prepare and cook as you would scallions, by trimming the root end and then slicing thinly. Use in cooking or in salads but remember the onion flavor is stronger, so use sparingly.

Buying and Storing

Buy leeks which look fresh and healthy. The white part should be firm and unblemished and the leaves green and lively. As leeks do not keep particularly well, it is best to buy them as and when you need them. If you need to store them, trim away the top of the leaves and keep them in the salad drawer of the fridge or in a cool place. After several days they will begin to shrivel.

Preparing

It is important to wash leeks thoroughly before cooking as earth and grit lodges itself between the white sections at the base. To prepare leeks, cut away the flags (leaves) and trim the base. Unless the leek is extremely fresh or home-grown, you will probably have to remove

Cooking

Leeks can be steamed or boiled and then added to your recipe, or you can fry sliced leeks gently in butter for a minute or so and then cover with a lid to sweat so they cook without browning. Unlike onions, leeks shouldn't be allowed to brown; they become tough and unappetizing. They can be stir-fried, however, with a little garlic and ginger. If they begin to cook too fiercely, splash in a little stock and soy sauce and simmer until tender.

Left: Leeks
Above: Ramp

ONION AND LEEK RECIPES

You'll never be at a loss for a meal idea when it comes to onions and leeks. Individual Onion Tarts with Goat Cheese, or Baked Onions Stuffed with Feta make fabulous appetizers, or for a main course try Leek Soufflé or Chicken with Shallots. Garlic doesn't have to have just a walk-on role either — give it star billing as with Roast Garlic with Croûtons. It's a dish your friends won't forget.

BAKED ONIONS STUFFED WITH FETA

FETA CHEESE COMBINED WITH PINE NUTS AND FRESH CILANTRO MAKES A PIQUANT STUFFING WHICH OFFERS A WONDERFUL CONTRAST OF FLAVOR WITH THE MELLOW RED ONION. FOR THE BEST TASTE MAKE SURE THAT YOU USE AUTHENTIC GREEK FETA CHEESE.

SERVES FOUR

INGREDIENTS
    4 large red onions
    1 tablespoon olive oil
    1 ounce pine nuts
    4 ounces feta cheese, crumbled
    1 ounce fresh white bread crumbs
    1 tablespoon chopped fresh cilantro
    salt and freshly ground black pepper

1 Preheat the oven to 350°F and lightly grease a shallow ovenproof dish. Peel the onions and cut a thin slice from the top and base of each. Place in a large saucepan of boiling water and cook for 10–12 minutes until just tender. Remove with a slotted spoon. Drain on paper towels and leave to cool slightly.

2 Using a small knife or your fingers, remove the inner sections of the onions, leaving about two or three outer rings. Finely chop the inner sections and place the shells in an ovenproof dish.

3 Heat the oil in a medium-size frying pan and fry the chopped onions for 4–5 minutes until golden, then add the pine nuts and stir-fry for a few minutes.

4 Place the feta cheese in a small bowl and stir in the onions and pine nuts, the bread crumbs and cilantro. Season well with salt and pepper and then spoon the mixture into the onion shells. Cover loosely with foil and bake in the oven for about 30 minutes and remove the foil for the last 10 minutes.

5 Serve as an appetizer or as a light lunch with warm olive bread.

ONION TARTS WITH GOAT CHEESE

A VARIATION OF A CLASSIC FRENCH DISH, TARTE A L'OIGNON, THIS DISH USES YOUNG GOAT CHEESE INSTEAD OF CREAM, AS IT IS MILD AND CREAMY AND COMPLEMENTS THE FLAVOR OF THE ONIONS. THIS RECIPE MAKES EITHER EIGHT INDIVIDUAL TARTS OR ONE LARGE 9-INCH TART.

SERVES EIGHT

INGREDIENTS
For the pastry
    6 ounces all-purpose flour
    2½ ounces butter
    1 ounce Cheddar cheese, grated
For the filling
    1–1½ tablespoons olive or
        sunflower oil
    3 onions, finely sliced
    6 ounces young goat cheese
    2 eggs, beaten
    1 tablespoon light cream
    2 ounces Cheddar cheese, grated
    1 tablespoon chopped fresh tarragon
    salt and freshly ground black pepper

1 To make the pastry, sift the flour into a bowl and rub in the butter until the mixture resembles fine bread crumbs. Stir in the grated cheese and add enough cold water to make a dough. Knead lightly, put in a plastic bag and chill. Preheat the oven to 375°F.

2 Roll out the dough on a lightly floured surface, and then cut into eight rounds using a 4½-inch pastry cutter and line eight 4-inch muffin pans. Prick the bases with a fork and bake in the oven for 10–15 minutes until firm but not browned. Reduce the oven temperature to 350°F.

3 Heat the olive or sunflower oil in a large frying pan and fry the onions over low heat for 20–25 minutes until they are a deep golden brown. Stir occasionally to prevent them burning.

4 Beat the goat cheese with the eggs, cream, Cheddar cheese and tarragon. Season with salt and pepper and then stir in the fried onions.

5 Pour the mixture into the part-baked pastry shells and bake in the oven for 20–25 minutes until golden. Serve warm or cold with a green salad.

GARLIC MUSHROOMS

GARLIC AND MUSHROOMS MAKE A WONDERFUL COMBINATION. THEY MUST BE SERVED PIPING HOT, SO IF POSSIBLE USE A BALTI PAN OR CAST-IRON FRYING PAN AND DON'T STAND ON CEREMONY — SERVE STRAIGHT FROM THE PAN.

SERVES FOUR

INGREDIENTS
2 tablespoons sunflower oil
1 ounce butter
5 scallions, thinly sliced
3 garlic cloves, crushed
1 pound white mushrooms
1½ ounces fresh white bread crumbs
1 tablespoon chopped fresh parsley
2 tablespoons lemon juice
salt and freshly ground black pepper

1 Heat the oil and butter in a balti pan, wok or cast-iron frying pan. Add the scallions and garlic and stir-fry over medium heat for 1–2 minutes.

2 Add the whole white mushrooms and fry over high heat for 4–5 minutes, stirring and tossing with a large wide spatula or wooden spoon, all the time.

3 Stir in the bread crumbs, parsley, lemon juice and seasoning. Stir-fry for a few minutes until the lemon juice has virtually evaporated and then serve.

ROAST GARLIC WITH CROÛTONS

YOUR GUESTS WILL BE ASTONISHED TO BE SERVED A WHOLE ROAST GARLIC FOR AN APPETIZER. ROAST GARLIC HAS A HEAVENLY FLAVOR AND IS SO IRRESISTIBLE THAT THEY WILL FORGIVE YOU THE NEXT DAY!

SERVES FOUR

INGREDIENTS
2 garlic bulbs
3 tablespoons olive oil
3 tablespoons water
sprig of rosemary
sprig of thyme
1 bay leaf
sea salt and freshly ground
black pepper
To serve
slices of Italian bread
olive or sunflower oil, for frying
6 ounces young goat cheese or soft
cream cheese
2 tablespoons chopped fresh herbs,
e.g. marjoram, parsley and chives

1 Preheat the oven to 375°F. Place the garlic bulbs in a small ovenproof dish and pour over the oil and water. Add the rosemary, thyme and bay leaf and sprinkle with sea salt and pepper. Cover with foil and bake in the oven for 30 minutes.

2 Remove the foil, baste the garlic heads with the juices from the dish and bake for a further 15–20 minutes until they feel soft when pressed.

3 Heat a little oil in a frying pan and fry the Italian bread on both sides until golden. Blend the cheese with the mixed herbs and place in a serving dish.

4 Cut each garlic bulb in half and open out slightly. Serve the garlic on small plates with the croûtons and soft cheese. Each garlic clove should be squeezed out of its papery shell, spread over a croûton and eaten with the cheese.

THAI NOODLES WITH GARLIC CHIVES

THIS RECIPE REQUIRES A LITTLE TIME FOR PREPARATION, BUT THE COOKING TIME IS VERY FAST.
EVERYTHING IS COOKED SPEEDILY IN A HOT WOK AND SHOULD BE EATEN AT ONCE.

SERVES FOUR

INGREDIENTS
    12 ounces dried rice noodles
    ½-inch piece fresh ginger, grated
    2 tablespoons light soy sauce
    3 tablespoons vegetable oil
    2 garlic cloves, crushed
    1 large onion, cut into thin wedges
    4 ounces fried bean curd,
      thinly sliced
    1 green chili, seeded
      and finely sliced
    6 ounces bean sprouts
    4 ounces garlic chives, cut into
      2-inch lengths
    2 ounces roasted peanuts, ground
    2 tablespoons dark soy sauce
    2 tablespoons chopped fresh
      cilantro
    1 lemon, cut into wedges

1 Place the noodles in a large bowl, cover with warm water and soak for 20–30 minutes, then drain. Blend the ginger, light soy sauce and 1 tablespoon of the oil in a bowl. Set aside for 10 minutes. Drain, reserving the marinade.

2 Heat 1 tablespoon of the oil in a wok or large frying pan. Fry the garlic for a few seconds, then remove from pan and discard.

5 When hot, spoon onto serving plates and garnish with the remaining ground peanuts, cilantro and lemon wedges.

COOK'S TIP
This is a vegetarian meal. However, thinly sliced pork or chicken could be used instead. Stir-fry the meat initially for 4–5 minutes.

3 Heat the remaining oil in the wok or frying pan and stir-fry the onion for 3–4 minutes until softened and tinged with brown. Add the bean curd and chili, stir-fry briefly and then add the noodles. Stir-fry for 4–5 minutes.

4 Stir in the bean sprouts, garlic chives and most of the ground peanuts, reserving a little for the garnish. Stir well, then add the dark soy sauce and the reserved marinade.

LEEK SOUFFLÉ

SOME PEOPLE THINK OF A SOUFFLÉ AS A DINNER PARTY DISH, AND A RATHER TRICKY ONE AT THAT. HOWEVER, OTHERS FREQUENTLY SERVE THEM FOR FAMILY MEALS BECAUSE THEY ARE QUICK AND EASY TO MAKE, AND PROVE TO BE VERY POPULAR AND SATISFYING.

SERVES TWO TO THREE

INGREDIENTS

    1 tablespoon sunflower oil
    1½ ounces butter
    2 leeks, thinly sliced
    about 1¼ cups milk
    1 ounce all-purpose flour
    4 eggs, separated
    3 ounces Gruyère or Emmenthal
      cheese, grated
    salt and freshly ground black pepper

1 Preheat the oven to 350°F and butter a large soufflé dish. Heat the oil and ½ ounce of the butter in a small saucepan or flameproof casserole and fry the leeks over low heat for 4–5 minutes until soft but not brown, stirring occasionally.

2 Stir in the milk and bring to boil. Cover and simmer for 4–5 minutes until the leeks are tender. Put the liquid through a strainer into a measuring jug.

3 Melt the remaining butter in a sauce-pan, stir in the flour and cook for 1 minute. Remove pan from the heat. Make up the reserved liquid with milk to 1¼ cups. Gradually stir the milk into the pan to make a smooth sauce. Return to the heat and bring to a boil, stirring. When thickened, remove from the heat. Cool slightly and then beat in the egg yolks, cheese and the leeks.

4 Whisk the egg whites until stiff and, using a large metal spoon, fold into the leek and egg mixture. Pour into the pre-pared soufflé dish and bake in the oven for about 30 minutes until golden and puffy. Serve immediately.

TAGLIATELLE WITH LEEKS AND PROSCIUTTO

LEEKS ARE A VERY VERSATILE VEGETABLE. THEIR DELICATE, MILDLY ONIONY FLAVOR MAKES THEM IDEAL TO USE IN STIR-FRIES, RISOTTOS, EGG DISHES, SOUPS AND SAUCES. IF USING OLDER LEEKS, MAKE SURE THEY HAVE NOT DEVELOPED A WOODY CORE.

SERVES FOUR

INGREDIENTS

5 leeks
1½ ounces butter or margarine
8 ounces tagliatelle, preferably
  green and white
4 teaspoons dry sherry
2 tablespoons lemon juice
2 teaspoons chopped fresh basil
4–5 ounces prosciutto, torn into strips
6 ounces ricotta cheese
salt and freshly ground black pepper
fresh basil leaves, to garnish
Parmesan cheese, to serve

4 Stir the sherry, lemon juice, basil and seasoning into the leek mixture and cook for 1–2 minutes so that the flavors can blend together. Add the prosciutto and ricotta cheese, stir and cook for about 1–2 minutes until heated through.

5 Drain the pasta and place in a warmed serving dish. Pour the leek and prosciutto mixture on top and mix lightly together. Garnish each serving with basil leaves and serve with shavings of Parmesan cheese.

1 Trim the leeks and then cut a slit from top to bottom, rinse well under cold water and cut into thin slices.

2 Melt the butter or margarine in a saucepan or flameproof casserole, add the leeks and fry over low heat for 3–4 minutes until tender but not too soft.

3 Add the tagliatelle to a large saucepan of boiling water and cook according to the instructions on the packet (about 3–5 minutes for fresh pasta; 8 minutes for dried pasta).

BAKED LEEKS WITH CHEESE AND YOGURT TOPPING

LIKE ALL VEGETABLES, THE FRESHER LEEKS ARE, THE BETTER THEIR FLAVOR, AND THE FRESHEST LEEKS AVAILABLE SHOULD BE USED FOR THIS DISH. SMALL, YOUNG LEEKS ARE AROUND AT THE BEGINNING OF THE SEASON AND ARE PERFECT TO USE HERE.

SERVES FOUR

INGREDIENTS

8 small leeks, about 1½ pounds
2 small eggs or 1 large one, beaten
5 ounces fresh goat cheese
⅓ cup plain yogurt
2 ounces Parmesan cheese, grated
1 ounce fresh white or brown bread crumbs
salt and freshly ground black pepper

1 Preheat the oven to 350°F and butter a shallow ovenproof dish. Trim the leeks, cut a slit from top to bottom and rinse well under cold water.

2 Place the leeks in a saucepan of water, bring to the boil and simmer gently for 6–8 minutes until just tender. Remove and drain well using a slotted spoon, and arrange in the prepared dish.

3 Beat the eggs with the goat cheese, yogurt and half the Parmesan cheese, and season well with salt and pepper.

4 Pour the cheese and yogurt mixture over the leeks. Mix the bread crumbs and remaining Parmesan cheese together and sprinkle over the sauce. Bake in the oven for 35–40 minutes until the top is crisp and golden brown.

CHICKEN WITH SHALLOTS

SERVES FOUR

INGREDIENTS

1 small chicken, about 3 pounds, or 4
  chicken pieces
seasoned all-purpose flour, for coating
2 tablespoons sunflower oil
1 ounce butter
4 ounces unsmoked lean bacon,
  chopped
1¾ cups red wine
1 bay leaf
2 thyme sprigs
2 garlic cloves
9 ounces shallots
4 ounces white mushrooms,
  halved if large
2 teaspoons plain flour
salt and freshly ground black pepper

1 Preheat the oven to 350°F. Remove
any excess skin or fat from the chicken
and cut into four or eight pieces. Place a
little seasoned flour in a large plastic
bag, add the chicken pieces and shake
to coat evenly.

2 Heat the oil and half the butter in
large flameproof casserole and fry the
bacon for 3–4 minutes. Add the chicken
pieces and fry, in batches if necessary,
until lightly browned. Add the wine, bay
leaf and thyme and bring to a boil. Cover
and cook in the oven for 1 hour.

3 Peel the shallots and boil them in
salted water for 10 minutes. Heat the
remaining oil in a small frying pan and
fry the shallots for 3–4 minutes until
beginning to brown. Add the mushrooms
and fry for a further 2–3 minutes.

4 Stir the shallots and mushrooms into
the casserole with the chicken and cook
for a further 8–10 minutes. Using a fork
blend the flour with the remaining butter
to make a thick paste.

5 Transfer the chicken pieces, shallots
and mushrooms to a serving dish and
keep warm. Bring the liquid to a boil and
then add small pieces of the flour paste,
stirring vigorously after each addition.
When all the paste has been added and
the sauce is thick, either pour over the
chicken pieces or return the chicken to
the casserole and serve.

GLAZED SHALLOTS

SERVES FOUR

INGREDIENTS

12–14 ounces shallots
1 tablespoon olive oil
1 ounce butter
1 tablespoon sugar
about ¾ cup water
salt and freshly ground black pepper

1 Peel the shallots and break in two if
the onions are joined. Heat the oil and
butter in a heavy-based saucepan and
gently fry the shallots over moderate heat
for 5–6 minutes until patches of brown
begin to appear. Stir occasionally.

2 Sprinkle the shallots with the sugar
and cook, stirring, for 1 minute.

3 Add enough water to just cover the
shallots and then cover and simmer over
low heat for about 25–35 minutes until
tender. Add a little extra water if necessary, to avoid the pan boiling dry. When
the onions are completely tender, remove
the lid and continue simmering gently
until the liquid at the bottom of the pan
has reduced to a thin syrup. Stir occasionally.

4 Spoon the shallots into a serving dish
and pour over the syrup. Serve with roast
meat or a baked vegetable dish.

SHOOTS
AND STEMS

Here are some of Nature's most tender vegetables.
Asparagus, fennel, samphire and fiddlehead fern have the taste
of early summer, while the artichoke arrives later but is no less
delicious for its tardiness. Celery and bean sprouts are available
all year round and, like other shoots and stems, add a fresh
taste to a meal.

ASPARAGUS

Asparagus is definitely a luxury vegetable. Its price, even in season, sets it apart from cabbages and cauliflowers, and it has a taste of luxury too. The spears, especially the thick, green spears, at their best in early summer, have an intense, rich flavor that is impossible to describe but easy to remember. If the gods eat, they will eat asparagus – served simply with a good hollandaise!

History

The ancient Greeks enjoyed wild asparagus, but it was not until the Roman period that we know it was cultivated. Even then asparagus was highly thought of: it is recorded that Julius Caesar liked to eat it with melted butter. There is little mention of asparagus being eaten in England until the seventeenth century. Mrs Beeton has 14 recipes for asparagus and from the prices quoted in her cookbook it is apparent that it was expensive even in Victorian times.

Nutrition

Asparagus provides vitamins A, B2 and C and is also a good source of potassium, iron and calcium. It is a well-known diuretic.

Varieties

There are many varieties of asparagus and many different ways of raising it too. Spanish and some Dutch asparagus is white with ivory tips; it is grown under mounds of soil and cut just as the tips begin to show. The purple variety is mostly grown in France, where the spears are cut once the tips are about 1½ inches above the ground. Consequently, the stalks are white and the tops tinged with green or purple. In contrast, American and English asparagus grows above the ground and the spears are entirely green. Arguments continue over which has the better flavor, most growers expressing a preference for their own asparagus!

Thin, short asparagus are excellent when briefly steamed or stir-fried and added to salads. In Italy, they are served by themselves, scattered with grated Parmesan cheese.

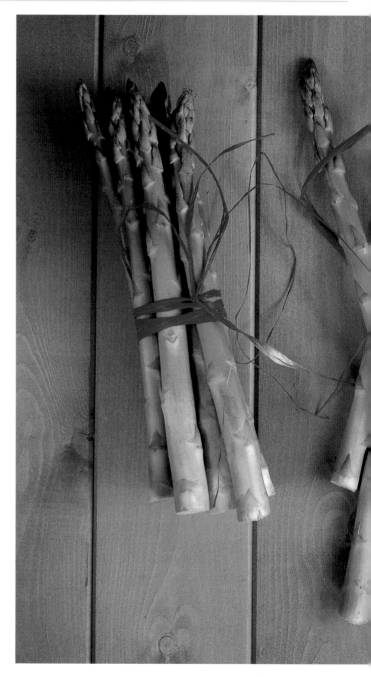

Preparing

Unless the asparagus comes straight from the garden, cut off the bottom of the stalk as it is usually hard and woody. If the bottom parts of the stem also feel hard, pare this away with a potato peeler *(below)*. However, if the asparagus is very fresh, this is not necessary, and thin asparagus rarely needs trimming at all.

Buying and Storing

Asparagus has a relatively short growing season, from late spring to early summer. Nowadays, it is available in stores almost all year through, but outside the season it will have been imported. It is still good, but it is expensive and will not have the flavor of home-produced asparagus, since it starts to lose its flavor once it is cut.

When buying asparagus, the tips should be tightly furled and fresh looking, and the stalks fresh and straight. If the stalks are badly scarred or droopy, it indicates that they have been hanging around for too long and it is not worth buying. Asparagus will keep for several days if necessary. Untie the bundles and store in the salad drawer of the fridge.

Cooking

The problem with cooking asparagus is that the stalks take longer to cook than the tender tips, which need to be only briefly steamed. Ideally, use an asparagus steamer. Place the asparagus spears with the tips upward in the wire basket and then lower into a little boiling salted water in the steamer. Cover and cook until the stems are tender.

Alternately, if you don't have an asparagus steamer, place the bundle upright in a deep saucepan of boiling salted water. (The bundle can be wedged into place with potatoes.) Cover with a dome of foil and cook for 5-10 minutes or until the spears are tender. The cooking time depends largely on the thickness of the spears, but it is important not to overcook; the spears should still have a "bite" to them.

Asparagus can also be roasted in a little olive oil. This cooking method intensifies the flavor and is gratifyingly simple. Serve with just a sprinkling of sea salt – it's quite delicious! If steaming asparagus, serve simply with melted butter, which perfectly complements the luxury of the vegetable.

Left: Asparagus
Above: White asparagus

ARTICHOKES

Artichokes have an exquisite flavor and are a very sociable food to eat. They grow in abundance in Brittany, and during July and August farmers can frequently be seen selling them by the roadside. The globes are huge hearty specimens and are extremely fresh, so they make a good buy.

History

It is not known for certain whether artichokes were eaten in antiquity. Although they are mentioned by writers, they could have been referring to the cardoon, which is the uncultivated form of artichoke. Cardoons grew wild in many southern European countries, and, as far as we know, cultivated artichokes first became a popular food in Italy. However, Goethe did not share the Italians' liking for the vegetable and remarks in his book, *Travels Through Italy*, that "the peasants eat thistles," something he didn't care for at all.

Nowadays, artichokes are grown all over southern Europe and in California. People in Italy, France and Spain eat artichokes while the vegetable is still young, before the choke has formed and the entire artichoke is edible. Unfortunately, such young delicacies are not exported, but look out for them if you are in these countries.

Buying and Storing

It is only worth buying artichokes when they are in season, although they are available in supermarkets almost all year through. In winter, however, they are sad looking specimens, small and rather dry, and are really not worth the bother of cooking. At their best, artichokes should be lively looking with a good bloom on their leaves, the inner leaves wrapped tightly round the choke and heart inside. Artichokes will keep for 2–3 days in the salad drawer of the fridge but are best eaten as soon as possible.

Preparing and Cooking

First twist off the stalk which should also remove some of the fibers at the base and then cut the base flat and pull away any small base leaves. If the leaves are very spiky, trim them with scissors if liked *(above)*, then rinse under running water. Cook in boiling water, acidulated with the juice of half a lemon. Large artichokes need to be simmered for 30–40 minutes until tender. To test if they are done, pull off one of the outer leaves. It should come away easily and the base of the leaf should be tender.

heart. Eat the heart with a knife and fork, dipping it in the garlic butter or vinaigrette.

CARDOONS

This impressively large vegetable is closely related to the globe artichoke and has a superb flavor, a cross between artichokes and asparagus. Cultivated plants frequently grow to 6 feet in height, and once mature, cardoons, like celery, are blanched as they grow. This process involves wrapping the stalks with newspaper and black bags for several weeks, so that when harvested, in late fall, before the frosts, the stalks are a pale green.

The cardoon is a popular vegetable in southern Europe but less commonly available elsewhere. In Spain, for instance, it is much appreciated and often appears on the table, poached and served with chestnuts or walnuts. Only the inner ribs and heart are used.

Artichokes and Drink

Artichokes contain a chemical called cynarin, which in many people (although surprisingly not all) affects the taste buds by enhancing sweet flavors. Among other things, this will spoil the taste of wine. Consequently, don't waste good wine with artichokes but drink ice water instead, which should taste pleasantly sweet.

Eating Artichokes

Artichokes are fun to eat. They have to be eaten with fingers, which does away with any pomp and ceremony, always a handicap for a good dinner party. Serve one artichoke between two, so that people can share the fun of pulling off the leaves and dipping them into garlic butter or vinaigrette. If you want to serve one each, serve them in succession. The dipping sauces are an essential part of eating artichokes; people can either spoon a little onto their plates or have a little bowl each. After dipping, draw the leaf through your teeth, eating the fleshy part.

When most of the leaves have been eaten, a few thin pointed leaves remain in the center, which can be pulled off altogether. Then pull or cut away the fine prickly choke and discard, leaving the

Far left: Artichokes
Top: Baby artichokes
Above: Cardoons

CELERY

Some people say that the very act of eating celery has a slimming effect because chewing it uses up more calories than the vegetable itself contains! Although it may be insubstantial, celery nevertheless has a distinct and individual flavor, sharp and savory, which makes it an excellent flavoring for soups and stuffings, as well as good on its own or in salads. The astringent flavor and crunchy texture of celery contrasts well with the other ingredients in salads such as Waldorf salad or Walnut and avocado salad.

History

Celery is known to have been commonly eaten in salads in Italy for hundreds of years.

Nutrition

Celery is very low in calories but contains potassium and calcium.

Varieties

Most grocers and supermarkets, depending on the time of year, sell both green and white celery. When celery is allowed to grow naturally, the stalks are green. However, by banking up earth against the shoots celery is blanched: the stalks are protected from sunlight and remain pale and white. Consequently, white celery is often "dirty" – covered loosely in soil – while green celery will always be clean. White celery, which is frost hardy, is only available in winter. It is more tender and less bitter than green celery and is generally considered superior. Celery is therefore thought of as a winter vegetable and is traditionally used at Christmas time, for stuffing and as a sauce to go with turkey or ham.

Buying and Storing

White celery is in season during the winter months. If possible, buy "dirty" celery which hasn't been washed. It has a better flavor than the pristine but rather bland supermarket variety. Look for celery with green fresh-looking leaves and straight stems. If the leaves or any outer stalks are missing, it is likely to be old, so worth avoiding.

Celery will keep for several days in the salad drawer of the refrigerator. Limp celery can be revived by wrapping it in absorbent paper and standing it in a jar of water.

Preparing

Wash if necessary and pull the stalks apart, trimming the base with a sharp knife. Cut into thick or thin slices according to the recipe. When served raw and whole, the coarse outer "strings" should be removed from each stalk by pulling them up from the base.

Cooking and Serving

Serve celery raw and finely sliced in salads, mixed with cream cheese or sour cream. Braised celery is tasty, either whole or sliced. Celery has a distinctive, savory, astringent flavor so is excellent in soups or stuffings.

CELERY ROOT

Strictly speaking, celery root is classified as a root vegetable rather than a shoot or stem. It is knobbly with a patchy brown/white skin and has a similar but less pronounced flavor than celery. Grated and eaten raw, it has a crunchy texture, but when cooked it is more akin to potatoes. Thin slices of potato and celery root cooked *au gratin* with cream is a popular way of serving this vegetable.

Buying and Preparing

If possible, buy smallish bulbs of celery root. The flesh discolors when exposed to light, so as soon as you have peeled, sliced, diced or grated the celery root, plunge it into a bowl of acidulated water (water with lemon juice added).

Cooking

Celery root can be used in soups and broths, or can be diced and boiled and eaten in potato salads.

Left: Green celery
Above: White celery
Right: Celery root

FIDDLEHEAD FERN

Sometimes called the ostrich fern, these shoots are a rich green color and are normally about 2 inches long. They have an unusual flavor, something like a cross between asparagus and okra, and have a slightly chewy texture, which makes them a popular choice for oriental dishes.

Preparing and Cooking

To prepare and cook, trim the ends and then steam or simmer in a little water or sauté in butter until tender. Use in salads or serve as a first course with a hollandaise sauce.

Right: Fiddlehead ferns
Below left: Alfalfa sprouts
Below right: Mung bean sprouts

ORIENTAL SHOOTS

BAMBOO SHOOTS

In the Far East, edible bamboo shoots are sold fresh in the market. The young shoots are stripped of their brown outer skins and the insides are then eaten. Although fresh bamboo shoots can occasionally be found in oriental stores, the most readily available variety is sold in cans. The flavor is undoubtedly spoiled. Fresh bamboo shoots have a mild but distinct taste, faintly reminiscent of artichokes, while canned ones really taste of nothing at all. However, the texture, which, in Chinese cuisine particularly, is as important as the flavor, is not so impaired, and bamboo shoots have a pleasantly crunchy bite.

Preparing and Cooking

Peel away the outer skin and then cook in boiling water for about half an hour. They should feel firm, but not "rock" hard. Once cooked, slice thinly and serve by themselves as a side dish, with garlic butter or a sauce, or add to stir-fries, spring rolls or any oriental dish

where you need a contrast of textures. Since canned bamboo shoots have been preserved in brine, always rinse well before using.

BEAN SPROUTS

Bean sprouts are a neglected vegetable, used almost carelessly for oriental dishes

but otherwise passed by as being insipid and not very interesting. It's a reputation they don't deserve: not only do they have a lovely fresh flavor, but they are also good for you.

All sorts of seeds can be sprouted, but the bean family are favorites among the sprouted vegetables. The bean sprouts most commonly available in the shops are sprouted mung beans, but aduki beans, alfalfa, lentils and soy beans can all be sprouted and taste delicious.

Nutrition

Beans sprouts contain a significant amount of protein, Vitamin C and many of the B vitamins. They have an excellent flavor too, best appreciated eaten raw in salads or sandwiches, and for slimmers they are an ideal food, low in calories, yet with sufficient substance to be filling, and with a flavor and texture that can be enjoyed without a dressing.

Buying and Storing

Bean sprouts should only be bought when absolutely fresh. They don't keep for long and they will taste sour if past their best. The sprouts should be firm, not limp, and and the tips should be green or yellow; avoid any that are beginning to turn brown.

Cooking

If stir-frying, add the bean sprouts at the last minute so they cook for the minimum period to keep plenty of crunch and retain their nutritional value. Most health food shops will have instructions on sprouting your own beans. Only buy seeds intended for sprouting.

PALM HEARTS

Fresh palm hearts are the buds of cabbage palm trees and are considered a delicacy in many parts of the world. They are available canned from oriental stores, but are most prized when fresh. These should be blanched before being cooked to eliminate any bitterness. They can be braised or sautéed and then served hot with a hollandaise sauce, or cold with a simple vinaigrette.

WATER CHESTNUTS

Water chestnut is the common name for a number of aquatic herbs and their nutlike fruit, the best known and most popular variety being the Chinese water chestnut, sometimes known as the Chinese sedge. In China they are grown in exactly the same way as rice, the

plants needing the same conditions of high temperatures, shallow water and good soil. In spring, the corms are planted in paddy fields which are then flooded to a depth of some 4 inches. These are drained in fall, and the corms are harvested and stored over the winter. Water chestnuts are much used in Chinese cooking and have a sweet crunchy flavor with nutty overtones. They are edible cooked or raw and are excellent in all sorts of Chinese dishes.

Above: Sprouting mung beans
Below (clockwise from top left): Canned water chestnuts, canned bamboo shoots, fresh water chestnuts, canned palm hearts

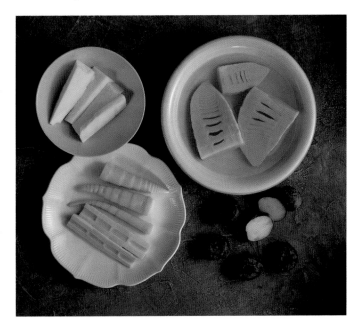

FENNEL

The vegetable fennel is closely related to the herb and spice of the same name. It is called variously bulb fennel, Florence fennel, sweet fennel, *finocchio dulce* or Italian fennel.

Like the herb, Florence fennel has the distinct flavor of anise, a taste that seems to go particularly well with fish, so the vegetable is often served with fish dishes while the herb or spice is commonly used in fish stocks, sauces or soups. The leaves are edible and can be used in soups and stocks as well as for garnishing.

History

Bulb fennel has only been popular for the last ten or so years, although it has a long history of cultivation, having been eaten by the ancient Egyptians, Greeks and Romans. In Italy, fennel has been eaten for several centuries: many of the best fennel recipes come from Italy and other parts of the Mediterranean.

Buying and Storing

If possible, buy small tender bulbs. The bulbs should be clean and white with no bruises or blemishes and the feathery leaves should be green and lively. Fennel will keep for a day or two in the salad drawer of the fridge.

Preparing

Unless the bulbs are very young and tender, remove the first layer of skin, as it is likely to be tough (this can be used for a stock). Fennel can then be sliced into slivers by cutting downward or into rings by cutting across the bulb. When used raw in salads, it must be cut into smaller pieces.

Cooking and Serving

Fennel can be served raw if it is thinly sliced and dressed with a light vinaigrette. In salads, its flavor contrasts well with apple, celery and other crunchy ingredients. Fennel is also excellent braised with onions, tomatoes and garlic.

Right: Bulb fennel
Far right: Marsh samphire

SAMPHIRE

There are two types of samphire. Marsh samphire grows in estuaries and salt marshes while rock samphire, sometimes called sea fennel, grows on rocky shores. The two are understandably confused since they are both connected with the sea, yet they are completely different plants.

The type likely to be sold by a fish dealer is marsh samphire. It is also known as glasswort and is sometimes called sea asparagus, as its shoots are similar to small asparagus shoots.

Although marsh samphire grows easily and is commonly found all over North America and Europe, it is not cultivated and is only available for a short time while it is in season, normally in late summer and early autumn.

Samphire has a distinctly salty, iodine flavor and a pleasant crisp texture. The flavor is reminiscent of the sea and goes particularly well with fish and seafood. However, samphire can be enjoyed simply steamed and dipped into melted butter.

Buying and Storing

When in season, good fish dealers get regular stocks of marsh samphire, and it should look bright and fresh. Buy it as you need it, as it will not keep for long.

Preparing and Cooking

If necessary, wash marsh samphire under cold running water. It is best steamed over a pan of boiling water for no more than 3 minutes. Alternately, blanch it in boiling water for 3-5 minutes and then drain. Samphire can be eaten raw but blanching it removes some of the saltiness.

To eat samphire, draw the shoots through the teeth to peel the succulent part from the thin central core.

SHOOT AND STEM RECIPES

If the season's right, you owe it yourself — and your guests — to make the most of shoots and stems. What could be a more perfect way to start a meal than with fresh Asparagus with Tarragon Hollandaise? Alternatively roast asparagus, French-style, for Roast Asparagus Crêpes. Other favorites include Celery, Avocado and Walnut Salad and Fennel and Mussel Provençal, while for something new, try Samphire with Chilled Fish Curry or Celery Root and Blue Cheese Roulade.

ASPARAGUS TART WITH RICOTTA

THIS DELICIOUS TART COMBINES THE SUBTLE FLAVOR OF ASPARAGUS WITH THE MILD TASTE OF CREAMY RICOTTA CHEESE TO GREAT EFFECT. SERVE WITH A GREEN SALAD AND TINY NEW POTATOES FOR A PERFECT WEEKEND LUNCH.

SERVES FOUR

INGREDIENTS
For the pastry
  3 ounces butter or margarine
  6 ounces all-purpose flour
  pinch of salt
For the filling
  8 ounces asparagus
  2 eggs, beaten
  8 ounces ricotta cheese
  2 tablespoons strained plain yogurt
  1½ ounces Parmesan cheese, grated
  salt and freshly ground black pepper

1 Preheat the oven to 400°F. Rub the butter or margarine into the flour and salt until the mixture resembles fine bread crumbs. Stir in enough cold water to form a smooth dough and knead lightly on a floured surface.

2 Roll out the pastry and line a 9-inch flan ring. Press firmly into the pan and prick all over with a fork. Bake in the oven for about 10 minutes until the pastry is pale but firm. Remove from the oven and reduce the temperature to 350°F.

3 To make the filling, trim the asparagus and cut 2 inches from the top and chop the remaining stalks into 1-inch pieces. Add the stalks to a saucepan of boiling water and after 1 minute add the tops. Simmer for 4–5 minutes until almost tender, then drain and refresh under cold water.

4 Beat together the eggs, ricotta, yogurt, Parmesan cheese and seasoning. Stir in the asparagus stalks and pour the mixture into the pastry case. Arrange the asparagus tips on top, pressing them down slightly into the ricotta mixture.

5 Bake in the oven for 35–40 minutes until golden. Serve warm or cold.

ASPARAGUS WITH TARRAGON HOLLANDAISE

THIS IS THE IDEAL STARTER FOR AN EARLY SUMMER DINNER PARTY WHEN THE NEW SEASON'S ASPARAGUS IS JUST IN AND AT ITS BEST. MAKING HOLLANDAISE SAUCE IN A BLENDER OR FOOD PROCESSOR IS INCREDIBLY EASY AND VIRTUALLY FOOLPROOF!

SERVES FOUR

INGREDIENTS
  1¼ pounds fresh asparagus
  salt
For the hollandaise sauce
  2 egg yolks
  1 tablespoon lemon juice
  4 ounces butter
  2 teaspoons finely chopped fresh
    tarragon
  salt and freshly ground black pepper

1 Prepare the asparagus, lay it in a steamer or in an asparagus steamer and place over a saucepan of rapidly boiling water. Cover and steam for 6–10 minutes until tender (the cooking time will depend on the thickness of the asparagus stems).

2 To make the hollandaise sauce, place the egg yolks, lemon juice and seasoning in a blender or food processor and process briefly. Melt the butter in a small pan until foaming and then, with the blender running, pour it on to the egg mixture in a slow, steady stream.

3 Stir in the tarragon by hand or process it (for a sauce speckled with green or a pale green sauce, respectively).

4 Arrange the asparagus on small plates and pour over some of the hollandaise sauce. Serve remaining sauce in a jug.

ASPARAGUS SOUP

HOME-MADE ASPARAGUS SOUP HAS A DELICATE FLAVOR, QUITE UNLIKE THAT FROM A CAN. THIS SOUP IS BEST MADE WITH YOUNG ASPARAGUS, WHICH IS TENDER AND BLENDS WELL. SERVE IT WITH WAFER-THIN SLICES OF BREAD.

SERVES FOUR

INGREDIENTS
   1 pound young asparagus
   1½ ounces butter
   6 shallots, sliced
   ½ ounce all-purpose flour
   2½ cups vegetable stock or water
   1 tablespoon lemon juice
   1 cup milk
   ½ cup light cream
   2 teaspoons chopped fresh chervil
   salt and freshly ground black pepper

1 Trim the stalks of the asparagus if necessary. Cut 1½ inches off the tops of half the asparagus and set aside for a garnish. Slice the remaining asparagus.

2 Melt 1 ounce of the butter in a large saucepan and gently fry the sliced shallots for 2–3 minutes until soft but not brown, stirring occasionally.

3 Add the sliced asparagus and fry over low heat for about 1 minute. Stir in the flour, cook for 1 minute. Stir in the stock or water, lemon juice and season to taste. Bring to a boil and then simmer, partially covered, for 15–20 minutes until the asparagus is very tender.

4 Cool slightly and then process the soup in a food processor or blender until smooth. Then press the puréed asparagus through a strainer placed over a clean saucepan. Add the milk by pouring and stirring it through the strainer with the asparagus so as to extract the maximum amount of asparagus purée.

5 Melt the remaining butter and fry the reserved asparagus tips gently for about 3–4 minutes to soften.

6 Heat the soup gently for 3–4 minutes. Stir in the cream and the asparagus tips. Heat gently and serve sprinkled with the chopped fresh chervil.

ROAST ASPARAGUS CRÊPES

ROAST ASPARAGUS IS DELICIOUS AND GOOD ENOUGH TO EAT JUST AS IT COMES. HOWEVER, FOR A REALLY SPLENDID STARTER, TRY THIS SIMPLE RECIPE. EITHER MAKE SIX LARGE OR TWICE AS MANY COCKTAIL-SIZE PANCAKES TO USE WITH SMALLER STEMS OF ASPARAGUS.

SERVES SIX

INGREDIENTS
    1 pound fresh asparagus
    6–8 tablespoons olive oil
    6 ounces mascarpone cheese
    4 tablespoons light cream
    1 ounce Parmesan cheese, grated
    sea salt
For the pancakes
    6 ounces all-purpose flour
    2 eggs
    1½ cups milk
    vegetable oil, for frying
    pinch of salt

1 To make the pancake batter, mix the flour with the salt in a large bowl, food processor or blender, then add the eggs and milk and beat or process to make a smooth, fairly thin, batter.

2 Heat a little oil in a large frying pan and add a small amount of batter, swirling the pan to coat the base evenly. Cook over moderate heat for about 1 minute, then flip over and cook the other side until golden. Set aside and cook the rest of the pancakes in the same way; the mixture makes about six large or 12 smaller pancakes.

3 Preheat the oven to 350°F and lightly grease a large shallow ovenproof dish or roasting pan with some of the olive oil.

4 Trim the asparagus by placing on a board and cutting off the bases. Using a small sharp knife, peel away the woody ends, if necessary.

5 Arrange the asparagus in a single layer in the dish, trickle over the remaining olive oil, rolling the asparagus to coat each one thoroughly. Sprinkle with a little salt and then roast in the oven for about 8–12 minutes until tender (the cooking time depends on the stem thickness).

6 Blend the mascarpone cheese with the cream and Parmesan cheese and spread a generous tablespoonful over each of the pancakes, leaving a little extra for the topping. Preheat the broiler.

7 Divide the asparagus spears among the pancakes, roll up and arrange in a single layer in an ovenproof dish. Spoon over the remaining cheese mixture and then place under a moderate broiler for 4–5 minutes, until heated through and golden brown. Serve at once.

CELERY ROOT GRATIN

ALTHOUGH CELERY ROOT HAS A RATHER UNATTRACTIVE APPEARANCE WITH ITS HARD, KNOBBLY SKIN, IT IS A VEGETABLE THAT HAS A VERY DELICIOUS SWEET AND NUTTY FLAVOR. THIS IS ACCENTUATED IN THIS DISH BY THE ADDITION OF THE SWEET YET NUTTY EMMENTAL CHEESE.

SERVES FOUR

INGREDIENTS

1 pound celery root
juice of ½ lemon
1 ounce butter
1 small onion, finely chopped
2 tablespoons all-purpose flour
1¼ cups milk
1 ounce Emmental cheese, grated
1 tablespoon capers
salt and cayenne pepper

1 Preheat the oven to 375°F. Peel the celery root and cut into ¼-inch slices, immediately plunging them into a saucepan of cold water acidulated with the lemon juice.

2 Bring the water to a boil and simmer the celery root for 10–12 minutes until just tender. Drain and arrange the celery root in a shallow ovenproof dish.

3 Melt the butter in a small saucepan and fry the onion over low heat until soft but not browned. Stir in the flour, cook for 1 minute and then slowly stir in the milk to make a smooth sauce. Stir in the cheese, capers and seasoning to taste and then pour over the celery root. Cook in the oven for 15–20 minutes until the top is golden brown.

VARIATION
For a less strongly flavored dish, alternate the layers of celery root with potato. Slice the potato, cook until almost tender, then drain well before assembling the dish.

CELERY ROOT AND BLUE CHEESE ROULADE

CELERY ROOT ADDS A DELICATE AND SUBTLE FLAVOR TO THIS ATTRACTIVE DISH. THE SPINACH ROULADE
MAKES AN ATTRACTIVE CONTRAST TO THE CREAMY FILLING, BUT YOU COULD USE A PLAIN OR CHEESE
ROULADE BASE INSTEAD. BE SURE TO ROLL UP THE ROULADE WHILE IT IS STILL WARM AND PLIABLE.

SERVES SIX

INGREDIENTS
    ½ ounce butter
    8 ounces cooked spinach, drained and
      chopped
    ⅔ cup light cream
    4 large eggs, separated
    ½ ounce Parmesan cheese, grated
    pinch of nutmeg
    salt and freshly ground black pepper
For the filling
    8 ounces celery root
    lemon juice
    3 ounces blue cheese
    4 ounces ricotta cheese
    freshly ground black pepper

1 Preheat the oven to 400°F and line a
13 x 9-inch jelly roll tin with non-stick
baking parchment.

2 Melt the butter in a saucepan and add
the spinach. Cook gently until all the
liquid has evaporated, stirring frequently.
Remove the pan from the heat and stir in
the cream, egg yolks, Parmesan cheese,
nutmeg and seasoning.

3 Whisk the egg whites until stiff, fold
them gently into the spinach mixture and
then spoon into the prepared pan.
Spread the mixture evenly and use a
metal spatula to smooth the surface.

4 Bake in the oven for 10–15 minutes
until the roulade is firm to the touch and
lightly golden on top. Carefully turn out
onto a sheet of wax paper and peel away
the lining paper. Roll it up with the paper
inside and leave to cool slightly.

5 To make the filling, peel and grate the
celery root into a bowl and sprinkle well
with lemon juice. Blend the blue cheese
and ricotta cheese together and mix with
the celery root and a little black pepper.

6 Unroll the roulade, spread with the
filling and roll up again. Serve at once or
wrap loosely and chill.

BRAISED CELERY WITH GOAT CHEESE

THE SHARP FLAVOR OF THE CELERY IN THIS DISH IS PERFECTLY COMPLEMENTED BY THE MILD YET TANGY
GOAT CHEESE. THIS RECIPE IS AN EXAMPLE OF QUICK AND EASY PREPARATION TO MAKE A DELICIOUS
ACCOMPANIMENT TO GRILLED MEAT OR STUFFED PANCAKES.

SERVES FOUR

INGREDIENTS
  1 ounce butter
  1 head of celery, thinly sliced
  6 ounces mild medium-fat
    goat cheese
  3–4 tablespoons light cream
  salt and freshly ground black pepper

1 Preheat the oven to 350°F and lightly
butter a medium-size shallow ovenproof
dish.

2 Melt the butter in a heavy-based
saucepan and fry the thinly sliced celery
for 2–3 minutes, stirring frequently. Add
3–4 tablespoons of water to the pan,
heat gently and then cover and simmer
over low heat for 5–6 minutes, until the
celery is nearly tender and the water has
almost evaporated.

3 Remove the pan from the heat and
stir in the goat cheese and cream. Taste
and season with salt and pepper, and
then turn into the prepared dish.

4 Cover the dish with buttered wax
paper and cook in the oven for 10–12
minutes. Serve at once.

CELERY, AVOCADO AND WALNUT SALAD

THE CRUNCHINESS OF THE CELERY AND WALNUTS CONTRASTS PERFECTLY WITH THE SMOOTH AVOCADO.
SERVE IT WITH A SOUR CREAM DRESSING AS SUGGESTED, OR SIMPLY DRESSED WITH A LITTLE OLIVE OIL
AND FRESHLY SQUEEZED LEMON JUICE.

SERVES FOUR

INGREDIENTS
  3 bacon strips (optional)
  8 tender white celery stalks,
    very thinly sliced
  3 scallions, finely chopped
  2 ounces walnut halves
  1 ripe avocado
  lemon juice
For the dressing
  ½ cup sour cream
  1 tablespoon olive oil
  pinch of cayenne pepper

1 Dry-fry the bacon, if using, until
golden and then chop into small pieces
and place in a salad bowl with the celery,
scallions and walnuts.

2 Halve the avocado and, using a very
sharp knife, cut into thin slices. Peel
away the skin from each slice and then
sprinkle generously with lemon juice and
add to the celery mixture.

3 Lightly beat the sour cream, olive oil
and cayenne pepper together in a jug or
small bowl. Either fold carefully into the
salad or serve separately.

STUFFED ARTICHOKES

THE AMOUNT OF STUFFING NEEDED FOR THIS DISH DEPENDS ON THE SIZE OF THE ARTICHOKES — IF THEY ARE SMALL YOU COULD SERVE ONE PER PERSON. TO INCREASE THE AMOUNT OF STUFFING, ADD EXTRA MOZZARELLA AND LEEK RATHER THAN BACON.

SERVES FOUR (as a starter)

INGREDIENTS
   2 artichokes, prepared
   lemon juice
For the stuffing
   1 ounce butter
   2–3 small leeks, sliced
   2–3 bacon strips, chopped (optional)
   3 ounces mozzarella cheese, cut into
     small cubes
   1–1½ ounces fresh brown or white
     bread crumbs
   1 teaspoon chopped fresh basil
   fresh basil leaves, to garnish
   salt and freshly ground black pepper

1 Place the artichokes in a large saucepan of salted water. Bring to a boil, cover and cook for 35–40 minutes or until a lower leaf comes away easily.

3 Drain the artichokes, upside down, and when cool enough to handle, cut in half from top to bottom using a sharp knife. Remove the inner leaves, pull out and discard the choke and then sprinkle the inside and base liberally with lemon juice to prevent discoloration.

4 Preheat the broiler. Spoon a little of the stuffing into each artichoke half and place them in a single layer in an oven-proof dish. Set under a moderately hot broiler and broiler for 5–6 minutes until the stuffing is golden brown. Serve on small plates garnished with basil leaves.

2 To make the stuffing, melt the butter in a saucepan and gently fry the leeks for 3–4 minutes. Add the bacon, if using, and continue frying until the leek is soft and the bacon lightly golden brown. Remove the pan from the heat and stir in the mozzarella cubes, bread crumbs, basil and seasoning to taste.

SAMPHIRE <u>WITH</u> CHILLED FISH CURRY

EVEN IF YOU'RE A BIG CURRY FAN, DON'T BE TEMPTED TO ADD TOO MUCH CURRY PASTE TO THIS DISH.
YOU NEED ONLY THE MEREST HINT OF MILD CURRY PASTE SO THAT THE FLAVOR OF THE SAMPHIRE AND
FISH CAN STILL BE APPRECIATED.

SERVES FOUR

INGREDIENTS
6 ounces samphire
12 ounces fresh salmon steak or fillet
12 ounces sole fillet
fish stock or water
4 ounces large peeled shrimp
1 ounce butter
1 small onion, very finely chopped
2 teaspoons mild curry paste
1–2 teaspoons apricot jam
⅔ cup sour cream
sprig of mint, to garnish (optional)

1 Trim the samphire and blanch in boiling water for about 5 minutes until tender. Drain and set aside.

2 Place the salmon and sole in a large frying pan, cover with fish stock or water and bring to the boil. Reduce the heat, cover and cook for 6–8 minutes until the fish is tender.

COOK'S TIP
As the samphire has a fresh salty tang of the sea, there is not really any need to add extra salt to this recipe.

3 Transfer the fish to a plate and when cool enough to handle, break the salmon and sole into bite-size pieces, removing any skin and bones. Place in a mixing bowl with the shrimp.

4 Melt the butter in a saucepan and gently fry the onion for 3–4 minutes until soft but not brown. Add the curry paste, cook for 30 seconds, then remove from the heat. Stir in the jam. Allow to cool and then stir in the sour cream.

5 Pour the curry cream over the fish. Arrange the samphire around the edge of a serving plate and spoon the fish into the center. Garnish with a sprig of mint.

FENNEL AND MUSSEL PROVENÇAL

SERVES FOUR

INGREDIENTS

2 large fennel bulbs
4–4½ pounds fresh mussels in their
  shells, well scrubbed under cold
  water and beards removed
¾ cup water
sprig of thyme
1 ounce butter
4 shallots, finely chopped
1 garlic clove, crushed
1 cup white wine
2 teaspoons all-purpose flour
¾ cup light cream
1 tablespoon chopped fresh parsley
salt and freshly ground black pepper
sprig of dill, to garnish

1 Trim the fennel and cut into slices
¼ inch thick and then cut into ½-inch
sticks. Cook in a little salted water until
just tender and drain.

2 Discard any mussels that are
damaged or do not close. Put in a large
saucepan, add the water and thyme,
cover tightly, bring to the boil and cook
for about 5 minutes until the mussels
open, shaking occasionally.

3 Transfer the mussels to a plate and
discard any that are unopened. When
cool enough to handle, remove them
from their shells, reserving a few in their
shells for a garnish.

4 Melt the butter in a saucepan and fry
the shallots and garlic for 3–4 minutes
until softened but not browned. Add the
fennel, fry briefly for 30–60 seconds and
then stir in the wine and simmer gently
until the liquid is reduced by half.

5 Blend the flour with a little extra wine
or water. Add the cream, parsley and
seasoning to the saucepan and heat
gently. Stir in the blended flour and the
mussels. Cook over low heat until the
sauce thickens. Season to taste and pour
into a warmed serving dish. Garnish with
dill and reserved mussels in their shells.

BRAISED FENNEL WITH TOMATOES

SERVES FOUR

INGREDIENTS

3 small fennel bulbs
2–3 tablespoons olive oil
5–6 shallots, sliced
2 garlic cloves, crushed
4 tomatoes, peeled and chopped
about ¾ cup dry white wine
1 tablespoon chopped fresh basil or
  ½ teaspoon dried
1½–2 ounces fresh white bread
  crumbs
salt and freshly ground black pepper

1 Preheat the oven to 300°F. Trim the
fennel bulbs and cut into slices about
½ inch thick.

2 Heat the olive oil in a large saucepan
and fry the shallots and garlic for about
4–5 minutes over moderate heat until
the shallots are slightly softened. Add the
tomatoes, stir-fry briefly and then stir in
⅔ cup of the wine, the basil and seasoning. Bring to a boil, add the fennel, then
cover and cook for 5 minutes.

3 Arrange the fennel in layers in an
ovenproof dish. Pour the tomato mixture
over and sprinkle the top with half the
bread crumbs. Bake in the oven for
about 1 hour. From time to time, press
down on the crumb crust with the back
of a spoon and sprinkle over another
layer of bread crumbs and a little more of
the wine. The crust slowly becomes gold-
en brown and very crunchy.

ROOTS

Roots are the mainstays of our winter meals. Parsnips, turnips, swedes and potatoes combine to make wonderful warming stews. Jerusalem artichokes are another winter favorite and, as winter turns to spring, young carrots and Jersey Royal potatoes appear. Exotic roots such as sweet potatoes and yams are available almost all year round, and look out too for salsify — a root vegetable that can be enjoyed whatever the season.

POTATOES

History

The potato originates from South America. Most people learned at school that Sir Walter Raleigh brought the tubers to England from Virginia, but this never convinced historians as the potato was completely unknown in North America until the eighteenth century. They now believe that Sir Francis Drake was responsible. In 1586, after battling against the Spaniards in the Caribbean, Drake stopped to pick up provisions from Cartegena in northern Colombia – and these included tobacco and potato tubers. En route home, he stopped off at Roanoke Island, off the coast of Virginia. The first group of English colonists had been sponsored to settle there by Sir Walter Raleigh, but by this time they had had enough. Drake brought them back to England, along with some of Raleigh's men and, of course, the provisions – including the potato tubers.

Potatoes apparently fascinated Queen Elizabeth and intrigued horticulturists, but they were not an overnight success among the people. The wealthy frequently reviled them as being flavorless and the food of the poor. People distrusted the fact that they reached maturity underground, believing them to be the work of

the devil. In Scotland, Presbyterian ministers darkly advised their congregations that there was no mention of potatoes in the Bible, and thus the eating of them was an ungodly act!

In spite of such a bad press, potatoes nevertheless were slowly recognized for their merit. By 1650 they were the staple food of Ireland, and elsewhere in Europe potatoes began to replace wheat as the most important crop, both for people and for livestock. In an early English cookbook, *Adam's Luxury and Eve's Cookery*, there are 20 different recipes for cooking and serving potatoes.

The first mention of potatoes in America is in 1719 in Londonderry, New Hampshire. They arrived not from the south, but via Irish settlers who brought their potatoes with them.

The current popularity of potatoes is probably thanks to a Frenchman called Antoine-Auguste Parmentier. A military pharmacist of the latter part of the eighteenth century, Parmentier recognized the virtues of the potato, both for its versatility and as an important food for the poor, and set out to improve its image. He persuaded Louis XVI to let him ostentatiously grow potatoes on royal land around the palace in Versailles to

impress the fashion-conscious Parisians. He also produced a court dinner in which each course contained potatoes. Gradually, eating potatoes became chic, first among people in the French court and then in French Society. Today, if you see *Parmentier* in a recipe or on a menu, it means "with potato."

Nutrition

Potatoes are an important source of carbohydrate. Once thought to be fattening, we now know that, on the contrary, potatoes can be an excellent part of a calorie-controlled diet – provided, of course, they are not fried in oil or mashed with too much butter. Potatoes are also a very good source of vitamin C, and during the winter potatoes are often the main source of this vitamin. They also contain potassium, iron and vitamin B.

Varieties

There are more than 400 international varieties of potato, but unless you are a gardener, you will find only some 15 varieties generally available. Thanks to labeling laws, packaged potatoes carry their names, which makes it easier to learn to differentiate between the varieties and find out which potato is good for what.

New Potatoes

Carlingford: Available as a new potato or as main crop, Carlingford has a close white flesh.

Jersey Royal: Often the first new potato of the season, Jersey Royals have been shipped from Jersey for over a hundred years and have acquired an enviable reputation among everyone who enjoys good food. Boiled or steamed and then served with butter and a sprinkling of parsley, they cannot be beaten.

Jersey Royals are kidney-shaped, with yellow firm flesh and a distinctive flavor. Don't confuse Jersey Royals with Jersey Whites, which are actually Maris Pipers, grown in Jersey.

Maris Bard: A regularly shaped, slightly waxy potato with white flesh.

Maris Peer: This variety has dry firm flesh and a waxy texture and doesn't disintegrate when cooked – consequently, it is good in salads.

Main Crop Potatoes

Desiree: A potato with a pink skin and yellow soft-textured flesh. It is good for baking, frying, roasting and mashing.

Yukon Gold: A good masher with yellow flesh and pale skin.

Idaho: A russet-skinned potato that was the original favorite for making chips. It has an excellent, distinctive flavor, and should you find them for sale, buy them at once for baked potatoes. They are also good boiled or roasted.

Kerr's Pink: A good cooking potato with pink skin and creamy flesh.

King Edward: Probably the best known of potatoes, although not the best in flavor. King Edwards are creamy white in color with a slightly floury texture.

Red King Edwards are virtually identical except for their red skin. Both are good roasted or baked. However, the flesh disintegrates when boiled, so while good for mashing do not use King Edwards if you want whole boiled potatoes.

Maris Piper: This is a widely grown variety of potato, popular with growers and cooks because it is good for all kinds of cooking methods – baking, frying, roasting and mashing. It has a pale, smooth skin and creamy white flesh.

Left: Maris Bard potatoes
Above: Kerr's pink (left) and Maris Piper (right) potatoes
Right: Romano potatoes

Pentland Dell: A long, oval-shaped potato with a floury texture that tends to disintegrate when boiled. For this reason, it is popular for roasting as the outside becomes soft when parboiled and then crisps up with the fat during roasting.

Romano: The Romano has a distinctive red skin with creamy flesh and is a good all-rounder, similar to Desiree.

Wilja: Introduced from Holland, this is a pale, yellow-fleshed potato with a good, sweet flavor and waxy texture.

Other Varieties

Although most of these varieties are also main crop, they are less widely available than those listed above but are increasingly sold in supermarkets. They are recommended for salads but many are also excellent sautéed or simply boiled.

Cara: A large main crop potato, which is excellent baked or boiled but is a good all-rounder.

Fingerlings: Thumb-sized, long baby potatoes are sometimes called finger potatoes. Among the many varieties are the German Lady's Finger. Since they are new crop potatoes, they need simply be boiled and then served either in salads or with a little butter and a sprinkling of parsley.

La Ratte: A French potato with a smooth skin and waxy yellow flesh. It has a chestnut flavor and is good in salads.

Linzer Delikatess: These small, kidney-shaped potatoes look a little like Jersey Royals but have a pale smooth skin. They do not have much taste and are best in salads where their flavor can be enhanced with other ingredients.

Pink Fir Apple: This is an old English variety, with pink skin and a smooth yellow flesh. It is becoming increasingly popular and has a distinctive flavor.

Above left: Cara (left) and Yukon Gold (right) potatoes
Left: Linzer Delikatess potatoes
Above: Desiree (left) and King Edward (right) potatoes
Right: Fingerlings

Blue: If you want to startle your friends, serve some of these striking purple-blue potatoes. There are several varieties of blue potato, ranging from a pale lavender to a wonderful deep purple. They have a dense texture, which makes them good for boiling. They are best served simply with a little butter and do retain their color when cooked.

Truffe de Chine: Another deep purple, almost black potato, of unknown origin but now grown in France. It has a nutty, slightly mealy flavor and is best served in a salad with a simple dressing. Like the Blue Potato, it retains its color after being cooked.

Recommended Varieties for Cooking

Baking: As for roasting, use potatoes with a floury texture, such as Idaho, Pentland Dell, King Edward and Maris Piper.

Boiling: Jersey Royal, Maris Bard and Maris Peer, or any of the Egyptian or Belgian new crop varieties. In addition, Pink Fir Apple, La Ratte and Linzer Delikatess are excellent.

Frying: King Edward, Idaho, Romano, Maris Piper and Desiree.

Mashing: Idaho, Maris Piper, King Edward, Wilja, Romano and Pentland Dell and Yukon Gold.

Roasting: Pentland Dell, Idaho, Maris Piper, King Edward, Desiree and Romano are among the best roasting potatoes. Ideally, use potatoes with a floury texture.

Salads: All the small, specialist potatoes, such as La Ratte, Pink Fir Apple and Linzer Delikatess as well as Fingerlings and small new potatoes.

Sautéing: Any waxy type of potato, such as Maris Bard, Maris Peer, any of the

specialist potatoes, and Romano and Maris Piper.

Buying and Storing

Potatoes should always be stored in a dark, cool, dry place. If they are stored exposed to the light, green patches will develop which can be poisonous, and they will go moldy if kept in the damp. When buying potatoes in bulk, it is best to buy them in paper sacks rather than plastic bags as humid conditions will cause them to go rotten. Similarly, if you buy potatoes in plastic bags, remove them when you get home and place them in a vegetable rack or in a paper bag, in a dark place.

Main crop potatoes will keep for several months in the right conditions but will gradually lose their nutritional value. New potatoes should be eaten within two or three days as they will go moldy if stored for too long.

Preparing

Most of the minerals and vitamins contained in potatoes are contained in or just below the skin. It is therefore better to eat potatoes in their skins. New potatoes need only be washed under running water; older potatoes need to be scrubbed.

If you peel potatoes, use a peeler that removes only the very top surface (*below left*) or, alternately, for salads and cold dishes, boil the potatoes in their skins and peel when cool.

Cooking

Baking: Cook baked potatoes in a low oven for well-browned and crunchy skins and fluffy flesh. Baked potatoes can be cooked more quickly in a microwave oven; for a crunchy texture to the skin place them in a hot oven for 10 minutes.

Boiling: It is impossible to generalize on how long to boil as it depends so much on the variety of potato. Try to cut potatoes to an even size (new potatoes should not need to be cut), salt the water if liked, cover and cook over a moderate heat. Don't boil potatoes too fiercely; old ones especially may disintegrate and leave you with a pan of starchy water.

French fries: Home-cooked French fries are a treat worth occasionally giving the family instead of the convenient but otherwise disappointing oven fries. However, they are fatty and therefore not good for you when eaten in great quantities or too often.

To make them, cut the potatoes into even-size pieces and place in a bowl of cold water for about 10 minutes before frying. Drain and then dry in a piece of muslin or an old dish towel before frying. Fry only as many pieces as will comfortably sit in the fat. Halfway through cooking, drain them and allow the oil to come back to temperature before plunging the fries back in. This browns the fries and they don't soak up excessive amounts of oil. Be warned; the cooking smells from making fries tend to linger!

Mashing: Boil the potatoes until tender, drain thoroughly and then tip them back into the pan; mash with a little milk and butter using a potato masher (*below right*), and season to taste with a little salt, if necessary, and pepper. Never use a food processor or blender: the potatoes will turn into an inedible thick gray paste. You may lightly whisk potatoes with a fork after mashing to fluff them up, but no more – for once modern machines have not improved on the basic utensil.

Roast Potatoes: The best roast potatoes are made using a floury textured potato such as Maris Piper or King Edward. Wash and cut them into even-size chunks and parboil them in lightly salted water until they begin to go tender and the outside looks soft. Drain them through a strainer or colander and then tip them back into the saucepan, put the lid on and shake the pan two or three times. This roughens up the surface of the potato. Place the potatoes in a dish of hot oil or fat, or around a joint of meat, and turn them over so that they are evenly coated. Roast them in the oven for 40-50 minutes until golden. Serve as soon as possible once cooked as the outsides become leathery if they are kept in a warm oven for too long.

Sautéing: There are various ways to sauté potatoes and no one way is better than another. For sautéed sliced potatoes, parboil whole potatoes for 5-10 minutes until they begin to soften. Drain them thoroughly and then slice into thick rounds. Using sunflower oil or a mixture of sunflower and olive oil (not butter as it will burn), fry them in a large frying pan. Turn the potatoes occasionally and cook until evenly browned. For sautéed, diced potatoes, cut the potatoes into small cubes, blanch for 2 minutes and then drain well. Either fry them on the stove or cook them in a little oil in the oven; turn them once or twice to brown evenly.

Steaming: New potatoes are excellent steamed. Place them on a bed of mint in a steamer or a colander over a pan of boiling water for 15-20 minutes.

Above left: Blue potatoes
Below left: Truffe de Chine (left) and Pink Fir Apple (right) potatoes

PARSNIPS

There's something very old-fashioned about parsnips. They conjure up images of cold winter evenings and warm comforting broths supped in front of a blazing wood fire. Nowadays parsnips are available all year through, but many people still feel they belong to winter, adding their characteristic flavor to soups and stews.

Parsnips are related to carrots, similarly sweet but with a distinct earthy flavor that blends well with other root vegetables and is also enhanced with spices and garlic.

History

Parsnips have a long history. The Romans grew and cooked them to make broths and stews. When they conquered Gaul and Britain, the Romans discovered that root vegetables grown in northerly areas had a better flavor than those grown in the south – they may have been the first to decree that parsnips should be eaten after the first frost!

Throughout the Dark Ages and early Middle Ages, parsnips were the main starchy vegetable for ordinary people (the potato had yet to be introduced). Parsnips were not only easy to grow but were a welcome food to eat during the lean winter months. They were also valued for their sugar content. Sweet parsnip dishes like jam and desserts became part of traditional English cooking, and they were also commonly used for making beer and wine. Parsnip wine is still one of the most popular of the country wines, with a beautiful golden color and a rich sherry-like flavor.

Nutrition

Parsnips contain moderate amounts of vitamins A and C, along with some of the B vitamins. They are also a source of calcium, iron and potassium.

Buying and Storing

Parsnips are really a winter crop, although nowadays they are available all year through. Tradition has it that parsnips are best after the first frost, but many people like the very young tender parsnips available in the early summer. When buying parsnips, choose small or

medium-size specimens as the large ones tend to be rather fibrous. They should feel firm and be a pale ivory color without any sprouting roots. Store parsnips in a cool place, ideally an airy larder or cool outhouse, where they will keep well for 8–10 days.

Preparing

Very small parsnips need little or no peeling; just trim the ends and cook according to your recipe. Medium-size and large parsnips must be peeled. Larger parsnips also must have the woody core removed; if it is cut out before cooking, the parsnips will cook more quickly and evenly.

Cooking

Roast parsnips are best parboiled for a few minutes before adding to the roasting dish. Very young parsnips can be roasted whole but larger ones are best halved or quartered lengthwise. Roast in butter or oil for about 40 minutes in an oven preheated to 400°F .

To boil parsnips, cut them into pieces about 2 inches long and boil for 15-20 minutes until tender. When boiled briefly like this, they keep their shape, but when added to a casserole or stew they eventually disintegrate. Don't worry if this happens; parsnips need plenty of cooking so that the flavor can blend with the other ingredients.

JERUSALEM ARTICHOKES

Jerusalem artichokes are related to the sunflower and have nothing to do with Jerusalem. One explanation for their name is that they were christened girasole, "Jerusalem," because their yellow flowers turned toward the sun. The Italian name for the Jerusalem artichoke is *girasole articocco*.

These small knobbly tubers have a lovely distinct flavor and are good in Palestine soup, a popular classic recipe. They are also delicious baked or braised.

History

Jerusalem artichokes are thought to have come from the central United States and Canada, where they were cultivated by the Native Americans as long ago as the fifteenth century. However, many writers have alluded to the fact that they cause "wind," which tempers their popularity.

Buying and Storing

Jerusalem artichokes are at their best during winter and early spring. They are invariably knobbly, but if possible buy neat ones with the minimum of knobs to save waste. The skins should be pale brown without any dark or soft patches. If they are stored in a cool dark place they will keep well for up to 10 days.

Preparing

The white flesh of artichokes turns purplish brown when exposed to light, so when peeling or slicing them raw, place them in a bowl of acidulated water (water to which the juice of about half a lemon has been added). Because artichokes are so knobbly, it is often easier to boil them in acidulated water in their skins and peel them afterward – the cooked skins should slip off easily.

Cooking

Jerusalem artichokes can be cooked in many of the ways in which you would cook potatoes or parsnips. They are excellent roasted, sautéed or dipped in batter and fried, but first parboil them for 10-15 minutes until nearly tender. For creamed artichokes, mix with potatoes in equal amounts; this slightly blunts their flavor, making a tasty side dish which is not too overpowering.

Left: Parsnips
Below: Jerusalem artichokes

TURNIPS AND RUTABAGAS

Turnips and rutabagas are both members of the cabbage family and are closely related to each other – so close that it is not surprising that their names are often confused. For instance, rutabagas are sometimes called Swedish turnips or swede-turnips and in Scotland, where they are thought of as turnips, they are called neeps.

Nowadays, the confusion is not so acute. Many grocers and supermarkets sell early or baby turnips or, better still, French turnips – *navets*.

Both are small and white, tinged either with green or in the case of *navets*, with pink or purple. Consequently, people are learning to tell their rutabagas from their turnips and also discovering what a delicious vegetable the turnip is.

History

Turnips have been cultivated for centuries, principally as an important livestock feed but also for humans. Although they were not considered the food of gourmets, they have been grown by poorer families as a useful addition to the winter table.

Rutabagas were known as turnip-rooted cabbages until the 1780s, when Sweden began exporting the vegetable to Britain and the shorter name resulted.

Until recently, turnips and rutabagas have not enjoyed a very high reputation among cooks in many parts of the world. This is partly because they are perceived as cattle food and partly because few people have taken the trouble to find acceptable ways of cooking them.

Many cooks tend to boil and then mash them to a watery pulp, and for many people this is the only way they have eaten either vegetable.

The French, in contrast, have had far more respect for the turnip, at least. For centuries they have devised recipes for their delicate *navets*, roasting them, caramelizing them in sugar and butter or simply steaming and serving with butter. Young, tender turnips have also been popular all over the Mediterranean region for many years, and there are many dishes using turnips with fish, poultry, or teamed with tomatoes, onions and spinach.

Nutrition

Both turnips and rutabagas are a good source of calcium and potassium.

Varieties

French *navets*, small round, squash-shaped turnips tinged with pink or purple, are increasingly available in grocers and supermarkets in the spring. Less common, but even more prized by the French, are the long carrot-shaped turnips, called *vertus*. English turnips are generally larger and are mainly green and white. Both have the characteristic peppery flavor, but this is less pronounced in *navets* which are generally sweeter.

Rutabagas generally have a more sub-stantial, fuller-bodied flavor than turnips but at their best have a subtle, pleasant taste. The Marian is a yellow fleshed variety with a distinct "rutabaga" flavor. White-fleshed swedes, like Merrick, have a more watery, turnip-like flavor.

Buying and Storing

Turnips: If possible, buy French *navets* or failing that, the smallest and youngest turnips, available in stores from spring. They should be firm, smooth and unblemished, ideally with fresh green tops. Store in a cool dry place.

Rutabagas: Unlike turnips, rutabagas generally seem to come large. However, if possible, choose small rutabagas with smooth and unblemished skins as large ones are likely to be tough and fibrous. Store as for turnips.

Preparing and Cooking

Turnips: Young turnips should not require peeling; simply trim, then simmer or steam until tender. They are delicious raw, thinly sliced or grated into salads.

Peel older turnips (*below*) and then slice or dice before cooking. Remember, turnips are members of the cabbage family and older specimens particularly can show signs of that unpleasant cabbage rankness if overcooked. To avoid this, blanch turnips if they are to be served as a vegetable dish, or add sparingly to soups and casseroles, so that the rank flavor is dispersed.

Rutabagas: Peel to remove the skin and then cut into chunks (*below*). Rutabagas will disintegrate if overcooked, and they are unpleasantly raw tasting if not cooked sufficiently. The only answer is to check frequently while they are cooking. Rutabagas are particularly good when teamed with other root vegetables in soups and casseroles, adding a pleasant, slightly nutty flavor.

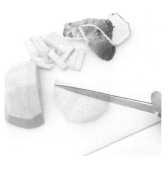

Far left: Navets and turnips
Below: Rutabagas

CARROTS

After potatoes, carrots are without doubt our best-known and best-loved root vegetable. In the days when vegetables were served merely as an accessory to meat, carrots always made an appearance – often overcooked but still eaten up because, we were told, they helped you to see in the dark.

Carrots have many different flavors, depending on how they are cooked. Young, new season carrots braised in butter and a splash of water are intensely flavored and sweet; when steamed, they are tender and melting. Carrots grated into salads are fresh and clean tasting, while in casseroles they are savory with the characteristic carrot flavor. In soups they are fragrant and mild, and in cakes their flavor can hardly be detected, yet their sweetness adds richness.

History

Until the Middle Ages, carrots were purple. The orange carrots came from Holland, from where they were exported in the seventeenth and eighteenth centuries. Although purple and white carrots continued to be eaten in France, nowadays they are something of a rarity.

Nutrition

Carrots contain large amounts of carotene and vitamin A, along with useful amounts of vitamins B3, C and E. When eaten raw, they also provide good quantities of potassium, calcium, iron and zinc, but these are reduced when carrots are boiled.

The idea that carrots are good for your night sight originated in the Second World War. Early radar stations were established along the south and east coasts of England in 1939 to detect aggressors in the air or at sea. The Germans attributed this sudden remarkable night vision to the British habit of eating carrots. Indeed, the vitamin A in carrots forms retinal, a lack of which brings on night blindness.

Buying and Storing

Home-grown carrots are so much nicer than shop bought ones. Almost all vegetables have a better flavor if grown organically, but this is particularly true of carrots.

When buying carrots, look out for the very young, pencil-thin ones, which are beautifully tender either eaten raw or steamed for just a few minutes. Young carrots are commonly sold with their feathery tops intact, which should be fresh and green. Older carrots should be firm and unblemished. Avoid tired looking carrots as they will have little nutritional value.

Carrots should not be stored for too long. They will keep for several days if stored in a cool, airy place or in the salad drawer of the fridge.

Preparing

Preparation depends on the age of the carrots. The valuable nutrients lie either in or just beneath the skin, so if the carrots are young, simply wash them under cold running water. Medium-size carrots may need to be scraped and large carrots will need either scraping or peeling.

Cooking

Carrots are excellent cooked or raw. Children often like raw carrots as they have a very sweet flavor. They can be cut into julienne strips, with a dressing added, or grated into salads and coleslaw – their juices run and blend wonderfully with the dressing. Carrots can be cooked in almost any way you choose. As an accompaniment, cut them into julienne strips and braise in butter and cider, or cook in the minimum of stock and toss in butter and a sprinkling of caraway seeds.

Roasted carrots are delicious, with a melt-in-the-mouth sweetness. Parboil large ones first, but younger carrots can be quickly blanched or added directly to the pan with a joint of meat.

HORSERADISH

Horseradish is grown for its pungent root, which is normally grated and mixed with cream or oil and vinegar and served with roast beef. Fresh horseradish is available in many supermarkets in the spring, and you can make your own horseradish sauce by simply peeling the root and then mixing 3 tablespoons of grated horseradish with $^2/_3$ cup heavy or whipping cream and adding a little Dijon mustard, vinegar and sugar to taste. As well as being excellent with hot or cold beef, horseradish sauce is delicious with smoked trout or mackerel or spread thinly on sandwiches with a fine pâté.

Left: Carrots
Right: Horseradish

BEETS

Experience of vinegar-sodden beets has doubtlessly put many people off them. Those who love them know to buy their beets fresh, so that they can cook them themselves. They can be served in a number of different ways: baked and served with sour cream, braised in a creamy sauce, grated in a salad or used for the classic soup *borscht*.

History

Beets are closely related to sugar beets and mangelwurzels. As the demand for sugar increased over the centuries, when sugar could successfully be extracted from beets, sugar production became a big industry in Britain and Europe.

Mangelwurzels were eaten in parts of Europe and in England in times of famine, although they were primarily grown as cattle fodder.

Beets, however, have probably been eaten since Roman times. By the mid-nineteenth century they were clearly a popular vegetable, and Mrs Beeton in her famous cookbook has 11 recipes for them, including a beet and carrot jam and beet fritters.

Nutrition

Beets are an excellent provider of potassium. The leaves, which have the flavor of spinach, are high in vitamin A, iron and calcium.

Buying and Storing

If possible, buy small beets which have their whiskers intact and have at least 2 inches of stalk at the top; if they are too closely cropped they will bleed during cooking. Beets will keep for several weeks if stored in a cool place.

Preparing

To cook beets whole, first rinse under cold running water. Cut the stalks to about 1 inch above the root and don't cut away the root or peel it – or the glorious deep red color will bleed away. When serving cold in salads, or where the recipe calls for chopped or grated beets, peel away the skin with a potato peeler or sharp knife.

Cooking

To bake in the oven, place the cleaned beet in a dish with a tight-fitting lid, and add 4-5 tablespoons of water. Lay a double layer of foil over the dish before covering with the lid, then bake in a low oven for 2-3 hours or until the beets are tender. Check occasionally to ensure the pan doesn't dry out and to see whether the beets are cooked. They are ready when the skin begins to wrinkle and can be easily rubbed away with your fingers. Alternately, simply wrap the beets in a double layer of foil and cook as above. To boil beets, prepare as above and simmer for about 1 1/2 hours.

BEET GREENS

The tops of several root vegetables are not only edible, but are also extremely nutritious. Beet greens are particularly good, being very high in vitamins A and C, and indeed have more iron and calcium than spinach itself. They are delicious, but not easily available unless you grow your own. If you are lucky enough to get some, boil the greens for a few minutes, then drain well and serve with butter or olive oil.

Left: Beets
Above right: Scorzonera
Below right: Salsify

SALSIFY AND SCORZONERA

These two root vegetables are closely related to each other as well as to members of the same family as dandelion and lettuce. All have long tapering roots.

Salsify has a white or pale brownish skin and scorzonera, sometimes called black salsify, has a black skin. They both have a pale creamy flesh and a fairly similar flavor reminiscent of artichokes and asparagus. Salsify is said to have the superior flavor and has been likened to oysters (it is sometimes referred to as the oyster plant), although many people fail to detect this.

Both salsify and scorzonera make an unusual and pleasant accompaniment, either creamed or fried in butter. They can also be also used in soups.

History

Salsify is native to the Mediterranean but now grows in most areas of North America and Europe. Scorzonera is a southern European plant.

Both roots are classified as herbs and, like many wild plants and herbs, their history is bound up with their use in medicines. The roots, together with their leaves and flowers, were used for the treatment of heartburn, loss of appetite and various liver diseases.

Buying and Storing

Choose specimens that are firm and smooth and, if possible, still with their tops on, which should look fresh and lively. Salsify will keep for several days stored in a cool dark place.

Preparing

Salsify and scorzonera are difficult to clean and peel. Either scrub the root under cold running water and then peel after cooking, or peel with a sharp stainless steel knife (*below*). As the flesh discolors quickly, place the trimmed pieces into acidulated water (water to which lemon juice has been added).

Cooking

Cut into short lengths and simmer for 20–30 minutes until tender. Drain well and sauté in butter, or serve with lemon juice, melted butter or chopped parsley.

Alternately, they can be puréed for soups or mashed. Cooked and cooled salsify and scorzonera can be served in a mustard or garlic vinaigrette with a simple salad.

EXOTIC ROOTS

Throughout the tropical regions of the world all sorts of tubers are grown and used for a fabulous variety of dishes. Yams, sweet potatoes, cassava and taro, to name but a few, are for many people a staple food, not only cooked whole as a vegetable accompaniment, but ground or pounded for bread and cakes. There is an enormous variety of these tropical and subtropical tubers, and while they cannot be cultivated in a moderate climate, the more common tubers are now widely available in specialist shops and in most supermarkets.

SWEET POTATOES

Sweet potatoes are another one of those vegetables that once tasted, are never forgotten. They are, as the name suggests, sweet, but they also have a slightly spicy taste. It's this distinct sweet and savory flavor which makes them such an excellent foil to many savory

dishes and they are fittingly paired with meat dishes that need a touch of sweetness, like turkey or pork.

History

Sweet potatoes are native to tropical America, but today they are grown all over the tropical world. They have been grown in South America from before the Inca civilizations and were introduced into Spain before the ordinary potato. They also have a long history of cultivation in Asia spreading from Polynesia to New Zealand in the fourteenth century.

They are an important staple food in the Caribbean and southern United States, and many famous recipes feature these vegetables. Candied sweet potatoes, for instance, are traditionally served with ham or turkey at Thanksgiving all over the United States, while Jamaica and the West Indies abound with sweet

potato dishes, from the simple baked potato to Caribbean pudding, a typically sweet and spicy dish with sweet potatoes, coconut, limes and cinnamon.

Sweet potatoes appear to have been introduced to England even earlier than regular potatoes. Henry VIII was said to have been very partial to them baked in a pie, believing they would improve his love life! If Henry VIII was eating sweet potatoes in the early/mid-sixteenth century, then it's likely he received them via the Spanish, who, thanks to Christopher Columbus, were busy conquering the New World, thus experiencing a whole range of tropical vegetables and fruit.

Varieties

The skin color ranges from white to pink to reddish brown. The red-skinned variety, which has a whitish flesh, is the one most commonly used in African and Caribbean cooking.

Buying and Storing

Choose small or medium-size ones if possible as larger specimens tend to be rather fibrous. They should be firm and evenly shaped; avoid those that seem withered, have damp patches or are sprouting. They will keep for several days in a cool place.

Preparing and Cooking

If baking, scrub the potatoes well and cook exactly as you would for ordinary potatoes. To boil, either cook in their skins and remove these after cooking, or peel and place in acidulated water (water to which lemon juice has been added). This prevents them turning brown and it's worth boiling them in lightly acidulated water for the same reason. Sweet potatoes can be cooked in any of the ways you would cook ordinary potatoes – roast, boiled, mashed or baked. However, avoid using them in creamy or gratin-type dishes. They are both too sweet and too spicy for that.

It is preferable to roast or sauté them with onions and other savory ingredients to bring out their flavor, or mash them and serve them over chunks of chicken for a crusted chicken pie.

Preparing

Peel away the skin thickly to remove the outer skin and the layer underneath that contains the poison dioscorine. This in fact is destroyed during cooking, but discard the peel carefully. Place the peeled yam in salted water because it discolors easily.

Cooking

Yams, like potatoes, are used as the main starchy element in a meal, boiled and mashed, fried, sautéed or roasted. They tend to have an affinity with spicy sauces and are delicious cut into discs, fried and sprinkled with a little salt and cayenne pepper. African cooks frequently pound boiled yam to make a dough which is then served with spicy stews and soups.

TARO/EDDO

Like yams, taro is another hugely important tuber in tropical areas, and for thousands of years it has been a staple food for many people. It goes under many different names; in South-east Asia, South and Central America, all over Africa and in the Caribbean it is called variously eddo and dasheen.

There are two basic varieties of taro – a large barrel-shaped tuber and a smaller variety, which is often called eddo or dasheen. They are all a dark mahogany brown with a rather shaggy skin, looking like a cross between a beet and a rutabaga.

Although they look very similar, taro belongs to a completely different family from yam and in flavor and texture is noticeably different. Boiled, it has a completely unique flavor, something like a floury water chestnut.

Buying and Storing

Try to buy small specimens; the really small smooth bulbs are tiny attachments to the larger taro and are either called eddoes, or rather sweetly, "sons of taro." Stored in a cool, dark place, they should keep for several weeks.

Left: Sweet potatoes
Above: Yams

YAMS

Yams have been a staple food for many cultures for thousands of years. There are today almost countless varieties, of different shapes, sizes and colors and called different names by different people. Most varieties are thought to have been native to China, although they found their way to Africa during a very early period and became a basic food, being easy to grow in tropical and subtropical conditions, and containing the essential carbohydrate of all staple foods.

Although cush-cush or Indian yam was indigenous to America, most yams were introduced to the New World as a result of the slave trade in the sixteenth century. Today with such a huge variety of this popular vegetable available, there are innumerable recipes for yam, many probably not printed and published, but handed down by word of mouth from mother to daughter and making their appearance at mealtimes all over the hot regions of the world.

Varieties

The greater yam, as the name suggests, can grow to a huge size. A weight of 137 pounds has been recorded. The varieties you are likely to find in stores will be about the size of a small marrow, although smaller yams are also available such as the sweet yam, which looks like a large potato and is normally covered with whiskery roots. All sizes have a coarse brown skin and can be white or red-fleshed.

In Chinese stores, you may find the Chinese yam, which is a more elongated, club-like shape and is covered with fine whiskers.

Buying

Look out for firm specimens with unbroken skins. The flesh inside should be creamy and moist and if you buy from a grocery, the storekeeper may well cut open a yam so you can check that it is fresh. They can be stored for several weeks in a cool, dark place.

Preparing

Taros, like yams, contain a poison just under the skin which produces an allergic reaction. Consequently, either peel taros thickly, wearing rubber gloves, or cook in their skins. The toxins are completely eliminated by boiling, and the skins peel off easily.

Cooking

Taros soak up large quantities of liquid during cooking, and this can be turned to advantage by cooking in well-flavored stock or with tomatoes and other vegetables. For this reason, they are excellent in soups and casseroles, adding bulk and flavor in a similar way to potatoes. They can also be steamed or boiled, deep-fried or puréed for fritters, but must be served hot as they become sticky if allowed to cool.

CALLALOO

Callaloo are the leaves of the taro plant, poisonous if eaten raw, but used widely in Asian and Caribbean recipes. They are cooked thoroughly, then used for wrapping meat and vegetables. Callaloo can also be shredded and cooked together with pork, bacon, crab, shrimp, okra, chili, onions and garlic, together with lime and coconut milk to make one of the Caribbean's most famous dishes, named after the leaves themselves, Callaloo.

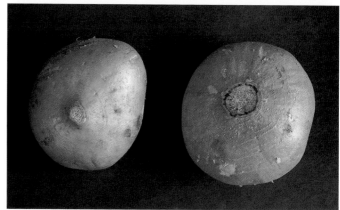

JICAMA

Also known as the Mexican potato, this large root vegetable is a native of central America. It has a thin brown skin and white, crunchy flesh which has a sweet, nutty taste. It can be eaten cooked in the same way as potatoes or sliced and added raw to salads.

Buy specimens that are firm to the touch. Jicama in good condition will keep for about two weeks if stored in a plastic bag in the refrigerator.

Top: Taros (eddoes)
Above: Jicama
Left: Callaloo

CASSAVA

This is another very popular West Indian root, used in numerous Caribbean dishes. It is native to Brazil, and found its way to the West Indies surprisingly via Africa, where it also became a popular vegetable. Known as cassava in the West Indies, it is called manioc or mandioc in Brazil, and juca or yucca is used in other parts of South America.

Cassava is used to make tapioca, and in South America a sauce and an intoxicating beverage are prepared from the juice. However, in Africa and the West Indies it is eaten as a vegetable either boiled, baked or fried, or cooked and pounded to a dough to make *fufu*, a traditional savory African pudding.

Right: Cassava
Below left: Ginger
Below right: Galangal

GINGER AND GALANGAL

GINGER

This is probably the world's most important and popular spice and is associated with a number of different cuisines – Chinese, Indian and Caribbean, to name but a few. It was known in Europe during the Roman period, but was still fairly rare until the spice routes opened up trade in the sixteenth and seventeenth centuries. Like many spices, ginger has the quality of enhancing and complementing both sweet and savory food, adding a fragrant spiciness to all sorts of dishes. However, while ground ginger is best in recipes which will be baked, and preserved ginger, where the ginger is preserved in syrup, tastes wonderful in desserts, for savory dishes, always use fresh ginger.

Nowadays, the pale, knobbly roots of fresh ginger are widely available in supermarkets and whenever possible, buy just a small quantity, as you will not need a great deal and fresh ginger will not keep indefinitely.

To prepare, simply peel away the skin with a sharp knife and grate or thinly slice according to the recipe.

GREATER GALANGAL

Galangal looks similar to ginger except that the rhizome is thinner and the young shoots are bright pink. The roots should be prepared as for ginger and can be used in curries and satay sauces.

ROOTS RECIPES

For tasty, nourishing meals, you don't need to look further than roots, whether it is carrots, beets or the ever popular potato. Potatoes Dauphinois or Artichoke Rösti are the stuff of winter evenings — warm and filling, simple to make, great to eat. For something with a more exotic flavor, try Yam Fritters or Mediterranean Chicken with Turnips.

PATATAS BRAVAS

THIS IS A CLASSIC SPANISH TAPAS DISH OF DEEP-FRIED CUBES OF POTATO WITH A SPICY TOMATO SAUCE. SERVING TAPAS IS A GOOD WAY OF PROVIDING YOUR GUESTS WITH A WONDERFUL RANGE OF FLAVORS AND TEXTURES.

SERVES FOUR

INGREDIENTS
  1½ pounds potatoes
  oil, for deep frying
For the sauce
  1 tablespoon olive oil
  1 small onion, chopped
  1 garlic clove, crushed
  14 ounce can tomatoes
  2 teaspoons Worcestershire
    sauce
  1 teaspoon wine vinegar
  about 1 teaspoon Tabasco sauce

1 Peel and cut the potatoes into small cubes and place in a large bowl of cold water to remove the excess starch.

2 Heat the oil in a medium-size frying pan and fry the onion and garlic for 3–4 minutes until the onion is soft and just beginning to brown.

3 Pour the tomatoes into a blender or food processor, process until smooth and then pour into the pan with the onion. Simmer, uncovered, over moderate heat for 8–10 minutes until the mixture is thick and reduced, stirring occasionally.

4 Heat the oil in a deep-fryer. Drain the potatoes and pat dry with paper towels. Fry the potatoes in the hot oil, in batches if necessary, until golden brown. Drain on paper towels.

5 Stir the Worcestershire sauce, vinegar and Tabasco sauce into the tomato mixture. Add the potatoes, stirring well so that all the potatoes are coated with the sauce. Spoon into individual serving dishes and serve at once.

POTATOES DAUPHINOIS

SERVES FOUR

INGREDIENTS
  1½ pounds potatoes, peeled and thinly
    sliced
  1 garlic clove
  1 ounce butter
  1¼ cups light cream
  ¼ cup milk
  salt and white pepper

1 Preheat the oven to 300°F. Place the potato slices in a bowl of cold water to remove the excess starch. Drain and pat dry with paper towels.

2 Cut the garlic in half and rub the cut side around the inside of a wide shallow ovenproof dish. Butter the dish generously. Blend the cream and milk in a jug.

3 Cover the bottom of the dish with a layer of potatoes. Dot a little butter over the potato layer, season with salt and pepper and then pour over a little of the cream and milk mixture.

4 Continue making layers, until all the ingredients have been used up, ending with a layer of cream.

5 Bake in the oven for about 1¼ hours. If the dish browns too quickly and seems to be drying out, cover with a lid or with a piece of foil. The potatoes are ready when they are very soft and the top is pale golden brown.

COOK'S TIP
For a slightly speedier version of this recipe, parboil the potato slices for 3–4 minutes. Drain well and assemble as above. Cook at 325°F for 45–50 minutes until potatoes are completely tender.

PARSNIP <u>AND</u> CHESTNUT CROQUETTES

THE SWEET NUTTY TASTE OF CHESTNUTS BLENDS PERFECTLY WITH THE SIMILARLY SWEET BUT EARTHY FLAVOR OF PARSNIPS. FRESH CHESTNUTS NEED TO BE PEELED BUT FROZEN CHESTNUTS ARE EASY TO USE AND ARE NEARLY AS GOOD AS FRESH FOR THIS RECIPE.

MAKES TEN TO TWELVE

INGREDIENTS
  1 pound parsnips, cut roughly into
    small pieces
  4 ounces frozen chestnuts
  1 ounce butter
  1 garlic clove, crushed
  1 tablespoon chopped fresh cilantro
  1 egg, beaten
  1½–2 ounces fresh white bread
    crumbs
  vegetable oil, for frying
  salt and freshly ground black pepper
  sprig of cilantro, to garnish

1 Place the parsnips in a saucepan with enough water to cover. Bring to a boil, cover and simmer for 15–20 minutes until completely tender.

2 Place the frozen chestnuts in a pan of water, bring to a boil and simmer for 8–10 minutes until very tender. Drain, place in a bowl and mash roughly.

3 Melt the butter in a small saucepan and cook the garlic for 30 seconds. Drain the parsnips and mash with the garlic butter. Stir in the chestnuts, chopped cilantro and season well.

4 Take about 1 tablespoon of mixture at a time and form into small croquettes, about 3 inches long. Dip each croquette into the beaten egg and then roll in the bread crumbs.

5 Heat a little oil in a frying pan and fry the croquettes for 3–4 minutes until golden, turning frequently so they brown evenly. Drain on paper towels and then serve at once, garnished with cilantro.

PARSNIP, EGGPLANT AND CASHEW BIRYANI

SERVES FOUR TO SIX

INGREDIENTS
 1 small eggplant, sliced
 10 ounces basmati rice
 3 parsnips
 3 onions
 2 garlic cloves
 1-inch piece fresh ginger, peeled
 about 4 tablespoons vegetable oil
 6 ounces unsalted cashew nuts
 1½ ounces golden raisins
 1 red bell pepper, seeded and sliced
 1 teaspoon ground cumin
 1 teaspoon ground coriander
 ½ teaspoon chili powder
 ½ cup plain yogurt
 1¼ cups vegetable or chicken stock
 1 ounce butter
 salt and freshly ground black pepper
 sprigs of cilantro, to garnish
 2 hard-boiled eggs, quartered

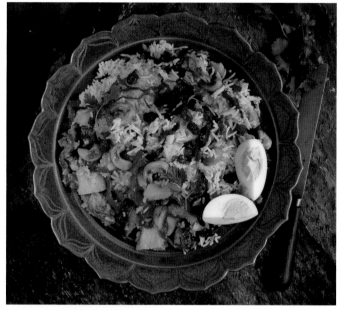

1 Sprinkle the eggplant with salt and leave for 30 minutes. Rinse, pat dry and cut into bite-size pieces. Soak the rice in a bowl of cold water for 40 minutes. Peel and core the parsnips. Cut into ½-inch pieces. Roughly chop 1 onion and put in a food processor or blender with the garlic and ginger. Add 2–3 tablespoons water and process to a paste.

2 Finely slice the remaining onions. Heat 3 tablespoons of the oil in a large flameproof casserole and fry gently for 10–15 minutes until deep golden brown. Remove and drain. Add 1½ ounces of the cashew nuts to the pan, stir-fry for 2 minutes. Add the golden raisins and fry until they swell. Remove and drain.

3 Add the eggplant and pepper to the pan and stir-fry for 4–5 minutes. Drain on paper towels. Fry the parsnips for 4–5 minutes. Stir in the remaining cashew nuts and fry for 1 minute. Transfer to the plate with the eggplants.

4 Add the remaining 1 tablespoon of oil to the pan. Add the onion paste. Cook, stirring over moderate heat for 4–5 minutes until the mixture turns golden. Stir in the cumin, cilantro and chili powder. Cook, stirring, for 1 minute, then reduce the heat and add the yogurt.

5 Bring the mixture slowly to a boil and stir in the stock, parsnips, eggplant and peppers. Season, cover and simmer for 30–40 minutes until the parsnips are tender and then transfer to an ovenproof casserole.

6 Preheat the oven to 300°F. Drain the rice and add to 1¼ cups of salted boiling water. Cook gently for 5–6 minutes until it is tender but slightly undercooked.

7 Drain the rice and pile it in a mound on top of the parsnips. Make a hole from the top to the base using the handle of a wooden spoon. Scatter the reserved fried onions, cashew nuts and golden raisins over the rice and dot with butter. Cover with a double layer of foil and then secure in place with a lid.

8 Cook in the oven for 35–40 minutes. To serve, spoon the mixture onto a warmed serving dish and garnish with cilantro sprigs and quartered eggs.

MEDITERRANEAN CHICKEN WITH TURNIPS

TURNIPS ARE POPULAR IN ALL PARTS OF THE MEDITERREAN, COOKED WITH TOMATOES AND SPINACH IN SIMPLE VEGETARIAN DISHES, OR TEAMED WITH FISH OR POULTRY FOR A MORE SUBSTANTIAL MEAL. THIS RECIPE COMES FROM THE EASTERN MEDITERRANEAN.

SERVES FOUR

INGREDIENTS

2 tablespoons sunflower oil
8 chicken thighs or 4 chicken pieces
4 small turnips
2 onions, chopped
2 garlic cloves, crushed
6 tomatoes, peeled and chopped
1 cup tomato juice
1 cup chicken stock
½ cup white wine
1 teaspoon paprika
good pinch of cayenne pepper
20 black olives, pitted
½ lemon, cut into wedges
salt and freshly ground black pepper
fresh parsley, to garnish
couscous, to serve

1 Preheat the oven to 325°F. Heat 1 tablespoon of the oil in a large frying pan and fry the chicken pieces until lightly browned. Peel the turnips and cut into julienne strips.

2 Transfer the chicken to a large casserole. Add the remaining oil to the pan and fry the onions and garlic for 4–5 minutes until lightly golden brown, stirring occasionally.

3 Add the turnip and stir-fry for about 2–3 minutes. Add the tomatoes, tomato juice, stock, wine, paprika, cayenne and seasoning. Bring to a boil. Pour over the chicken. Stir in the olives and lemon.

4 Cover tightly and cook in the oven for 1–1¼ hours until the chicken is tender.

5 Garnish with fresh parsley and serve on a bed of couscous.

RUTABAGA CRISPS

TENDER SLICES OF RUTABAGA WITH A CRUNCHY BREADCRUMB COATING PROVIDE A FEAST FOR THE SENSES. THE SLIGHTLY PEPPERY FLAVOR OF RUTABAGA IS COMPLEMENTED BY THE SPICY BREADCRUMB MIXTURE.

SERVES FOUR

INGREDIENTS

1 small rutabaga
2 ounces fresh brown or white
 bread crumbs
1 tablespoon all-purpose flour
½ teaspoon paprika
½ teaspoon ground coriander
½ teaspoon ground cumin
pinch of cayenne pepper
1 egg, beaten
salt and freshly ground black pepper
oil, for deep frying
mango chutney, to serve

3 Heat the oil in a deep fryer or wok and fry the rutabaga discs, in batches if necessary, for 4–5 minutes until golden on the outside and soft inside. Drain on paper towels and serve with mango chutney.

COOK'S TIP
Fry the discs until the rutabaga is tender, so that the crunchiness of the bread-crumb coating contrasts with the soft vegetable.

1 Peel the rutabaga, cut in half and slice thinly. Cook in boiling water for 3–5 minutes until just tender. Drain well.

2 Mix together the bread crumbs, flour, paprika, coriander, cumin, cayenne pepper and seasoning. Dip the rutabaga slices first in the egg and then in the breadcrumb mixture.

GLAZED CARROTS WITH CIDER

THIS RECIPE IS EXTREMELY SIMPLE TO MAKE. THE CARROTS ARE COOKED IN THE MINIMUM OF LIQUID TO BRING OUT THE BEST OF THEIR FLAVOR, AND THE CIDER ADDS A PLEASANT SHARPNESS.

SERVES FOUR

INGREDIENTS
1 pound young carrots
1 ounce butter
1 tablespoon brown sugar
½ cup cider
4 tablespoons vegetable stock or water
1 teaspoon French mustard
1 tablespoon finely chopped fresh
   parsley

1 Trim the tops and bottoms off the carrots. Peel or scrape them. Using a sharp knife cut the carrots into julienne.

2 Melt the butter in a saucepan, add the carrots and sauté for 4–5 minutes, stirring frequently. Sprinkle over the sugar and cook, stirring for 1 minute or until the sugar has dissolved.

3 Add the cider and stock or water, bring to a boil and stir in the French mustard. Partially cover the pan and simmer for about 10–12 minutes until the carrots are just tender. Remove the lid and continue cooking until the liquid has reduced to a thick sauce.

4 Remove the saucepan from the heat, stir in the parsley and then spoon into a warmed serving dish. Serve as an accompaniment to broiled meat or fish or with a vegetarian dish.

COOK'S TIP
If the carrots are cooked before the liquid in the saucepan has reduced, transfer the carrots to a serving dish and rapidly boil the liquid until thick. Pour over the carrots and sprinkle with parsley.

CARROT, APPLE AND ORANGE COLESLAW

THIS DISH IS AS DELICIOUS AS IT IS EASY TO MAKE. THE GARLIC AND HERB DRESSING ADDS THE NECESSARY CONTRAST TO THE SWEETNESS OF THE SALAD.

SERVES FOUR

INGREDIENTS
12 ounces young carrots,
   finely grated
2 eating apples
1 tablespoon lemon juice
1 large orange
For the dressing
3 tablespoons olive oil
4 tablespoons sunflower oil
3 tablespoons lemon juice
1 garlic clove, crushed
4 tablespoons plain yogurt
1 tablespoon chopped mixed fresh
   herbs: tarragon, parsley, chives
salt and freshly ground black pepper

1 Place the carrots in a large serving bowl. Quarter the apples, remove the core and then slice thinly. Sprinkle with the lemon juice to prevent them discoloring and then add to the carrots.

2 Using a sharp knife, remove the peel and pith from the oranges and then separate into segments.

3 To make the dressing, place all the ingredients in a jar with a tight-fitting lid and shake vigorously to blend.

4 Just before serving, pour the dressing over the salad and toss well together.

CARROT AND CILANTRO SOUP

NEARLY ALL ROOT VEGETABLES MAKE EXCELLENT SOUPS AS THEY PURÉE WELL AND HAVE AN EARTHY FLAVOR WHICH COMPLEMENTS THE SHARPER FLAVORS OF HERBS AND SPICES. CARROTS ARE PARTICULARLY VERSATILE AND THIS SIMPLE SOUP IS ELEGANT IN BOTH FLAVOR AND APPEARANCE.

SERVES FOUR TO SIX

INGREDIENTS
  1 pound carrots, preferably young and
    tender
  1 tablespoon sunflower oil
  1½ ounces butter
  1 onion, chopped
  1 celery stalk, sliced plus 2–3 pale
    leafy celery tops
  2 small potatoes, chopped
  4 cups chicken stock
  2–3 teaspoons ground coriander
  1 tablespoon chopped fresh cilantro
  ⅞ cup milk
  salt and freshly ground black pepper

1 Trim the carrots, peel if necessary and cut into chunks. Heat the oil and 1 ounce of the butter in a large flame-proof casserole or heavy-based saucepan and fry the onion over a gentle heat for 3–4 minutes until slightly softened but not browned.

2 Cut the celery stalk into slices. Add the celery and potato to the onion in the pan, cook for a few minutes and then add the carrots. Fry over low heat for 3–4 minutes, stirring frequently, and then cover. Reduce the heat even further and sweat for about 10 minutes. Shake the pan or stir occasionally so the vegetables do not stick to the bottom.

3 Add the stock, bring to a boil and then partially cover and simmer for a further 8–10 minutes until the carrots and pota-to are tender.

4 Remove 6–8 tiny celery leaves for a garnish and finely chop the remaining celery tops (about 1 tablespoon once chopped). Melt the remaining butter in a small saucepan and fry the ground coriander for about 1 minute, stirring constantly.

5 Reduce the heat and add the chopped celery and fresh cilantro and fry for about 1 minute. Set aside.

6 Process the soup in a food processor or blender and pour into a clean saucepan. Stir in the milk, coriander/cilantro mixture and seasoning. Heat gently, taste and adjust the seasoning. Serve garnished with the reserved celery.

COOK'S TIP
For a more piquant flavor, add a little lemon juice just before serving.

PAN-FRIED SWEET POTATOES <u>WITH</u> BACON

THIS IS A COMFORTING DISH TO EAT ON A COLD WINTER'S EVENING. BACON AND ONION COUNTERACT THE SWEETNESS OF THE POTATO, AND THE CAYENNE PEPPER GIVES THE NECESSARY EXTRA "BITE."

SERVES FOUR

INGREDIENTS

1½–2 pounds sweet potatoes
juice of 1 lemon
1 tablespoon all-purpose flour
a good pinch of cayenne pepper
about 3 tablespoons sunflower oil
1 large onion, chopped
4 ounces lean bacon, chopped
2 ounces fresh brown or white bread
  crumbs
salt

1 Peel the sweet potatoes and cut into chunks about 1½ inches square. Place in a pan of boiling water with the lemon juice and a little salt and simmer for 8–10 minutes until cooked but not soft.

2 Mix together the flour, cayenne pepper and a pinch of salt. Drain the potatoes and then dust with the seasoned flour, coating the pieces well.

3 Heat 1 tablespoon of the oil in a large frying pan and fry the onion for about 2 minutes. Add the bacon and fry over low heat for 6–8 minutes until the onion and bacon are golden. Transfer to a plate using a slotted spoon.

4 Add the bread crumbs and fry, stir-ring, for about 1–2 minutes until golden. Add to the plate with the bacon.

5 Heat the remaining oil in the pan and fry the potatoes for 5–6 minutes, turning occasionally, until evenly browned. Stir in the breadcrumb and bacon mixture and cook for 1 minute. Serve at once.

ARTICHOKE RÖSTI

SERVES FOUR TO SIX

INGREDIENTS
1 pound Jerusalem artichokes
juice of 1 lemon
1 pound potatoes
about 2 ounces butter
salt

1 Peel the Jerusalem artichokes and place in a saucepan of water together with the lemon juice and a pinch of salt. Bring to a boil and cook for about 5 minutes until barely tender.

2 Peel the potatoes and place in a separate pan of salted water. Bring to a boil and cook until barely tender – they will take slightly longer than the artichokes.

3 Drain and cool both the artichokes and potatoes, and then grate them into a bowl. Mix them with your fingers, without breaking them up too much.

4 Melt the butter in a large heavy-based frying pan. Add the artichoke mixture, spreading it out with the back of a spoon. Cook gently for about 10 minutes.

5 Invert the "cake" onto a plate and slide back into the pan. Cook for about 10 minutes until golden. Serve at once.

ARTICHOKE TIMBALES WITH SPINACH SAUCE

SERVES SIX

INGREDIENTS
2 pounds Jerusalem artichokes
juice of 1 lemon
1 ounce butter
1 tablespoon oil
1 onion, finely chopped
1 garlic clove, crushed
2 ounces fresh white bread crumbs
1 egg
4–5 tablespoons vegetable stock
   or milk
1 tablespoon chopped fresh parsley
1 teaspoon finely chopped sage
salt and freshly ground black pepper
For the sauce
8 ounces fresh spinach, prepared
½ ounce butter
2 shallots, finely chopped
⅔ cup light cream
¾ cup vegetable stock
salt and freshly ground black pepper

1 Preheat the oven to 350°F. Grease six ⅔-cup ramekin dishes, and then place a circle of wax paper in the bottom of each.

2 Peel the artichokes and put in a saucepan with the lemon juice and water to cover. Bring to a boil and simmer for about 10 minutes until tender. Drain and mash with the butter.

3 Heat the oil in a small frying pan and fry the onion and garlic until soft. Place in a food processor or blender with the bread crumbs, egg, stock, parsley, sage and seasoning. Process to a smooth purée, add the artichokes and process again briefly using the pulse button.

4 Put the mixture in the prepared dishes. Smooth the tops. Cover with wax paper, place in a roasting pan half-filled with boiling water and bake for 35–40 minutes.

5 To make the sauce, cook the spinach without water, in a large covered saucepan, for 2–3 minutes. Shake the pan occasionally. Strain and press out the excess liquid.

6 Melt the butter in a small saucepan and fry the shallots gently until slightly softened but not browned. Place in a food processor or blender and process to make a smooth purée. Pour back into the pan, add the cream and seasoning, and keep warm over very low heat. Do not allow the mixture to boil.

7 Allow the timbales to stand for a few minutes after cooking and then turn out onto warmed serving plates. Spoon the warm sauce over them and serve.

COOK'S TIP
When puréeing the artichokes in a food processor or blender, use the pulse button and process for a very short time. The mixture will become cloying if it is over-processed.

YAM FRITTERS

YAMS HAVE A SLIGHTLY DRIER FLAVOR THAN POTATOES AND ARE PARTICULARLY GOOD WHEN MIXED WITH SPICES AND THEN FRIED. THE FRITTERS CAN ALSO BE MOLDED INTO SMALL BALLS AND DEEP-FRIED. THIS IS A FAVORITE AFRICAN WAY OF SERVING YAMS.

MAKES ABOUT 18–20

INGREDIENTS
    1½ pounds yams
    milk, for mashing
    2 small eggs, beaten
    3 tablespoons chopped tomato flesh
    3 tablespoons finely chopped
       scallions
    1 green chili, seeded and finely sliced
    flour, for shaping
    1½ ounces white bread crumbs
    vegetable oil, for shallow frying
    salt and freshly ground black pepper

1 Peel the yams and cut into chunks. Place in a saucepan of salted water and boil for 20–30 minutes until tender. Drain and mash with a little milk and about 3 tablespoons of the beaten eggs.

2 Add the chopped tomato, scallions, chili and seasoning and stir well.

3 Using floured hands shape the yam and vegetable mixture into round fritters, about 3 inches in diameter.

4 Dip each in the remaining beaten egg and then coat evenly with the bread crumbs. Heat a little oil in a large frying pan and fry the yam fritters for about 4–5 minutes until golden brown. Turn the fritters over once during cooking. Drain well on paper towels and serve.

EDDO, CARROT AND PARSNIP MEDLEY

EDDO (TARO), LIKE YAMS, IS WIDELY EATEN IN AFRICA AND THE CARIBBEAN, OFTEN AS A PURÉE. HERE, IT IS ROASTED AND COMBINED WITH MORE COMMON ROOT VEGETABLES TO MAKE A COLORFUL DISPLAY.

SERVES FOUR TO SIX

INGREDIENTS
    1 pound eddoes or taros
    12 ounces parsnips
    1 pound carrots
    1 ounce butter
    3 tablespoons sunflower oil
For the dressing
    2 tablespoons fresh orange juice
    2 tablespoons brown sugar
    2 teaspoons soft green peppercorns
    salt
    fresh parsley, to garnish

1 Preheat the oven to 400°F. Peel the eddoes and cut into pieces about 2 x ¾ inches, and place in a large bowl.

2 Peel the parsnips, halve lengthwise and remove the inner core if necessary. Cut into the same size pieces as the eddo and add to the bowl. Blanch in boiling water for 2 minutes and then drain. Peel or scrub the carrots, and halve or quarter them according to their size.

3 Place the butter and sunflower oil in a roasting pan and heat in the oven for 3–4 minutes. Add the vegetables, turning them in the oil to coat evenly. Roast in the oven for 30 minutes.

4 Meanwhile, blend the orange juice, sugar and soft green peppercorns in a small bowl. Remove the roasting pan from the oven and allow to cool for a minute or so and then carefully pour the mixture over the vegetables, stirring to coat them all. (If the liquid is poured on immediately, the hot oil will spit.)

5 Return the tin to the oven and cook for a further 20 minutes until the vegetables are crisp and golden. Transfer to a warmed serving plate and sprinkle with salt. Garnish with parsley to serve.

GREENS

Whatever the season, there is something for everyone when it comes to greens. Cauliflowers, kale, broccoli and Brussels sprouts are all members of the cabbage family and like the cabbage itself are among the most nutritious of all vegetables. Spinach too is full of vitamins and minerals and is wonderfully versatile, and if you want to ring the changes, Oriental cabbages, such as Chinese cabbage or pak-choi are widely available and quite delicious.

SPINACH

For many people, spinach is inextricably linked with Popeye, the cartoon character who used to eat huge amounts of spinach. It is a wonderfully versatile vegetable, popular worldwide, with nearly every cuisine featuring spinach somewhere in its repertoire. The Italians are particularly partial to spinach and have hundreds of dishes using the vegetable. The words *à la florentine* mean the dish contains spinach.

As well as being delicious on its own, chopped or puréed spinach can be mixed with a range of other ingredients with superb results. It has a particular affinity with dairy products and in the Middle East, feta or helim cheese is used to make boreks or other spinach pies. The Italians mix spinach with ricotta or Parmesan cheese for a huge range of recipes, and the English use eggs and sometimes Cheddar for a spinach soufflé.

History

Spinach was first cultivated in Persia several thousands of years ago. It came to Europe via the Arab world; the Moors introduced it to Spain, and Arabs in the Middle East took it to Greece. It first appeared in England in the fourteenth century, probably via Spain. It is mentioned in the first known English cookbook, where it is referred to as *spynoches*, which echoes the Spanish word for spinach, *espinacas*. It quickly became a popular vegetable, probably because it is quick and easy to grow and similarly easy and quick to cook.

Nutrition

Spinach is an excellent source of vitamin C if eaten raw, as well as vitamins A and B, calcium, potassium and iron. Spinach was originally thought to provide far more iron than it actually does, but the iron is "bound" up by oxalic acid in cooked spinach, which prevents the body absorbing anything but the smallest amounts. Even so, it is still an extremely healthy vegetable whether eaten cooked or raw.

Buying and Storing

Spinach grows all year through, so you should have no difficulty in buying it fresh. Frozen spinach is a poor substitute, mainly because it has so little flavor, so it is worth the effort to use the fresh product.

Spinach leaves should be green and lively; if they look tired and the stalks are floppy, shop round until you find something in better condition. Spinach reduces significantly when cooked: about 1 pound will serve two people. Store it in the salad drawer of the fridge, where it will keep for 1–2 days.

Preparing

Wash well in a bowl of cold water and remove any tough or large stalks.

Cooking

Throw the leaves into a large pan with just the water that clings to the leaves and place over a low heat with a sprinkling of salt. Cover the pan so the spinach steams in its own liquid and shake the pan occasionally to prevent the spinach sticking to the bottom. It cooks in 4-6 minutes, wilting down to about an eighth of its former volume. Drain and press out the remaining liquid with the back of a spoon.

Spinach can be used in a variety of ways. It can be chopped and served with lots of butter, or similarly served with other spring vegetables such as

BRUSSELS SPROUTS

baby carrots or young fava beans. For frittatas, chop the spinach finely, stir in a little Parmesan cheese, a good sprinkling of salt and pepper and a dash of cream, if liked, and stir into the omelet before cooking. Alternately, purée it for sauces or blend it for soups. Spinach is also delicious raw, served with chopped bacon or croûtons. A fresh spinach salad is delicious as the leaves have just the right balance of flavor – sharp but not overpowering.

Below: Spinach
Below right: Brussels sprouts

Brussels sprouts have a pronounced and sweet nutty flavor, quite unlike cabbage, although the two are closely related. They are traditionally served at Christmas with chestnuts and indeed have a definite affinity for certain nuts – particularly the sweet flavored nuts, e.g. almonds, pair well rather than hazelnuts or walnuts.

History

Brussels sprouts were cultivated in Flanders (now Belgium) during the Middle Ages. They are basically miniature cabbages which grow in a knobbly row on a long tough stalk. The Germans call sprouts *rosenkohl* – rose cabbage – a pretty and descriptive name as they look like small rosebuds.

Buying and Storing

Buy Brussels sprouts as fresh as possible as older ones are more likely to have that strong unpleasant "cabbage" flavor. They should be small and hard with tightly wrapped leaves. Avoid any

that are turning yellow or brown or have loose leaves.

Brussels sprouts will keep for several days in a cool place such as a larder or salad drawer of a fridge, but it is far better to buy them as you need them.

Preparing

Cut away the bottom of the stalk and remove the outer leaves. Some people cut a cross through the bottom of the stalk although this is not really necessary. If you haven't been able to avoid buying big Brussels sprouts, cut them in half or into quarters, or slice them thinly for stir-frying.

Cooking

As with cabbage, either cook Brussels sprouts very briefly or braise slowly in the oven. Cook in small amounts of fast boiling water for about 3 minutes until just tender. To stir-fry Brussels sprouts, slice into three or four pieces and then fry in a little oil and butter – they taste great with onions and ginger.

CAULIFLOWER

Cauliflower is a member of the cabbage family, *Brassica oleracea*. Like all cabbages, cauliflower suffers terribly from overcooking. A properly cooked cauliflower has a pleasant fresh flavor but when overcooked it turns grey and becomes unpalatably soft, taking on a nasty rank flavor with an unpleasant aftertaste. Children often like raw cauliflower even though they may not connect it with the same vegetable served up as boiled.

History

Cauliflower is thought to have come originally from China and thence to the Middle East. The Moors introduced it to Spain in the twelfth century and from there it found its way to England via established trading routes. The early cauliflower was the size of a tennis ball but is has gradually been cultivated to the enormous sizes we see today. Ironically, baby cauliflowers are now fashionable.

Varieties

Green and occasionally purple cauli-flowers are available in the stores. The purple variety was originally grown in Sardinia and Italy but is increasingly grown by other market gardeners. They look pretty and unusual but are otherwise similar to white cauliflower. Dwarf varieties of cauliflower are now commonly available in stores.

Broccoli Romanescoes: As well as baby white cauliflowers, broccoli romanescoes are also avaliable.These pretty green or white vegetables look like a cross between broccoli and cauliflower, but are more closely related to cauliflower. They taste very much like cauliflower, but since they are quite small, they are less likely to be overcooked and consequently retain their excellent flavor.

Broccoflower: A cross between broccoli and cauliflower, this looks like a pale green cauliflower. It has a mild flavor and should be cooked in the same way as you would cauliflower.

Right: Baby cauliflowers
Far right top: Broccoli romanescoes
Far right bottom: Green cauliflowers

Nutrition

Cauliflower contains potassium, iron and zinc, although cooking reduces the amounts. It is also a good source of vitamins A and C.

Buying and Storing

In top condition, a cauliflower is a creamy white color with the outer leaves curled round the flower. The head should be unblemished with no black or discolored areas and the outer leaves should look fresh and crisp. Keep cauliflower in a cool place for no longer than 1–2 days; after that it will deteriorate and valuable nutrients will be lost.

Preparing

To cook a cauliflower whole, first trim away the coarse bottom leaves (leave the inner ones on, if liked). Very large cauliflowers are best halved or broken into florets, as the outside will overcook before the inside is tender. Some people trim away the stalk, but others like this part and only trim off the very thick stalk at the bottom of the plant.

Cooking

Cauliflowers are excellent steamed, either whole or in florets. Place in a steamer or colander over a pan of boiling water, cover and steam until just tender and immediately remove from the heat. The florets can then be fried in olive oil or butter for a few minutes to give a lightly browned finish.

When cooking a cauliflower whole, start testing it after 10 minutes; it should feel tender but still have plenty of "bite" left in it. Cauliflower is a popular vegetable accompaniment, either served with just a little butter, or with a tomato or cheese sauce. It is also good stir-fried with onions and garlic together with a few tomatoes and capers.

Cauliflower is excellent in salads or used for crudités. Either use it raw or blanch it in boiling water for 1–2 minutes, then refresh under cold running water.

Small cauliflowers and broccoli romanescoes are intended to be cooked whole, and can be steamed or boiled, covered with a lid, in the minimum of water for 4-5 minutes until just tender.

SPROUTING BROCCOLI <u>AND</u> CALABRESE

Varieties

Calabrese Broccoli: This is the vegetable we today commonly call broccoli, with large beautiful, blue-green heads on succulent stalks. It is named after the Italian province of Calabria where this variety was first developed.

Purple Sprouting Broccoli: The original variety – it has long thin stalks with small flowerheads that are normally purple but can be white or green. Heads, stalks and tender leaves are all edible. The purple heads turn green when cooked but the others keep their color. Purple sprouting broccoli is more seasonal than the easily available calabrese; it is usually available from late winter onward.

Buying and Storing

If possible, buy loose broccoli rather than the pre-wrapped bundles, because it is easier to check that it is fresh and also because wrapped vegetables tend to deteriorate more quickly.

Purple sprouting broccoli can also be sold loose or prepacked. Check that the stalk, flower head and leaves all look fresh and that the florets are tightly closed and bright green. Neither type will keep for long.

Broccoli or calabrese is a relatively modern vegetable and is one of the most popular. It is quick and easy to prepare with little or no waste and similarly easy to cook. It is attractive, whether served raw or cooked, and you can buy it in the quantity you require, unlike cauliflower or cabbage.

History

Before calabrese came into our stores, people bought and ate purple sprouting broccoli. This is basically an "untidy" version of calabrese, with long shoots and clusters of flowerheads at the end – the broccoli we know today has neat tidy heads. The stalks of purple sprouting broccoli have a faint asparagus flavor.

The Romans cooked purple sprouting broccoli in wine or served it with sauces and it is still a popular vegetable today in Italy, cooked in the oven with anchovies and onions or served with pasta in a garlic and tomato sauce.

Preparing and Cooking

Trim the ends and remove any discolored leaves.

Calabrese Broccoli: Break into even-size pieces, dividing the stem and floret lengthwise if they are thick. Cook in a little boiling water for 4–5 minutes until just tender and then drain. Do not steam this variety of broccoli as its vibrant green color tends to turn gray.

Purple Sprouting Broccoli: Either steam in long, even-size lengths in a steamer or, if you have an asparagus steamer, cook as you would asparagus. Alternately, tie the stems loosely together and stand in a little water – if necessary, wedge it in with a potato or rolled up piece of foil. Cover with a dome of foil and steam for 4–5 minutes until tender.

Serving

Serve both varieties simply with butter and lemon juice or with a hollandaise or béarnaise sauce as an accompaniment. They are also excellent stir-fried.

Above far left: Purple cauliflower
Below far left: Purple sprouting broccoli
Above: Calabrese broccoli
Below: Turnip tops

TURNIP TOPS

Turnip tops, like beet greens, are both delicious and nutritious. They are not widely available but if you are able to buy some or if you grow your own, slice them *(below)* and boil or steam for a few minutes, then drain and serve with butter.

CABBAGE

Cabbage, sliced and cooked, can be one of two things: deliciously crisp, with a mild pleasant flavor – or overcooked and horrible! Cabbage and other brassicas contain the chemical hydrogen sulphide, which is activated during cooking at about the point the vegetable starts to soften. It eventually disappears, but during the in-between time, cabbage acquires its characteristic rank smell and flavor. So, either cook cabbage briefly, or cook it long and slow, preferably with other ingredients so that flavors can mingle.

History

Cabbage has a long and varied history. However, because there are many varieties of cabbage under the general heading of "brassica", it is difficult to be sure whether the variety the Greeks and Romans enjoyed is the same as today's round cabbage, or something more akin to kale or even Chinese cabbage.

The round cabbages we know today were an important food during the Dark Ages, and by the Middle Ages they were in abundance, as you will see if you study the paintings of that period. These commonly show kitchen tables or baskets at market positively groaning with fruit and vegetables, and cabbages in all their shapes and sizes were often featured.

Medieval recipes suggest cooking cabbages with leeks, onions and herbs. In the days when all except the very wealthy cooked everything in one pot, it is fair to assume that cabbages were cooked long and slow.

Varieties

Savoy Cabbage: This is a variety of green cabbage with crimped or curly leaves. It has a mild flavor and is particularly tender, thus needing less cooking than other varieties.

Spring Greens: These have fresh loose heads with a pale yellow-green heart. They are available in spring and are delicious simply sliced, steamed and served with butter.

Right: Savoy cabbage
Above far right: Green cabbage
Below far right: Spring greens

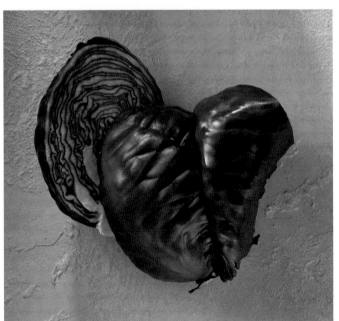

Green Cabbage: The early green, or spring, cabbages are dark green, loose-leafed and have a slightly pointed head. They have little or no heart as they are picked before this has had time to de-velop. Nevertheless, they are a very good cabbage and all but the very outside leaves should be tender. As the season progresses, larger, firmer and more pale green cabbages are available. These are a little tougher than the spring cabbages and need longer cooking.

Red Cabbage: A beautifully colored cabbage with smooth firm leaves. The color fades during cooking unless a little vinegar is added to the water. Red cabbage can be pickled or stewed with spices and flavorings.

White Cabbage: Sometimes called Dutch cabbages, white cabbages have smooth firm pale green leaves. They are available throughout the winter. They are good cooked or raw. To cook, slice them thinly, then boil or steam and serve with butter. To serve raw, slice thinly and use in a coleslaw.

Buying and Storing

Cabbages should be fresh looking and unblemished. When buying, avoid any with wilted leaves or those that look or feel puffy. Savoys and collard greens will keep in a cool place for several days; firmer cabbages will keep happily for much longer.

Preparing

Remove the outer leaves, if necessary, and then cut into quarters. Remove the stalk and then slice or shred according to your recipe or to taste.

Cooking

For green or white cabbages, place the shredded leaves in a pan with a pat of butter and a couple of tablespoons of water to prevent burning. Cover and cook over a medium heat until the leaves are tender, occasionally shaking the pan or stirring.

Red cabbage is cooked quite differently and is commonly sautéed in oil or butter and then braised in a low oven for up to 1 1/2 hours with apples, currants, onions, vinegar, wine, sugar and spices.

KALE AND CURLY KALE

Kale is the name used for a variety of green-leafed vegetables of the brassica family. Most kales have thick stems and robust leaves that do not form a head. Many kales have curly leaves, which are the variety most commonly eaten. Large coarse-leafed kales are grown for cattle and sheep feeds.

History

Kale is thought to be one of the first cultivated brassicas. Colewort, the wild ancestor, still grows along the coasts of western Europe.

Varieties

Collards: Collards, or collard greens, are a popular green vegetable in the southern United States. They are grown in summer and autumn for harvesting in the spring and are a good source of vitamin A.

Curly Kale: With its crimped, curly leaves, this is the most commonly available kale, although even this can be quite hard to come by. If you are a big fan and don't grow your own, try farm stores in early spring.

Purple or Silver Kale: This is an ornamental variety, and is grown almost exclusively for display.

Preparing and Cooking

Kale is probably the strongest tasting of the brassicas and is best cooked simply, paired with a bland-flavored vegetable, such as potatoes. To prepare, break the leaves from the stalk and then cut out any thick stalk from the leaf. This can then be rolled and sliced or cooked whole. Boil the leaves in a little salted water for 3-5 minutes until tender. Owing to its robust nature, kale is frequently teamed with fairly hot spices and is consequently popular in many Indian dishes.

Above far left: White cabbage
Below far left: Red cabbage
Left: Collards
Above: Curly kale

GARDEN AND WILD LEAVES

VINE LEAVES

All leaves from vines that produce grapes can be eaten when young. They make an ideal wrapping for various meats and vegetables as they are surprisingly strong and of course edible. Most countries that produce wine will have dishes where vine leaves appear. *Dolmades*, commonly eaten in Greece and the Middle East is perhaps the best known dish, but in France, Spain and Italy, there are recipes using vine leaves to wrap small birds, like quail or snipe.

Vine leaves have a faintly lemon/cabbage flavor which can be detected at its best in a good *dolmades*. The leaves must be cooked briefly before using, so that they are pliable and don't crack or break as you wrap the food. Bring to the boil and simmer for about 1 minute. The leaves should then be drained and separated until you are ready to use them.

DANDELION

Any child who has picked dandelions for his or her rabbits or guinea pigs and has watched them gobble them up greedily will know that this weed, though hated by the gardener in the family, has something going for it. Some gardeners, of course, are very partial to dandelion and raise the plant carefully so that the leaves are fresh and tender for the salad, and in France dandelions can often be seen for sale at market.

Look in any book of herbal remedies,

and dandelions will feature prominently. They are a well-known diuretic, their French name – *pissenlits* (wet-a-bed) – attesting to this in no uncertain terms.

Although it's gratifying to pick your own vegetables for free, it is generally recommended, if you like dandelions, that you buy the domestic seeds and grow your own. These are likely to be the juiciest

and least bitter plants. If you do pick your own, do so well away from the road-side and wash the leaves carefully.

Dandelion leaves can be added to salads or used in *pissenlits au lard*, where whole young dandelion plants are dressed in vinaigrette and then covered in finely chopped pieces of salt pork or bacon and bacon fat.

SORREL

Sorrel is not always available commercially, although it is in France and is greatly prized. However, it grows wild in cool soils, or can be grown in your own garden. Young leaves are delicious in salads, or, later in the year, can be used in soups or sauces to accompany fish. It has a sharp, distinct, lemon flavor and is commonly teamed with eggs and cream.

ORACHE

Although not related to spinach, this beautiful red or golden-leafed plant is called mountain spinach and its large leaves can be treated like spinach.

GOOD KING HENRY AND FAT HEN

These are both members of the goosefoot family and were popular vegetables in Europe in the sixteenth century. Today, Good King Henry has all but disappeared, and Fat Hen only grows wild as a weed. Both were superseded by spinach, which they are said to resemble in taste, although Fat Hen is milder.

NETTLES

Wild food enthusiasts get very excited about nettles as food, perhaps because they are plentiful and free and maybe because they take pleasure in eating something that everyone else avoids. Of course, once cooked, the sting completely disappears. They should be picked when they are very young and are good used in soups.

Above far left: Fresh vine leaves
Above left: Dandelion
Below left: Sorrel
Right: Good King Henry
Below: Nettles

CHINESE GREENS

CHINESE CABBAGE/LEAVES (PE-TSAI)

Chinese cabbage, also called Napa cabbage, has pale green, crinkly leaves with long, wide, white ribs. Its shape is a little like a very fat head of celery, which gives rise to another of its alternative names, celery cabbage. It is pleasantly crunchy with a faint cabbage flavor, and, since it is available all year through, it makes a useful winter salad component. Chinese cabbage is also very good stir-fried with a tasty sauce. It is an essential ingredient of many oriental recipes.

Buying and Storing

For some reason, Chinese leaves almost always look fresh and perky when on sale in the supermarket, which probably indicates that they travel well and are transported quickly. Avoid any with discoloured or damaged stems. The leaves should be pale green and straight without blemishes or bruises. They will keep for up to six days in the salad drawer of the fridge.

Preparing

Remove the outside leaves and slice as much as you need.

Many Chinese greens are members of the brassica family. If you go into a popular and reasonably large Chinese supermarket, you'll be astonished at the varieties of green vegetables for sale. Discovering the names of these vegetables, on the other hand, can be a bit of a hit-and-miss undertaking, as the storekeepers, although always well intentioned, rarely know the English name, if indeed there is one.

CHINESE MUSTARD GREENS

Mustard greens are worth buying if you can, as they are very good to eat. The plant is a member of the cabbage family, but is grown in Europe solely for its mustard seed. In India and Asia it has long been grown for its oil seed, but the Chinese developed the plant for its leaves as well. These are deep green and slightly puckered-looking and have a definite mustard flavor, which can be quite fiery.

If you grow your own, then you'll be able to enjoy the young leaves which can be added to lettuce to spice up salads. Older leaves are best stir-fried and then dressed with a light Chinese sauce. They are also good cooked with onion and garlic and served as a side dish to accompany pork or bacon.

Cooking and Serving

If adding to salads, combine Chinese cabbage with something fairly forceful, like Belgian endive or arugula, and add a well-flavored dressing. If adding to a stir-fry, cook with garlic, ginger and other fairly strong flavors. While the faint cabbage flavor will be lost, you will still get the pleasant crunchy "bite" of the stalk, and the leaves will carry the sauce.

PAK-CHOI

If you frequent your local Chinese super-market, you will almost certainly have come across *Pak-Choi*. In English it should correctly be called Chinese celery cabbage and its thick stalks, joined at the end in a small root, are vaguely celery-like. Its leaves, on the other hand, are generally large and spoon shaped. There are many different species of this vegetable, and smaller specimens look more like the tops of radishes and have small slim stalks. Consequently the vegetable can be known by all sorts of picturesque names, like "horse's ear" and "horse's tail." There's no rule for discovering exactly what you are buying, but the important thing is to choose a fresh plant whatever its size: look for fresh green leaves and crisp stalks.

Preparing and Cooking

Break apart the stalks, rinse, then cut both stalks and leaves into thick or thin slices. These can then be stir-fried with garlic and onions, or cooked and served as you would chard. It has a pleasant flavor, milder than mustard greens, yet with more bite than the bland Chinese cabbage.

CHINESE BROCCOLI

This is another leafy vegetable, but with slender heads of flowers that look a little like our own broccoli, except that the flowers are usually white or yellow. Once the thicker stalks are trimmed, the greens can be sliced and cooked and served in the same way as Chinese mustard greens.

Far left: Chinese mustard greens
Left: Chinese leaves
Above: Chinese broccoli
Below: Pak-choi

KOHLRABI

Kohlrabi looks like a cross between a cabbage and a turnip and is often classified as a root vegetable, even though it grows above ground. It is a member of the brassica family, but, unlike cabbages, it is the bulbous stalk that is edible rather than the flowering heads.

There are two varieties of kohlrabi: one is purple and the other pale green. They both have the same mild and fresh tasting flavor, not dissimilar to water chestnuts. Kohlrabi is neither as peppery as turnip nor as distinctive as cabbage, but it is easy to see why people think it a little like both. It can be served as an alternative to carrots or turnips.

History

Although kohlrabi is not a very popular vegetable in North America, it is commonly eaten in Europe, as well as in China, India and Asia. In Kashmir, where it is grown, there are many recipes – the bulbs are often finely sliced and eaten in salads and the greens are cooked in mustard oil with garlic and chilies.

Buying and Storing

Kohlrabi is best when small and young, since larger specimens tend to be coarse and fibrous. It keeps well for 7–10 days if stored in a cool place.

Preparing

Peel the skin with a knife and then cook whole or slice.

Cooking

Very small kohlrabies are tender and can be cooked whole. However, if they are any bigger than 2 inches in diameter, they can be stuffed. To do this, hollow out a little before cooking and then stuff with fried onions and tomatoes, for instance. For sliced kohlrabi, cook until just tender and serve with butter or a creamy sauce. They can also be cooked long and slow in gratin dishes, with, for instance, potatoes as a variation of *gratin Dauphinois*. Alternately, parboil them and bake in the oven covered with a cheese sauce.

CHARD

Chard is one of those vegetables that needs plenty of water when growing, which explains why it is a popular garden vegetable in many places which have a high rainfall. Gardeners are very fond of chard, not only because it is delicious to eat but also because it is so very striking.

Chard is often likened to spinach. The leaves have similarities, although they are not related and chard is on an altogether larger scale. Chard leaves are large and fleshy with distinctive white ribs, and the flavor is stronger and more robust than spinach. It is popular in France where it is baked with rice, eggs and milk in *tians*, and cooked in a celebrated pastry from Nice – *tourte de blettes* – which is a sweet tart filled with raisins, pine nuts, apples and chard bound together with eggs. It is also often combined with eggs in frittatas and tortillas.

Chard is a member of the beet family and is called by several names on this theme, including sea kale beet and spinach beet.

Ruby or rhubarb chard has striking red ribs and leaf beet is often cultivated as a decorative plant, but they both have the same flavor, and unlike sugar beet and beets, they are cultivated only for their leaves.

Buying and Storing

Heads of chard should be fresh and bright green; avoid those with withered leaves or flabby stems. It keeps better than spinach but should be eaten within a couple of days.

Preparing

Some people buy or grow chard for the white stems alone and discard the leaves (or give them to pet guinea pigs), but this is a waste of a delicious vegetable. The leaf needs to be separated from the ribs, and this can be done roughly with a sharp knife (*right*) or more precisely using scissors. The ribs can then be sliced. Either shred the leaves, or blanch them and use them to wrap little parcels of fragrant rice or other food. If the chard is young and small, the ribs do not need to be removed.

Cooking

For pies, frittatas and gratins, the leaves and ribs can be cooked together. Gently sauté the ribs in butter and oil and then add the leaves a minute or so later. Alternately, the ribs can be simmered in a little water until tender and the leaves added a few minutes later or steamed over the top.

Above far left: Kohlrabi
Left: Purple kohlrabi
Above: Chard

GREENS
RECIPES

Greens are so good for you we really should eat lots more. They're also versatile and quite delicious, so there's no excuse either! Broccoli Crumble and Balti-style Cauliflower with Tomatoes are quick and easy dishes, or try Broccoli and Chicken Lasagne or Spinach in Filo with Three Cheeses for great family eating. Stir-fried Brussels Sprouts presents sprouts in whole new and delicious light, while the traditional Greek dish, Dolmades, is surprisingly simple to prepare.

BROCCOLI AND CHICKEN LASAGNE

DEFINITELY DIFFERENT FROM TRADITIONAL LASAGNE, THIS DISH IS TOPPED WITH MOUTHWATERING MELTING MOZZARELLA.

SERVES SIX

INGREDIENTS
1 pound broccoli, broken into florets
1 pound chicken breasts, skinned and boned
1 tablespoon sunflower oil
1 ounce butter
1 onion, finely chopped
1 garlic clove, chopped
2½ cups passata or creamed strained tomatoes
½ teaspoon thyme
½ teaspoon oregano
about 12 sheets precooked lasagne
10 ounces fromage frais
3 ounces Parmesan cheese, grated
8 ounces mozzarella cheese, thinly sliced
salt and freshly ground black pepper

1 Preheat the oven to 350°F and butter a large shallow ovenproof dish. Steam or boil the broccoli until nearly tender. Strain and set aside.

2 Cut the chicken into thin strips. Heat the oil and butter in a frying pan and fry the chicken for a few minutes until lightly browned. Transfer to a plate using a slotted spoon and set aside.

3 Add the onion and garlic to the pan and fry for 3–4 minutes until the onion has softened and is lightly golden brown. Stir in the passata or creamed tomatoes, thyme, oregano and seasoning, and cook for about 3–4 minutes over moderate heat until the sauce is slightly thickened, stirring regularly.

4 Spoon half the tomato sauce into the prepared dish. Add a layer of lasagne and then half the chicken and half the broccoli. Dot with half the fromage frais and sprinkle with half the Parmesan cheese. Put another layer of lasagne on top and spoon over the remaining tomato sauce, chicken, broccoli and fromage frais. End with a layer of lasagne.

5 Arrange the mozzarella cheese slices on top and sprinkle with the remaining Parmesan cheese. Bake in the oven for 30–35 minutes until the top is golden.

BROCCOLI CRUMBLE

SERVES FOUR

INGREDIENTS
1 ounce butter or margarine
2 leeks, thinly sliced
1 ounce all-purpose flour
⅔ cup milk
½ cup water
8 ounces broccoli, broken into florets
1 ounce Parmesan cheese
salt and freshly ground black pepper
For the topping
4 ounces all-purpose flour
1 teaspoon dried basil
3 ounces butter or margarine
2 ounces fresh brown or white bread crumbs
pinch of salt

1 Preheat the oven to 375°F. Melt the butter in a flameproof casserole or saucepan and fry the leeks for 2–3 minutes until softened. Stir in the flour and then gradually add the milk and water. Bring to a boil, add the broccoli, season and simmer, half-covered, over low heat for 5 minutes.

2 Stir in the Parmesan cheese, season with salt and pepper and pour into a medium ovenproof dish.

3 To make the topping, mix the flour with the basil and salt. Rub in the butter or margarine and then stir in the bread crumbs. Sprinkle over the broccoli and then bake in the oven for 20–25 minutes until the topping is golden.

SPINACH AND CANNELLINI BEANS

THIS HEARTY DISH CAN BE MADE WITH ALMOST ANY DRIED BEAN OR PEA, SUCH AS BLACK-EYED PEAS, HARICOTS OR CHICK-PEAS. IT IS A GOOD DISH TO SERVE ON A COLD EVENING.

SERVES FOUR

INGREDIENTS
    8 ounces cannellini beans,
      soaked overnight
    3 tablespoons olive oil
    1 slice white bread
    1 onion, chopped
    3–4 tomatoes, peeled and chopped
    a good pinch of paprika
    1 pound spinach
    1 garlic clove, halved
    salt and freshly ground black pepper

1 Drain the beans, place in a saucepan and cover with water. Bring to a boil and boil rapidly for 10 minutes. Cover and simmer for about 1 hour until the beans are tender. Drain.

2 Heat 2 tablespoons of the oil in a frying pan and fry the bread until golden brown. Transfer to a plate.

3 Fry the onion in the remaining oil over low heat until soft but not brown, then add the tomatoes and continue cooking over low heat.

4 Heat the remaining oil in a large pan, stir in the paprika and then add the spinach. Cover and cook for a few minutes until the spinach has wilted.

5 Add the onion and tomato mixture to the spinach, mix well and stir in the cannellini beans. Place the garlic and fried bread in a food processor and process until smooth. Stir into the spinach and bean mixture. Add ⅔ cup cold water and then cover and simmer gently for 20–30 minutes, adding more water if necessary.

SPINACH IN FILO WITH THREE CHEESES

A GOOD CHOICE TO SERVE WHEN VEGETARIANS AND MEAT EATERS ARE GATHERED FOR A MEAL, AS WHATEVER THEIR PREFERENCE, EVERYONE SEEMS PARTIAL TO THIS TASTY DISH.

SERVES FOUR

INGREDIENTS
- 1 pound spinach
- 1 tablespoon sunflower oil
- ½ ounce butter
- 1 small onion, finely chopped
- 6 ounces ricotta cheese
- 4 ounces feta cheese, cut into small cubes
- 3 ounces Gruyère or Emmenthal cheese, grated
- 1 tablespoon fresh chopped chervil
- 1 teaspoon fresh chopped marjoram
- salt and freshly ground black pepper
- 5 large or 10 small sheets filo pastry
- 1½–2 ounces butter, melted

1 Preheat the oven to 375°F. Cook the spinach in a large saucepan over moderate heat for 3–4 minutes until the leaves have wilted, shaking the saucepan occasionally. Strain and press out the excess liquid.

2 Heat the oil and butter in a saucepan and fry the onion for 3–4 minutes until softened. Remove from the heat and add half of the spinach. Combine using a metal spoon, breaking up the spinach.

3 Add the ricotta cheese and stir until evenly combined. Stir in the remaining spinach, again chopping it into the mixture with a metal spoon. Fold in the feta and Gruyère or Emmenthal cheeses, chervil, marjoram and seasoning.

4 Lay a sheet of filo pastry measuring about 12 inches square on a work surface. (If you have small filo sheets, lay them side by side, overlapping by about 1 inch in the middle.) Brush with melted butter and cover with a second sheet; brush this with butter and build up five layers of pastry in this way.

5 Spread the filling over the pastry, leaving a 1-inch border. Fold the two shorter sides inward and then roll up.

6 Place the roll, seam side down, on a greased baking sheet and brush with the remaining butter. Bake in the oven for about 30 minutes until golden brown.

CAULIFLOWER AND MUSHROOM GOUGÈRE

THIS IS AN ALL-ROUND FAVORITE VEGETARIAN DISH. WHEN COOKING THIS DISH FOR MEAT LOVERS, CHOPPED ROAST HAM OR FRIED BACON CAN BE ADDED.

SERVES FOUR TO SIX

INGREDIENTS
1¼ cups water
4 ounces butter or margarine
5 ounces all-purpose flour
4 eggs
4 ounces Gruyère or Cheddar cheese, finely diced
1 teaspoon French mustard
salt and freshly ground black pepper
For the filling
14-ounce can tomatoes
1 tablespoon sunflower oil
½ ounce butter or margarine
1 onion, chopped
4 ounces white mushrooms, halved if large
1 small cauliflower, broken into small florets
sprig of thyme
salt and freshly ground black pepper

1 Preheat the oven to 400°F and butter a large oval ovenproof dish. Place the water and butter together in a large saucepan and heat until the butter has melted. Remove from the heat and add all the flour at once. Beat well with a wooden spoon for about 30 seconds until smooth. Allow to cool slightly.

2 Beat in the eggs, one at a time, and continue beating until the mixture is thick and glossy. Stir in the cheese and mustard and season with salt and pepper. Spread the mixture around the sides of the ovenproof dish, leaving a hollow in the center for the filling.

3 To make the filling, purée the tomatoes in a blender or food processor and then pour into a measuring jug. Add enough water to make up to 1¼ cups of liquid.

4 Heat the oil and butter in a flameproof casserole and fry the onion for about 3–4 minutes until softened but not browned. Add the mushrooms and cook for 2–3 minutes until they begin to be flecked with brown. Add the cauliflower florets and stir-fry for 1 minute.

5 Add the tomato liquid, thyme and seasoning. Cook, uncovered, over low heat for about 5 minutes until the cauliflower is only just tender.

6 Spoon the mixture into the hollow in the ovenproof dish, adding all the liquid. Bake in the oven for about 35–40 minutes, until the outer pastry is well risen and golden brown.

COOK'S TIP

For a variation, ham or bacon can be added. Use about 4–5 ounces thickly sliced roast ham and add to the sauce at the end of step 5.

BALTI-STYLE CAULIFLOWER WITH TOMATOES

BALTI IS A TYPE OF MEAT AND VEGETABLE COOKING FROM PAKISTAN AND NORTHERN INDIA. IT CAN REFER BOTH TO THE PAN USED FOR COOKING, WHICH IS LIKE A LITTLE WOK, AND THE SPICES USED. IN THE ABSENCE OF A GENUINE BALTI PAN, USE EITHER A WOK OR A HEAVY FRYING PAN.

SERVES FOUR

INGREDIENTS

2 tablespoons vegetable oil
1 onion, chopped
2 garlic cloves, crushed
1 cauliflower, broken into florets
1 teaspoon ground coriander
1 teaspoon ground cumin
1 teaspoon ground fennel seeds
½ teaspoon garam masala
pinch of ground ginger
½ teaspoon chili powder
4 plum tomatoes, peeled, seeded
  and quartered
6 fluid ounces water
6 ounces fresh spinach, roughly
  chopped
1–2 tablespoons lemon juice
salt and freshly ground black pepper

1 Heat the oil in a balti pan, wok, or large frying pan. Add the onion and garlic and stir-fry for 2–3 minutes over high heat until the onion begins to brown. Add the cauliflower florets and stir-fry for a further 2–3 minutes until the cauliflower is flecked with brown.

2 Add the coriander, cumin, fennel seeds, garam masala, ginger and chili powder and cook over high heat for 1 minute, stirring all the time; then add the tomatoes, water and salt and pepper. Bring to a boil and then reduce the heat, cover and simmer for 5–6 minutes until the cauliflower is just tender.

3 Stir in the chopped spinach, cover and cook for 1 minute until the spinach is tender. Add enough lemon juice to sharpen the flavor and adjust the seasoning to taste.

4 Serve straight from the pan, with an Indian meal or with chicken or meat.

HOT BROCCOLI TARTLETS

APART FROM THE UBIQUITOUS QUICHE, VEGETABLE TARTS ARE NOT VERY COMMON IN NORTH AMERICA. HOWEVER, IN FRANCE YOU CAN FIND A WHOLE VARIETY OF SAVORY TARTLETS, FILLED WITH ONIONS, LEEKS, MUSHROOMS AND BROCCOLI.

MAKES EIGHT TO TEN

INGREDIENTS
    1 tablespoon oil
    1 leek, finely sliced
    6 ounces broccoli, broken into florets
    ½ ounce butter
    ½ ounce all-purpose flour
    ⅔ cup milk
    2 ounces Cheddar cheese, grated
    fresh chervil, to garnish
For the pastry
    6 ounces all-purpose flour
    3 ounces butter
    1 egg
    pinch of salt

1 To make the pastry, place the flour and salt in a large bowl and rub in the butter and egg to make a dough. Add a little cold water if necessary, knead lightly, then cover with plastic wrap and leave to rest in the fridge for 1 hour.

2 Preheat the oven to 375°F. Let the dough return to room temperature for 10 minutes and then roll out on a lightly floured surface and line 8–10 deep muffin pans. Prick the bases with a fork and bake in the oven for about 10–15 minutes until the pastry is firm and lightly golden. Increase the oven temperature to 400°F.

3 Heat the oil in a small saucepan and sauté the leek for 4–5 minutes until soft. Add the broccoli, stir-fry for about 1 minute and then add a little water. Cover and steam for 3–4 minutes until the broccoli is just tender.

4 Melt the butter in a separate saucepan, stir in the flour and cook for a minute, stirring all the time. Slowly add the milk and stir to make a smooth sauce. Add half of the cheese and season with salt and pepper.

5 Spoon a little broccoli and leek into each tartlet case and then spoon over the sauce. Sprinkle each tartlet with the remaining cheese and then bake in the oven for about 10 minutes until golden.

6 Serve the tartlets as part of a buffet or as a starter, garnished with chervil.

CHARD PASTIES

CHARD, LIKE SPINACH, GOES PARTICULARLY WELL IN PASTIES. UNLIKE SOME GREEN VEGETABLES, IT CAN SURVIVE A LITTLE EXTRA COOKING AND IS SUBSTANTIAL ENOUGH TO BE THE PRINCIPAL INGREDIENT.

SERVES FOUR

INGREDIENTS
   1½ pounds chard
   1 ounce butter or margarine
   1 onion, finely chopped
   3 ounces lean bacon, chopped
   2 ounces Gruyère cheese, grated
   1 ounce fresh brown or white
      bread crumbs
   6 tablespoons light cream
   salt and freshly ground black pepper
For the pastry
   10 ounces all-purpose flour
   5 ounces butter or margarine
   pinch of salt
   beaten egg for glazing

1 To make the pastry, place the flour and salt in a mixing bowl and rub in the butter or margarine. Add a little cold water and mix to a soft dough. Knead lightly on a floured surface. Cover with plastic wrap and chill for 30 minutes.

2 Trim the stalks of the chard and then chop both the leaves and stalk. Place in a heavy-based pan, cover and cook over low heat for 6–8 minutes until the stalks are tender and the leaves wilted. Shake the pan occasionally. Strain and press out the excess liquid, then place in a mixing bowl and leave to cool.

3 Melt the butter in a small frying pan and fry the onion and bacon for about 4–5 minutes until the onion is lightly golden and the bacon browned.

4 Add the onion and bacon to the chard and stir in the cheese, bread crumbs, cream and seasoning to taste. Preheat the oven to 400°F.

5 Divide the pastry into four and roll out into rounds. Spoon the filling onto the center of each and dampen the edges with water. Bring the sides together over the filling and press together to seal. Brush with beaten egg and then put on an oiled baking sheet. Bake for about 15–20 minutes until the pastry is golden.

KALE WITH PARMESAN AND GARLIC

KALE IS A ROBUST, FULL-BODIED TYPE OF CABBAGE. IT HAS A VERY PRONOUNCED FLAVOR AND IS GOOD WHEN COOKED WITH OTHER STRONG-FLAVORED INGREDIENTS SUCH AS ONIONS, GARLIC AND PARMESAN CHEESE. IT DOES NOT NEED LONG COOKING AS THE LEAVES ARE QUITE TENDER.

SERVES FOUR

INGREDIENTS

    3 tablespoons olive oil
    2 garlic cloves, crushed
    4 scallions, sliced
    12 ounces curly kale, thinly sliced,
      tough stalk removed
    2 ounces Parmesan cheese, grated
    salt and freshly ground black pepper
    shavings of Parmesan cheese,
      to garnish

1 Heat the olive oil in a large saucepan or wok and fry the garlic gently for a few seconds. Add the scallions, stir-fry for 2 minutes and then add the kale.

2 Stir-fry for a few minutes so that the kale is coated in oil, and then add about ¼ cup water. Bring to a boil, cover and simmer until the kale is tender. Stir occasionally during cooking and do not allow the pan to boil dry.

3 Bring the liquid to the boil and allow the excess to evaporate and then stir in the Parmesan cheese. Serve at once with extra shavings of cheese, if liked.

PASTA WITH SAVOY CABBAGE AND GRUYÈRE

THIS IS AN INEXPENSIVE AND SIMPLE DISH WITH A SURPRISING TEXTURE AND FLAVOR. THE CABBAGE IS COOKED SO THAT IT HAS PLENTY OF "BITE" TO IT, CONTRASTING WITH THE SOFTNESS OF THE PASTA.

SERVES FOUR

INGREDIENTS

1 ounce butter
1 small Savoy or green cabbage,
  thinly sliced
1 small onion, chopped
12 ounces pasta, e.g. tagliatelle,
  fettucine, penne, etc.
1 tablespoon cnopped fresh parsley
⅔ cup light cream
2 ounces Gruyère or Cheddar cheese,
  grated
about 1¼ cups hot vegetable or
  chicken stock
salt and freshly ground black pepper

1 Preheat the oven to 350°F and butter a large casserole. Place the cabbage in a mixing bowl.

2 Melt the butter in a small frying pan and fry the onion until softened. Stir into the cabbage in the bowl.

3 Cook the pasta according to the instructions, until *al dente*.

4 Drain well and stir into the bowl with the cabbage and onion. Add the parsley and mix well and then pour into the prepared casserole.

5 Beat together the cream and Gruyère or Cheddar cheese and then stir in the hot stock. Season well and pour over the cabbage and pasta, so that it comes about halfway up the casserole. If necessary, add a little more stock.

6 Cover tightly and cook in the oven for 30–35 minutes, until the cabbage is tender and the stock is bubbling. Remove the lid for the last 5 minutes of the cooking time to brown the top.

STIR-FRIED BRUSSELS SPROUTS

SERVES FOUR

INGREDIENTS
1 pound Brussels sprouts
1 tablespoon sunflower oil
6–8 scallions, cut into 1-inch lengths
2 slices fresh ginger
1½ ounces slivered almonds
⅔–¾ cup vegetable or chicken stock
salt

1 Remove any large outer leaves and trim the bases of the Brussels sprouts. Cut into slices about ½ inch thick.

2 Heat the oil in a wok or heavy frying pan and fry the scallions and the ginger for 2–3 minutes, stirring frequently. Add the almonds and stir-fry over moderate heat until both the onions and almonds begin to brown.

3 Remove and discard the ginger, reduce the heat and stir in the Brussels sprouts. Stir-fry for a few minutes and then pour in the stock and cook over low heat for 5–6 minutes or until the sprouts are nearly tender.

4 Add a little salt, if necessary, and then increase the heat to boil off the excess liquid. Spoon into a warmed serving dish and serve immediately.

BRUSSELS SPROUT GRATIN

SERVES FOUR

INGREDIENTS
⅔ cup heavy or whipping cream
⅔ cup milk
1 ounce Parmesan cheese, grated
1½ pounds Brussels sprouts, thinly sliced
½ ounce butter
1 garlic clove, finely chopped
salt and freshly ground black pepper

1 Preheat the oven to 300°F and butter a shallow ovenproof dish. Blend together the cream, milk, Parmesan cheese and seasoning.

2 Place a layer of Brussels sprouts in the bottom of the prepared dish, sprinkle with a little garlic and pour over about a quarter of the cream mixture. Add another layer of sprouts and continue building layers in this way, ending with the remaining cream and milk

3 Cover loosely with wax paper and bake for 1–1¼ hours. Halfway through cooking, remove the paper and press the sprouts under the liquid in the dish. Return to the oven to brown.

CHINESE CABBAGE WITH LIME DRESSING

FOR THIS THAI RECIPE, THE COCONUT DRESSING IS TRADITIONALLY MADE USING FISH SAUCE, BUT VEGETARIANS COULD USE MUSHROOM SAUCE INSTEAD. BEWARE, THIS IS A FIERY DISH!

SERVES FOUR

INGREDIENTS
    6 scallions
    ½ Chinese cabbage, finely shredded
    2 tablespoons oil
    3 fresh red chilies, cut into thin strips
    4 garlic cloves, thinly sliced
    1 tablespoon crushed peanuts
For the dressing
    1–2 tablespoons fish sauce
    2 tablespoons lime juice
    1 cup coconut milk

1 To make the dressing, blend together the fish sauce and lime juice, and then stir in the coconut milk.

2 Cut the scallions diagonally into slices, including all but the very tips of the green parts.

3 Using a large sharp knife, cut the Chinese cabbage into very fine shreds.

4 Heat the oil in a wok and stir-fry the chilies for 2–3 minutes until crisp. Transfer to a plate using a slotted spoon.

5 Stir-fry the garlic for 30–60 seconds until golden brown and transfer to the plate with the chilies.

6 Stir-fry the white parts of the scallions for about 2–3 minutes and then add the green parts and stir-fry for a further 1 minute. Add to the plate with the chilies and garlic.

7 Bring a large pan of salted water to the boil and add the cabbage; stir twice and then drain immediately.

8 Place the warmed cabbage in a large bowl, add the coconut dressing and stir well. Spoon into a large serving bowl and sprinkle with the crushed peanuts and the stir-fried chili mixture. Serve either warm or cold.

COOK'S TIP
Coconut milk is available in cans from large supermarkets and Chinese stores. Alternately, creamed coconut is available in packets. To use creamed coconut, place about 4 ounces in a jug and pour over 1 cup boiling water. Stir well until dissolved.

DOLMADES

DOLMADES ARE STUFFED VINE LEAVES, A TRADITIONAL GREEK DISH. IF YOU CAN'T OBTAIN FRESH VINE LEAVES, USE A PACKET OF BRINED VINE LEAVES. SOAK THE LEAVES IN HOT WATER FOR 20 MINUTES THEN RINSE AND DRY WELL ON PAPER TOWELS BEFORE USE.

MAKES 20–24

INGREDIENTS

20–30 fresh young vine leaves
2 tablespoons olive oil
1 large onion, finely chopped
1 garlic clove, crushed
8 ounces cooked long grain rice,
  or mixed white and wild rice
about 3 tablespoons pine nuts
1 tablespoon slivered almonds
1½ ounces golden raisins
15ml/ 1 tablespoon snipped chives
1 tablespoon finely chopped
  fresh mint
juice of ½ lemon
⅔ cup white wine
hot vegetable stock
salt and freshly ground black pepper
sprig of mint, to garnish
Greek yogurt, to serve

1 Bring a large pan of water to a boil and cook the vine leaves for about 2–3 minutes. They will darken and go limp after about 1 minute and simmering for a further minute or so ensures they are pliable. If using leaves from a packet, place them in a large bowl, cover with boiling water and leave for a few minutes until the leaves can be easily separated. Rinse them under cold water and drain on paper towels.

2 Heat the oil in a small frying pan and fry the onion and garlic for 3–4 minutes over low heat until soft.

3 Spoon the onion and garlic mixture into a bowl and add the cooked rice.

4 Stir in 2 tablespoons of the pine nuts, the almonds, golden raisins, chives, mint, lemon juice and seasoning and mix well.

5 Lay a vine leaf on a clean work surface, veined side uppermost. Place a spoonful of filling near the stem, fold the lower part of the leaf over it and roll up, folding in the sides as you go. Continue stuffing the vine leaves in the same way.

6 Line the bottom of a deep frying pan with four large vine leaves. Place the stuffed vine leaves close together in the pan, seam side down, in a single layer.

7 Add the wine and enough stock to just cover the vine leaves. Place a plate directly over the leaves, then cover and simmer gently for 30 minutes, checking to make sure the pan does not boil dry.

8 Chill the vine leaves garnished with the remaining pine nuts and a sprig of mint and serve with a little yogurt.

BEANS, PEAS AND SEEDS

Sweet and succulent, beans and peas are the vegetables we first turn to when we need a tasty accompaniment. Okra, like snow peas and most fresh beans, come complete with pods. Podded peas are best when absolutely fresh, dried beans give us another huge dimension of vegetable dishes, while corn is a delight, whether kept on the cob or served as kernels on the side.

FAVA BEANS

One of the delights of having a garden is discovering how truly delicious some vegetables are when garden fresh. This seems particularly true of fava beans, which have a superb sweet flavor that sadly can never be reproduced in the frozen product. If you're lucky enough to grow or be given fresh fava beans, don't worry about recipes; just cook them until tender and serve with butter. It will be a revelation! However, if you're not one of those lucky few, don't dismiss fava beans, as they are still a wonderfully versatile vegetable. They can be used in soups or casseroles, and, since they have a mealy texture, they also purée well.

History

People have been eating fava beans almost since time began. A variety of wild fava bean grew all over southern Europe, North Africa and Asia, and it would have been a useful food for early man. There is archaeological evidence that by Neolithic times fava beans were being farmed, making them one of the first foods to be cultivated.

Fava beans will grow in most climates and most soils. They were a staple food for people throughout the Dark Ages and the Middle Ages, grown for feeding people and livestock until being replaced by the potato in the seventeenth and eighteenth centuries. Fava beans were an important source of protein for the poor, and because they dry well, they would have provided nourishing meals for families until the next growing season.

Nutrition

Beans are high in protein and carbohydrates and are also a good source of vitamins A, B1 and B2. They also provide potassium and iron as well as several other minerals.

Buying and Storing

Buy beans as fresh as possible. The pods should preferably be small and tender. Use as soon as possible.

Preparing

Very young beans in tender pods, no more than 3 inches in length, can be eaten pod and all; top and tail, and then slice roughly. Usually, however, you will need to shell the beans. Elderly beans are often better skinned after they are cooked to rid them of the strong, bitter flavor that puts many people off this vegetable.

Cooking

Plunge shelled beans (or in their pods if very young) into rapidly boiling water and cook until just tender. They can also be parboiled and then finished off braised in butter. For a simple broad bean purée, blend the cooked beans with garlic cooked in butter, cream and a pinch of fresh herbs, such as savory or thyme.

LIMA BEANS

These are popular in the US, named after the capital of Peru, and are sold mainly shelled. They are an essential ingredient in the Native American dish *succotash*. Lima beans should be cooked in a little boiling water until tender. Elderly beans need skinning after they are cooked. The dried bean, also known as the butter bean, can be large or small. These large beans tend to become mushy when cooked so are best used in soups or purées.

Above: Fava beans
Below: Lima beans
Right: Wax beans

WAX BEANS

The wax bean is native to South America, where it has been cultivated for more than 2000 years, and there is archaeological evidence of its existence much earlier than that.

It is a popular vegetable to grow. Most home vegetable gardeners have a patch of wax beans – they are easy to grow and, like all legumes, their roots contain bacteria that help renew nitrogen supplies in the soil.

They have a more robust flavor and texture than French beans and are distinct from green beans in several ways: they are generally much larger with long, flattened pods; their skin is rough textured, although in young beans this softens during cooking; and they contain purple beans within the pods, unlike green beans whose beans are mostly white or pale green. Nevertheless, runner beans belong to the same family as all the green beans.

Buying and Storing

Always buy young beans as the pods of larger beans are likely to be tough. The pods should feel firm and fresh; if you can see the outline of the bean inside the pod it is likely to be fibrous – although you could leave the beans to dry out and use the dried beans later in the season. Ideally, the beans inside should be no larger than your small fingernail.

Use as soon as possible after buying; they do not store well.

Preparing

Wax beans need to be topped and tailed and may also need stringing. Carefully put your knife through the top of the bean without cutting right through, and then pull downward; if a thick thread comes away, the beans need stringing, so do the same on the other side. The beans can then be sliced either using a sharp knife or a slicer.

Slice through lengthwise, not diagonally, so that you will be able to serve the beans with just a little skin and lots of succulent flesh.

Cooking

Plunge the beans into boiling salted water and cook until *al dente*.

PEAS

Fresh peas are wonderful – try tasting them raw, straight from the pod. Unfortunately, the season for garden peas is short, and frozen peas, which are the next best thing, never quite come up to the mark. If you grow your own peas, for three or four weeks in early summer, you can eat like a king; otherwise you can buy them from a good grocer, who may be able to keep you supplied all through the early summer.

History

Peas have an even longer history than fava beans, with archaeological evidence showing they were cultivated as long ago as 5700 BC. High in protein and carbohydrates, they would have been another important staple food and were eaten fresh or dried for soups or potage.

"Pease" porridge is mentioned in a Greek play written in 5 BC. "Pease pudding," probably something similar, made with split peas with onion and herbs, is an old-fashioned but still very popular dish, especially in the north of England, traditionally eaten with ham and pork.

One of the first recipes for peas, however, comes from *Le Cuisinier Français*, which was translated into English in the middle of the seventeenth century and gives a recipe for *petits pois à la française* (peas cooked with small-hearted lettuces) – still a popular recipe today.

Varieties

Snow Peas: These are eaten whole and have a delicate flavor, providing they are not overcooked. Unfortunately, they are easy to overcook and the texture then becomes rather slippery. Alternately, blanch or stir-fry them. They are also good served raw in salads.

Petits Pois: These are not, as you might expect, immature peas but are a dwarf variety. Gardeners grow their own, but they are not available fresh in the stores as they are mainly grown commercially for canning or freezing.

Sugar Peas, Sugar Snaps: These have the distinct fresh flavor of raw peas and are more plump and have more snap than snow peas.

Buying and Storing

Only buy fresh peas; if they are old they are bound to be disappointing and you would be better off buying them frozen. In top condition, the pods are bright green and lively looking; the more withered the pod, the longer they have been hanging around. It is possible to surreptitiously sample peas on occasion, to check if they are fresh (grocers don't seem to mind if you buy some). Use fresh peas as soon as possible.

Preparing

Shelling peas can be very relaxing. Press open the pods and use your thumb to push out the peas *(below)*. Snow peas and sugar snaps just need to be topped and tailed *(below right)*.

Left: Peas
Above right: Sugar snap peas

Cooking

Cook peas with a sprig of mint in a pan of rapidly boiling water or in a covered steamer until tender. Alternately, melt butter in a flameproof casserole, add the peas and then cover and sweat over low heat for 4–5 minutes. Cook snow peas and sugar snaps in any of these ways but for a shorter time.

GREEN BEANS

slim in shape. They should be eaten when very young, no more than 2¹⁄₂-3 inches in length.

Thai Beans: These long beans are similar to French beans and can be prepared and cooked in the same way.

Yellow Wax Beans: This is also a French bean and has a mild, slightly buttery taste.

Buying and Storing

Whatever variety, beans should be bright and crisp. Avoid wilted ones, or those with overly mature pods which feel spongy when lightly squeezed. They do not keep well, so use as soon as possible after buying or picking.

Preparing

To remove the ends of the beans: gather them together in one hand and then slice away the top ¹⁄₄ inch *(below)*, then do the same at the other end. If necessary, pull off any stringy bits.

Whether you call beans French beans, haricots or green beans, they all belong to a large and varied family.

History

The bean is a New World vegetable that had been cultivated for thousands of years by native peoples in both the north and south of the continent, which accounts for its wide diversity.

Varieties

One variety or another is available all year through and so they are one of the most convenient fresh green vegetables.

French Beans: This name encompasses a range of green beans, including the snap bean and bobby bean. They are mostly fat and fleshy, and when fresh, should be firm so that they break in half with a satisfying snapping sound.

Haricots Verts: These are considered the best French beans and are delicate and

Cooking

Plunge beans into rapidly boiling salted water and cook until *al dente*. When overcooked, beans have a flabby texture and also lose much of their flavor. Drain and toss them in butter or serve in a sauce with shallots and bacon. For salads, cook until just tender and then refresh under cold water. They are excellent with a garlicky vinaigrette. Serve with carrots or other root vegetables and savor the contrast in flavors.

Above left: Bobby beans
Below left: Yellow wax beans
Right: Haricots verts
Below: Thai beans

CORN

Fresh corn, eaten on the cob with salt and a little butter, is deliciously sweet. Some gardeners who grow it have a pan ready on the boil, so that when they cut the corn it goes into the pan in only the time it takes to race up from the garden to the kitchen. Buying it from the supermarket is inevitably a bit hit-or-miss, although if purchased in season, corn can be very good indeed.

History

In 1492, as Christopher Columbus disembarked on the island now called Cuba, he was met by Native Americans offering two gifts of hospitality – one was tobacco and the other something the Native Americans called *maïs*. The English word for staple food was then corn, so that when Columbus and his crew saw that maize was the staple food for the Native Americans, it was dubbed "Indian corn."

Corn originated in South America and had enormous significance to the Native Americans of the whole continent, who were said to have lived and died by corn. They referred to it as their "first mother and father, the source of life." By far their most important food, corn was used in many other ways as well. They used the plant for their shelters and for fences, and they wore it and decorated their bodies with it.

The Aztecs had corn planting ceremonies that included human sacrifices, and other tribes had similar customs to appease the god "corn." Countless myths and legends have been woven around corn, each tribe telling a slightly different story, but each on the same theme of planting and harvesting corn. For anthropologists and historians, they make compelling study.

Nutrition

Corn is a good carbohydrate food and is rich in vitamins A, B and C. It contains protein, but less so than most other cereals. It is also a good source of potassium, magnesium, phosphorus and iron.

Varieties

There are five main varieties of corn – popcorn, sweet corn, dent corn, flint corn and flour corn. Dent corn is the

most commonly grown worldwide, for animal feeds and oil, and the corn we eat on the cobs is sweet corn. Baby corn cobs are picked when immature and are cooked and eaten whole.

Buying and Storing

As soon as corn is picked, its sugar begins to turn to starch and therefore the sooner it goes into the pot, the better. Wherever possible, buy locally grown corn.

Look for husks that are clean and green and tassels which are golden, with no sign of matting. The corn itself should look plump and yellow. Avoid cobs with pale or white kernels or those with older shriveled kernels which will undoubtedly be disappointing.

Preparing

Strip away the husks. To use the kernels for recipes, cut downward using a sharp knife from top to bottom *(left)*.

Cooking

Cook corn on the cob in plenty of boiling salted water until tender. Timing depends on the size of the cobs but 10-15 minutes will normally be enough. Serve them with sea salt and butter, but if the cobs are really sweet, leave out the butter. Stir-fry baby corn cobs briefly and serve in oriental dishes.

Far left: Corn cobs
Below: Baby corn cobs

OKRA

History

Okra originated in Africa. In the sixteenth century, when African people were enslaved by the Spanish and shipped to the New World, they took with them the few things they could, including the plants and seeds from home – dried peas, yams, ackee – and okra. This lantern-shaped pod containing rows of seeds oozes a sticky mucilaginous liquid when cooked, and it was popular not only for its subtle flavor but also for thickening soups and stews.

The plant thrived in the tropical climate and by the early nineteenth century, when the slave trade was finally abolished, okra was an important part of the cuisine of the Caribbean and the southern United States. In and around New Orleans, the Creoles, the American-born descendants of European-born settlers, adopted a popular Native American dish called *gumbo*. An essential quality of this famous dish was its thick gluey consistency. The Native Americans used filé powder (the dry pounded leaves of the sassafras tree), but okra was welcomed as a more satisfactory alternative.

Gumbos are now the hallmark of Creole cooking, and in some parts of America, the word "gumbo" is an alternative word for okra itself.

Buying and Storing

Choose young, small pods as older ones are likely to be fibrous. They should be bright green, firm and slightly springy when squeezed. Avoid any that are shriveled or bruised. They will keep for a few days in the salad drawer of the fridge.

Preparing

When cooking whole, trim the top but don't expose the seeds inside or the viscous liquid will ooze into the rest of the dish. If, however, this is what you want, slice thickly or thinly according to the recipe *(right)*. If you want to eliminate some of this liquid, first soak the whole pods in acidulated water (water to which lemon juice has been added) for about an hour.

Cooking

The pods can be steamed, boiled or lightly fried, and then added to or used

with other ingredients. If cooked whole, okra is not mucilaginous but is pleasantly tender. Whether cooked whole or sliced, use garlic, ginger or chili to perk up the flavor, or cook Native American-style, with onions, tomatoes and spices.

Above: Okra

DRIED BEANS AND PEAS

Dried beans feature in traditional cuisines all over the world, from Mexican refried beans to Italy's *pasta e fagioli*. They are nutritious, providing a good source of protein when combined with rice, and are a marvelous store cupboard standby.

Black-eyed Peas: Sometimes called black-eyed beans, these small cream-colored beans have a black spot or eye. When cooked, they have a tender, creamy texture and a mildly smoky flavor. Black-eyed beans are widely used in Indian cooking.

Chana Dhal: Chana dhal is very similar to yellow split peas but smaller in size and with a slightly sweeter taste. It is used in a variety of vegetable dishes.

Chickpeas: These round beige-colored pulses have a strong, nutty flavor when cooked. As well as being used for curries, chickpeas are also ground into a flour which is widely used in many Indian dishes such as *pakoras* and *bhajees*.

Flageolet Beans: Small oval beans which are either white or pale green in color. They have a very mild, refreshing flavor and feature in classic French dishes.

Green Lentils: Also known as continental lentils, these have quite a strong flavor and retain their shape during cooking. They are very versatile and are used in a number of dishes.

Haricot Beans: Small, white oval beans which come in different varieties. Haricot beans are ideal for Indian cooking because not only do they retain their shape but they also absorb the flavors of the spices.

Kidney Beans: Kidney beans are one of the most popular pulses. They are dark red/brown, kidney-shaped beans with a strong flavor.

Mung Beans: These are small, round green beans with a slightly sweet flavor and creamy texture. When sprouted they produce the familiar bean sprouts.

Red Split Lentils: A readily available lentil that can be used for making dhal. Use instead of toovar dhal.

Toovar Dhal: A dull orange-colored split pea with a very distinctive earthy flavor. Toovar dhal is available plain and in an oily variety.

Soaking and Cooking Tips

Most dried pulses, except lentils, need to be soaked overnight before cooking. Wash the beans thoroughly and remove any small stones and damaged beans. Put into a large bowl and cover with plenty of cold water. When cooking, allow double the volume of water to beans and boil for 10 minutes. This initial boiling period is essential to remove any harmful toxins. Drain, rinse and cook in fresh water. The cooking time for all pulses varies depending on the type and their freshness. Pulses can be cooked in a pressure cooker to save time. Lentils, on the whole, do not need soaking. They should be washed in several changes of cold water before being cooked.

Left (clockwise from bottom right): Mung beans, flageolet beans, chickpeas, haricot beans, black-eyed peas, kidney beans
Above (clockwise from top): Red split lentils, green lentils, toovar dhal, chana dhal

BEAN, PEA AND SEED RECIPES

Whether you're looking for classic side dishes, or for
something more unusual, peas and beans are a great
choice. Fava Beans à la Paysanne or Peas with Baby
Onions and Cream are favorites everywhere;
Indian-style Okra or Wax Beans with Garlic will
please the more adventurous. Corn is particularly
versatile; use it for snacks such as Corn and Cheese
Pasties, or for a delicious main course soup,
Corn and Scallop Chowder.

LAMB AND FAVA BEAN COUSCOUS

THIS SIMPLE-TO-MAKE STEW INCLUDES BOTH LAMB AND CHICKEN. IT IS SERVED ON A BED OF COUSCOUS WITH A SPICY SAUCE FOR POURING OVER.

SERVES FOUR

INGREDIENTS

2–3 tablespoons vegetable oil
12 ounces lean lamb, cut into cubes
3 skinless chicken pieces, cut into
   large chunks
1 large onion, chopped
2 garlic cloves, crushed
3 carrots, cut into 1½-inch lengths
1 small parsnip, cut into chunks
4 tomatoes, skinned and chopped
1⅔ cups chicken stock
1 cinnamon stick
½ teaspoon ground ginger
sprig of thyme
1 small red or green bell pepper,
   seeded and sliced
8 ounces shelled fava beans
1–2 teaspoons Tabasco or chili sauce
salt and freshly ground black pepper
For the couscous
8 ounces couscous
1 tablespoon olive oil
pinch of salt

1 Heat the oil in a large flameproof casserole and fry the cubes of lamb until evenly browned. Drain and transfer to a plate. Add the chicken pieces and cook until brown. Drain and put on the plate.

2 Heat a further 1 tablespoon oil and fry the onion and garlic over low heat for 4–5 minutes until softened. Add the carrots and parsnip, stir-fry for a few minutes and then add the tomatoes, stock, cinnamon stick, ginger, thyme and seasoning, together with the meat. Bring to a boil, stirring occasionally, and then reduce the heat, cover and simmer gently for about 45–60 minutes until the meat is cooked and very tender.

3 Meanwhile, in a large bowl rub the olive oil and salt into the couscous. Stir in boiling water to cover and leave to soak for at least 10 minutes.

4 Add the pepper and fava beans to the stew and simmer for 10 minutes until the vegetables are cooked.

5 Place the soaked couscous in a colander and make five or six "holes" in the grain using the handle of a wooden spoon. Set the couscous over the stew, cover and steam for 10 minutes.

6 Just before serving, ladle about ⅔ cup of the cooking liquid into a small pan. Add a little Tabasco sauce and heat gently. Taste and add more Tabasco sauce, if liked, for a hotter and spicier sauce, and then pour into a warmed serving jug.

7 Spoon the couscous onto a large warmed serving plate and pour the stew over. Serve with the hot sauce.

FAVA BEANS À LA PAYSANNE

SERVES FOUR

INGREDIENTS

1 tablespoon olive oil
1 onion, finely chopped
3 ounces lean ham in a thick slice,
   finely diced
12 ounces shelled fava beans
2 Bibb lettuces, chopped
⅓ cup chicken or vegetable stock
¼ cup light cream
salt and freshly ground black pepper
sprigs of mint or chervil, to garnish

1 Heat the oil in a saucepan. Fry the onion and ham until soft. Add the beans and lettuce. Cover, cook gently for 6–8 minutes, stirring occasionally.

2 Stir in the stock, cream and seasoning and cook over very low heat for 20–30 minutes. Stir occasionally, taking care not to break up the beans.

3 Turn into a warmed serving dish and garnish with a sprig of mint or chervil. Serve with broiled meat or an omelet.

COOK'S TIP
Larger fava beans sometimes have a tough outer skin. It is a good idea to cook them briefly, peel off the outer skin and use the tender green centers.

PEAS WITH BABY ONIONS AND CREAM

IDEALLY, USE FRESH PEAS AND FRESH BABY ONIONS. FROZEN PEAS ARE AN ACCEPTABLE SUBSTITUTE IF FRESH ONES AREN'T AVAILABLE, BUT FROZEN ONIONS TEND TO BE INSIPID AND ARE NOT WORTH USING. ALTERNATELY, USE THE WHITE PART OF SCALLIONS.

SERVES FOUR

INGREDIENTS
  6 ounces baby onions
  ½ ounce butter
  2 pounds fresh peas (about 12 ounces shelled or frozen)
  ⅔ cup heavy cream
  ½ ounce all-purpose flour
  2 teaspoons chopped fresh parsley
  1–2 tablespoons lemon juice (optional)
  salt and freshly ground black pepper

1 Peel the onions and halve them if necessary. Melt the butter in a flame-proof casserole and fry the onions for 5–6 minutes over moderate heat, until they begin to be flecked with brown.

3 Using a small whisk, blend the cream with the flour. Remove the pan from the heat and stir in the combined cream and flour, parsley and seasoning to taste.

4 Cook over low heat for about 3–4 minutes, until the sauce is thick. Taste and adjust the seasoning; add a little lemon juice to sharpen, if liked.

2 Add the peas and stir-fry for a few minutes. Add ¼ cup water and bring to a boil. Partially cover and simmer for about 10 minutes until both the peas and onions are tender. There should be a thin layer of water on the bottom of the pan – add a little more water if necessary or if there is too much liquid, remove the lid and increase the heat until the liquid is reduced.

SNOW PEAS WITH CHICKEN AND CILANTRO

SNOW PEAS ARE SO DELICATE AND FRESH-TASTING THAT IT SEEMS A CRIME TO DO ANYTHING AT ALL WITH THEM, BARRING FLASH COOKING AND SERVING THEM HOT OR COLD WITH A LITTLE BUTTER OR A VINAIGRETTE DRESSING. THEY ARE EXCELLENT IN STIR-FRIES, ADDING COLOR AND TEXTURE.

SERVES FOUR

INGREDIENTS

4 boned and skinned chicken breasts
8 ounces snow peas
3 tablespoons vegetable oil, plus
  oil for deep frying
3 garlic cloves, finely chopped
1-inch piece fresh ginger, freshly
  grated
5–6 scallions, cut into 1½-inch
  lengths
2 teaspoons sesame oil
For the marinade
1 teaspoon cornstarch
1 tablespoon light soy sauce
1 tablespoon medium dry sherry
1 tablespoon vegetable oil
For the sauce
1 teaspoon cornstarch
2–3 teaspoons dark soy sauce
½ cup chicken stock
2 tablespoons oyster sauce
boiled rice, to serve

1 Cut the chicken into strips about ½ x 1½ inches. To make the marinade, blend together the cornstarch and soy sauce. Stir in the sherry and oil. Pour over the chicken, turning the pieces over to coat evenly, and leave for 30 minutes.

2 Trim the snow peas and plunge into a pan of boiling salted water. Bring back to the boil and then drain and refresh them under cold running water.

3 To make the sauce, mix together the cornstarch, soy sauce, stock and oyster sauce and set aside.

4 Heat the oil in a deep fryer. Drain the chicken strips and fry, in batches if necessary, for about 30 seconds to brown. Drain and transfer to a plate using a slotted spoon.

5 Heat 1 tablespoon of the vegetable oil in a wok and add the garlic and ginger. Stir-fry for 30 seconds. Add the snow peas and stir-fry for 1–2 minutes. Transfer to a plate and keep warm.

6 Heat the remaining vegetable oil in the wok, add the scallions and stir-fry for 1–2 minutes. Add the chicken and stir-fry for 2 minutes. Pour in the sauce, reduce the heat and cook until it thickens and the chicken is cooked through.

7 Stir in the sesame oil, and pour over the snow peas. Serve with boiled rice.

GREEN BEAN SALAD

ALTHOUGH BEAN SALADS ARE DELICIOUS SERVED WITH A SIMPLE VINAIGRETTE DRESSING, THIS DISH IS A LITTLE MORE ELABORATE. IT DOES, HOWEVER, ENHANCE THE FRESH FLAVOR OF THE BEANS.

SERVES FOUR

INGREDIENTS

1 pound green beans
1 tablespoon olive oil
1 ounce butter
½ garlic clove, crushed
2 ounces fresh white bread crumbs
1 tablespoon chopped fresh parsley
1 egg, hard-boiled and finely chopped
For the dressing
2 tablespoons olive oil
2 tablespoons sunflower oil
2 teaspoons white wine vinegar
½ garlic clove, crushed
¼ teaspoon Dijon mustard
pinch of sugar
pinch of salt

1 Trim the green beans and cook in boiling salted water for 5–6 minutes until tender. Drain the beans and refresh them under cold running water and place in a serving bowl.

2 Make the salad dressing by blending the oils, vinegar, garlic, mustard, sugar and salt thoroughly together. Pour over the beans and toss to mix.

COOK'S TIP
For a more substantial salad, boil about 1 pound scrubbed new potatoes until tender, cool and then cut them into bite-size chunks. Stir into the green beans and then add the dressing.

3 Heat the oil and butter in a frying pan and fry the garlic for 1 minute. Stir in the bread crumbs and fry over moderate heat for about 3–4 minutes until golden brown, stirring frequently.

4 Remove the pan from the heat and stir in the parsley and then the egg. Sprinkle the breadcrumb mixture over the green beans. Serve warm or at room temperature.

GREEN BEANS WITH BACON AND CREAM

SERVES FOUR

INGREDIENTS
    12 ounces green beans
    2–3 ounces bacon, chopped
    1 ounce butter or margarine
    1 tablespoon all-purpose flour
    1½ cups milk and light cream, mixed
    salt and freshly ground black pepper

1 Preheat the oven to 375°F. Trim the beans and cook in lightly salted boiling water for about 5 minutes until just tender. Drain and place them in an oven-proof dish.

2 Dry-fry the bacon until crisp, chop into small pieces and stir into the beans.

3 Melt the butter or margarine in a saucepan, stir in the flour and then add the milk and cream to make a smooth sauce. Season well with salt and pepper.

4 Pour the sauce over the beans and carefully mix it in. Cover lightly with a piece of foil and bake in the oven for 15–20 minutes until hot.

WAX BEANS WITH GARLIC

DELICATE AND FRESH TASTING FLAGEOLET BEANS AND GARLIC ADD A DISTINCT FRENCH FLAVOR TO THIS SIMPLE SIDE DISH. SERVE TO ACCOMPANY ROAST LAMB OR VEAL.

SERVES FOUR

INGREDIENTS
   8 ounces flageolet beans
   1 tablespoon olive oil
   1 ounce butter
   1 onion, finely chopped
   1–2 garlic cloves, crushed
   3–4 tomatoes, peeled and chopped
   12 ounces wax beans, prepared and
      sliced
   ⅔ cup white wine
   ⅔ cup vegetable stock
   2 tablespoons chopped fresh parsley
   salt and freshly ground black pepper

1 Place the flageolet beans in a large saucepan of water, bring to a boil and simmer for ¾–1 hour until tender. Drain.

2 Heat the oil and butter in a large frying pan and sauté the onion and garlic for 3–4 minutes until soft. Add the chopped tomatoes and continue cooking over low heat until they are soft.

3 Stir the flageolet beans into the onion and tomato mixture, then add the wax beans, wine, stock, and a little salt. Stir well. Cover and simmer for 5–10 minutes until the wax beans are tender.

4 Increase the heat to reduce the liquid, then stir in the parsley and season with a little more salt, if necessary, and pepper.

INDIAN–STYLE OKRA

WHEN OKRA (BHINDI) IS SERVED IN INDIAN RESTAURANTS IT IS OFTEN FLAT AND SOGGY BECAUSE IT HAS BEEN OVERCOOKED OR LEFT STANDING. HOWEVER, WHEN YOU MAKE THIS DISH YOURSELF, YOU WILL REALIZE HOW DELICIOUS OKRA CAN BE.

SERVES FOUR

INGREDIENTS
    12 ounces okra
    2 small onions
    2 garlic cloves, crushed
    ½-inch piece fresh ginger
    1 green chili, seeded
    2 teaspoons ground cumin
    2 teaspoons ground coriander
    2 tablespoons vegetable oil
    juice 1 lemon

3 Reduce the heat and add the garlic and ginger mixture. Cook for about 2–3 minutes, stirring frequently, and then add the okra, lemon juice and 7 tablespoons water. Stir well, cover tightly and simmer over low heat for about 10 minutes until tender. Transfer to a serving dish, sprinkle with the fried onion rings and serve at once.

1 Trim the okra and cut into ½-inch lengths. Roughly chop one of the onions and place in a food processor or blender with the garlic, ginger, chili and 6 tablespoons water. Process to a paste. Add the cumin and coriander and blend again.

2 Thinly slice the remaining onion into rings and fry in the oil for 6–8 minutes until golden brown. Transfer to a plate using a slotted spoon.

CORN <u>AND</u> CHEESE PASTIES

THESE TASTY PASTIES ARE REALLY SIMPLE TO MAKE AND IRRESISTIBLE — WHY NOT MAKE DOUBLE THE AMOUNT, AS THEY'LL GO LIKE HOTCAKES.

<u>MAKES 18–20</u>

INGREDIENTS
    9 ounces corn
    4 ounces feta cheese
    1 egg, beaten
    2 tablespoons heavy or whipping
        cream
    ½ ounce Parmesan cheese, grated
    3 scallions, chopped
    8–10 small sheets filo pastry
    4 ounces butter, melted
    freshly ground black pepper

1 Preheat the oven to 375°F and butter two muffin pans.

2 If using fresh corn, strip the kernels from the cob using a sharp knife and simmer in a little salted water for 3–5 minutes until tender. For canned corn, drain and rinse well under cold running water.

3 Crumble the feta cheese into a bowl and stir in the corn. Add the egg, cream, Parmesan cheese, scallions and ground black pepper, and stir well.

4 Take one sheet of pastry and cut it in half to make a square. (Keep the remaining pastry covered with a damp cloth to prevent it drying out.) Brush with melted butter and then fold into four, to make a smaller square (about 3 inches).

5 Place a heaped teaspoon of mixture in the center of each pastry square and then squeeze the pastry around the filling to make a "money bag" casing.

6 Continue making pasties until all the mixture is used up. Brush the outside of each "bag" with any remaining butter and then bake in the oven for about 20–25 minutes until golden. Serve hot.

CORN AND SCALLOP CHOWDER

FRESH HOME-GROWN CORN IS IDEAL FOR THIS CHOWDER, ALTHOUGH CANNED OR FROZEN CORN ALSO WORKS WELL. THIS SOUP IS ALMOST A MEAL IN ITSELF AND MAKES A PERFECT LUNCH DISH.

SERVES FOUR TO SIX

INGREDIENTS

2 ears of corn or 7 ounces frozen or
    canned corn
2½ cups milk
½ ounce butter or margarine
1 small leek or onion, chopped
1 small garlic clove, crushed
1½ ounces smoked lean bacon,
    finely chopped
1 small green bell pepper, seeded
    and diced
1 celery stalk, chopped
1 medium potato, diced
1 tablespoon all-purpose flour
1¼ cups chicken or vegetable stock
4 scallops
4 ounces cooked fresh mussels
pinch of paprika
⅔ cup light cream (optional)
salt and freshly ground black pepper

1 Using a sharp knife, slice down the ears of the corn to remove the kernels. Place half of the kernels in a food processor or blender and process with a little of the milk.

2 Melt the butter or margarine in a large saucepan and gently fry the leek or onion, garlic and bacon for 4–5 minutes until the leek is soft but not browned. Add the green bell pepper, celery and potato and sweat over low heat for a further 3–4 minutes, stirring frequently.

3 Stir in the flour and cook for about 1–2 minutes until the mixture is golden and frothy. Gradually stir in the milk and corn mixture, stock, the remaining milk and corn kernels and seasoning.

4 Bring to a boil and then reduce the heat to a gentle simmer, and cook, partially covered, for 15–20 minutes until the vegetables are tender.

5 Pull the corals away from the scallops and slice the white flesh into ¼-inch slices. Stir the scallops into the soup, cook for 4 minutes and then stir in the corals, mussels and paprika. Allow to heat through for a few minutes and then stir in the cream, if using. Adjust the seasoning to taste and serve.

SQUASHES

In their bright and beautiful colors, these are the vegetables that say autumn. Locally grown zucchini are available from mid to late summer, as are the pretty pattypans. Marrows follow in late summer and then come the winter squashes — acorn squash, kabocha, onion squash and pumpkins — just in time for Halloween and pumpkin pie.

ZUCCHINI

Zucchini are the best loved of all the squashes as they are so versatile. They are quick and easy to cook and are succulent and tender with a delicate, unassuming flavor. Unlike other squashes, they are available all year through.

Vegetables taste best when eaten immediately after they have been picked, and this particularly applies to zucchini. They have a long season and are good to grow since the more you cut, the more the plants produce. Left unchecked, they turn into marrows.

Varieties

The zucchini is classified as a summer squash, *cucurbita pepo*, along with marrows and pattypan squashes.

Zucchini: Sometimes called courgettes, zucchini are basically immature marrows. The word is a diminutive of the Italian *zucca*, meaning gourd, and similarly courgette means miniature *courge*, French for marrow. Zucchini have a deep green skin, with firm pale flesh. The seeds and pith found in marrows have yet to form but are visible in more mature zucchini. Conversely, the prized baby zucchini have no suggestion of seeds or pith and the flesh is completely firm.

Yellow Zucchini: These are bright yellow and somewhat straighter than green zucchini. They have a slightly firmer flesh than green zucchini but are otherwise similar.

Pattypan Squashes: These little squashes look like tiny custard squashes. They can be pale green, yellow or white and have a slightly firmer texture than zucchini, but a similar flavor. They can be sliced and broiled in the same way as zucchini but, to make the most of their size and shape, steam them whole until tender.

Summer Crooknecks: Pale yellow with curves at the neck and a bumpy skin, crooknecks are prepared and cooked in the same way as zucchini.

Italian Zucchini: These very long, thin zucchini are grown in Italy. They are treated liked ordinary zucchini but are strictly a bottle gourd.

Buying and Storing

Zucchini should be firm with a glossy, healthy looking skin. Avoid any that feel soft or generally look limp, as they will be dry and not worth using. Choose small zucchini whenever possible and buy in small quantities as needed.

Preparing

The tiny young zucchini need no preparation at all, and if they still have their flowers, so much the better. Other zucchini should be topped and tailed and then prepared according to the recipe, either sliced or slit for stuffing.

Cooking

Baby zucchini need little or no cooking. Steam them whole or just blanch them. Sliced larger zucchini can be steamed or boiled but take care that they do not overcook as they go soggy very quickly. Alternately, grill, roast or fry them. Try dipping slices in a light batter and then shallow frying in a blend of olive and sunflower oil. To roast, place them in a ovenproof dish, scatter with crushed garlic and a few torn basil leaves and sprinkle with olive oil; then bake in a very hot oven until tender, turning the slices occasionally.

Top left: Pattypan squashes
Far left: Baby zucchini
Left: Yellow zucchini
Right: Italian zucchini beside white and green zucchini

MARROWS AND SUMMER SQUASHES

Vegetable marrow is classified as a summer squash yet it is rather the poor relation of squashes. Most of the edible flesh is water and at best it is a rather bland vegetable, with a slightly sweet flavor. At worst, it is insipid and if cooked to a mush (which isn't unheard of), it is completely tasteless.

Marrows can be stuffed, although it involves a lot of energy expended for very little reward; but marrow cooked over low heat in butter with no added water (so that it steams in its own juice) brings out the best in it.

History

Marrows, like all the summer and winter squashes, are native to America. Squashes were eaten by Native Americans, traditionally with corn and beans, and in an Iroquois myth the three vegetables are represented as three inseparable sisters. Although the early explorers would almost certainly have come into contact with them, they were not brought back home, and vegetable marrow was not known in England until the nineteenth century. Once introduced, however, it quickly became very popular. Mrs Beeton gives eight recipes for vegetable marrow and observes that "it is now extensively used." No mention at all is made of zucchini, which of course are simply immature marrows, as any gardener will know.

Varieties

The word "marrow" as a general term tends to refer to the summer squashes. At the end of summer and in the early fall a good variety of the large summer squashes is available.

Vegetable Marrows: This is the proper name for the large prize marrows, beloved of harvest festivals and country fairs. Buy small specimens whenever possible.

Spaghetti Squashes/Marrows: Long and pale yellow, like all marrows these squashes can grow to enormous sizes, but buy small specimens for convenience as well as flavor. They earned their name from the resemblance of the cooked flesh to spaghetti.

To boil a spaghetti squash, first pierce the end, so that the heat can reach the middle, then cook for about 25 minutes or until the skin feels tender. Cut the squash in half lengthwise, remove the seeds, and then fork the strands of flesh out onto a plate. It has a fragrant, almost honey and lemon flavor and tastes good with garlic butter or pesto.

Custard Marrows: These are pretty, pale green squashes with scalloped edges and a similar flavor to zucchini. If possible, buy small specimens, about 4 inches across. Boil these whole until tender, then cut a slice off the tops, scoop out the seeds and serve with a pat of butter.

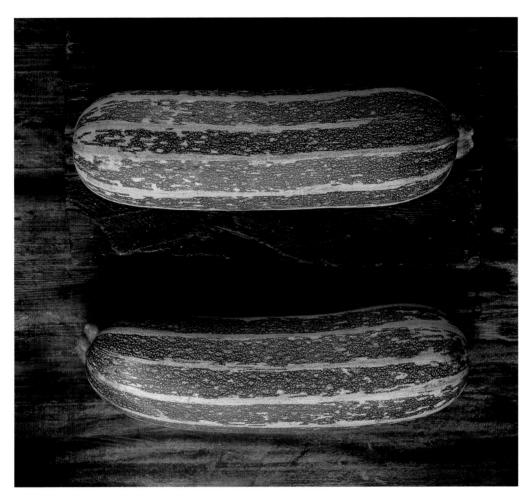

Buying and Storing

Buy vegetables that have clear, unblemished flesh and avoid any with soft or brown patches. Vegetable marrows and spaghetti squashes will keep for several months provided they are kept in a cool, dark place. Custard marrows will keep up to a week.

Preparing

Wash the skin. For sautéing or steaming, or if the skin is tough, peel it away. For braised marrow, cut into chunks and discard the seeds and pith (*right*). For

stuffing, cut into thick slices or cut length-wise and discard the seeds and pith.

Cooking

Place chunks of marrow in a heavy-based pan with a little butter, cover and cook until tender. It can then be livened up with garlic, herbs or tomatoes. For stuffed marrow, blanch first, stuff, then cover or wrap it in foil to cook.

Above: Vegetable marrows
Far left: Spaghetti squashes
Left: Custard marrows

PUMPKINS AND WINTER SQUASHES

Pumpkins are the most famous of the winter squashes; aesthetically they are one of nature's most pleasing vegetables for their huge size, their color and the smoothness of their skin. They originated in America and, from a culinary point of view, they have their home here.

The name squash comes from America and as well as pumpkins, the family includes acorn, butternut and turban squashes to name but a few. There are simply hundreds of different squashes, including Sweet Dumpling, Queensland Blue (from Australia), Calabaza, Cushaw and Golden Nugget.

History

The tradition of eating pumpkin at Thanksgiving came from when the Pilgrim Fathers, who had settled in New England and proclaimed a day of thanks-giving and prayer for the harvest. The early tradition was to serve the pumpkin with its head and seeds removed, the cavity filled with milk, honey and spices, and baked until tender. The custom of eating pumpkin at Thanksgiving has remained, but it is now served in a dif-ferent way: puréed pumpkin, either fresh or canned, is used to make golden tarts.

Varieties

There are a huge number of varieties of winter squashes and, confusingly, many are known by several different names. However, from a cooking point of view, most are interchangeable, although it is best to taste dishes as you cook them, as seasoning may differ from one to the other. In general, they all have a floury and slightly fibrous flesh and a mild, almost bland flavor tinged with sweet-ness. Because of this blandness, they harmonize well with other ingredients.

Acorn Squashes: These are small and heart-shaped with a beautiful deep green or orange skin, or a mixture of the two. Peel, then use as for pumpkins or bake whole, then split and serve with butter.

Butternut Squashes: Perfectly pear-shaped, these are a buttery color. Use in soups or in any pumpkin recipe.

Delicata Squashes: This pretty pale yellow squash has a succulent yellow

flesh, tasting like a cross between sweet potato and butternut squash.

English Pumpkins: These have a softer flesh than the American variety and are good for soups or, if puréed, combined with potatoes or other root vegetables.

Hubbard Squashes: These large winter squashes have a thick, bumpy, hard shell which can range in color from bright orange to dark green. If they are exceptionally large, they are sometimes sold in halves or large wedges. They have a grainy texture and are best mashed with butter and seasoning.

Kabocha Squashes: Attractive bright green squashes with a pale orange flesh.

They are similar in flavor and texture to acorn squashes and can be prepared and cooked in the same way.

Onion Squashes: Round, yellow or pale orange, onion squashes have a mild flavor, less sweet than pumpkin but still with a slightly fruity or honey taste. They are good in risottos or in most pumpkin recipes, but taste for flavor – you may need to add extra seasoning or sugar.

Above (clockwise from right): A pumpkin hybrid, kabocha squash, acorn squash Right (clockwise from top right): Hybrid squash, two golden acorn squashes, two small and one large pumpkin

Pumpkins: Large, bright yellow or orange squashes, with a deep orange flesh. They have a sweet, slightly honeyed, flavor and are very much a taste North Americans and Australians grow up with. However, they are not to everyone's liking and some people find them rather cloying. Pumpkin soup, pumpkin bread and pumpkin pie are part of the American tradition, as are faces carved from the shell at Halloween.

Buying and Storing

All winter squashes may be stored for long periods. Buy firm, unblemished vegetables with clear smooth skins.

Preparing

For larger squashes, or for those being used for soups or purées, peel and cut into pieces, removing the seeds (*left*).

Cooking

Boil in a little water for about 20 minutes until tender, then mash and serve with butter and plenty of salt and pepper. Smaller squashes can be baked whole in their skins, then halved, seeded and served with butter and maple syrup. Pumpkin and other squashes can also be lightly sautéed in butter before adding stock, cream or chopped tomatoes.

EXOTIC GOURDS

While the squashes are native to America, most gourds originated in the Old World – from Africa, India and the Far East. However, over the millennia, seeds crossed water and, over the centuries, people crossed continents so that squashes and gourds are now common all over the world. Both belong to the family *Cucurbitacea*, and both are characterised by their rapid-growing vines.

Bottle Gourds: Bottle gourds are still a familiar sight in Africa, where they are principally grown not for their fruit, but for their dried shells. The gourds can grow to enormous sizes and the shells are used for water bottles, cups and musical instruments. The young fruit can be eaten, but it is extremely bitter and is normally only added to highly flavored stews, like curries.

Chayotes: The chayote (pronounced chow-chow) is a popular gourd in all sorts of regions of the world and can be found in just about any ethnic supermarket, be it Chinese, African, Indian or Caribbean. In each it is known by a different name, christophine being the Caribbean term, but choko, shu-shu and chinchayote among its many other names used elsewhere. Unlike most gourds, it originated in Mexico but was widely grown throughout the tropics after the invasions of the Spanish.

It is a pear-shaped fruit with a large central pit and has a cream-colored or green skin. It has a bland flavor, similar to marrow, and a slightly firmer texture something like pumpkin. It is commonly used in Caribbean cooking, primarily as a side dish or in soufflés. Alternately it can be used raw in salads.

Chinese Bitter Melons: These are a common vegetable in all parts of Asia and go by a myriad of names – bitter gourd and bitter cucumber to name but two. They are popular throughout Asia, eaten when very young, but are extremely bitter and rarely eaten in the West. They are easily recognized as they have warty, spiny skins, looking like a toy dinosaur. The skins are white when young but will probably have ripened to a dark green by the time they appear in the shops.

Most recipes from China suggest halving the gourd, removing the pulp and then slicing before boiling for several minutes to remove their bitterness. They can then be added to stir-fries or other oriental dishes.

Far left: Sweet dumpling
Left: Pumpkin
Top right: Chinese bitter melon
Middle right: Loofah
Below: Chayote

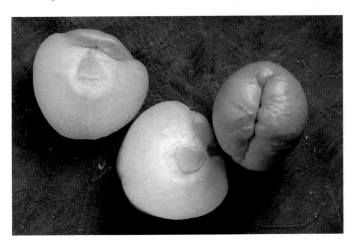

Smooth and Angled Loofahs: The smooth loofah must be one of the strangest plants. When young it can be eaten, although it is not much valued. However, the plant is grown almost exclusively for sponges, used everywhere as a back rub in the bath. The ripe loofahs are picked and, once the skin has been stripped off and the seeds shaken out, allowed to dry. The plant then gradually dries to a fibrous skeleton and thence to bathrooms everywhere - so now you know!

Angled or ribbed loofahs are more commonly eaten but again are only edible when young as they become unpleasantly bitter when mature. They taste something like zucchini and are best cooked in a similar way, either fried in butter or cooked with tomatoes, garlic and oil.

CUCUMBERS

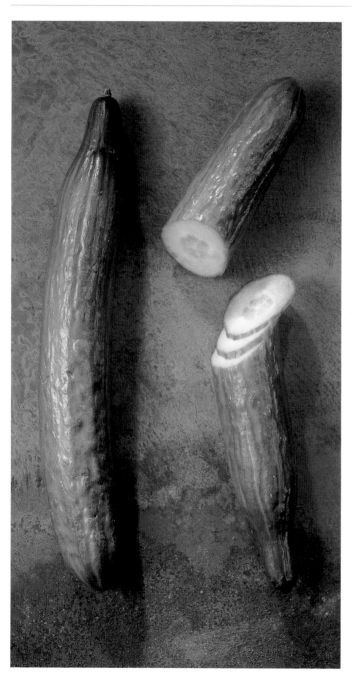

The Chinese say food should be enjoyed for its texture as well as flavor; cucumbers have a unique texture and refreshing cool taste. An afternoon tea with cucumber sandwiches, thinly sliced cucumber between wafer thin brown buttered bread, provides a delight of contrasts – the soft bread, the smooth butter and the cool crisp cucumber.

Varieties

English Cucumbers: These are the cucumbers the English are most familiar with. They have fewer seeds and thinner skin than the ridged cucumber.
Gherkins: These are tiny cucumbers with bumpy, almost warty skins and are mostly pickled in vinegar and eaten with cold meats or chopped into mayonnaise.
Kirbys: Small cucumbers, available in the United States and used for pickling.
Ridged Cucumbers: These are smaller than most cucumbers with more seeds and a thick, bumpy skin. The waxed ones need to be peeled before eating but most ridged cucumbers on the European Continent are unwaxed and good without peeling.

Buying and Storing

Cucumbers should be firm from top to bottom. They are often sold prewrapped in plastic and can be stored in the salad drawer of the fridge for up to a week. Remove the plastic packaging once you've "started" a cucumber. Discard once it begins to go soggy.

Preparing

Whether you peel a cucumber or not is a matter of personal preference, but wash it if you don't intend to peel it. Some producers use wax coatings to give a glossy finish and these cucumbers must be peeled. If you are in doubt, buy organic cucumbers. Special citrus peelers can remove strips of peel to give an attractive striped effect when sliced.

Left: Cucumbers
Above right: Ridged cucumbers
Above far right: Baby cucumbers
Below right: Kirbys

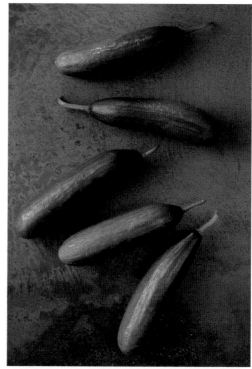

Serving

Thinly sliced cucumber is most frequently served with a light dressing or sour cream. In Greece cucumber is an essential part of a Greek country salad, *horiatiki salata*, cut into thick chunks and served with tomatoes, peppers and feta and dressed simply with olive oil and a little wine vinegar.

Iced cucumber soup is delicious, and cucumber can also be puréed with yogurt, garlic and herbs and served with sour cream stirred in.

Cooking

Cucumbers are normally served raw, but are surprisingly good cooked. Cut the cucumber into wedges, remove the seeds and then simmer for a few minutes until tender. Once drained, return the cucumber to the pan and stir in a little cream and seasoning.

SQUASH
RECIPES

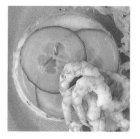

Pumpkins and squashes need long slow cooking, which
is why these are the vegetables you need for warming
dishes such as Pumpkin Soup, Onion Squash Risotto
and Baked Marrow in Parsley Sauce. Zucchini on the
other hand are best cooked quickly. Baked Zucchini,
stuffed with goat cheese, and Zucchini Italian-style,
are cooked so that maximum flavor is retained,
and the result is perfection.

ONION SQUASH RISOTTO

THIS RISOTTO PROVIDES A WARM AND COMFORTING MEAL AFTER A TIRING DAY. FOR A VEGETARIAN ALTERNATIVE SIMPLY OMIT THE BACON AND USE VEGETABLE STOCK.

SERVES FOUR

INGREDIENTS
1 pumpkin, about 2–2¼ pounds
2 tablespoons olive oil
1 onion, chopped
1–2 garlic cloves, crushed
4 ounces lean bacon, chopped
4 ounces arborio rice
2½–3 cups chicken stock
1½ ounces Parmesan cheese, grated
1 tablespoon chopped fresh parsley
salt and freshly ground black pepper

1 Halve or quarter the pumpkin, remove the seeds and skin, and then cut into chunks about ½–¾ inches in size.

2 Heat the oil in a flameproof casserole and fry the onion and garlic for about 3–4 minutes, stirring frequently. Add the bacon and continue frying until both the onion and bacon are lightly golden.

3 Add the pumpkin, stir-fry for a few minutes. Add the rice and cook for about 2 minutes, stirring all the time.

4 Pour in about half of the stock and season. Stir well and then half cover and simmer gently for about 20 minutes, stirring occasionally. As the liquid is absorbed, add more stock and stir to prevent the mixture sticking to the bottom.

5 When the pumpkin and rice are nearly tender, add a little more stock. Cook uncovered for 5–10 minutes. Stir in the Parmesan cheese and parsley and serve.

PUMPKIN SOUP

THE SWEET FLAVOR OF PUMPKIN IS GOOD IN SOUPS, TEAMING WELL WITH OTHER MORE SAVORY INGREDIENTS SUCH AS ONIONS AND POTATOES TO MAKE A WARM AND COMFORTING DISH.

SERVES FOUR TO SIX

INGREDIENTS
1 tablespoon sunflower oil
1 ounce butter
1 large onion, sliced
1½-pound pumpkin, cut into
  large chunks
1 pound potatoes, sliced
2½ cups vegetable stock
good pinch of nutmeg
1 teaspoon chopped fresh tarragon
2½ cups milk
about 1–2 teaspoons lemon juice
salt and freshly ground black pepper

1 Heat the oil and butter in a heavy-based saucepan and fry the onion for 4–5 minutes over low heat until soft but not browned, stirring frequently.

2 Add the pumpkin and potato, stir well and then cover and sweat over low heat for about 10 minutes until the vegetables are almost tender, stirring occasionally to prevent them from sticking to the pan.

3 Stir in the stock, nutmeg, tarragon and seasoning. Bring to a boil and then simmer for about 10 minutes until the vegetables are completely tender.

4 Allow to cool slightly, then pour into a food processor or blender and process until smooth. Pour back into a clean saucepan and add the milk. Heat gently and then taste, adding the lemon juice and extra seasoning if necessary. Serve piping hot with country brown bread.

BAKED ZUCCHINI

WHEN VERY SMALL AND VERY FRESH ZUCCHINI ARE USED FOR THIS RECIPE IT IS WONDERFUL, BOTH SIMPLE AND DELICIOUS. THE CREAMY YET TANGY GOAT CHEESE CONTRASTS WELL WITH THE VERY DELICATE FLAVOR OF THE YOUNG ZUCCHINI.

SERVES FOUR

INGREDIENTS
8 small zucchini, about 1 pound total weight
1 tablespoon olive oil, plus extra for greasing
3–4 ounces goat cheese, cut into thin strips
small bunch fresh mint, finely chopped
freshly ground black pepper

1 Preheat the oven to 350°F. Cut out eight rectangles of foil large enough to encase each zucchini and brush each with a little oil.

2 Trim the zucchini and cut a thin slit along the length of each.

3 Insert pieces of goat cheese in the slits. Add a little mint and sprinkle over the olive oil and black pepper.

4 Wrap each zucchini in the foil rectangles, place on a baking sheet and bake for about 25 minutes until tender.

COOK'S TIP
Almost any cheese could be used in this recipe. Mild cheeses, however, such as a mild cheddar or mozzarella, will best allow the flavor of the zucchini to be appreciated.

ZUCCHINI ITALIAN-STYLE

IF YOU GROW YOUR OWN ZUCCHINI AND HAVE HUGE QUANTITIES TO USE UP, THIS IS A QUICK AND EASY RECIPE. ITS SIMPLICITY BELIES ITS EXCELLENCE.

SERVES FOUR

INGREDIENTS

1 tablespoon virgin olive oil
1 tablespoon sunflower oil
1 large onion, chopped
1 garlic clove, crushed
4–5 medium zucchini, cut into ½-inch slices
⅔ cup chicken or vegetable stock
½ teaspoon chopped fresh oregano
salt and freshly ground black pepper
chopped fresh parsley, to garnish

3 Stir in the stock, oregano and seasoning and simmer gently for 8–10 minutes, until the liquid has almost evaporated. Spoon the zucchini into a serving dish, sprinkle with parsley and serve.

1 Heat the oils in a large frying pan and fry the onion and garlic over moderate heat for 5–6 minutes until the onion has softened and is beginning to brown.

2 Add the zucchini and fry for about 4 minutes until they just begin to be flecked with brown. Stir frequently.

M ARROWS <u>WITH</u> G NOCCHI

A SIMPLE WAY WITH MARROW, THIS DISH MAKES AN EXCELLENT ACCOMPANIMENT TO BROILED MEAT BUT IT IS ALSO GOOD WITH A VEGETARIAN DISH, OR SIMPLY SERVED WITH GRILLED TOMATOES.

SERVES FOUR

INGREDIENTS
  1 small marrow, cut into
    bite-size chunks
  2 ounces butter
  14-ounce packet gnocchi
  ½ garlic clove, crushed
  salt and freshly ground black pepper
  chopped fresh basil, to garnish

1 Preheat the oven to 350°F and butter a large ovenproof dish. Place the marrow, more or less in a single layer, in the dish. Dot all over with the remaining butter.

2 Place a double piece of buttered wax paper over the top. Cover with an ovenproof plate or lid so that it presses the marrow down, and then place a heavy, ovenproof weight on top of that. (Use a couple of old-fashioned scale weights.)

3 Put in the oven to bake for about 15 minutes, by which time the marrow should just be tender.

4 Cook the gnocchi in a large saucepan of boiling salted water for 2–3 minutes, or according to the instructions on the packet. Drain well.

5 Stir the garlic and gnocchi into the marrow. Season and then place the wax paper over the marrow and return to the oven for 5 minutes (the weights are not necessary).

6 Just before serving, sprinkle the top with a little chopped fresh basil.

BAKED MARROW <u>IN</u> PARSLEY SAUCE

THIS IS A REALLY GLORIOUS WAY WITH A SIMPLE AND MODEST VEGETABLE. TRY TO FIND A SMALL, FIRM AND UNBLEMISHED MARROW FOR THIS RECIPE, AS THE FLAVOR WILL BE SWEET, FRESH AND DELICATE.

SERVES FOUR

INGREDIENTS
1 small young marrow, about 2 pounds
2 tablespoons olive oil
½ ounce butter
1 onion, chopped
1 tablespoon all-purpose flour
1¼ cups milk and light cream mixed
2 tablespoons chopped fresh parsley
salt and freshly ground black pepper

1 Preheat the oven to 350°F and cut the marrow into pieces measuring about 2 x 1 inches.

2 Heat the oil and butter in a flameproof casserole and fry the onion over a gentle heat until very soft.

3 Add the marrow and sauté for 1–2 minutes and then stir in the flour. Cook for a few minutes and then stir in the milk and cream mixture.

4 Add the parsley and seasoning, stir well and then cover and cook in the oven for 30–35 minutes. If liked, remove the lid for the final 5 minutes of cooking to brown the top. Alternately, serve the marrow in its rich pale sauce.

COOK'S TIP
Chopped fresh basil or a mixture of basil and chervil also tastes good in this dish.

CUCUMBER AND TROUT MOUSSE

THIS IS A VERY LIGHT, REFRESHING MOUSSE, MAKING THE MOST OF THE CLEAN TASTE OF CUCUMBER.
SERVE IT AS A STARTER OR FOR A LIGHT LUNCH WITH A GREEN SALAD.

SERVES SIX

INGREDIENTS

1 small cucumber
3 smoked trout fillets, about 5 ounces
  total weight
4 ounces ricotta cheese
1 tablespoon powdered gelatin
⅔ cup vegetable stock
12–14 pimiento stuffed olives, sliced
2 tablespoons lemon juice
1 teaspoon finely chopped fresh
  tarragon
⅔ cup heavy or whipping cream
2 egg whites
salt and freshly ground black pepper
peeled shrimp and lemon wedges,
  to garnish
For the topping
1 tablespoon powdered gelatin
6 tablespoons vegetable stock

1 Lightly oil six ramekin dishes. To prepare the topping, take one quarter of the cucumber and slice thinly . Sprinkle the gelatin over the stock, leave to soak for a few minutes and then place over a saucepan of simmering water and stir until completely dissolved.

2 Spoon a little of the gelatin mixture into each dish and arrange two or three cucumber slices on top. Put in the fridge to set. Pour over the remaining gelatin mixture and return to the fridge to set.

3 To make the mousse, peel and very finely dice the remaining cucumber and put in a bowl. Flake the fish, discarding the skin and any bones and add to the cucumber. Beat in the ricotta cheese.

4 Sprinkle the gelatin over 2 tablespoons of water in a bowl and leave to soak for a few minutes. Place over a saucepan of simmering water and stir until dissolved.

5 Heat the stock. Stir in the dissolved gelatin and leave until cool but not set. Pour over the trout and stir in the olives, lemon juice, tarragon and seasoning.

6 Lightly whip the cream and whisk the egg whites until stiff. Fold the cream into the trout mixture, followed by the egg whites. Spoon the mousse into the ramekin dishes, leveling the surface. Cover and chill for 1–2 hours and then unmold onto serving plates.

7 Garnish with any remaining cucumber slices together with a few peeled shrimp and some lemon wedges.

LOOFAH AND EGGPLANT RATATOUILLE

LOOFAHS HAVE A SIMILAR FLAVOR TO ZUCCHINI AND CONSEQUENTLY TASTE EXCELLENT WITH EGGPLANT AND TOMATOES. THE CILANTRO ADDS AN EXTRA EXOTIC TOUCH.

SERVES FOUR

INGREDIENTS

1 large or 2 medium eggplants
1 pound young loofahs or
   sponge gourds
1 large red bell pepper, cut into
   large chunks
8 ounces cherry tomatoes
8 ounces shallots, peeled
2 teaspoons ground coriander
4 tablespoons olive oil
2 garlic cloves, finely chopped
a few cilantro leaves
salt and freshly ground black pepper

1 Cut the eggplants into thick chunks and sprinkle the pieces with salt. Set aside in a colander for about 45 minutes and then rinse well under cold running water and pat dry.

2 Preheat the oven to 425°F. Slice the loofahs into ¾-inch pieces. Place the eggplant, loofah and pepper pieces, together with the tomatoes and shallots in a roasting pan which is large enough to take all the vegetables in a single layer.

3 Sprinkle with the ground coriander and olive oil and then scatter the chopped garlic and cilantro leaves on top. Season to taste.

4 Roast for about 25 minutes, stirring the vegetables occasionally, until the loofah is golden brown and the peppers are beginning to char at the edges.

CHOCOLATE ZUCCHINI CAKE

THE RECIPE FOR THIS MOIST CHOCOLATE CAKE COMES FROM AMERICA. PERHAPS AN UNLIKELY COMBINATION, IT IS A DELICIOUS VARIATION WELL WORTH TRYING.

SERVES FOUR TO SIX

INGREDIENTS

   4 ounces margarine
   ½ cup sunflower oil
   4 ounces caster sugar
   8 ounces soft brown sugar
   3 eggs, beaten
   ½ cup milk
   12 ounces all-purpose flour
   2 teaspoons baking powder
   4 tablespoons cocoa powder
   ½ teaspoon ground allspice
   1 pound zucchini, peeled and grated
   1 teaspoon vanilla extract
   8 ounces semisweet chocolate dots

1 Preheat the oven to 375°F and line a 9 x 13-inch baking pan with wax paper.

2 Cream the margarine, oil and sugars together until light and fluffy, then gradually beat in the eggs and milk.

3 Sift the flour, baking powder, cocoa powder and ground allspice together and fold gently into the mixture.

4 Stir in the grated zucchini and vanilla extract and spoon the mixture into the prepared pan. Smooth the top using a metal spatula and sprinkle the chocolate dots over the top.

5 Bake in the oven for 35–45 minutes until the cake is firm and a knife comes out clean. Cut into squares while still warm and then leave to cool.

PUMPKIN AND HAM FRITTATA

A FRITTATA IS AN ITALIAN VERSION OF THE SPANISH TORTILLA, A SUBSTANTIAL OMELET MADE OF EGGS AND VEGETABLES. IT IS CUT LIKE A CAKE AND CAN BE EATEN HOT, COLD OR WARM.

SERVES FOUR

INGREDIENTS

2 tablespoons sunflower oil
1 large onion, chopped
1 pound pumpkin, chopped into bite-size pieces
7 fluid ounces chicken stock
4 ounces smoked ham, chopped
6 eggs
2 teaspoons chopped fresh marjoram
salt and freshly ground black pepper

1 Preheat the oven to 375°F and oil a large shallow ovenproof dish. Heat the oil in a large frying pan and fry the onion for 3–4 minutes until softened.

2 Add the pumpkin and fry over a brisk heat for 3–4 minutes, stirring frequently. Stir in the stock, cover and simmer over low heat for 5–6 minutes until the pumpkin is slightly tender. Add the ham.

3 Pour the mixture into the prepared dish. Beat the eggs with the marjoram and a little seasoning. Pour into the dish and then bake for 20–25 minutes until the frittata is firm and lightly golden.

VEGETABLE FRUITS

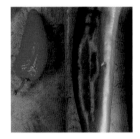

What would we do without our fabulous range of vegetable

fruits? Here are the most colorful, and probably most versatile

of all our vegetables. Tomatoes and peppers are the basis of

countless dishes, with chilies adding their particular personality

to any dish where a little extra something is required.

Eggplants too are wonderfully versatile and for a Caribbean

flavor, there are plantains and green bananas.

TOMATOES

Next to onions, tomatoes are one of the most important fresh ingredients in the kitchen. In Mediterranean cooking, they are fundamental. Along with garlic and olive oil, they form the basis of so many Italian, Spanish and Provençal recipes that it is hard to find many dishes in which they are not included.

History

Tomatoes are related to potatoes, eggplant and sweet and chili peppers, and all are members of the nightshade family. Some very poisonous members of this family may well have deterred our ancestors from taking to tomatoes. Indeed, the leaves of tomatoes are toxic and can result in a very bad stomach ache.

Tomatoes are native to western South America. By the time of the Spanish invasions in the sixteenth century, they were widely cultivated throughout the whole of South America and Mexico. Hernán Cortés, conqueror of the Aztecs, sent the first tomato plants, a yellow variety, to Spain (no doubt along with the plundered Aztec gold).

However, people did not instinctively take to this "golden apple." English horticulturists mostly grew them as ornamental plants to adorn their gardens and had little positive to say about them as food. Spain is recorded as the first country to use tomatoes in cooking, stewing them with oil and seasoning. Italy followed suit, but elsewhere they were treated with suspicion.

The first red tomatoes arrived in Europe in the eighteenth century, brought to Italy by two Jesuit priests. They were gradually accepted in northern Europe where, by the mid-nineteenth century, they were grown extensively, eaten raw, cooked or used for pickles.

Above right: Red and yellow cherry tomatoes
Below right: Yellow pear tomatoes
Opposite above: Round or salad tomatoes on the vine
Opposite below: Beefsteak tomatoes

Varieties

There are countless varieties of tomatoes, ranging from the huge beef tomatoes that measure 4 inches across, to tiny cherry tomatoes, not much bigger than a thumb nail. They come in all shapes, too – elongated, plum-shaped or slightly squarish and even pear-shaped.

Beefsteak Tomatoes: Large, ridged and deep red or orange in color, these have a good flavor so are good in salads.

Canned Tomatoes: Keep a store of canned tomatoes, especially in the winter when fresh ones tend to taste insipid. Tomatoes are one of the few vegetables that take well to canning, but steer clear of any that are flavored with garlic or herbs. It is far better to add flavoring yourself.

Cherry Tomatoes: These small, dainty tomatoes were once the prized treasures of gardeners but are now widely available. Although more expensive than round tomatoes, they have a delightful

sweet flavor and are worth paying the extra money for serving in salads or for cooking whole.

Plum Tomatoes: Richly flavored with fewer seeds than regular tomatoes, these Italian-grown tomatoes are usually recommended for cooking, although they can be used in salads.

Round or Salad Tomatoes: These are the common tomatoes found in grocers and supermarkets. They vary in size according to the exact type and season. Sun-ripened tomatoes have the best flavor, however; for through-the-year availability the fruit is often picked and ripened off the plant. These tomatoes are versatile in everyday cooking. Adding a pinch of sugar and taking care to season the dish well helps to overcome any weakness in flavor.

Sun-dried Tomatoes: This is one of the fashionable foods of the late Eighties and early Nineties. They add an evocative flavor to many Mediterranean dishes, but don't use them too indiscriminately.

Tomato Paste: This is good for adding an intense tomato flavor, but use carefully or the flavor will be overpowering. Tubes have screw tops and are better than cans as, once opened, they can be kept for up to 4–6 weeks in the fridge.

Yellow Tomatoes: These are exactly like red tomatoes - they may be round, plum or cherry-sized - except they are yellow.

Buying and Storing

Ideally, tomatoes should be allowed to ripen slowly on the plant so that their flavor can develop. Consequently, home-grown tomatoes are best, followed by those grown and sold locally. When buying from a supermarket or grocer, look at the leafy green tops; the fresher they look the better. Buy locally grown beefsteak or cherry tomatoes for salads and plum tomatoes for rich sauces. Paler tomatoes or those tinged with green will redden if kept in a brown paper bag or the salad drawer of the fridge, but if you intend to use tomatoes right away, buy bright red specimens. Overripe tomatoes, where the skin has split and they seem to be bursting with juice, are excellent in soups. However, check for any sign of mold or decay, as this will spoil all your good efforts.

Preparing

Slice tomatoes across rather than downward for salads and pizza toppings. For wedges, cut downward; halve or quarter and cut into two or three depending on the size of the tomato.

Cooking

Among the many classic tomato dishes is tomato soup, cooked to a delicate orange color with stock or milk, or simmered with vegetables, garlic and basil. Recipes *à la provençale* indicate that tomatoes are in the dish; in Provençal cooking and Italian dishes, tomatoes are used with fish, meat and vegetables, in sauces and stuffings, with pasta and in superb salads. The Italian *tri colore salata* is a combination of large tomatoes, mozzarella and basil (the three colors of the Italian flag). The natural astringency of tomatoes means that, in salads, they need only be sprinkled with a fruity olive oil.

Chopped Tomatoes

Chopped tomatoes add a depth of flavor to all sorts of meat and vegetarian dishes. Ideally, even in fairly rustic meals, the tomatoes should be peeled, since the skin can be irritating to eat once cooked. Some sauces also recommend seeding tomatoes, in which case cut the tomato into halves and scoop out the seeds before chopping (*above*).

Skinning Tomatoes

Cut a cross in the tops of the tomatoes, then place in a bowl and pour over boiling water. Leave for a minute (*above*), then use a sharp knife to peel away the skin, which should come away easily. Do a few at a time (five at most) otherwise they will begin to cook while soaking; boil water for the next batch when you have finished peeling. The water must be boiling.

EGGPLANTS

Many varieties of eggplants are cultivated and cooked all over the world. In Europe, Asia or America, they feature in a multitude of different dishes.

History

Although eggplant is a member of the nightshade family and thus related to potatoes, tomatoes and peppers, it was not discovered in the New World. The first mention of its cultivation is in China in 5 BC, and it is thought to have been eaten in India long before that. The Moors introduced the eggplant to Spain some 1200 years ago and it was grown in Andalucia. It is likely that they also introduced it to Italy, and possibly from there to other southern and eastern parts of Europe.

In spite of their popularity in Europe, eggplants did not become popular in the United States or Britain until very recently; although previous generations of food writers knew about them, they gave only the occasional recipe for cooking with them.

Above left: Plum tomatoes
Top: Eggplants
Above: Baby eggplants
Left: Japanese eggplants

Meanwhile, in the southern and eastern parts of Europe, eggplant had become extremely well liked, and today it is one of the most popular vegetables in the Mediterranean. Indeed, Italy, Greece and Turkey claim to have 100 ways of cooking it. In the Middle East, eggplant is also a central part of their cuisine.

Varieties

There are many different varieties of eggplants, differing in color, size and shape according to their country of origin. Small ivory-white and plump eggplants look like large eggs (hence their name in the States; they are called aubergines in the UK). Pretty striped eggplants may be either purple or pink and flecked with white irregular stripes. The Japanese or Asian eggplant is straight and very narrow, ranging in color from a pretty variegated purple and white to a solid purple. It has a tender, slightly sweet flesh. Most eggplants, however, are either glossy purple or almost black and can be long and slim or fat like zeppelins. All eggplants have a similar

flavor and texture; they taste bland yet slightly smoky when cooked, and the flesh is spongy to touch when raw, but soft after cooking.

Buying and Storing

Eggplants should feel heavy and firm to the touch, with glossy, unblemished skins. They will keep well in the salad drawer of the fridge for up to two weeks.

Preparing

When frying eggplants for any dish where they need slicing (e.g. ratatouille), it is a good idea to salt the slices first in order to draw out some of their moisture, otherwise, they absorb enormous quantities of oil during cooking (they absorb copious amounts anyway, but

salting reduces this slightly). Salting also used to be advised to reduce their bitterness but today's varieties are rarely bitter.

To salt eggplants, cut into slices, about ¹/₂ inch thick for fried slices, *(top right)* or segments *(above right)* and sprinkle generously with salt. Leave them to drain in a colander for about one hour, then rinse well and gently squeeze out the moisture from each slice or carefully pat dry with a piece of cheesecloth.

Cooking

Eggplant slices can be fried in olive oil, as they are or first coated in batter – both popular Italian and Greek starters.

For moussaka, *parmigiana* and other dishes where eggplant is layered with

other ingredients, fry the slices briefly in olive oil. This gives them a tasty crust, while the inside stays soft.

To make a purée, such as for Poor Man's Caviar, first prick the eggplant all over with a fork and then roast in a moderately hot oven for about 30 minutes until tender. Scoop out the flesh and mix with scallions, lemon juice and olive oil. One of the most famous eggplant dishes is *Imam Bayaldi* – "the Iman fainted" – fried eggplant stuffed with onions, garlic, tomato, spices and lots of olive oil.

Above left: White eggplants
Below left: Striped eggplants
Above: Thai eggplants, including white,
yellow and pea eggplants

PEPPERS

In spite of their name, peppers have nothing to do with the spice pepper used as a seasoning, although early explorers may have been mistaken in thinking the fruit of the shrubby plant looked like the spice they were seeking. It is thanks to this 400-year-old mistake that the name "pepper" has stuck.

History

The journeys Christopher Columbus and the conquistadors made were partly to find the spices Marco Polo had found a hundred years earlier in the Far East. Instead of the Orient, however, Columbus discovered the Americas, and instead of spices, he found maize, potatoes and tomatoes. He would have noted, though, that the Native Americans flavored their food with ground peppers, and since it was hot, like pepper, perhaps wishful thinking colored his objectivity. In any case, he returned with the new vegetables, describing them as peppers and advertising them as more pungent than those from Caucasus.

Varieties

Peppers and chilies are both members of the capsicum family. To distinguish between them, peppers are called sweet peppers, bell peppers and even bullnose peppers and come in a variety of colors – red, green, yellow, white, orange and a dark purple-black.

The color of the pepper tells you something about its flavor. Green peppers are the least mature and have a fresh "raw" flavor. Red peppers are ripened green peppers and are distinctly sweeter. Yellow/orange peppers taste more or less like red peppers, although perhaps slightly less sweet and if you have a fine palate you may be able to detect a difference. Black peppers have a similar flavor to green peppers but when cooked are a bit disappointing as they turn green; so if you buy them for their dramatic color, they are best used in salads.

In Greece and other parts of southern Europe, longer, slimmer peppers are often available which have a more pronounced sweet and pungent flavor than the bell-shaped peppers in the US – although this may be because they are locally picked and therefore absolutely fresh. Whichever is the case, they are quite delicious.

Buying and Storing

Peppers should look glossy and sprightly and feel hard and crisp; avoid any that look wrinkled or have damp soft patches. They will keep for a few days at the bottom of the fridge.

Preparing

To prepare stuffed peppers, cut off the top and then cut away the inner core and pith, and shake out the seeds. The seeds and core are easily removed when halving, quartering or slicing.

Cooking

There are countless ways of cooking peppers. Sliced, they can be fried with onions and garlic in olive oil and then braised with tomatoes and herbs. This is the basic ratatouille; other vegetables, such as zucchini and eggplant, can of course be added.

Peppers can be roasted, either with ratatouille ingredients or with only onions and garlic. Cut into large pieces, place in a roasting pan and sprinkle with olive oil, torn basil and seasoning. Roast in a very hot oven (425°F) for about 30 minutes, turning occasionally. Broiled peppers are another superb dish. Once broiled they can be skinned to reveal a soft, luxurious texture and added to salads.

Above far left: Red, green and orange bell peppers
Below far left: Yellow bell peppers
Above left: White bell peppers
Above right: Purple bell peppers

Skinning Peppers

Cut the pepper into quarters lengthwise and broil, skin side up (*above*), until the skin is charred and evenly blistered. Place the pieces immediately into a plastic bag (you will need tongs or a fork as they will be hot) and close the top of the bag with a tie or a loose knot. Leave for a few minutes and then remove from the bag and the skin will peel off easily.

CHILIES

Some people apparently become so addicted to the taste of hot food that they carry little jars of chopped dried chilies around with them and scatter them over every meal. Although this is a bit extreme, it is chilies more than any other ingredient that spice up our mealtimes.

Varieties

Chilies are the most important seasoning in the world after salt. Unlike peppers, to which they are closely related, the different varieties of chili can have widely different heat values – from the "just about bearable" to the "knock your head off" variety.

Anaheim Chili: A long, thin chili with a blunt end, named after the Californian city. It can be red or green and has a mild, sweet taste.

Ancho Chili/Pepper: These look like tiny peppers. They are mild enough to taste their underlying sweetness.

Birdseye or Bird Chili: These small red chilies are fiery hot. Also known as pequin chilies.

Cayenne Pepper: This is made from the dried, ground seeds and pods of chilies. The name comes from the capital of French Guiana, north of Brazil, although the cayenne chili does not grow any longer and the pepper is made from chilies grown all over the world.

Early Jalapeño: A popular American chili, which starts dark green and gradually turns to red.

Habañero: Often called Scotch Bonnet, this is the hottest of all chilies and is small and can be green, red or yellow. Color is no real guide to its heat properties, so don't be fooled into thinking that green ones are mild. They are all *very* hot. The habañero comes from Mexico and is frequently used in Mexican and Caribbean dishes.

Hot Gold Spike: A large, pale, yellow-green fruit grown in the southwestern United States: it is very hot.

Above: Birdseye chilies
Left: Habañero chilies (in and below bowl) and Yellow wax peppers

Preparing

The capsaicin in chilies is most concentrated in the pith inside the pod and this, together with the seeds, should be cut away (*below*) unless you want maximum heat. Capsaicin irritates the skin and especially the eyes, so take care when preparing chilies. Either wear gloves or wash your hands thoroughly after handling chilies.If you rub your eyes, even if you have washed your hands carefully, it will be painful.

Cooking

In Mexican cooking chilies play a vital, and almost central role. It is difficult to think of any savory Mexican dish that does not contain either fresh chilies or some form of processed chili, whether canned, dried or ground. Other cuisines, however, are equally enthusiastic about chilies. They are essential in curries and similar dishes from India and the Far East, and in Caribbean and Creole food they are also used extensively.

If you have developed a tolerance for really hot food, then there is no reason why you shouldn't add as many as you wish. In general, however, use chilies discreetly, if for no better reason than you can't take the heat away if you make a mistake.

Above: Ancho chilies (left) and Anaheim chilies (on board)

Poblano: A small, dark green chili, served whole in Spain either roasted or broiled. They are mostly mild but you can get the rogue fiery one, so beware if eating them whole.
Red Chili: These are long, rather wrinkled chilies which are green at first and then gradually ripen to red. They are of variable hotness and, because they are so long and thin, are rather difficult to prepare.
Serrano Chili: A long, red and extremely hot chili.
Tabasco: A sauce made with chilies, salt and vinegar and first made in New Orleans. It is a fiery sauce, popular in Creole, Caribbean and Mexican cookery – or indeed in any dish requiring last minute heat.
Yellow Wax Pepper: Pale yellow to green, these can vary from mild to hot.

Buying and Storing

Some fresh chilies look wrinkled even in their prime and therefore this is not a good guide to their freshness. They should, however, be unblemished, and avoid any which are soft or bruised.

The substance which makes the chili hot is a volatile oil called capsaicin. This differs not only from one type to another but also from plant to plant, depending on growing conditions; the more the plant has to struggle to survive in terms of light, water, soil, etc, the more capsaicin will be produced. It is therefore impossible to tell how hot a chili will be before tasting, although some types are naturally hotter than others. The belief that green chilies are milder than red ones does not necessarily follow; generally red chilies will have ripened for longer in the sun with the result that they will only be sweeter for all that sunshine. Chilies can be stored in a plastic bag in the fridge for a few days.

PLANTAINS AND GREEN BANANAS

While bananas are well and truly fruit, eaten almost exclusively as a dessert or by themselves as fruit, plantains can reasonably be considered among the vegetable fraternity as they have a definite savory flavor, are normally eaten as a first or main course and can only be eaten once cooked.

Varieties

Plantains: Also known as cooking bananas, these have a coarser flesh and more savory flavor than sweet bananas. While superficially they look exactly like our own bananas, they are, on closer inspection, altogether larger and heavier looking. They can vary in color from the unripe fruit, which is green, through yellow to a mottled black color, which is when the fruit is completely ripe.

Green Bananas: Only certain types of green bananas are used in African and Caribbean cooking, and the "greenish" bananas you find in most western supermarkets are normally eating bananas, just waiting to ripen. If you need green bananas for a recipe, look out for them in West Indian or African stores.

Preparing

Plantains: These are inedible raw and must be cooked before eating. Unless very ripe, the skin can be tricky to remove. With yellow and green plantains, cut the fruit into short lengths, then slit the skin along the natural ridge of each piece of plantain. Gently ease the skin away from the flesh and pull the skin until it peels off completely (*below*).

Once peeled, plantains can be sliced horizontally or into lengths and then roasted or fried. Like bananas, plantains will discolor if exposed to the air so, if not using immediately, sprinkle with lemon juice or place in a bowl of salted water.

Green Bananas: These should be prepared in a similar way. As with plantains, green bananas should not be eaten raw and are usually boiled, either in their skins or not, according to the recipe.

If making green banana crisps, use a potato peeler to produce the thinnest slices (*left*).

If cooking plantains or green bananas in their skins, slit the skin lengthwise along the sides and place in a saucepan of salted water. Bring to the boil, simmer gently for about 20 minutes until tender and then cool. The peel can then easily be removed before slicing.

Cooking and Serving

Plantains and green bananas both have an excellent flavor. In many African and Caribbean recipes they are roasted or fried and then served simply with salt. However, if boiled, they can be sliced

and served in a simple salad with a few sliced onions, or added to something far more elaborate like a gado gado salad, with mango, avocado, lettuce and shrimp.

Plantains also make a delicious soup, where they are often teamed with corn. After frying an onion and a little garlic, add two sliced and peeled plantains, together with tomatoes, if liked. Fry gently for a few minutes and then add vegetable stock to cover and one or two sliced chilies, together with about 6 ounces of corn. Simmer gently together until the plantain is tender.

Above left: Plantains
Below left: Green bananas
Below: Canned ackee

ACKEE

Ackee is a tropical fruit which is used in a variety of savory dishes, mainly of Caribbean origin, where the fruit is very popular. The fruit itself is bright red and, when ripe, bursts open to reveal three large black seeds and a soft, creamy flesh resembling scrambled eggs. It has a slightly lemony flavor and is traditionally served with saltfish to make one of Jamaica's national dishes. Only buy ripe fruit as, when under-ripe, certain parts of the fruit are toxic.

However, unless you are visiting the Caribbean you are probably only likely to find ackee in cans, and indeed most recipes call for canned ackee which is a good substitute for the fresh fruit.

Jamaican cooks also use ackee to add a subtle flavor to a variety of vegetable and bean dishes. The canned ackee needs very little cooking, and should be added to dishes in the last few minutes of cooking. Take care when stirring into a dish as it breaks up very easily.

AVOCADOS

The avocado has been known by many names – butter pear and alligator pear to name but two. It earned the title butter pear clearly because of its consistency, but alligator pear was the original Spanish name. Although you would be forgiven for thinking this was due to its knobbly skin (among some varieties anyway), the name in fact derives from the Spanish which was based on the Aztec word, the basically unpronounceable *ahuacatl.* From this to the easily-said alligator and thence to avocado was but a short step.

History

The avocado is a New World fruit, native to Mexico, but while it would have been "discovered" by the Old World explorers, it didn't become a popular food in Europe until the middle of this century, when modern transport meant that growers in California, who started farming avocados in the middle of the nineteenth century, could market this fruit worldwide. Avocados are now also exported by South Africa and Australia.

Nutrition

The avocado is high in protein and carbohydrate. It is one of the few fruits that contains fat, and it is also rich in potassium, Vitamin C, some B vitamins and Vitamin E. Its rich oils, particularly its Vitamin E content, mean that it is not only useful as food, but for skin and hair

care too, something the Aztecs and Incas were aware of a thousand years ago. The cosmetic industry may have been in its infancy, but it still knew a good thing when it saw it.

Because of their valuable protein and vitamin content, avocados are a popular food for babies. They are easily blended, and small children generally enjoy their creamy texture and pleasant flavor.

Varieties

There are four varieties: Hass, the purple-black small knobbly avocado, the Ettinger and Fuerte, which are pear-shaped and have smooth green skin, and the Nabal, which is rounder in shape. The black-colored Hass has golden-yellow flesh, while green avocados have pale green to yellow flesh.

Buying and Storing

The big problem in buying avocados is that they're never ripe when you want them to be. How often do you see shoppers standing by the avocado shelves, feeling around for that rare creature, the perfectly ripe avocado? Most times they all feel as hard as rocks; that or else they're hopelessly soft and squashy and clearly past their best. The proper and sensible thing to do is buy fruit a few days before you need it. An unripe avocado will ripen in 4–7 days at room temperature. Once it is ripe, it will keep well in the fridge for a few days, but you still need to plan well in advance if you want to be sure of the perfect avocado.

The alternative is to hope for the best and keep feeling around until you find a ripe fruit. A perfect avocado should have a clean, unblemished skin without any brown or black patches. If ripe, it should "give" slightly if squeezed gently in the hand, but not so much that it actually feels soft. Over-ripe avocados are really not worth bothering with, however persuasive and generous the offer from the man on the market. The flesh will be unattractively brown and stringy and the bits of good flesh you do manage to salvage will be soft and pulpy. Good for a dip, but nothing much else.

Preparing

Although they are simple fruits, avocados can be the devil to prepare. Once peeled, you are left with a slippery object which is then almost impossible to remove from the stone.

If you intend to eat the avocados in halves, it's fairly simple to just prise out the pit once halved. If you want to slice the fruit, use this tip. The only thing you need is a very sharp knife. Cut the avocado in half, remove the stone and then, with the skin still on, cut through the flesh and the skin to make slices. It is then relatively simple to strip off the peel.

Remember to sprinkle the slices with lemon juice as the flesh discolors once exposed to the air.

Cooking

Most popular raw, avocados can also be baked, broiled or used in sautéed and sauced dishes.

Serving Ideas

As well as shrimp or vinaigrette, a half avocado can hold a mixture of chopped tomatoes and cucumber, a mild garlic cheese dip or a sour cream potato salad. Slices of avocado are delicious served with sliced tomatoes and mozzarella, sprinkled simply with olive oil, lemon juice and plenty of black pepper. Avocado can be chopped and added to a salad, or puréed for a rich dressing.

In Mexico, where avocados grow in abundance, there are countless avocado recipes. Guacamole is perhaps the best known, but they are also eaten in soups and stews and commonly used to garnish tacos and enchiladas.

BREADFRUIT

Breadfruit is the name for a tropical tree that grows on the islands of the South Pacific ocean. The fruit of the tree is about the size of a small melon with a rough rind and a pale, mealy flesh.

Preparing

The fruit should be peeled and the core removed.

Cooking

Breadfruit can be treated like potatoes: the flesh may be boiled, baked or fried. It is a staple food for the people of the Pacific islands who bake the flesh, or dry and grind it for biscuits, bread and puddings. It has a sweet flavor and soft texture when ripe.

Left (clockwise from the right): Fuerte, Hass and Nabal avocados
Right: Breadfruit

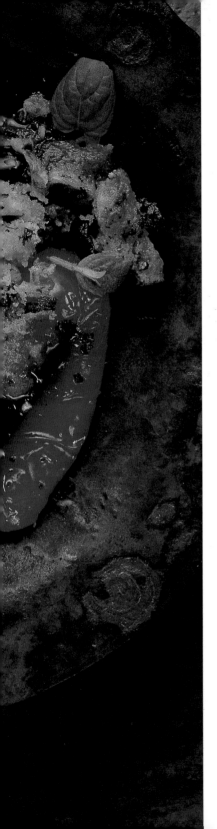

VEGETABLE
FRUIT
RECIPES

Vegetable fruits are the perfect excuse for letting
your cook's imagination run riot. Tomatoes, peppers,
chilies and eggplants have a wonderful affinity, and
by simply putting two or three of these ingredients
together, almost by magic you have a superb summer
supper. Whether it's Eggplant and Zucchini Bake,
Gazpacho, Spinach and Pepper Pizza or Eggs
Flamenco, our favorite vegetable fruits play
a starring role. And if you fancy sampling
Caribbean cuisine, try Plantain Appetizer,
served with piquant Guacamole.

EGGPLANT AND ZUCCHINI BAKE

THIS IS A WONDERFULLY WARMING DISH FOR A WINTER'S DAY. USE
FRESH BASIL, IF AVAILABLE, AS THE TASTE IS FAR SUPERIOR.

SERVES FOUR TO SIX

INGREDIENTS
1 large eggplant
2 tablespoons olive oil
1 large onion, chopped
1–2 garlic cloves, crushed
2 pounds tomatoes, peeled
  and chopped
a handful of basil leaves, shredded
  or 1 teaspoon dried basil
1 tablespoon chopped fresh parsley
2 zucchini, sliced lengthwise
all-purpose flour, for coating
5–6 tablespoons sunflower oil
12 ounces mozzarella, sliced
1 ounce Parmesan cheese, grated

1 Slice the eggplant, sprinkle with salt and set aside for 45–60 minutes.

2 Heat the olive oil in a large frying pan. Fry the onion and garlic for 3–4 minutes until softened. Stir in the tomatoes, half the basil, the parsley and seasoning. Bring to a boil. Reduce the heat and cook, stirring, for 25–35 minutes until thickened. Mash the tomatoes to a pulp.

3 Rinse and dry the eggplant. Dust the eggplant and zucchini with flour.

4 Heat the sunflower oil in another frying pan and fry the eggplant and zucchini until golden brown. Set aside.

5 Preheat the oven to 350°F. Butter an ovenproof dish. Put a layer of eggplant and then zucchini in the dish, pour over half the sauce and scatter with half the mozzarella. Sprinkle over most of the remaining basil and a little parsley. Repeat the layers, ending with mozzarella. Sprinkle the Parmesan cheese and remaining herbs on top and bake for 30–35 minutes. Serve at once.

EGGPLANT WITH TZATZIKI

SERVES FOUR

INGREDIENTS
2 medium-sized eggplants
oil, for deep frying
salt
For the batter
3 ounces all-purpose flour
1 egg
½–⅔ cup milk, or ½ milk, ½ water
pinch of salt
For the tzatziki
½ cucumber, peeled and diced
⅔ cup plain yogurt
1 garlic clove, crushed
1 tablespoon chopped fresh mint

1 To make the tzatziki, place the cucumber in a colander, sprinkle with salt and leave for 30 minutes. Rinse, drain well and pat dry on kitchen paper. Mix the yogurt, garlic, mint and cucumber in a bowl. Cover and chill. Slice the eggplant lengthwise. Sprinkle with salt. Leave for 1 hour.

2 To make the batter, sift the flour and salt into a large bowl add the egg and milk and beat until smooth.

3 Rinse the eggplant slices and pat dry. Heat ½ inch of oil in a large frying pan. Dip the eggplant slices in the batter and fry them for 3–4 minutes until golden, turning once. Drain on paper towels and serve with the tzatziki.

GAZPACHO

GAZPACHO IS A CLASSIC SPANISH SOUP. IT IS POPULAR ALL OVER SPAIN BUT NOWHERE MORE SO THAN IN ANDALUCIA, WHERE THERE ARE HUNDREDS OF VARIATIONS. IT IS A COLD SOUP OF TOMATOES, TOMATO JUICE, GREEN BELL PEPPER AND GARLIC, WHICH IS SERVED WITH A SELECTION OF GARNISHES.

SERVES FOUR

INGREDIENTS
3–3½ pounds ripe tomatoes
1 green bell pepper, seeded and
   roughly chopped
2 garlic cloves, crushed
2 slices white bread, crusts removed
4 tablespoons olive oil
4 tablespoons tarragon wine vinegar
⅔ cup tomato juice
good pinch of sugar
salt and freshly ground black pepper
ice cubes, to serve
For the garnishes
   2 tablespoons sunflower oil
   2–3 slices white bread, diced
   1 small cucumber, peeled and
      finely diced
   1 small onion, finely chopped
   1 red bell pepper, seeded and finely diced
   1 green bell pepper, seeded and finely
      diced
   2 hard-boiled eggs, chopped

1 Skin the tomatoes, then quarter them and remove the cores.

2 Place the pepper in a food processor and process for a few seconds. Add the tomatoes, garlic, bread, olive oil and vinegar and process again. Add the tomato juice, sugar, seasoning and a little extra tomato juice or cold water and process. The consistency should be thick but not too stodgy.

3 Pour into a bowl and chill for at least 2 hours but no more than 12 hours, otherwise the textures deteriorate.

4 To prepare the bread cubes to use as a garnish, heat the oil in a frying pan and fry them until golden brown. Drain well.

5 Place each garnish in a separate small dish, or alternately arrange them in rows on a large plate.

6 Just before serving, stir a few ice cubes into the soup and then spoon into serving bowls. Serve with the garnishes.

TOMATO AND BASIL TART

IN FRANCE, PATISSERIES DISPLAY MOUTH-WATERING SAVORY TARTS IN THEIR WINDOWS. THIS IS A VERY SIMPLE YET EXTREMELY TASTY TART MADE WITH RICH PIECRUST PASTRY, FILLED WITH SLICES OF MOZZARELLA CHEESE AND TOMATOES AND TOPPED WITH OLIVE OIL AND BASIL LEAVES.

SERVES FOUR

INGREDIENTS
    5 ounces young mozzarella,
        thinly sliced
    4 large tomatoes, thickly sliced
    about 10 basil leaves
    2 tablespoons olive oil
    2 garlic cloves, thinly sliced
    sea salt and freshly ground
        black pepper
For the pastry
    4 ounces all-purpose flour
    pinch of salt
    2 ounces butter or margarine
    1 egg yolk

1 To prepare the pastry, mix together the flour and salt, then rub in the butter or margarine and egg yolk. Add enough cold water to make a smooth dough and knead lightly on a floured surface. Place in a plastic bag and chill for about 1 hour.

2 Preheat the oven to 375°F. Remove pastry from the fridge and allow about 10 minutes for it to return to room temperature and then roll out into an 8-inch round. Press into the bottom of an 8-inch flan dish or pan. Prick all over with a fork and then bake in the oven for about 10 minutes until firm but not brown. Allow to cool slightly. Reduce the oven temperature to 350°F.

3 Arrange the mozzarella slices over the pastry base. On top, arrange a single layer of the sliced tomatoes, overlapping them slightly. Dip the basil leaves in olive oil and arrange them on the tomatoes.

4 Scatter the garlic on top, drizzle with the remaining olive oil and season with a little salt and a good sprinkling of black pepper. Bake for 40–45 minutes, until the tomatoes are well cooked. Serve hot.

ITALIAN ROAST PEPPERS

SIMPLE AND EFFECTIVE, THIS DISH WILL DELIGHT ANYONE WHO LIKES PEPPERS. IT CAN BE EATEN EITHER AS A STARTER SERVED WITH ITALIAN BREAD, OR AS A LIGHT LUNCH WITH COUSCOUS OR RICE.

SERVES FOUR

INGREDIENTS
    4 small red bell peppers, halved,
      cored and seeded
    2–3 tablespoons capers, chopped
    10–12 black olives, pitted
      and chopped
    2 garlic cloves, finely chopped
    2–3 ounces mozzarella, grated
    1–1½ ounces fresh white bread
      crumbs
    ½ cup white wine
    3 tablespoons olive oil
    1 teaspoon finely chopped fresh mint
    1 teaspoon chopped fresh parsley
    freshly ground black pepper

1 Preheat the oven to 350°F and butter a shallow ovenproof dish. Place the peppers tightly together in the dish and sprinkle over the chopped capers, black olives, garlic, mozzarella and bread crumbs.

2 Pour over the wine and olive oil and then sprinkle with the mint, parsley and freshly ground black pepper.

3 Bake for 30–40 minutes until the topping is crisp and golden brown.

SWEET PEPPER CHOUX WITH ANCHOVIES

*THE RATATOUILLE VEGETABLES IN THIS DISH ARE ROASTED INSTEAD OF STEWED, AND HAVE A
WONDERFUL AROMATIC FLAVOR. ANY COMBINATION OF RED, GREEN OR YELLOW BELL PEPPERS CAN BE
USED. FOR VEGETARIANS, OMIT THE ANCHOVIES.*

SERVES SIX

INGREDIENTS

  1¼ cups water
  4 ounces butter or margarine
  5 ounces all-purpose flour
  4 eggs
  4 ounces Gruyère or Cheddar cheese,
    finely diced
  1 teaspoon Dijon mustard
  salt

For the filling

  3 bell peppers; red, yellow and green
  1 large onion, cut into eighths
    or sixteenths
  3 tomatoes, peeled and quartered
  1 zucchini, sliced
  6 basil leaves, torn in strips
  1 garlic clove, crushed
  2 tablespoons olive oil
  about 18 black olives, pitted
  3 tablespoons red wine
  ¾ cup passata or puréed canned
    tomatoes
  2-ounce can anchovy fillets, drained
  salt and freshly ground black pepper

1 Preheat the oven to 475°F and grease
six individual ovenproof dishes. To
prepare the filling, halve the peppers,
discard the seeds and core and cut into
1-inch chunks.

2 Place the peppers, onion, tomatoes
and zucchini in a roasting pan. Add the
basil, garlic and olive oil, stirring so the
vegetables are well coated. Sprinkle with
salt and pepper and then roast for about
25–30 minutes until the vegetables are
just beginning to blacken at the edges.

3 Reduce the oven temperature to
400°F. To make the choux pastry, put the
water and butter or margarine together in
a large saucepan, heat until the butter
melts. Remove from the heat and add all
the flour immediately. Beat well with a
wooden spoon for about 30 seconds until
smooth. Allow to cool slightly.

4 Beat in the eggs, one at a time, and
then continue beating until the mixture is
thick and glossy. Stir in the cheese and
mustard, then season with salt and
pepper. Spoon the mixture around the
sides of the prepared dishes.

5 Spoon the vegetables into a large
mixing bowl, together with any juices or
scrapings from the bottom of the pan.
Add the olives and stir in the wine and
passata or puréed tomatoes. (Or, you can
stir these into the roasting pan but allow
the pan to cool slightly otherwise the
liquid will boil and evaporate.)

6 Divide the pepper mixture between
the six dishes and arrange the drained
anchovy fillets on top. Bake in the oven
for about 25–35 minutes until the choux
pastry is puffy and golden. Serve hot with
a fresh green salad.

EGGS FLAMENCO

A VARIATION OF THE POPULAR BASQUE DISH PIPERADE, THE EGGS ARE COOKED WHOLE INSTEAD OF BEATING THEM BEFORE ADDING TO THE PEPPER MIXTURE. THE RECIPE IS KNOWN AS CHAKCHOUKA IN NORTH AFRICA AND MAKES A GOOD LUNCH OR SUPPER DISH.

SERVES FOUR

INGREDIENTS
2 red bell peppers, seeded
1 green bell pepper, seeded
2 tablespoons olive oil
1 large onion, finely sliced
2 garlic cloves, crushed
5–6 tomatoes, peeled and chopped
½ cup puréed canned tomatoes or
    tomato juice
good pinch of dried basil
4 eggs
8 teaspoons light cream
pinch of cayenne pepper (optional)
salt and freshly ground black pepper

1 Preheat the oven to 350°F. Thinly slice the red and green peppers. Heat the olive oil in a large frying pan. Fry the onion and garlic gently for about 5 minutes, stirring, until softened.

2 Add the peppers to the onions and fry for 10 minutes. Stir in the tomatoes and tomato purée or juice, the basil and seasoning. Cook gently for a further 10 minutes until the peppers are soft.

3 Spoon the mixture into four ovenproof dishes, preferably earthenware. Make a hole in the centre and break an egg into each. Spoon 2 teaspoons cream over the yolk of each egg and sprinkle with a little black pepper or cayenne, as preferred.

4 Bake in the oven for 12–15 minutes until the white of the egg is lightly set. Serve at once with chunks of crusty warm Italian bread.

SPINACH AND PEPPER PIZZA

MAKES TWO 12-inch PIZZAS

INGREDIENTS
 1 pound fresh spinach
 4 tablespoons light cream
 1 ounce Parmesan cheese, grated
 1 tablespoon olive oil
 1 large onion, chopped
 1 garlic clove, crushed
 ½ green bell pepper, seeded and thinly
   sliced
 ½ red bell pepper, seeded and thinly
   sliced
 6–8 fluid ounces passata sauce or
   puréed tomatoes
 2 ounces black olives, pitted and
   chopped
 1 tablespoon chopped fresh basil
 6 ounces mozzarella cheese, grated
 6 ounces Cheddar cheese, grated
 salt
For the dough
 1 ounce fresh yeast or 1 tablespoon
   dried yeast and 1 teaspoon sugar
 12 ounces unbleached all-purpose flour
 2 tablespoons olive oil
 1 teaspoon salt
 about ⅞ cup warm water

1 To make the dough, cream together the fresh yeast and ⅔ cup of the water and set aside until frothy. If using dried yeast, stir the sugar into ⅔ cup water, sprinkle over the yeast and leave until frothy.

2 Place the flour and salt in a large bowl, make a well in the center and pour in the olive oil and yeast mixture. Add the remaining water, mix to make a stiff but pliable dough. Knead on a lightly floured surface for about 10 minutes until smooth and elastic.

3 Shape the dough into a ball and place in a lightly oiled bowl, cover with plastic wrap and leave in a warm place for about 1 hour until it has doubled in size.

4 To prepare the topping, cook the spinach over moderate heat for 4–5 minutes until the leaves have wilted. Strain and press out the excess liquid. Place in a bowl and mix with the cream, Parmesan cheese and salt to taste.

5 Heat the oil in a frying pan and fry the onion and garlic over moderate heat for 3–4 minutes until the onion has slightly softened. Add the peppers and continue cooking until the onion is lightly golden, stirring regularly.

6 Preheat the oven to 425°F. Knead the dough briefly on a lightly floured surface. Divide the dough and roll out into two 12-inch rounds.

7 Spread each base with the passata sauce or puréed tomatoes. Add the onions and peppers and then spread over the spinach mixture. Scatter the olives and basil leaves and sprinkle with the mozzarella and Cheddar cheeses.

8 Bake in the oven for 15–20 minutes, or until the crust is lightly browned and the top is beginning to turn golden. Allow to cool slightly before serving.

ENCHILADAS WITH HOT CHILI SAUCE

IN MEXICO, CHILIES APPEAR IN ALMOST EVERY SAVORY DISH, EITHER IN THE FORM OF CHILI POWDER OR CHOPPED, SLICED OR WHOLE. BY MEXICAN STANDARDS, THIS IS A LOW-HEAT VERSION OF THE POPULAR CHICKEN ENCHILADAS. IF YOU LIKE YOUR FOOD HOT, ADD EXTRA CHILIES TO THE SAUCE.

SERVES FOUR

INGREDIENTS
  8 wheat tortillas
  6 ounces Cheddar cheese, grated
  1 onion, finely chopped
  12 ounces cooked chicken, cut into
    small chunks
  1¼ cups sour cream
  1 avocado, sliced and tossed in lemon
    juice, to garnish
  For the salsa picante
  1–2 green chilies
  1 tablespoon vegetable oil
  1 onion, chopped
  1 garlic clove, crushed
  14 ounce-can chopped tomatoes
  2 tablespoons tomato paste
  salt and freshly ground black pepper

3 Preheat the oven to 350°F and butter a shallow ovenproof dish. Take one tortilla and sprinkle with a good pinch of cheese and chopped onion, about 1½ ounces of chicken and 1 tablespoon of salsa picante. Pour over 1 tablespoon of sour cream, roll up and place, seam side down, in the dish. Make seven more enchiladas.

4 Pour the remaining salsa over the top and sprinkle with the remaining cheese and onion. Bake in the oven for about 25–30 minutes until the top is golden. Serve with the remaining sour cream either poured over, or in a separate jug, and garnish with the sliced avocado.

1 To make the salsa picante, cut the chilies in half lengthwise and carefully remove the cores and seeds. Slice the chilies very finely. Heat the oil in a frying pan and fry the onion and garlic for about 3–4 minutes until softened. Add the tomatoes, tomato paste and chilies. Simmer gently, uncovered, for about 12–15 minutes, stirring frequently.

2 Pour the sauce into a food processor or blender, and process until smooth. Return to the heat and cook very gently, uncovered, for a further 15 minutes. Season to taste then set aside.

HOT SOUR CHICKPEAS

THIS DISH, KHATTE CHOLE, IS EATEN AS A SNACK ALL OVER INDIA, SOLD BY ITINERANT STREET VENDORS. THE HEAT OF THE CHILIES IS DAMPENED PARTLY BY THE CILANTRO, WHILE THE LEMON JUICE ADDS A WONDERFUL SOURNESS.

SERVES FOUR

INGREDIENTS
    12 ounces chickpeas, soaked
        overnight
    4 tablespoons vegetable oil
    2 medium onions, very finely chopped
    8 ounces tomatoes, peeled and finely
        chopped
    1 tablespoon ground coriander
    1 tablespoon ground cumin
    1 teaspoon ground fenugreek
    1 teaspoon ground cinnamon
    1–2 hot green chilies, seeded
        and finely sliced
    about 1-inch piece fresh ginger,
        grated
    4 tablespoons lemon juice
    1 tablespoon chopped fresh cilantro
    salt

1 Drain the chickpeas and place them in a large saucepan, cover with water and bring to a boil. Cover and simmer for 1–1¼ hours until tender, making sure the chickpeas do not boil dry. Drain, reserving the cooking liquid.

2 Heat the oil in a large flameproof casserole. Reserve about 2 tablespoons of the chopped onions and fry the remainder in the casserole over moderate heat for 4–5 minutes, stirring frequently, until tinged with brown.

3 Add the tomatoes and continue cooking over moderately low heat for 5–6 minutes until soft. Stir frequently, mashing the tomatoes to a pulp.

4 Stir in the coriander, cumin, fenugreek and cinnamon. Cook for 30 seconds and then add the chickpeas and 12 fluid ounces of the reserved cooking liquid. Season with salt, cover and simmer very gently for about 15–20 minutes, stirring occasionally and adding more cooking liquid if the mixture becomes too dry.

5 Meanwhile, mix the reserved onion with the chili, ginger and lemon juice.

6 Just before serving, stir the onion and chili mixture and the cilantro into the chickpeas, and adjust the seasoning.

GUACAMOLE

THIS IS QUITE A FIERY VERSION OF A POPULAR MEXICAN DISH, ALTHOUGH PROBABLY NOWHERE NEAR AS HOT AS YOU WOULD BE SERVED IN MEXICO, WHERE IT SEEMS HEAT KNOWS NO BOUNDS!

SERVES FOUR

INGREDIENTS
2 ripe avocados, peeled and pitted
2 tomatoes, peeled, seeded and finely
  chopped
6 scallions, finely chopped
1–2 chilies, seeded and finely
  chopped
2 tablespoons fresh lime or lemon
  juice
1 tablespoon chopped fresh cilantro
salt and freshly ground black pepper
coriander sprig, to garnish

1 Put the avocado halves into a bowl and mash roughly with a large fork.

2 Add the remaining ingredients. Mix well and season according to taste. Serve garnished with fresh cilantro.

PLANTAIN APPETIZER

PLANTAINS ARE A TYPE OF COOKING BANANA WITH A LOWER SUGAR CONTENT THAN DESSERT BANANAS. THEY ARE UNSUITABLE FOR EATING RAW AND CAN BE USED IN A WIDE RANGE OF DISHES. THIS DELICIOUS ASSORTMENT OF SWEET AND SAVORY PLANTAINS IS A POPULAR DISH IN AFRICA.

SERVES FOUR

INGREDIENTS

2 green plantains
3 tablespoons vegetable oil
1 small onion, very thinly sliced
1 yellow plantain
½ garlic clove, crushed
salt and cayenne pepper
vegetable oil, for frying

1 Peel one of the green plantains and cut into wafer-thin rounds, preferably using a swivel-headed potato peeler.

2 Heat about 1 tablespoon of the oil in a large frying pan and fry the plantain slices for 2–3 minutes until golden, turning occasionally. Transfer to a plate lined with paper towels and keep warm.

3 Coarsely grate the other green plantain and mix with the onion.

4 Heat 1 tablespoon of the remaining oil in the pan and fry the plantain and onion mixture for 2–3 minutes until golden, turning occasionally. Transfer to the plate with the plantain slices.

5 Peel the yellow plantain, cut into small chunks. Sprinkle with cayenne pepper. Heat the remaining oil and fry the yellow plantain and garlic for 4–5 minutes until brown. Drain and sprinkle with salt.

SALAD
VEGETABLES

Color is the name of the game these days when it comes to

salads. No longer do we have to suffer the limp green salads of

old. The choice of radicchio, lamb's lettuce, arugula and escarole,

not to mention the many varieties of lettuce, mean that today's

salads are bursting with different flavors and textures — a treat

for the eye and the palette.

LETTUCE

One aspect of lettuce that sets it apart from any other vegetable is that you can only buy it in one form – fresh.

History

Lettuce has been cultivated for thousands of years. In Egyptian times it was sacred to the god Min, and tubs of lettuce were ceremoniously carried before this fertility god. It was then considered a powerful aphrodisiac, yet for the Greeks and the Romans lettuce was thought to have quite the opposite effect, making one sleepy and generally soporific. Chemists today confirm that lettuce contains a hypnotic similar to opium, and in herbal remedies lettuce is recommended for insomniacs.

Varieties

There are hundreds of different varieties of lettuce. Today, an increasing variety is available in stores so that the salad bowl can contain a wealth of color and texture.

Round Lettuces

Sometimes called head or cabbage lettuces, round lettuces have cabbage-like heads and include:
Butterheads: These are the classic lettuces seen in kitchen gardens. They have a pale heart and floppy, loosely packed leaves. They have a pleasant flavor as long as they are fresh.
Crispheads: Crisp lettuces, such as Iceberg, have an excellent crunchy texture and will keep their vitality long after butterheads have faded and died.
Looseheads: These are non-hearting lettuce with loose leaves and include *lollo rosso* and *lollo biondo*, oakleaf lettuce and Red Salad Bowl. Although they are not particularly remarkable for their flavor, they look superb.

Cos Lettuces

The romaine is the only lettuce that would have been known in antiquity. It is known

Above: Butterhead lettuce
Right: Lollo rosso lettuce
Above far right: Romaine lettuce
Below far right: Lamb's lettuce
Below extreme right: Bibb lettuce

by two names: cos, derived from the Greek island where it was found by the Romans; and romaine, the name used by the French after it was introduced to France from Rome. There are two romaine lettuces, both with long, erect heads.

Romaine: Considered the most delicious lettuce, this has a firm texture and a faintly nutty taste. It is the correct lettuce for Caesar Salad, one of the classic salads.

Bibb: In appearance Bibbs look like something between a baby romaine and a tightly furled butterhead. They have firm hearts and are enjoyed for their distinct flavor. Like other lettuce hearts, they cope well with being cooked.

LAMB'S LETTUCE OR CORN SALAD

This popular winter leaf does not actually belong to the lettuce family (it is related to Fuller's teasel), but as it makes a lovely addition to salads, this seems a good place to include it. Called *mâche* in France, it has spoon-shaped leaves and an excellent nutty flavor.

Nutrition

As well as containing vitamins A, C and E, lettuce provides potassium, iron and calcium and traces of other minerals.

Buying and Storing

The best lettuce is that fresh from the garden. The next best thing is to buy lettuce from a farm store or pick-your-own (although if fertilizers and pesticides are used, their flavor will be disappointing compared to the organic product).

Nowadays, lettuce is frequently sold ready shredded and packed with herbs etc, an acceptable and convenient form of buying lettuce. Whether you buy lettuce prepacked or from the shelf, it must be fresh. Soil and bugs can be washed off but those with limp or yellow leaves are of no use. Eat lettuce as soon as possible after purchasing; in the meantime keep it in a cool dark place, such as the salad drawer of the fridge.

Making Salads

Salads can be made using only one lettuce or a mixture of many. There are no rules but, when mixing salads, choose leaves to give contrast in texture and color as well as flavor. Fresh herbs, such as parsley, cilantro and basil also add an interesting dimension.

Tear rather than cut the leaves of loose-leafed lettuce; icebergs and other large lettuces are commonly sliced or shredded. Eat as soon as possible after preparing.

Dressings should be well-flavored with a hint of sharpness, but never too astringent. Make them in a blender, a screw-top jar or in a large bowl so that the ingredients can be thoroughly blended. Always use the best possible oils and vinegars, in roughly the proportion of five oil to one vinegar or lemon juice. Use half good olive oil and half sunflower oil, or for a more fragrant dressing, a combination of walnut oil and sunflower oil. A pinch of salt and pepper is essential, French mustard is optional and the addition of a little sugar will blunt the flavor.

Add the dressing to the salad when you're ready to serve – never before.

ARUGULA

Arugula, also called rocket, has a wonderful peppery flavor and is excellent in a mixed green salad. It has small, bright green dandelion-shaped leaves. The Greeks and Romans commonly ate *arugula* in mixed salads, apparently to help counterbalance the dampening effect lettuce had on the libido – arugula's aphrodisiac properties in antiquity are well cataloged. It used to be sown around the statues of Priapus, the mythological Greek god of fertility and protector of gardens and herbs and son of Aphrodite and Dionysus.

Buying and Storing

Arugula is to be found either among the salads or fresh herbs in supermarkets. Buy fresh green leaves and use soon after purchasing. If necessary, the leaves can be kept immersed in cold water.

Preparing and Serving

Discard any discolored leaves. Add arugula to plain green salads, or grind with garlic, pine nuts and olive oil for a dressing for pasta.

Since it has such a striking flavor, a little arugula goes a long way, making it an excellent leaf for garnishing. It tastes superb contrasted with grilled goat cheese, or one or two leaves can be added to sandwiches, or loosely packed into pita bread pockets along with tomatoes, avocado, peanuts and bean sprouts.

Above left: Oak Leaf lettuce
Below left: Frisée
Below: Arugula

CHICORY AND RADICCHIO

Chicory, radicchio, endive and escarole are all related to each other and when they are tasted together you can easily detect their family resemblance. Their names are occasionally interchanged: chicory is often referred to as Belgian or French endive, and French and Belgian *chicorée* as the English curly endive and the American frisée.

CHICORY

During the late eighteenth century, chicory was grown in Europe for its root, which was added to coffee. A Belgian, M. Brezier, discovered that the white leaves could be eaten, a fact he kept secret during his lifetime; but after his death chicory became a popular vegetable, first in Belgium and later elsewhere in Europe. Its Flemish name is *witloof*, meaning "white leaf," and its characteristic pale leaf is due to its being grown in darkness; the paler it is, the less bitter its flavor.

Chicory can be eaten raw but is commonly cooked, either baked, stir-fried or poached. To eat raw, separate the leaves and serve with fruit, such as oranges or grapefruit, which counteract chicory's slight bitterness.

RADICCHIO

This is one of many varieties developed from wild chicory. It looks like a small lettuce with deep wine-red leaves and striking cream ribs and owes its splendid foliage to careful shading. If it is grown completely in the dark the leaves are marbled pink, and those that have been exposed to some light can be patched with a green or copper color. Its flavor tends to be bitter but contrasts well with green salads. Radicchio can be stir-fried or poached, although the leaves turn dark green when cooked.

FRISÉE AND ESCAROLE

These are robust salad ingredients in both flavor and texture. The curly-leaved frisée looks like a green frizzy mop and the escarole is broad-leaved, but both have a distinct bitter flavor. Serve mixed with each other and a well-flavored dressing. This dampens down the bitter flavor but gives the salad a pleasant "bite."

Preparing

To prepare chicory, take out the core at the base with a sharp knife (*left*) and discard any wilted or damaged leaves. Rinse thoroughly, then dry the leaves.

Above: Chicory
Above right: Radicchio
Below right: Escarole

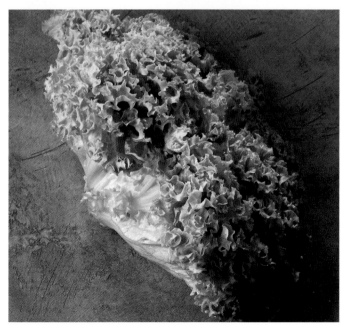

Preparing Salad Leaves

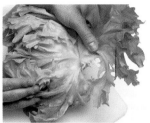

Pull the leaves away from the stalk, discarding any wilted or damaged leaves.

Wash the leaves in plenty of cold water, swirling gently to make sure all dirt and any insects are washed away.

Place the washed leaves in a soft dish towel and then gently pat dry.

Place in a dry dish towel in a large plastic bag. Chill in the fridge for about 1 hour.

RADISHES

Radishes have a peppery flavor that can almost be felt in the nostrils as you bite into one. Their pungency depends not only on the varieties but also on the soil in which they are grown. Freshly harvested radishes have the most pronounced flavor and crisp texture.

Varieties

Radishes were loved throughout antiquity and consequently there are many varieties worldwide. Both the small red types and the large white radishes are internationally popular.

Red Radishes: These small red orbs have many pretty names, but are mostly sold simply as radishes. They are available all year round, have a deep pink skin, sometimes paler or white at the roots and a firm white flesh. Their peppery flavor is milder in the spring and they are almost always eaten raw. Finely sliced and sandwiched in bread and butter, they make an interesting *hors d'oeuvre*.

French Breakfast Radishes: These are red and white and slightly more elongated than the red radish. They tend to be milder than the red radishes and are popular in France either eaten on their own or served with other raw vegetables as *crudités*.

Daikon or Mooli Radishes: Sometimes known as the oriental radish, the daikon is a smooth-skinned, long, white radish. Those bought in stores have a mild flavor, less peppery than the red radish – perhaps because they lose their flavor after long storage (daikons straight from the garden are hot and peppery). They can be eaten raw or pickled, or added to stir-fries.

Buying and Storing

Buy red radishes that are firm with crisp leaves. If at all possible, buy daikons or moolis which still have their leaves; this is a good indication of their freshness as they wilt quickly. The leaves should be green and lively and the skins clear with no bruises or blemishes. They can be stored in the fridge for a few days.

Preparing and Serving

Red radishes need only to be washed. They can then be sliced or eaten whole by themselves or in salads. You can make a feature of them by slicing into a salad of, say, oranges and walnuts, perhaps with a scattering of arugula and dressed with a walnut oil vinaigrette. To use daikon in a stir-fry, cut into slices and add to the dish for the last few minutes of cooking. It adds not only flavor but also a wonderfully juicy and crunchy texture.

Left: Red radishes
Above: French breakfast radishes
Right: Daikon, or mooli, radishes

WATERCRESS

Watercress is perhaps the most robustly flavored of all the salad ingredients and a handful of watercress is all you need to perk up a rather dull green salad. It has a distinctive "raw" flavor, both peppery and slightly pungent and this, together with its bright green leaves, make it a popular garnish.

Watercress, as the name suggests, grows in water. It needs fast flowing clean water to thrive and is really only successful around freshwater springs on chalk hills. The first watercress beds were cultivated in Europe, but watercress is now grown worldwide.

WINTER CRESS

Winter cress or land cress is often grown as an alternative to watercress, when flowing water is not available. It looks like a robust form of watercress and indeed has a similar if even more assertive flavor, with a distinct peppery taste. Use as you would use watercress, either in salads or in soups.

Nutrition

Watercress is extremely rich in vitamins A, B2, C, D and E. It is also rich in calcium, potassium and iron and provides significant quantities of sulphur and chloride.

Buying and Storing

Only buy fresh-looking watercress – the darker and larger the leaves the better. Avoid any with wilted or yellow leaves. It will keep for several days in the fridge or better still, submerged in a bowl, or arranged in a jar of cold water, and kept in a cool place.

Preparing and Cooking

Discard any yellow leaves and remove thick stalks which will be too coarse for salads or soups. Small sprigs can be added to salads.

For soups and purées, either blend watercress raw or cook briefly in stock, milk or water. Cooking inevitably destroys some of the nutrients but cooked watercress has a less harsh flavor, while still retaining its characteristic peppery taste.

MUSTARD AND CRESS

Mustard and cress are often grown together, to provide spicy greenery as a garnish or for salads. They are available all year through.

Mustard seedlings germinate 3-4 days sooner than the cress, so if you buy mustard and cress from the supermarket, or grow your own on the windowsill, initially the punnets will only show mustard seedlings.

History

Cress has been grown for thousands of years, known first to the Persians. There is a story that the Persians would always eat cress before they baked bread, and there are other references in antiquity to people eating cress with bread.

Serving

Today mustard and cress are often enjoyed in sandwiches, either served simply on buttered bread, or with avocado or cucumber added. Cress probably wouldn't be substantial enough as a salad in itself, but, with its faint spicy flavor, it can perk up a plain green salad, and it is also excellent in a tomato salad, dressed simply with olive oil and tarragon vinegar.

Above left: Watercress
Below left: Winter cress
Above right: Mustard seedlings
Right: Cress seedlings

SALAD
VEGETABLE
RECIPES

Salads can be as simple or complicated as you like.
Main meal salads such as Chicken Livers and Green
Salad or Warm Duck Salad with Orange would make
an excellent lunch or supper dish. But, if you're
looking for a something less elaborate, choose a
Caesar Salad or the Arugula and Grilled Goat
Cheese Salad, and serve as an appetizer or side salad.
Salad leaves can even be cooked. Baked Chicory with
Prosciutto is a famous classic, while Radicchio Pizza
gives a modern twist to an old favorite.

CHICKEN LIVERS AND GREEN SALAD

CHICKEN LIVERS HAVE A WONDERFULLY ROBUST FLAVOR THAT COMPLEMENTS A SALAD WITH A PIQUANT DRESSING. IF YOU ARE SHORT OF TIME YOU CAN BUY READY PREPARED SALADS WHICH ARE AVAILABLE FROM MOST SUPERMARKETS.

SERVES FOUR

INGREDIENTS
a selection of fresh salad leaves
4 scallions, finely sliced
1 tablespoon roughly chopped
   Italian parsley
4 ounces unsmoked lean bacon,
   chopped
1 pound chicken livers
seasoned all-purpose flour, for dusting
1 tablespoon sunflower oil
1 ounce butter or margarine
salt and freshly ground black pepper
sprigs of fresh parsley, to garnish
For the dressing
⅓ cup sunflower oil
2–3 tablespoons lemon juice
1 teaspoon French mustard
1 small garlic clove, crushed
salt and freshly ground black pepper

1 To make the dressing, place the oil, lemon juice, mustard, garlic and seasoning in a screw-top jar and shake vigorously to mix.

2 Place the salad leaves in a large bowl with the scallions and parsley. Pour over the dressing, toss briefly and then arrange on four individual serving plates.

3 Dry-fry the bacon in a frying pan until golden brown. Transfer to a plate using a slotted spoon and keep warm.

4 Trim the chicken livers, pat dry on paper towels and then dust them thoroughly with the seasoned flour.

5 Heat the oil and butter in a frying pan and fry the livers over a fairly high heat for about 8 minutes, turning occasionally until cooked to your preference, either cooked through or slightly pink inside.

6 Arrange the chicken livers on the salad leaves and scatter the crisp bacon pieces over the top.

CAESAR SALAD

A CLASSIC SALAD WITH AN EGG YOLK DRESSING, THIS MUST BE MADE USING ROMAINE LETTUCE. THE ORIGINS OF ITS NAME ARE A MYSTERY. SOME PEOPLE SAY IT WAS INVENTED BY AN ITALIAN, CAESAR CARDINI, IN MEXICO, AND OTHERS THAT IT COMES FROM CALIFORNIA.

SERVES FOUR

INGREDIENTS
4–5 tablespoons olive oil
1 garlic clove, crushed
3 ounces stale white bread,
   cut into cubes
1 romaine lettuce
8 anchovies, chopped
1½ ounces shavings of Parmesan
   cheese
For the dressing
2 egg yolks
½ teaspoon French mustard
¼ cup olive oil
¼ cup sunflower oil
1 tablespoon white wine vinegar
a pinch of salt

1 Place the garlic in the oil and set aside for about 30 minutes for the garlic flavor to infuse into the oil.

2 To make the dressing, place the egg yolks, French mustard, olive oil, sunflower oil, vinegar and salt in a screw-top jar and shake well.

3 To make the croûtons, strain the garlic oil into a frying pan and discard the garlic. When hot, fry the bread until golden and then drain on paper towels.

4 Arrange the lettuce leaves in a salad bowl. Pour over the dressing and gently fold in the anchovies and croûtons. Scatter with Parmesan shavings.

RADICCHIO PIZZA

THIS UNUSUAL PIZZA TOPPING CONSISTS OF CHOPPED RADICCHIO WITH LEEKS, TOMATOES AND PARMESAN AND MOZZARELLA CHEESES. THE BASE IS A SCONE DOUGH, MAKING THIS A QUICK AND EASY SUPPER DISH TO PREPARE. SERVE WITH A CRISP GREEN SALAD.

SERVES TWO

INGREDIENTS

14-ounce can chopped tomatoes
2 garlic cloves, crushed
pinch of dried basil
1½ tablespoons olive oil, plus extra
    for dipping
2 leeks, sliced
3½ ounces radicchio, roughly chopped
¾ ounces Parmesan cheese, grated
4 ounces mozzarella cheese, sliced
10–12 black olives, pitted
basil leaves, to garnish
salt and freshly ground black pepper
For the dough
8 ounces self-rising flour
½ teaspoon salt
2 ounces butter or margarine
about ½ cup milk

1 Preheat the oven to 425°F and grease a baking sheet. Mix the flour and salt in a bowl, rub in the butter or margarine and gradually stir in the milk and water and mix to a soft dough.

4 Heat the olive oil in a large frying pan and fry the leeks and remaining garlic for 4–5 minutes until slightly softened. Add the radicchio and cook, stirring continuously for a few minutes, and then cover and simmer gently for about 5–10 minutes. Stir in the Parmesan cheese and season with salt and pepper.

5 Cover the dough base with the tomato mixture and then spoon the leek and radicchio mixture on top. Arrange the mozzarella slices on top and scatter over the black olives. Dip a few basil leaves in olive oil, arrange on top and then bake the pizza for 15–20 minutes until the scone base and top are golden brown.

2 Roll the dough out on a lightly floured surface to make a 10–11-inch round. Place on the baking sheet.

3 Purée the tomatoes and then pour into a small saucepan. Stir in one of the crushed garlic cloves, together with the dried basil and seasoning, and simmer over moderate heat until the mixture is thick and reduced by about half.

WARM DUCK SALAD WITH ORANGE

THE DISTINCT, SHARP FLAVOR OF RADICCHIO, FRISÉE AND FRESH ORANGES COMPLEMENTS THE RICH TASTE OF THE DUCK TO MAKE THIS A SUPERB DISH. IT IS GOOD SERVED WITH STEAMED NEW POTATOES FOR AN ELEGANT MAIN COURSE.

SERVES FOUR

INGREDIENTS
2 boneless duck breasts
salt
2 oranges
frisée, radicchio and lamb's lettuce
2 tablespoons medium dry sherry
2–3 teaspoons dark soy sauce

1 Rub the skin of the duck breasts with salt and then slash the skin several times with a sharp knife.

2 Heat a heavy cast-iron frying pan and fry the duck breasts, skin side down at first, for 20–25 minutes, turning once, until the skin is well browned and the flesh is cooked to your preference. Transfer to a plate to cool slightly and pour off the excess fat from the pan.

3 Peel the oranges. Separate the oranges into segments and use a knife to remove all the pith, catching the juice in a small bowl. Arrange the lettuces in a shallow serving bowl.

4 Heat the duck juices in the pan and stir in 3 tablespoons of the reserved orange juice. Bring to a boil, add the sherry and then just enough soy sauce to give the sauce a piquant, spicy flavor.

5 Cut the duck into thick slices and arrange over the salad. Pour over the warm dressing and serve.

BAKED CHICORY <u>WITH</u> PROSCIUTTO

*ALTHOUGH CHICORY IS SOMETIMES TOO HARSHLY FLAVORED FOR SOME PEOPLE'S TASTES, SIMMERING IT
BEFORE BRAISING ELIMINATES ANY BITTERNESS SO THAT THE FLAVOR IS PLEASANTLY MILD.*

SERVES FOUR

INGREDIENTS
    4 heads of chicory
    1 ounce butter
    1 cup vegetable or chicken stock
    4 slices prosciutto
    3 ounces mascarpone cheese
    2 ounces Emmenthal or Cheddar
      cheese, sliced
    salt and freshly ground black pepper

4 Remove the chicory using a slotted spoon. Lay out the prosciutto slices and place one piece of chicory on each of the slices. Roll up and place, side by side, in a single layer in the prepared dish.

5 Simmer the stock until it is reduced by about half and then remove from the heat. Stir in the mascarpone cheese and pour the sauce over the chicory. Lay the slices of Emmenthal or Cheddar cheese over the top and bake in the oven for about 15 minutes until the top is golden and the sauce is bubbling.

1 Preheat the oven to 350°F. Grease an ovenproof dish. Trim the chicory and remove the central core.

2 Melt the butter in a large saucepan and gently sauté the chicory over a moderate heat for 4–5 minutes, turning occasionally, until the outer leaves begin to turn transparent.

3 Add the stock and a little seasoning, bring to a boil and then cover and simmer gently for 5–6 minutes until the chicory is almost tender.

ARUGULA AND GRILLED GOAT CHEESE SALAD

GOAT CHEESE CAN BE BOUGHT IN MANY DIFFERENT FORMS. FOR THIS RECIPE, LOOK OUT FOR CYLINDER-SHAPED GOAT CHEESE FROM A DELICATESSEN OR FOR SMALL ROLLS THAT CAN BE CUT INTO PIECES WEIGHING ABOUT 2 OUNCES.

SERVES FOUR

INGREDIENTS
    about 1 tablespoon olive oil
    about 1 tablespoon vegetable oil
    4 slices Italian bread
    3 tablespoons walnut oil
    1 tablespoon lemon juice
    8-ounce cylinder-shape goat cheese
    generous handful of arugula leaves
    about 4 ounces frisée
For the sauce
    3 tablespoons apricot jam
    4 tablespoons white wine
    2 teaspoons Dijon mustard

1 Heat the olive and vegetable oils in a frying pan and fry the slices of Italian bread on one side only, until lightly golden brown. Transfer to a plate lined with paper towels.

4 Preheat the broiler a few minutes before serving the salad. Cut the goat cheese into 2-ounce rounds and place each piece on a croûton, untoasted side up. Place under the broiler and cook for 3–4 minutes until the cheese melts.

5 Toss the arugula and frisée in the walnut oil dressing and arrange attractively on four individual serving plates. When the croûtons are ready, arrange on each plate and pour over a little of the apricot sauce.

2 To make the sauce, heat the jam in a small saucepan until warm but not boiling. Push through a strainer, into a clean pan, to remove the pieces of fruit, and then stir in the white wine and mustard. Heat gently and then keep warm until ready to serve.

3 Blend the walnut oil and lemon juice and season with a little salt and pepper.

STIR-FRIED CHINESE LEAVES WITH SCALLOPS

A SPEEDY STIR-FRY MADE USING SALAD VEGETABLES AND SCALLOPS. BOTH THE CHINESE RADISH AND CHINESE LEAVES HAVE A PLEASANT CRUNCHY "BITE," AND THE CHINESE LEAVES CARRY THE SAUCE.

SERVES FOUR

INGREDIENTS
   10 prepared scallops
   4–5 tablespoons vegetable oil
   3 garlic cloves, finely chopped
   ½-inch piece fresh ginger, finely sliced
   4–5 scallions, cut lengthwise into
     1-inch pieces
   2 tablespoons medium dry sherry
   ½ Chinese radish (daikon), cut into
     ½-inch slices
   1 Chinese cabbage, chopped
     lengthwise into thin strips
   For the marinade
   1 teaspoon cornstarch
   1 egg white, lightly beaten
   pinch of white pepper
   For the sauce
   1 teaspoon cornstarch
   3 tablespoons oyster sauce

1 Rinse the scallops and separate the corals from the white meat. Cut each scallop into 2–3 pieces and slice the corals. Place them on two dishes.

2 For the marinade, blend together the cornstarch, egg white and white pepper. Pour half over the scallops and the rest over the corals. Leave for 10 minutes.

3 To make the sauce, blend the cornstarch with 4 tablespoons of water and the oyster sauce and set aside.

4 Heat about 2 tablespoons of the oil in a wok, add half of the garlic and let it sizzle, and then add half the ginger and half of the scallions. Stir-fry for about 30 seconds and then stir in the scallops (not the corals).

5 Stir-fry for ½–1 minute until the scallops start to become opaque and then reduce the heat and add 1 tablespoon of the sherry. Cook briefly and then spoon the scallops and the cooking liquid into a bowl and set aside.

6 Heat another 2 tablespoons of oil in the wok, add the remaining garlic, ginger and scallions and stir-fry for 1 minute. Add the corals, stir-fry briefly and transfer to a dish.

7 Heat the remaining oil and add the daikon. Stir-fry for about 30 seconds and then stir in the cabbage. Stir-fry for about 30 seconds and then add the oyster sauce mixture and about 4 tablespoons of water. Allow the cabbage to simmer briefly and then stir in the scallops and corals, together with all their liquid and cook briefly to heat through.

RADISH, MANGO AND APPLE SALAD

RADISH IS AVAILABLE ALL YEAR THROUGH AND THIS SALAD CAN BE SERVED ANY TIME OF YEAR, WITH ITS CLEAN, CRISP TASTES AND MELLOW FLAVORS. SERVE WITH SMOKED FISH, SUCH AS ROLLS OF SMOKED SALMON OR WITH CONTINENTAL HAM OR SALAMI.

SERVES FOUR

INGREDIENTS
  10–15 radishes
  1 eating apple, peeled cored and
    thinly sliced
  2 celery stalks, thinly sliced
  1 small ripe mango, peeled and cut
    into small chunks
For the dressing
  ½ cup sour cream
  2 teaspoons creamed horseradish
  1 tablespoon chopped fresh dill
  salt and fresh ground black pepper
  sprig of dill, to garnish

3 Cut through the mango lengthwise either side of the pit. Make even criss-cross cuts through each side section. Take each one and bend it back to separate the cubes. Remove the mango cubes with a small knife and add to the bowl. Pour the dressing over the vegetables and fruit and stir gently so that all the ingredients are coated in the dressing. When ready to serve, spoon the salad into an attractive salad bowl and garnish with a sprig of dill.

1 To prepare the dressing, blend together the sour cream, horseradish and dill in a small jug or bowl and season with a little salt and pepper.

2 Remove the ends of the radishes and then slice them thinly. Add to a bowl together with the thinly sliced apple and celery.

WATERCRESS SOUP

SERVES FOUR

INGREDIENTS

1 tablespoon sunflower oil
½ ounce butter
1 medium onion, finely chopped
1 medium potato, diced
about 6 ounces watercress
1⅔ cups chicken or vegetable stock
1⅔ cups milk
lemon juice
salt and freshly ground black pepper
sour cream, to serve (optional)

1 Heat the oil and butter in a large saucepan and fry the onion over low heat until soft but not browned. Add the potato, fry gently for 2–3 minutes and then cover and sweat for 5 minutes over low heat, stirring occasionally.

2 Strip the watercress leaves from the stalks and roughly chop the stalks.

3 Add the stock and milk to the pan, stir in the chopped stalks and season with salt and pepper. Bring to a boil and then simmer gently, partially covered, for 10–12 minutes until the potatoes are tender. Add all but a few of the watercress leaves and simmer for 2 minutes.

4 Process the soup in a food processor or blender, and then pour into a clean saucepan and heat gently with the reserved watercress leaves. Taste when hot and add a little lemon juice and adjust the seasoning.

5 Pour the soup into warmed soup dishes and swirl in a little sour cream, if using, just before serving.

COOK'S TIP
Provided you leave out the cream, this is a low calorie but nutritious soup, which, served with crusty bread, makes a satisfying meal.

WATERCRESS AND TWO-FISH TERRINE

THIS IS A PRETTY, DELICATE DISH, IDEAL FOR A SUMMER BUFFET PARTY OR PICNIC. SERVE WITH LEMON MAYONNAISE OR SOUR CREAM, AND A WATERCRESS AND GREEN SALAD.

SERVES SIX TO EIGHT

INGREDIENTS

12-ounce monkfish, filleted
6-ounce sole, filleted
1 egg and 1 egg white
3–4 tablespoons lemon juice
1½–2 ounces fresh white bread crumbs
1¼ cups heavy or whipping cream
3 ounces smoked salmon
6 ounces watercress, roughly chopped
salt and freshly ground black pepper

1 Preheat the oven to 350°F and line a 6¼-cup loaf pan with wax paper.

2 Cut the fish into rough chunks, discarding the skin and bones. Put the fish into a food processor.

3 Process briefly and add the egg and egg white, lemon juice, bread crumbs and cream. Process to a paste. Put the mixture into a bowl. Take 5 tablespoons of the mixture and process with the smoked salmon. Transfer to a separate bowl. Take 5 tablespoons of the white fish mixture and process with the watercress.

4 Spoon half of the white fish mixture into the base of the prepared loaf pan and smooth the surface with a metal spatula.

5 Spread over the watercress mixture, then the smoked salmon mixture and finally spread over the remaining white fish mixture and smooth the top.

6 Lay a piece of buttered non-stick baking paper on top of the mixture and then cover with foil. Place the loaf tin in a roasting pan, half-filled with boiling water and cook in the oven for 1¼–1½ hours. Toward the end of the cooking time the terrine will begin to rise, which indicates that it is ready.

7 Allow to cool in the pan and then turn onto a serving plate and peel away the wax paper. Chill for 1–2 hours.

MUSHROOMS

*Delicious, succulent, soft, chewy — all sorts of adjectives can be
used when describing mushrooms. There are now so many to
choose from and each has its own particular flavor and
character. From firm favorites such as white and field
mushrooms, to ceps, morels and oyster mushrooms that grow
in woodlands, these delicacies deserve a starring role in a
multitude of dishes.*

WHITE MUSHROOMS

Mushrooms are generally cooked, although some white mushrooms are served raw in salads. Eat them quickly; after frying they can go soft and flabby.

History

In the past, mushrooms have had a firm association with the supernatural and even today their connection with the mysterious side of life hasn't completely disappeared. Fairy rings – circles of mushrooms – inexplicably appear overnight in woods and fields and thunder is still thought to bring forth fresh crops of mushrooms.

Many types of mushrooms and fungi are either poisonous or hallucinogenic, and in the past their poisons have been distilled for various murderous reasons.

The use of the term mushroom to mean edible species, and toadstool to mean those considered poisonous, has no scientific basis, and there is no simple rule for distinguishing between the two. Picking wild mushrooms is not safe unless you are confident about identifying edible types. In France during the autumn, people take the wild mushrooms they have gathered to the local pharmacy, where safe mushrooms are identified.

Varieties

White/Button Mushrooms: Cultivated mushrooms are widely available in stores and are sold when very young and tiny. The slightly larger ones are known as closed cap, while larger ones still are open capped, or open cup, mushrooms. They have ivory or white caps with pinky/beige gills that darken as they mature. All have a pleasant flavor.

Cremini Mushrooms: These have a thicker stem and a darker, pale brown cap. They have a more pronounced "mushroomy" flavor and a meatier texture than white mushrooms.

Buying and Storing

It is easy to see whether or not white mushrooms are fresh – their caps will be clean and white, without bruises or blemishes. The longer they stay on the shelves, the darker and more discolored the caps become, while the gills underneath turn from pink to brown.

If possible, use the paper bags provided in many supermarkets nowadays when buying mushrooms. Mushrooms in plastic bags sweat in their own heat, eventually turning slippery and unappetizing. If you have no choice or you buy mushrooms in cellophane-wrapped cartons, transfer loose to the bottom of the fridge as soon as possible. They will keep only for a day or two.

Preparing

Mushrooms should not be washed but wiped with a damp cloth or a piece of paper towel (*below*). This is partly because you don't want to increase their water content, and also because they should be fried as dry as possible.

Unless the skins are very discolored, it should not be necessary to peel them, although you probably will need to trim the very base of the stem.

Cooking

Mushrooms are largely composed of water and shrink noticeably during cooking. They also take up a lot of fat as they cook so it is best to use butter or a good olive oil for frying. Fry mushrooms briskly over a moderately high heat so that as they shrink the water evaporates and they don't stew in their own juice. For the same reason do not fry too many mushrooms at once in the same pan.

Most of the recipes in this book use fried mushrooms as their base and they are completely interchangeable – so if you can't get wild mushrooms or cremini mushrooms for instance, white mushrooms can be used instead.

Above: White mushrooms
Top right: Flat mushrooms
Far right: Field mushrooms
Right: Cremini mushrooms (top) and open capped or cup mushrooms

FIELD MUSHROOMS

Field mushrooms are the wild relatives of the cultivated mushroom and when cooked have a wonderful aroma. Flat mushrooms, although indistinguishable from field mushrooms in appearance, have probably been cultivated and are also excellent. Connoisseurs say that only wild mushrooms have any flavor but many would argue against this. However, if you know where to find field mushrooms, keep the secret to yourself (most mushroom devotees seem to know this) and count yourself lucky!

Buying and Storing

Field mushrooms are sometimes available during the autumn in farm stores. Since they are likely to have been picked recently, they should be fresh unless obviously wilting. Unless you intend to stuff them, don't worry if they are broken in places as you will be slicing them anyway. Use as soon as possible after purchase.

Preparing

Trim the stalk bottoms if necessary and wipe the caps with a damp cloth. Slice according to the recipe.

Cooking

For true field mushrooms, you need do nothing more complicated than simply fry them in butter or olive oil with a suggestion of garlic if liked. However, like flat mushrooms, field mushrooms can be used for stuffing, in soups or indeed any mushroom recipe. They are darker than white mushrooms and will color soups and sauces brown, but the flavor will be extremely good.

When stuffing mushrooms, gently fry the caps on both sides for a few minutes. The stalks can be chopped and added to the stuffing or can be used for soups or stocks.

WOODLAND MUSHROOMS

Varieties

Ceps: Popular in France, where they are known as *cèpes* and in Italy where they are called *porcini*, these meaty, bun-shaped mushrooms have a fine almost suede-like texture and a good flavor. Instead of gills they have a spongy texture beneath the cap and unless they are very young it is best to scrape this away as it goes soggy when cooked. Ceps are excellent fried in oil or butter over a brisk heat to evaporate the liquid and then added to omelets.

Alternately, an Italian way of cooking is to remove the stalk and the spongy tubes, and brush the tops with olive oil. Broil for about 10 minutes under a moderate broiler and then turn them over and pour olive oil and a sprinkling of garlic into the center. Broil for a further 5 minutes and then serve sprinkled with seasoning and parsley.

Chanterelles: Frilly, trumpet-shaped chanterelles are delicate mushrooms which range in color from cream to a vivid yellow. Later, winter chanterelles have grayish-lilac gills on the underside of their dark caps. Chanterelles have a delicate, slightly fruity flavor and a firm, almost rubbery texture. They are difficult to clean as their tiny gills tend to trap grit and earth. Rinse them gently under cold running water and then shake dry. Fry in butter over a gentle heat to start with so they exude their liquid and then increase the heat to boil it off. They are delicious with scrambled eggs, or served by themselves with finely cut toast.

Horn of Plenty/Black Trumpets: Taking its name from its shape, this mushroom ranges in color from mid-brown to black. As it is hollow, it will need to be brushed well to clean or, if a large specimen, sliced in half. It is very versatile, but goes particularly well with fish.

Hedgehog Fungus: This mushroom is difficult to find either on sale or on the woodland floor, but it has great culinary value and is much sought after. Small, young specimens can be cooked whole or sliced, or even used raw in salads. More mature mushrooms may be bitter and are best cooked with butter and herbs. They go well with both meat and fish.

Morels: These are the first mushrooms of the year, appearing not in autumn but in spring. In Scandinavia they are called the "truffles of the north" and are considered among the great edible fungi. They are cone-shaped with a crinkled spongy cap but are hollow inside. You will need to wash them well under running water as insects tend to creep into their dark crevices. Morels need longer cooking than most mushrooms: sauté them in butter, add a squeeze of lemon and then cover and simmer for up to an hour until tender. The juices can then be thickened with cream or egg yolks.

Dried Mushrooms: Most wild mushrooms are available dried. To reconstitute, soak in warm water for about 20-30 minutes; in the case of morels when they are added to stews, soak for about 10 minutes. Dried wild mushrooms, particularly ceps, have an intense flavor.

Left: Clockwise from the top: Hedgehog fungus, Horn of Plenty, chanterelles
Above right: Dried mushrooms
Above left: Morels
Right: Winter chanterelles

WILD MUSHROOMS AND OTHER FUNGI

Mushroom gathering, a seasonal event throughout Eastern Europe, Italy and France, is increasingly popular. The French are particularly enthusiastic: in autumn whole families drive to secret locations to comb the ground for prizes like shaggy ink caps or ceps. Wild mushrooms are sold in supermarkets.

OYSTER MUSHROOMS

These ear-shaped fungi grow on rotting wood. Cap, gills and stem are all the same color, which can be grayish brown, pink or yellow. They are now widely cultivated, although they are generally thought of as wild mushrooms. Delicious both in flavor and texture, they are softer than the white mushroom when cooked but seem more substantial, having more "bite" to them.

Buying and Storing

Fresh specimens are erect and lively looking with clear gills and smooth caps. They are often sold packed in plastic boxes under cellophane wrappings and

will wilt and go soggy if left on the shelf for too long. Once purchased, remove them from the plastic packaging and use as soon as possible.

Preparing

Oyster mushrooms rarely need trimming at all but if they are large, tear rather than cut them into pieces. In very large specimens the stems can be tough and should be discarded.

Cooking

Fry in butter until tender – they take less time to cook than white mushrooms. Do not overcook oyster mushrooms as the flavor will be lost and the soft texture will become more rubbery.

Left: Pink and yellow oyster mushrooms
Above: Gray oyster mushrooms

ENOKITAKI MUSHROOMS

This is another Japanese mushroom. The wild variety is orangy-brown with shiny caps but outside Japan, you will probably only be able to find the cultivated variety, which are similarly fine, with pin-size heads, but are pale colored with snowy white caps. They have a fine, sweet and almost fruity flavor. In Japanese cookery they are added to salads or used as a garnish for soups or hot dishes. Since they become tough if overcooked, add enokitaki mushrooms at the very last minute of cooking.

SHIITAKE MUSHROOMS

These Japanese fungi are now commonly available in supermarkets. They are among a variety of tree mushrooms (called *take* in Japan, the *shii* being the hardwood tree from which they are harvested). They have a meaty, slightly acid flavor and a distinct slippery texture. Shiitake mushrooms, though once only available in oriental stores, are now widely available in most supermarkets. Unlike white mushrooms that can be flash-fried, shiitake need to be cooked through, although even this only takes 3–5 minutes. Add them to stir-fries for a delicious flavor and texture. Alternatively, fry them in oil until tender. Sprinkle with sesame oil and then serve with a little soy sauce.

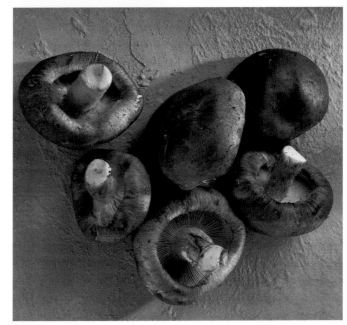

Above: Enokitaki mushrooms
Right: Shiitake mushrooms

MUSHROOM RECIPES

Nearly everyone has a favorite mushroom dish. Mushrooms have the ability to go with almost anything, which is why there is always such a range of dishes when it comes to these fungi. Cream of Mushroom Soup, Soufflé Omelet with Mushroom Sauce, Stuffed Mushrooms and Boeuf en Croûte, with a mushroom filling, will appeal to traditional tastes but for those who fancy something different, try Gnocchi with Oyster Mushrooms or Tagliatelle Fungi.

CREAM OF MUSHROOM SOUP

A GOOD MUSHROOM SOUP MAKES THE MOST OF THE SUBTLE AND SOMETIMES RATHER ELUSIVE FLAVOR OF MUSHROOMS. WHITE MUSHROOMS ARE USED HERE FOR THEIR PALE COLOR; CREMINI OR, BETTER STILL, FIELD MUSHROOMS GIVE A FULLER FLAVOR BUT TURN THE SOUP BROWN.

SERVES FOUR

INGREDIENTS
   10 ounces white mushrooms
   1 tablespoon sunflower oil
   1½ ounces butter
   1 small onion, finely chopped
   1 tablespoon all-purpose flour
   1¾ cups vegetable stock
   1¾ cups milk
   pinch of dried basil
   2–3 tablespoons light cream
      (optional)
   fresh basil leaves, to garnish
   salt and freshly ground black pepper

1 Separate the mushroom caps from the stalks. Finely slice the caps and finely chop the stalks.

2 Heat the oil and half the butter in a heavy-based saucepan and add the onion, mushroom stalks and ½–¾ of the sliced mushroom caps. Fry for about 1–2 minutes, stirring frequently, and then cover and sweat over low heat for 6–7 minutes, stirring occasionally.

3 Stir in the flour and cook for about 1 minute. Gradually add the stock and milk, to make a smooth thin sauce. Add the basil, and season with salt and pepper. Bring to a boil and then simmer, partly covered, for 15 minutes.

4 Cool slightly and then pour the soup into a food processor or blender and process until smooth. Melt the rest of the butter in a frying pan and fry the remaining mushrooms gently for 3–4 minutes until they are just tender.

5 Pour the soup into a clean saucepan and stir in the sliced mushrooms. Heat until very hot and adjust the seasoning. Add a little cream, if using. Serve sprinkled with fresh basil leaves.

SOUFFLÉ OMELET WITH MUSHROOM SAUCE

A SOUFFLÉ OMELET INVOLVES A LITTLE MORE PREPARATION THAN AN ORDINARY OMELET BUT THE RESULT IS LIGHT AND SPRINGY TO TOUCH. THIS DISH MAKES A DELICIOUS LIGHT LUNCH.

SERVES ONE

INGREDIENTS
   2 eggs, separated
   ½ ounce butter
   sprig of parsley or cilantro
   For the mushroom sauce
   ½ ounce butter
   3 ounces white mushrooms,
      thinly sliced
   1 tablespoon all-purpose flour
   ½ cup milk
   1 teaspoon chopped fresh parsley
      (optional)
   salt and freshly ground black pepper

1 To make the mushroom sauce, melt the butter in a saucepan or frying pan and fry the sliced mushrooms for 4–5 minutes until tender. •

2 Stir in the flour and then gradually add the milk, stirring all the time, to make a smooth sauce. Add the parsley, if using, and season with salt and pepper. Keep warm to one side.

3 Beat the egg yolks with 1 tablespoon of water and season with a little salt and pepper. Whisk the egg whites until stiff and then fold into the egg yolks using a metal spoon. Preheat the broiler.

4 Melt the butter in a large frying pan and pour the egg mixture into the pan. Cook over a gentle heat for 2–4 minutes. Place the frying pan under the broiler and cook for a further 3–4 minutes until the top is golden brown.

5 Slide the omelet onto a warmed serving plate, pour over the mushroom sauce and fold the omelet in half. Serve garnished with a sprig of parsley or fresh cilantro leaves.

STUFFED MUSHROOMS

*THIS IS A CLASSIC MUSHROOM DISH, STRONGLY FLAVORED WITH GARLIC. IF YOU PREFER A MORE
SUBTLE GARLIC FLAVOR, BRIEFLY FRY THE GARLIC FIRST.*

SERVES FOUR

INGREDIENTS

1 pound large flat mushrooms
butter, for greasing
3 tablespoons finely chopped fresh
    parsley
1½–2 ounces fresh white bread crumbs
2 garlic cloves, minced or very
    finely chopped
about 5 tablespoons olive oil
salt and freshly ground black pepper
sprig Italian parsley, to garnish

1 Preheat the oven to 350°F. Cut off the
mushroom stalks and reserve on one
side.

2 Arrange the mushroom caps in a
buttered shallow dish, gill sides upward.

3 Finely chop the mushroom stalks and
mix with the parsley, bread crumbs,
garlic, 2 tablespoons of the olive oil and
seasoning to taste, and then pile a little
of the mixture into each mushroom.

4 Add the remaining oil to the dish and
cover the mushrooms with buttered wax
paper. Bake for about   15–20 minutes,
removing the paper for the last 5 minutes
to brown the tops. Garnish with a sprig of
Italian parsley.

COOK'S TIP
The cooking time for the mushrooms
depends on their size and thickness. If
they are fairly thin, cook for slightly less
time. They should be tender but not too
soft when cooked. If preferred, the garlic
may be cooked before adding to the
bread crumb mixture. Heat about
1 tablespoon of oil in a frying pan and fry
the garlic very briefly and then stir into
the breadcrumb mixture.

BOEUF ᴱᴺ CROÛTE

A DUXELLES FILLING OF FINELY CHOPPED MUSHROOMS, SHALLOTS, GARLIC AND PARSLEY IS THE CLASSIC FILLING FOR BOEUF EN CROÛTE. THESE INDIVIDUAL VERSIONS ARE GOOD SERVED WITH BOILED OR STEAMED NEW POTATOES AND A GREEN VEGETABLE.

SERVES FOUR

INGREDIENTS

    4 fillet steaks, about 4–5 ounces each
    a little Dijon mustard
    1 ounce butter
    10 ounces puff pastry
    1 ounce fresh white bread crumbs
    beaten egg, for glazing
    salt and freshly ground black pepper
    sprigs of parsley or chervil, to garnish
For the duxelles filling
    4 shallots, finely chopped
    1–2 garlic cloves, crushed
    8–10 ounces flat mushrooms, finely
      chopped
    1 tablespoon finely chopped parsley

1 Preheat the oven to 425°F. Rub a little mustard over each of the steaks and season with pepper. Melt the butter in a heavy-based frying pan and fry the steaks for about 1–2 minutes each side, so that they are browned on the outside but still red in the center. Transfer to a plate to cool.

2 To make the filling, add the shallots and garlic to the pan and fry briefly. Stir in the finely chopped mushrooms.

3 Fry over fairly high heat for about 3–4 minutes, stirring, until the juices run. Lower the heat and cook gently for 4–5 minutes until the mixture is dry. Add the parsley and seasoning and cool.

4 Cut the pastry into four and roll out each piece very thinly to a 7-inch square. Cut the corners from each square and spread a spoonful of the mushroom mixture in the center. Top with a steak and sprinkle with a spoonful of fresh bread crumbs.

5 Bring the sides of the pastry up to the center and seal with water. Place seam side down on a baking sheet.

6 Decorate with pastry trimmings and brush each with beaten egg. Bake for about 20 minutes, until golden brown.

GNOCCHI <u>WITH</u> OYSTER MUSHROOMS

GNOCCHI MAKES AN UNUSUAL AND PLEASANT ALTERNATIVE TO PASTA. IT IS BLAND ON ITS OWN BUT BRINGS OUT THE OYSTER MUSHROOM FLAVOR IN THIS DISH AND ITS SOFT TEXTURE CONTRASTS WITH THE FIRMNESS OF THE MUSHROOMS.

SERVES FOUR

INGREDIENTS
    8 ounces oyster mushrooms
    1 tablespoon olive oil
    1 ounce butter, plus extra to serve
    1 medium onion, finely chopped
    1 garlic clove, crushed
    4 plum tomatoes, peeled and chopped
    3–4 tablespoons vegetable stock or
        water
    11-ounce packet plain potato gnocchi
    2 teaspoons chopped fresh parsley
    Parmesan cheese, cut in shavings,
        to serve

1 Trim the mushrooms and cut into halves or quarters, if they are large. Heat the oil in a large frying pan and fry the onion and garlic over low heat for about 4–5 minutes until softened but not browned, stirring frequently.

2 Increase the heat, add the mushrooms to the pan and sauté for about 3–4 minutes, stirring constantly.

3 Stir in the chopped tomatoes, stock or water and seasoning and then cover and simmer for about 8 minutes until the tomatoes are very soft and reduced to a pulp. Stir occasionally.

4 Cook the gnocchi in a large pan of salted boiling water for 2–3 minutes (or according to the instructions on the packet) and then drain well. Place in a large warmed serving bowl and stir in the butter and chopped parsley.

5 Pour the mushroom and tomato mixture over the top, stir briefly and sprinkle with the Parmesan cheese.

COOK'S TIP
If the mushrooms are very large, the stalks are likely to be tough, therefore they should be discarded. Always tear rather than cut oyster mushrooms.

SEAFOOD <u>AND</u> OYSTER MUSHROOM APPETIZER

THIS DISH IS A REMARKABLY QUICK TO PREPARE. IT CAN BE MADE INTO A MORE SUBSTANTIAL DISH BY STIRRING 10–12 OUNCES OF COOKED PASTA SHELLS INTO THE SAUCE AT THE END.

SERVES FOUR

INGREDIENTS
    1 tablespoon olive oil
    ½ ounce butter
    1 garlic clove, crushed
    6 ounces oyster mushrooms,
        halved or quartered
    4–6 ounces peeled shrimp
    4 ounces cooked mussels, optional
    juice of ½ lemon
    1 tablespoon medium dry sherry
    ⅔ cup heavy cream
    salt and freshly ground black pepper

1 Heat the oil and butter in a frying pan and sauté the garlic for a few minutes, then add the mushrooms. Cook over moderate heat for 4–5 minutes until soft, stirring from time to time.

2 Reduce the heat and stir in the shrimp, mussels and lemon juice. Cook for 1 minute, stirring continuously. Stir in the sherry and cook for 1 minute.

3 Add the cream and cook gently until heated through but not boiling. Taste and adjust the seasoning and then spoon into warmed serving dishes. Serve immediately with chunks of Italian bread.

TAGLIATELLE FUNGI

THE MUSHROOM SAUCE IS QUICK TO MAKE AND THE PASTA COOKS VERY QUICKLY; BOTH NEED TO BE COOKED AS NEAR TO SERVING AS POSSIBLE SO CAREFUL COORDINATION IS REQUIRED. PUT THE PASTA IN TO COOK WHEN THE MASCARPONE CHEESE IS ADDED TO THE SAUCE.

SERVES FOUR

INGREDIENTS
about 2 ounces butter
8–12 ounces chanterelles or other
    wild mushrooms
1 tablespoon all-purpose flour
⅔ cup milk
6 tablespoons crème fraiche or sour
    cream
1 tablespoon chopped fresh parsley
10 ounces fresh tagliatelle
olive oil
salt and freshly ground black pepper

3 Add the crème fraiche or sour cream, parsley, mushrooms and seasoning and stir well. Cook gently to heat through and then keep warm while cooking the pasta.

4 Cook the pasta in a large saucepan of boiling water for 4–5 minutes (or according to the instructions on the packet). Drain well, toss in a little olive oil and then turn onto a warmed serving plate. Pour the mushroom sauce over and serve immediately.

COOK'S TIP
Chanterelles are a little tricky to wash, as they are so delicate. However, since these are woodland mushrooms, it's important to clean them thoroughly. Hold each one by the stalk and let cold water run under the gills to dislodge hidden dirt. Shake gently to dry.

1 Melt 1½ ounces of the butter in a frying pan and fry the mushrooms for about 2–3 minutes over low heat until the juices begin to run, then increase the heat and cook until the liquid has almost evaporated. Transfer the mushrooms to a bowl using a slotted spoon.

2 Stir in the flour, adding a little more butter if necessary, and cook for about 1 minute, and then gradually stir in the milk to make a smooth sauce.

SHIITAKE FRIED RICE

SHIITAKE MUSHROOMS HAVE A STRONG MEATY MUSHROOMY AROMA AND FLAVOR. THIS IS A VERY EASY RECIPE TO MAKE, AND ALTHOUGH IT IS A SIDE DISH IT CAN ALMOST BE A MEAL IN ITSELF.

SERVES FOUR

INGREDIENTS
2 eggs
3 tablespoons vegetable oil
12 ounces shiitake mushrooms
8 scallions, sliced diagonally
1 garlic clove, crushed
½ green bell pepper, chopped
1 ounce butter
12 ounces cooked long grain rice
1 tablespoon medium dry sherry
2 tablespoons dark soy sauce
1 tablespoon chopped fresh cilantro
salt

1 Beat the eggs with 1 tablespoon of cold water and season with a little salt.

2 Heat 1 tablespoon of the oil in a wok or large frying pan, pour in the eggs and cook to make a large omelet. Lift the sides of the omelet and tilt the wok so that the uncooked egg can run underneath and be cooked. Roll up the omelet and slice thinly.

3 Remove and discard the mushroom stalks if tough and slice the caps thinly, halving them if they are large.

4 Heat 1 tablespoon of the remaining oil in the wok and stir-fry the scallions and garlic for 3–4 minutes until softened but not brown. Transfer them to a plate using a slotted spoon.

5 Add the pepper, stir-fry for about 2–3 minutes, then add the butter and the remaining 1 tablespoon of oil. As the butter begins to sizzle, add the mushrooms and stir-fry over moderate heat for 3–4 minutes until soft.

6 Loosen the rice grains as much as possible. Pour the sherry over the mushrooms and then stir in the rice.

7 Heat the rice over moderate heat, stirring all the time to prevent the rice sticking. If the rice seems very dry, add a little more oil. Stir in the reserved onions and omelet slices, the soy sauce and cilantro. Cook for a few minutes until heated through and serve.

COOK'S TIP
Unlike risotto, for which rice is cooked along with the other ingredients, Chinese fried rice is always made using cooked rice. If you use 6–8 ounces uncooked long grain, you will get about 16–20 ounces of cooked rice, enough for four people.

WILD MUSHROOMS ᴵᴺ BRIOCHE

SERVES FOUR

INGREDIENTS
4 small brioches
olive oil, for glazing
4 teaspoons lemon juice
sprigs of parsley, to garnish
For the mushroom filling
1 ounce butter
2 shallots
1 garlic clove, crushed
6–8 ounces assorted wild mushrooms,
  halved if large
3 tablespoons white wine
3 tablespoons double cream
1 teaspoon chopped fresh basil
1 teaspoon chopped fresh parsley
salt and freshly ground black pepper

1 Preheat the oven to 350°F. Using a serrated or grapefruit knife, cut a circle out of the top of the brioche and reserve. Scoop out the bread inside to make a small cavity.

2 Place the brioches and the tops on a baking sheet and brush inside and out with olive oil. Bake for 7–10 minutes until golden and crisp. Squeeze 1 teaspoon of lemon juice inside each brioche.

3 To make the filling, melt the butter in a frying pan and fry the shallots and garlic for 2–3 minutes until softened.

4 Add the mushrooms and cook gently for about 4–5 minutes, stirring.

5 When the juices begin to run, reduce the heat and continue cooking for about 3–4 minutes, stirring occasionally, until the pan is fairly dry.

6 Stir in the wine. Cook for a few more minutes and then stir in the cream, basil, parsley and seasoning to taste.

7 Pile the mushroom mixture into the brioche shells and return to the oven and reheat for about 5–6 minutes. Serve as a starter, garnished with a sprig of parsley.

WILD MUSHROOMS ᵂᴵᵀᴴ PANCAKES

SERVES SIX

INGREDIENTS
8–10 ounces assorted wild
  mushrooms
2 ounces butter
1–2 garlic cloves
splash of brandy (optional)
freshly ground black pepper
sour cream, to serve
For the pancakes
4 ounces self-rising flour
¾ ounce buckwheat flour
½ teaspoon baking powder
pinch of salt
2 eggs
about 1 cup milk
oil, for frying

1 To make the pancakes, mix together the flours, baking powder and salt in a large bowl or food processor. Add the eggs and milk and beat or process to make a smooth batter, about the consistency of light cream.

2 Grease a large griddle or frying pan with a little oil and when hot, pour small amounts of batter (about 1–2 tablespoons per pancake) onto the griddle, well spaced apart.

3 Fry for a few minutes until bubbles begin to appear on the surface and the underside is golden, and then flip over. Cook for about 1 minute until golden. Keep warm, wrapped in a clean dish towel. (Makes about 18–20 pancakes.)

4 If the mushrooms are large, cut them in half. Melt the butter in a frying pan and add the garlic and mushrooms. Fry over moderate heat for a few minutes until the juices begin to run and then increase the heat and cook, stirring frequently, until nearly all the juices have evaporated. Stir in the brandy, if using, and season with a little black pepper.

5 Arrange the warm pancakes on a serving plate and spoon over a little sour cream. Top with the hot mushrooms and serve immediately.

COOK'S TIP
This makes a delicious and elegant starter for a dinner party. Alternatively, make cocktail-size pancakes and serve as part of a buffet supper.

INDEX

A

ackee, 443
acorn squashes, 412
alcohol, preserving fruit in, 17
almonds
  almond cookies, 41
  cold lemon soufflé with
    caramelized almond
    topping, 159
  crunchy-topped fresh apricot
    cake, 89
  fresh lemon tart, 163
  moist orange and almond
    cake, 166
  yellow plum tart, 86
Alphonse Lavalle grapes, 232
Alphonsine mangoes, 186
Alphonso mangoes, 186
Alpine strawberries, 95
Amarelle cherries, 71
Anaheim chilies, 440
Ancho chilies, 440
anchovies
  Caesar salad, 474
  sweet pepper choux with
    anchovies, 453
Anjou pears, 30
apple bananas, 172
apple corers, 12
apple processors, 12
apple segmenters, 12
apples, 20-9
  apple and cider sauce, 56
  apple and red onion
    marmalade, 56
  apple charlottes, 47
  apple crêpes with butterscotch
    sauce, 44
  baked stuffed apples, 42
  carrot, apple and orange
    coleslaw, 340
  cider apples, 29
  crab apples, 29
  Dutch apple cake, 54
  filo-topped apple pie, 51
  French apple tart, 53
  hot blackberry and apple
    soufflés, 115
  radish, mango and apple
    salad, 481
  spiced apple crumble, 42
  tarte Tatin, 50
apricots, 63
  apricot parcels, 88
  caramelized apricots with
    French toast, 80
  crunchy-topped fresh apricot
    cake, 89

arbutus, 96
artichokes *see* globe artichokes;
    Jerusalem artichokes
argula, 465
arugula and grilled goat cheese
    salad, 479
Ashmead's Kernel apples, 21
Asian pears, 35
asparagus, 288-9
  asparagus soup, 302
  asparagus tart with ricotta, 300
  asparagus with tarragon
    hollandaise, 300
  roast asparagus crêpes, 303
aubergines, 435-7
avocados, 444-5
  celery, avocado and walnut
    salad, 306
  guacamole, 458

B

babacos, 175
bacon
  French beans with bacon and
    cream, 401
  onion squash risotto, 420
  pan-fried sweet potatoes with
    bacon, 343
baking
  fruit, 16
  potatoes, 318, 319
balti-style cauliflower with
    tomatoes, 373
bamboo shoots, 294
bananas, 172-4
  banana and mascarpone
    creams, 212
  banana and pecan
    bread, 222
  bananas with lime and
    cardamom sauce, 212
  rum and banana waffles, 216
  toffee bananas, 214
Barbillone figs, 236
basil
  tomato and basil tart, 451
Beach plums, 65
bean sprouts, 294-5
beans
  dried, 393

see also individual types
    of bean
Beauty of Bath apples, 21
beef
  boeuf en croûte, 497
  beefsteak tomatoes, 433
beets, 326
beet greens, 326
bergamots, 141
Bermuda onions, 266
berries, 93-133
  berry brûlée tarts, 130
  recipes, 113-33
  summer berry crêpes, 116
  summer pudding, 114
Beth pears, 30
Beurré Bosc pears, 30
Beurré Hardi pears, 30
Beurré Superfin pears, 30
Bigarade oranges, 145
Bigarreau cherries, 70
bilberries, 103
Bing cherries, 70
bird's-eye chilies, 440
biryani
  parsnip, eggplant and cashew
    biryani, 337
bitter oranges, 145
black cherry clafoutis, 78
black currants, 110-11
  black currant sorbet, 123
  fresh currant bread-and-butter
    pudding, 126
black-eyed peas, 393
black grapes, 232
black mulberries, 102
Black Tartarian cherries, 70
black trumpets, 488
blackberries, 99-100
  blackberry jelly, 132
  blackberry Kir Royale, 100
  coconut jelly with star anise
    fruits, 204
  hot blackberry and apple
    soufflés, 115
blaeberries, 103
blanching vegetables, 261

blenders, 257
Blenheim Orange apples, 21
Blonde oranges, 144
blood oranges, 144-5
blueberries, 103
  blueberry pie, 129
  cranberry and blueberry
    streusel cake, 127
  fresh berry pavlova, 118
  fresh blueberry muffins, 128
  fruits of the forest, 120
boeuf en croûte, 497
boiling
  potatoes, 319
  vegetables, 260
Bombay mangoes, 186
bottle gourds, 414
bottled figs, 237
box graters, 12
boysenberries, 101
Braeburn apples, 21
Bramley's Seedling apples, 27
bread
  croutons, 278
  fresh currant bread-and-butter
    pudding, 126
  summer pudding, 114
breadfruit, 176, 445
brioche
  caramelized apricots with
    French toast, 80
  wild mushrooms in
    brioche, 502
broccoflower, 352
broccoli, 354-5
  broccoli and chicken
    lasagne, 368
  broccoli crumble, 368
  hot broccoli tartlets, 374
broccoli, Chinese, 363
broiling fruit, 16
brownies, date and walnut, 222
Brussels sprouts, 351
  Brussels sprout gratin, 378
  stir-fried Brussels sprouts, 378
Buissone figs, 236
bullaces, 69
Burbank plums, 64
butterhead lettuces, 462
butternut squashes, 412
butterscotch sauce, apple crêpes
    with, 44
button mushrooms, 486

C

cabbage, 356-8
  pasta with Savoy cabbage and
    Gruyère, 377

Caesar salad, 474
cakes
  chocolate zucchini cake, 428
  cranberry and blueberry
    streusel cake, 127
  crunchy-topped fresh apricot
    cake, 89
  Dutch apple cake, 54
  Greek yogurt and fig cake, 249
  lemon and lime syrup
    cake, 167
  moist orange and almond
    cake, 166
  pear and polenta cake, 54
calabrese, 354-5
callaloo, 330
Cambridge Favorite
  strawberries, 95
candied orange peel, 147
candying fruit, 17
canelle knives, 12
canned fruit and vegetables
  apricots, 63
  bananas, 173
  figs, 237
  mandarin oranges, 143
  mangoes, 186
  peaches, 61
  pears, 34
  pineapple, 193
  tomatoes, 433
cannellini beans, spinach and, 370
cantaloupe melons, 228
Cape gooseberries, 191
Cara potatoes, 316
carambolas, 176
caramel
  baked lattice peaches, 82
  berry brûlée tarts, 130
  caramelized apricots with
    French toast, 80
  caramelizing fruit, 17
  caramelizing grapes, 235
  citrus fruit flambé with pistachio
    praline, 158
  cold lemon soufflé with
    caramelized almond
    topping, 159
  passion fruit crème caramels
    with dipped physalis, 201
  toffee bananas, 214
Cardinal grapes, 232
cardoons, 291
Carlingford potatoes, 314
carrots, 324-5
  carrot and cilantro soup, 342
  carrot, apple and orange
    coleslaw, 340

eddo, carrot and parsnip
    medley, 346
  glazed carrots with cider, 340
  julienne, 260
Casaba melons, 229
cashew nuts
  parsnip, eggplant and cashew
    biryani, 337
cassava, 331
casseroles, cast-iron/
    flameproof, 257
cauliflower, 352-3
  balti-style cauliflower with
    tomatoes, 373
  cauliflower and mushroom
    gougère, 372
cayenne pepper, 440
celery, 292-3
  braised celery with goat
    cheese, 306
  celery, avocado and walnut
    salad, 306
celery root, 293
  celery root and blue cheese
    roulade, 305
  celery root gratin, 304
ceps, 488
Champagne
  blackberry Kir Royale, 100
chana dhal, 393
chanterelles, 488
  tagliatelle fungi, 500
chard, 365
  chard pasties, 375
Charentais melons, 228
Chasselas grapes, 233
chayotes, 414-15
cheese, savory recipes
  arugula and grilled goat cheese
    salad, 479
  asparagus tart with ricotta, 300
  baked chicory with
    prosciutto, 478
  baked zucchini, 422
  baked leeks with cheese and
    yogurt topping, 283

baked onions stuffed with
    feta, 276
braised celery with goat
    cheese, 306
broccoli and chicken
    lasagne, 368
celery root and blue cheese
    roulade, 305
corn and cheese pasties, 404
eggplant and zucchini
    bake, 448
enchiladas with hot chili
    sauce, 456
kale with Parmesan and
    garlic, 376
leek soufflé, 281
onion tarts with goat
    cheese, 276
pasta with Savoy cabbage and
    Gruyère, 377
radicchio pizza, 476
roast asparagus crêpes, 303
spinach and pepper pizza, 455
spinach in filo with three
    cheeses, 371
stuffed artichokes, 308
tomato and basil tart, 451
cheese, sweet recipes
  banana and mascarpone
    creams, 212
  exotic fruit tart, 219
  lemon coeur à la crème with
    Cointreau oranges, 150
  lemon grass skewers with lime
    cheese, 204
  red grape and cheese
    tartlets, 246
cheesecakes
  lemon and lime cheesecake,
    155
  pomegranate jeweled
    cheesecake, 211
cherimoyas, 177
cherries, 70-1
  black cherry clafouti, 78
  fresh cherry and hazelnut
    strudel, 81
  spiced fruits jubilee, 75
cherry guavas, 182
cherry pitters, 13
cherry plums, 65
cherry tomatoes, 433
chestnut mushrooms, 486
chestnuts
  cranberry and chestnut
    stuffing, 109
  parsnip and chestnut
    croquettes, 336

chicken
  broccoli and chicken
    lasagne, 368
  chicken with shallots, 284
  enchiladas with hot chili
    sauce, 456
  Mediterranean chicken with
    turnips, 338
  snow peas with chicken and
    cilantro, 399
chicken livers and green
    salad, 474
chickpeas, 393
  hot sour chickpeas, 457
chicory, 466
  baked chicory with
    prosciutto, 478
chilies, 440-1
  enchiladas with hot chili
    sauce, 456
  hot sour chickpeas, 457
  pickled peach and chili
    chutney, 90
Chinese bitter melons, 415
Chinese broccoli, 363
Chinese cabbage, 362-3
  stir-fried Chinese leaves with
    scallops, 480
Chinese chives, 269
  Thai noodles with Chinese
    chives, 280
Chinese greens, 362-3
Chinese leaves with scallops,
    stir-fried, 480
Chinese mustard greens, 362
chives, 269
chocolate
  chocolate and mandarin truffle
    slice, 154
  chocolate, pear and pecan
    pie, 52
  chocolate zucchini cake, 428
  date and walnut brownies, 222
  fruits of the forest with white
    chocolate creams, 120
chopping vegetables, 260

choux pastry
  sweet pepper choux with
    anchovies, 453
chowder, corn and scallop, 405
chutney
  apple and red onion
    marmalade, 56
  fig and date chutney, 251
  mango chutney, 224
  pickled peach and chili
    chutney, 90
cider
  apple and cider sauce, 56
  glazed carrots with cider, 340
cider apples, 29
cilantro
  carrot and cilantro soup, 342
citron, 139
citrus fruits, 135-69
  citrus fruit flambé with pistachio
    praline, 158
  preparation, 15
  recipes, 149-69
citrus presses, 13
citrus zesters, 12
civet fruit, 180
clafouti, black cherry, 78
clementines, 142
  clementine jelly, 151
cloudberries, 98
coconut milk

  coconut jelly with star anise
    fruits, 204
  exotic fruit sushi, 203
  pak-choi with lime dressing, 380
coeur à la crème, lemon, 150
Cointreau
  crêpes Suzette, 156
  lemon coeur à la crème with
    Cointreau oranges, 150
colanders, 257
coleslaw
  carrot, apple and orange
    coleslaw, 340
collards, 359
Comice pears, 31

Conference pears, 31
cookies
  almond cookies, 41
  ginger cookies, 242
cooking apples, 27-8
cooking methods
  fruit, 16
  vegetables, 260-1
coring fruit, 12, 14
corn, 390-1
  corn and cheese pasties, 404
  corn and scallop chowder, 405
corn salad, 463
cos lettuces, 462-3
coulis, raspberry, 98
courgettes, 408-9
couscous, lamb and fava
    bean, 396
cowberries, 108
Cox's Orange Pippin apples, 22
crab apples, 29
cranberries, 108-9
  cranberry and blueberry
    streusel cake, 127
  cranberry and chestnut stuffing,
    109
  cranberry sauce, 109
crème caramels, passion fruit, 201
Crenshaw melons, 229
crêpes
  apple crêpes with butterscotch
    sauce, 44
  crêpes Suzette, 156
  roast asparagus crêpes, 303
  summer berry crêpes, 116
  see also pancakes
cress, 471
crisphead lettuces, 462
Crispin apples, 22
crisps, rutabaga, 338
croquettes, parsnip and
    chestnut, 336
croutons, roast garlic with, 278
crumbles
  broccoli crumble, 368
  spiced apple crumble, 42
crystallized fruits, 17
crystallized pineapple, 193
cucumbers, 416-17
  cucumber and trout
    mousse, 426
  eggplant with tzatziki, 448
curly endive, 466
curly kale, 359
currants (dried), 235
curry, samphire with chilled
    fish, 309
curuba, 177

custard
  gooseberry and elderflower
    fool, 119
  plum and custard creams, 74
custard apples, 177
custard marrows, 410
Czar plums, 65

D
daikon radishes, 468
  stir-fried Chinese leaves and
    scallops, 480
damsons, 68
  damson cheese, 68
  iced gin and damson soufflés, 79
dandelion, 360
Danish pastries
  plum and marzipan pastries, 85
dasheen, 329-30
date plums, 190
dates, 178-9
  date and walnut brownies, 222
  fig and date chutney, 251
  hot date puddings with toffee
    sauce, 215
  pickled peach and chili
    chutney, 90
  stuffed dates, 179
Dauphine Violette figs, 236
deep-frying
  fruit, 16
  vegetables, 261
Delicata squashes, 412
Denniston's Superb plums, 64
Desirée potatoes, 315
dewberries, 99-100
discoloration, preventing, 14
Discovery apples, 22
dolmades, 381
Doyenné du Comice pears, 31
dragon fruit, 180
dried fruit and vegetables, 17
  apples, 27-8
  apricots, 63
  bananas, 173
  beans, 393

dates, 178
figs, 237
grapes, 235
mangoes, 187
mushrooms, 489
peaches, 61
pears, 34
peas, 393
persimmons, 190
pineapple, 193
drinks, apple, 29
duck
  duck in bitter orange sauce, 147
  warm duck salad with
    orange, 477
durians, 180
Dutch apple cake, 54

E
Early Rivers cherries, 70
Early Sulphur gooseberries, 106
eddo, 329-30
  eddo, carrot and parsnip
    medley, 346
eggplants, 435-7
  eggplant and zucchini
    bake, 448
  eggplant with tzatziki, 448
  loofah and eggplant
    ratatouille, 427
  parsnip, eggplant and cashew
    biryani, 337
eggs
  eggs flamenco, 454
  pumpkin and ham frittata, 429
  soufflé omelet with mushroom
    sauce, 494
Egremont Russet apples, 22
Ein d'Or melons, 229
elderberries, 104
elderflowers, 104
  gooseberry and elderflower
    fool, 119
  lychee and elderflower
    sorbet, 202
electric juice extractors, 13
elephant garlic, 271
Elsanta strawberries, 95
Elstar apples, 22
Elvira strawberries, 95
Empire apples, 22

enchiladas with hot chili sauce, 456
endive, curly, 466
  arugula and grilled goat cheese salad, 479
English cherries, 71
English cucumbers, 416
English pumpkins, 412
enokitaki mushrooms, 491
equipment
  fruit preparation, 12-13
  vegetables, 256-7
escarole, 466
Estima potatoes, 315
exotic fruits, 171-225
  exotic fruit salad with passion fruit dressing, 207
  exotic fruit sushi, 203
  exotic fruit tart, 219
  recipes, 199-225
  tropical fruit gratin, 208
exotic gourds, 414-15
exotic root vegetables, 328-31

F
fava beans, 384
  fava beans à la paysanne, 396
  lamb and fava bean couscous, 396
fat hen, 361
feijoas, 181
fennel, 296
  braised fennel with tomatoes, 310
  fennel and mussel Provençal, 310
fiddlehead ferns, 294
field mushrooms, 487
figs, 236-8
  fig and date chutney, 251
  fig and walnut torte, 244
  fresh fig filo tart, 248
  Greek yogurt and fig cake, 249
filo-topped apple pie, 51
finger potatoes, 316
flageolet beans, 393
  wax beans with garlic, 402
Flame Seedless grapes, 232
Florence fennel, 296
fondant icing, physalis in, 191
food processors, 257
fool, gooseberry and elderflower, 119
Forelle pears, 31
fraises des bois, 95
freezing blackberries, 99
French apple tart, 53
French beans, 388

French breakfast radishes, 468
French fries, 318, 319
French toast, caramelized apricots with, 80
frittata, pumpkin and ham, 429
fritters, 261
  pear and cinnamon fritters, 45
  yam fritters, 346
frosting fruit, 17
fruit
  buying, 14
  cooking methods, 16-17
  equipment, 12-13
  preparation, 14
fruit salads
  exotic fruit salad with passion fruit dressing, 207
fruits of the forest with white chocolate creams, 120
frying pans, 257
frying vegetables, 261
Fuji apples, 23
funnels, 13

G
Gala apples, 23
galangal, 331
Galia melons, 228
garden leaves, 360
garlic, 270-1
  garlic mushrooms, 278
  kale with Parmesan and garlic, 376
  roast garlic with croutons, 278
garlic chives, 269
garlic presses, 256
garnishes
  citrus fruit, 15
  fig flowers, 238
Gaviota plums, 64
gazpacho, 450
geans, cherries, 70
gherkins, 416
gin and damson soufflés, iced, 79
ginger, 331
  ginger baskets, 152
  ginger cookies, 242
  papaya baked with ginger, 206
ginup, 181

glacé cherries, 71
glacé fruits, 17
glacé peaches, 61
globe artichokes, 290-1
  stuffed artichokes, 308
gnocchi
  gnocchi with oyster mushrooms, 498
  marrows with gnocchi, 424
goat cheese
  arugula and grilled goat cheese salad, 479
  baked leeks with cheese and yogurt topping, 283
  baked zucchini, 422
  braised celery with goat cheese, 306
  onion tarts with goat cheese, 276
Golden Delicious apples, 23
golden raspberries, 97
golden watermelons, 231
Golden Wonder potatoes, 315
Goldendrop gooseberries, 106
good King Henry, 361
gooseberries, 106-7
  gooseberry and elderflower fool, 119
Gorella strawberries, 95
gougère, cauliflower and mushroom, 372
gourds, 414-15
granadillas, 181
Granny Smith apples, 23
grape juice, 234
grapefruit, 136-7
  citrus fruit flambé with pistachio praline, 158
  three-fruit marmalade, 168
grapefruit knives, 13
grapefruit segmenters, 13
grapes, 232-5
  caramelizing grapes, 235
  red grape and cheese tartlets, 246
grapeseed oil, 234
graters, 256
grating
  citrus zest, 15
  graters, 12
  lemons, 138
gratins
  Brussels sprout gratin, 378
  celery root gratin, 304
Greek yogurt and fig cake, 249
green bananas, 173, 174, 442-3
green beans, 388
  green bean salad, 400

green beans with bacon and cream, 401
green cabbage, 358
greengages, 68
greens, 349-81
  recipes, 367-81
Greensleeves apples, 23
Grenadier apples, 27
guacamole, 458
guavas, 182
guines, cherries, 70

H
habañero chilies, 440
hairy lychees, 196
ham
  fava beans à la paysanne, 396
  pumpkin and ham frittata, 429
  see also prosciutto
haricot beans, 393
haricots verts, 388
Hautbois strawberries, 95
haws, 105
hazelnuts
  fresh cherry and hazelnut strudel, 81
  nectarine and hazelnut meringues, 76
Heritage raspberries, 97
hips, rose, 105
hollandaise sauce
  asparagus with tarragon hollandaise, 300
honeydew melons, 229
horned cucumbers, 183
horned melons, 183
horns of plenty, 488
horseradish, 325
Hosui pears, 35
hot gold spike chilies, 440
hot sour chickpeas, 457
Howgate Wonder apples, 27
Hubbard squashes, 412
huckleberries, 102
hybrid berries, 101

I
ice cream, fresh strawberry, 122
iced gin and damson soufflés, 79
Ida Red apples, 23
Indian figs, 195
Indian-style okra, 403
Italia grapes, 232
Italian fennel, 296
Italian roast peppers, 452
Italian zucchini, 409

J
jackfruit, 182
Jaffa oranges, 144
jalapeño chilies, 440
Jamaican fruit trifle, 210
Jamaican plums, 183
James Grieve apples, 23
jams
   melon and star anise jam, 250
   strawberry jam, 133
Japonica quinces, 37
jelly
   bramble jelly, 132
   clementine jelly, 151
   coconut jelly with star anise
      fruits, 204
   quince jelly, 36
   redcurrant jelly, 111
jelly bags, 13
jelly melons, 183
Jersey Royal potatoes, 314
Jersey White potatoes, 314
Jerusalem artichokes, 321
   artichoke rösti, 344
   artichoke timbales with spinach
      sauce, 344
jicama, 330
Jonagold apples, 23-4
Jonathan apples, 24
Josephine de Malines pears, 31
juca, 331
juice
   grape, 234
   lemon, 139

pomegranate, 195
jujubes, 183
Julie mangoes, 186
julienne strips
   carrots, 260
   citrus rind, 140
   zest, 15

K
Kabocha squashes, 412
Kadota figs, 236
kaffir limes, 140
kaki plums, 190
kale, 359
   kale with Parmesan and
      garlic, 376
Katy apples, 24
Kent mangoes, 186
Kerr's Pink potatoes, 315
Key lime pie, 164
Key limes, 140
Khoob melons, 228
Kidd's Orange Red apples, 24
kidney beans, 393
King Edward potatoes, 315
Kir Royale, blackberry, 100
Kirbys, 416
kiwanos, 183
kiwi fruit, 184
knives, 256
kohlrabi, 364
kubos, 184
kumquats, 141
   spiced poached
      kumquats, 168

L
La Ratte potatoes, 316
lady finger bananas, 172
lamb and fava bean
   couscous, 396
lamb's lettuce, 463
land cress, 470
Langley's Industry
   gooseberries, 106
lasagne, broccoli and chicken, 368
Laxton's Fortune apples, 24
Laxton's Superb apples, 24
leeks, 272-3
   baked leeks with cheese and
      yogurt topping, 283
   leek soufflé, 281
   preparing, 258
   radicchio pizza, 476
   stuffed artichokes, 308
   tagliatelle with leeks and
      prosciutto, 282
lemon, 138-9

cold lemon soufflé with
   caramelized almond
      topping, 159
fresh lemon tart, 163
lemon and lime
   cheesecake, 155
lemon and lime syrup
   cake, 167
lemon coeur à la crème with
   Cointreau oranges, 150
lemon meringue pie, 162
lemon roulade with lemon curd
   cream, 160
lemon surprise pudding, 156
papaya and lemon relish, 225
three-fruit marmalade, 168
lemon sole
   samphire with chilled fish
      curry, 309
   watercress and two-fish
      terrine, 482
lemon squeezers, 12
lemon taps, 13
lemongrass skewers with lime
   cheese, 204
lentils, 393
lettuce, 462-4
   fava beans à la
      paysanne, 396
   Caesar salad, 474
Leveller gooseberries, 106
lima beans, 384
limequats, 141
limes, 140
   bananas with lime and
      cardamom sauce, 212
   Key lime pie, 164
   lemon and lime
      cheesecake, 155
   lemon and lime syrup
      cake, 167
   lemon grass skewers with lime
      cheese, 204
   pak-choi with lime
      dressing, 380
lingonberries, 108
Linzer Delikatess potatoes, 317
liquidizers, 257
Little Gem lettuces, 463
liver
   chicken livers and green
      salad, 474
loganberries, 101
London gooseberries, 106
longans, 184
loofahs, 415
   loofah and eggplant
      ratatouille, 427

loosehead lettuces, 462
loquats, 185
lychees, 185
   coconut jelly with star anise
      fruits, 204
   lychee and elderflower
      sorbet, 202

M
mâche, 463
McIntosh apples, 24
Malling Jewel raspberries, 97
mandarins, 142, 143
   chocolate and mandarin truffle
      slice, 154
mandolines, 256
mangoes, 186-7
   cold mango soufflés topped
      with toasted coconut, 200
   Jamaican fruit trifle, 210
   lemon grass skewers with lime
      cheese, 204
   mango and tamarillo
      pastries, 218
   mango chutney, 224
   mango pie, 220
   radish, mango and apple
      salad, 481
mangosteens, 188
manioc, 331
maracoyas, 188
Maraschino cherries, 71
Marian rutabagas, 323
Maris Bard potatoes, 314
Maris Peer potatoes, 314
Maris Piper potatoes, 314-315
Marjorie's Seedling plums, 64
marmalade, three-fruit, 168
marrows, 410-11
   baked marrow with parsley
      sauce, 425
   marrows with gnocchi, 424
marsh samphire, 297
marzipan
   baked lattice peaches, 82
   plum and marzipan pastries, 85

mashers, 256
mashing potatoes, 318-319
Mediterranean chicken with
    turnips, 338
medlars, 37
melon ballers, 13
melons, 228-30
    melon and star anise jam, 250
    melon trio with ginger
        cookies, 242
meringues
    fresh berry pavlova, 118
    lemon meringue pie, 162
    nectarine and hazelnut
        meringues, 76
Merrick rutabagas, 323
Merton Pride pears, 31
Mexican limes, 140
Mexican potatoes, 330
microwave cooking, fruit, 16
mincemeat
    apricot parcels, 88
minneolas, 143
Mirabelles, 65
monkfish
    watercress and two-fish
        terrine, 482
Montmorency cherries, 71
mooli, 468
Morello cherries, 71
morels, 489
mousses
    cucumber and trout mousse, 426
    quince and ginger mousse, 41
    white chocolate creams, 120
muffins, fresh blueberry, 128
mulberries, 102
mung beans, 393
Muscat grapes, 232, 233
mushrooms, 485-502
    boeuf en croûte with mushroom
        filling, 497
    cauliflower and mushroom
        gougère, 372
    cream of mushroom soup, 494
    garlic mushrooms, 278
    gnocchi with oyster
        mushrooms, 498
    preparing, 258
    seafood and oyster mushroom
        appetizer, 498
    soufflé omelet with mushroom
        sauce, 494
    stuffed mushrooms, 496
    tagliatelle fungi, 500
    wild mushrooms in brioche, 502
    wild mushrooms with
        pancakes, 502

musk melons, 228
mussels
    fennel and mussel
        Provençal, 310
    seafood and oyster mushroom
        appetizer, 498
mustard and cress, 471
mustard greens, 362

N
Napa cabbage, 362
Napoleon cherries, 70
Napoleon grapes, 232
Nashi pears, 35
Navel oranges, 144
Navelina oranges, 144
navets, 323
nectarines, 62
    nectarine and hazelnut
        meringues, 76
    nectarine relish, 90
    spiced fruits jubilee, 75
nettles, 361
new potatoes, 314
noodles
    Thai noodles with Chinese
        chives, 280

O
Ogen melons, 228

okra, 392
    Indian-style okra, 403
omelets
    soufflé omelet with mushroom
        sauce, 494
one-crust rhubarb pie, 247
onion squashes, 412
    onion squash risotto, 420
onions, 264-7
    apple and red onion
        marmalade, 56
    baked onions stuffed with
        feta, 276
    onion tarts with goat
        cheese, 276
    peas with baby onions and
        cream, 398
Onward pears, 31
orache, 360

oranges, 144-7
    candied orange peel, 147
    citrus fruit flambé with pistachio
        praline, 158
    cranberry sauce, 109
    crêpes Suzette, 156
    duck in bitter orange sauce, 147
    lemon coeur à la crème with
        Cointreau oranges, 150
    moist orange and almond
        cake, 166
    ruby orange sherbet in ginger
        baskets, 152
    three-fruit marmalade, 168
    warm duck salad with
        orange, 477
oriental shoots, 294-5
Orleans Reinette apples, 24
ortaniques, 143
ostrich ferns, 294
oyster mushrooms, 490
    gnocchi with oyster
        mushrooms, 498
    seafood and oyster mushroom
        appetizer, 498

P
Packham's Triumph pears, 31
pak-choi, 363
    pak-choi with lime dressing, 380
palm hearts, 295
pancakes
    wild mushrooms with
        pancakes, 502
    see also crêpes
pans, 257
papayas, 189-90
    grilled pineapple with papaya
        sauce, 208
    Jamaican fruit trifle, 210
    lemongrass skewers with lime
        cheese, 204
    papaya and lemon relish, 225
    papaya baked with ginger, 206
paring knives, 12
parsnips, 320

eddo, carrot and parsnip
    medley, 346
parsnip and chestnut
    croquettes, 336
parsnip, eggplant and cashew
    biryani, 337
Parvin mangoes, 186
Passacrena pears, 31
passion fruit, 189
    exotic fruit salad with passion
        fruit dressing, 207
    passion fruit crème caramels
        with dipped physalis, 201
pasta with Savoy cabbage and
    Gruyère, 377
pasties
    chard pasties, 375
    corn and cheese pasties, 404
pastries
    apricot parcels, 88
    baked lattice peaches, 82
    fig and walnut torte, 244
    mango and tamarillo
        pastries, 218
    plum and marzipan pastries, 85
    see also pies; tarts
patatas bravas, 334
pattypan squashes, 409
pavlova, fresh berry, 118
paw-paws see papayas
pe-tsai, 362-3
peaches, 60-2
    baked lattice peaches, 82
    peach and red currant
        tartlets, 84
    peach Melba syllabub, 76
    pickled peach and chili
        chutney, 90
pears, 30-5
    chocolate, pear and pecan
        pie, 52
    iced pear terrine with Calvados
        and chocolate sauce, 40
    pear and cinnamon fritters, 45
    pear and polenta cake, 54
    poached pears in port syrup, 46
peas, 386-7
    peas with baby onions and
        cream, 398
peas, dried, 393
pecan nuts
    banana and pecan bread, 222
    chocolate, pear and pecan
        pie, 52
peel
    candied orange peel, 147
    julienne strips, 140
    lemon, 139

peelers, 256
peeling
    fruit, 12, 14, 15
    vegetables, 259
Pentland Dell potatoes, 316
pepinos, 191
peppers, 438-9
    eggs flamenco, 454
    gazpacho, 450
    Italian roast peppers, 452
    skinning, 260, 439
    spinach and pepper pizza, 455
    sweet pepper choux with
        anchovies, 453
Perlette grapes, 232
perpetual strawberries, 95
Perry pears, 35
persimmons, 190
petits pois, 387
physalis, 191
    passion fruit crème caramels
        with dipped physalis, 201
pickled peach and chili
    chutney, 90
Piel de Sapo melons, 229
pies
    blueberry pie, 129
    boeuf en croûte, 497
    chard pasties, 375
    corn and cheese
        pasties, 404
    filo-topped apple pie, 51
    lemon meringue pie, 162
    mango pie, 220
    one-crust rhubarb pie, 247
    spinach in filo with three
        cheeses, 371
pineapple easy slicers, 12
pineapple melons, 228
pineapples, 192-3
    grilled pineapple with papaya
        sauce, 208
    Jamaican fruit trifle, 210
pink currants, 111
Pink Fir Apple potatoes, 317
Pink Lady apples, 24
pistachio nuts
    citrus fruit flambé with pistachio
        praline, 158

pitihayas, 180
pizzas
    radicchio pizza, 476
    spinach and pepper pizza, 455
plantains, 173, 174, 442-3
    plantain appetizer, 459
plum tomatoes, 433
plums, 64-7
    plum and custard creams, 74
    plum and marzipan
        pastries, 85
    spiced fruits jubilee, 75
    yellow plum tart, 86
poaching fruit, 16
poblano chilies, 441
polenta
    pear and polenta cake, 54
pomegranates, 194-5
    pomegranate jeweled
        cheesecake, 211
pomelos, 136, 137
Pomme d'Api apples, 24
port
    poached pears in port syrup, 46
    port-stewed rhubarb with vanilla
        desserts, 243
potato mashers, 256
potato peelers, 256
potatoes, 314-19
    artichoke rösti, 344
    patatas bravas, 334
    potatoes Dauphinois, 334
praline
    citrus fruit flambé with pistachio
        praline, 158
preserving fruit, 17
preserving pans, 13
prickly pears, 195
prosciutto
    baked chicory with
        prosciutto, 478
    tagliatelle with leeks and
        prosciutto, 282
prunes, 66, 67
pumpkins, 412, 414
    pumpkin and ham frittata, 429
    pumpkin soup, 420
puréeing
    apples, 28
    fruit, 17
Purple Congo potatoes, 318
purple kale, 359
purple sprouting broccoli, 354-5

Q
Quetsch plums, 65
quinces, 36-7
    hot quince soufflés, 48

quince and ginger mousse, 41
quince jelly, 36

R
radicchio, 466
    radicchio pizza, 476
radishes, 468-9
    radish, mango and apple
        salad, 481
raisins, 235
rambutans, 196
ramp, 273
Ranier cherries, 70
raspberries, 97-8
    fresh berry pavlova, 118
    fruits of the forest with white
        chocolate creams, 120
    peach Melba syllabub, 76
    raspberry and rose petal
        shortcakes, 124
    raspberry coulis, 98
    raspberry sauce, 203
ratatouille, loofah and
    eggplant, 427
reamers, 13
red bananas, 173
red cabbage, 358
red chilies, 441
red currants, 110, 111
    fresh currant bread-and-butter
        pudding, 126
    peach and red currant
        tartlets, 84
    red currant jelly, 111
Red Delicious apples, 24-5
red onions, 265
red radishes, 468
Red Williams pears, 32
relishes
    nectarine relish, 90
    papaya and lemon relish, 225
remontant strawberries, 95
Reverend W. Wilkes apples, 27
rhubarb, 239
    one-crust rhubarb pie, 247

port-stewed rhubarb with vanilla
    desserts, 243
rhubarb chard, 365
rice
    dolmades, 381
    exotic fruit sushi, 203
    onion squash risotto, 420
    parsnip, eggplant and cashew
        biryani, 337
    shiitake fried rice, 501
ridged cucumbers, 416
risotto, onion squash, 420
roast potatoes, 318-319
Rocha pears, 32
rock samphire, 297
rocket, 465
romaine lettuces, 463
romanescoes, 352
Romano potatoes, 316
root vegetables, 313-47
    preparing, 258
    recipes, 333-47
rose hips, 105
rösti, artichoke, 344
roulades
    celery root and blue cheese
        roulade, 305
    lemon roulade with lemon curd
        cream, 160
round lettuces, 462
round tomatoes, 433
rowanberries, 105
Royal Gala apples, 23
ruby chard, 365
ruby mangoes, 186
ruby orange sherbet in ginger
    baskets, 152
rum and banana waffles, 216
runner beans, 385
rutabaga, 322-3
    rutabaga crisps, 338

S
salad tomatoes, 433
salad vegetables, 461-83
    recipes, 473-83
salads
    arugula and grilled goat cheese
        salad, 479
    Caesar salad, 474
    carrot, apple and orange
        coleslaw, 340
    celery, avocado and walnut
        salad, 306
    chicken livers and green
        salad, 474
    green bean salad, 400
    preparing, 259

radish, mango and apple
  salad, 481
warm duck salad with
  orange, 477
salak, 197
salmon
  samphire with chilled fish
    curry, 309
salsify, 327
Salustianas oranges, 144
samphire, 297
  samphire with chilled fish
    curry, 309
Santa Rosa plums, 64
sapodillas, 196
satsumas, 142
saucepans, 257
sauces
  apple and cider sauce, 56
  cranberry sauce, 109
  raspberry coulis, 98
  raspberry sauce, 203
sautéing
  fruit, 16

potatoes, 319
vegetables, 261
Savoy cabbage, 356
  pasta with Savoy cabbage
    and Gruyère, 377
scallions, 267
scallops
  corn and scallop
    chowder, 405
  stir-fried Chinese leaves with
    scallops, 480
scorzonera, 327
seafood and oyster mushroom
  appetizer, 498
segmenting fruit, 14, 15
  grapefruit, 136
  oranges, 145
Serrano chilies, 441
Seville oranges, 145
shaddock, 136
shallots, 268
  chicken with shallots, 284

glazed shallots, 284
Shamouti oranges, 144
Sharon fruit, 190
sherbet
  ruby orange sherbet in ginger
    baskets, 152
shiitake mushrooms, 491
  shiitake fried rice, 501
shoots and stems, 287-311
  recipes, 299-311
shortcakes, raspberry and rose
  petal, 124
shredding vegetable
  leaves, 260
shrimp
  seafood and oyster mushroom
    appetizer, 498
sieves, 257
silver kale, 359
skinning
  peppers, 439
  tomatoes, 434
sloes, 69
smoked trout
  cucumber and trout
    mousse, 426
smooth loofahs, 415
snake fruit, 197
snow peas, 387
  snow peas with chicken and
    cilantro, 399
soft fruit *see* berries; stone fruits
sole
  samphire with chilled fish
    curry, 309
  watercress and two-fish
    terrine, 482
sorbets
  blackcurrant sorbet, 123
  lychee and elderflower
    sorbet, 202
sorrel, 360
soufflé omelet with mushroom
  sauce, 494
soufflés
  cold lemon soufflé with
    caramelized almond
    topping, 159
  cold mango soufflés topped
    with toasted coconut, 200
  hot blackberry and apple
    soufflés, 115
  hot quince soufflés, 48
  iced gin and damson
    soufflés, 79
  leek soufflé, 281
soups
  asparagus soup, 302

carrot and cilantro soup, 342
corn and scallop chowder, 405
cream of mushroom soup, 494
gazpacho, 450
pumpkin soup, 420
watercress soup, 482
sour cherries, 71
soursops, 177
spaghetti squashes, 410
Spanish limes, 181
Spanish onions, 264
Spartan apples, 25
spiced fruits jubilee, 75
spiced poached kumquats, 168
spinach, 350-1
  artichoke timbales with spinach
    sauce, 344
  celery root and blue cheese
    roulade, 305
  spinach and cannellini
    beans, 370
  spinach and pepper pizza, 455
  spinach in filo with three
    cheeses, 371
spring greens, 356
spring onions, 267
sprouting broccoli, 354-5
squashes, 407-29
  recipes, 419-29
star fruit, 176
steamers, 257
steaming
  potatoes, 319
  vegetables, 261
stems and shoots, 287-311
  recipes, 299-311
stewing fruit, 16
stir-frying vegetables, 261
stone fruits, 59-91
  peeling, 15
  recipes, 73-91
  removing pits, 15, 61
stoning equipment, 13
storing
  fruit, 14
  vegetables, 258
strawberries, 94-6
  fresh strawberry ice cream, 122
  fruits of the forest with white
    chocolate creams, 120
  strawberry jam, 133
strawberry guavas, 182
streusel cake, cranberry and
  blueberry, 127
strudel, fresh cherry and
  hazelnut, 81
stuffing, cranberry and
  chestnut, 109

Sugar Baby watermelons, 231
sugar bananas, 172
sugar peas, 387
sugar snaps, 387
sugar thermometers, 13
Sultana grapes, 232
sultanas, 235

summer berry crêpes, 116
summer crookneck
  squashes, 409
summer melons, 228
summer pudding, 114
summer squashes, 410-11
sun-dried tomatoes, 433
sunberries, 101
sweating vegetables, 261
swedes, 322-3
Sweet Gold pineapples, 192
sweet potatoes, 328
  pan-fried sweet potatoes with
    bacon, 343
sweetcorn, 390-1
Sweetie grapefruit, 136
Swiss chard, 365
syllabub, peach Melba, 76

T
Tabasco sauce, 441
tagliatelle
  tagliatelle fungi, 500
  tagliatelle with leeks and
    prosciutto, 282
Tahitian limes, 140
tamarillos, 197
  mango and tamarillo
    pastries, 218
tangelos, 143
tangerines, 142-3
tangleberries, 102
taro, 329-30
tarragon hollandaise, asparagus
  with, 300
tarts
  asparagus tart with ricotta, 300

berry brûlée tarts, 130
chocolate, pear and pecan
    pie, 52
exotic fruit tart, 219
French apple tart, 53
fresh fig filo tart, 248
fresh lemon tart, 163
hot broccoli tartlets, 374
Key lime pie, 164
onion tarts with goat
    cheese, 276
peach and redcurrant tartlets, 84
red grape and cheese
    tartlets, 246
tarte Tatin, 50
tomato and basil tart, 451
yellow plum tart, 86
see also pastries; pies
tayberries, 101
tea breads
    banana and pecan bread, 222
tempura, 261
terrines
    iced pear terrine, 40
    watercress and two-fish
        terrine, 482
Thai beans, 388
Thai noodles with Chinese
    chives, 280
thermometers, 13
Thompson Seedless grapes, 232
three-fruit marmalade, 168
Tientsin pears, 35
Tiger watermelons, 231
toffee bananas, 214
toffee sauce, hot date puddings
    with, 215
tomato purée, 433-4
tomatoes, 432-4
    balti-style cauliflower with
        tomatoes, 373
    braised fennel with
        tomatoes, 310
    eggplant and zucchini
        bake, 448
    eggs flamenco, 454
    gazpacho, 450

patatas bravas, 334
radicchio pizza, 476
skinning, 260, 434
tomato and basil tart, 451
Tommy Atkins mangoes, 186
toovar dhal, 393
tortillas
    enchiladas with hot chili
        sauce, 456
tree melon, 191
tree strawberries, 96
tree tomatoes, 197
trifle, Jamaican fruit, 210
tropical fruit gratin, 208
Truffe de Chine potatoes, 318
tummelberries, 101
turnip tops, 355
turnips, 322-3
    Mediterranean chicken with
        turnips, 338
tzatziki, eggplant with, 448

U
Ugli fruit, 137

V
Valencia oranges, 145
vanilla desserts, port-stewed
    rhubarb with, 243
vegetable fruits, 430-59
    recipes, 447-59
vegetable peelers, 12
vegetables
    buying, 258

cooking methods, 260-1
equipment, 256-7
history, 254
nutrition, 254-5
preparing, 258-60
storing, 258
vertus, 323
Victoria plums, 64
Vidalia onions, 266
vine leaves, 360
    dolmades, 381

W
waffles, rum and banana, 216
walnuts
    date and walnut brownies, 222
    fig and walnut torte, 244
water chestnuts, 295
watercress, 470
    watercress and two-fish
        terrine, 482
    watercress soup, 482
watermelons, 231
    melon trio with ginger
        biscuits, 242
wax beans, 385
    wax beans with garlic, 402
whinberries, 103
white cabbage, 358
white currants, 110, 111
white grapes, 232
white mulberries, 102
white mushrooms, 486
white onions, 266
whortleberries, 103
wild leaves, 360-1
wild mushrooms, 490-1
    wild mushrooms in
        brioche, 502
    wild mushrooms with
        pancakes, 502
wild raspberries, 97
wild strawberries, 95
Wilja potatoes, 316
Williams Bon Chrétien pears, 32
wine
    blackberry Kir Royale, 100

wineberries, 101
winter cress, 470
winter melons, 229
Winter Nelis pears, 32
winter squashes, 412-14
woks, 257
woodland mushrooms, 488-9
Worcester Pearmain apples, 25
Worcestershire berries, 107

Y
yams, 329
    yam fritters, 346
yellow onions, 264
yellow plum tart, 86
yellow raspberries, 97
yellow tomatoes, 434
yellow wax beans, 388
yellow wax peppers, 441
yellow zucchini, 408
yogurt
    baked leeks with cheese and
        yogurt topping, 283
    eggplant with tzatziki, 448
    Greek yogurt and fig cake, 249
youngberries, 101

Z
zest
    grating, 15
    lemons, 138, 139
zesters, 12
zucchini, 408-9
    baked zucchini, 422
    chocolate zucchini cake, 428
    eggplant and zucchini
        bake, 448
    zucchini Italian-style, 423

ACKNOWLEDGMENTS

Photographs are by Don Last
William Lingwood, Patrick
McLeavey and Thomas
Odulate/© Anness Publishing
except for: p27 ml Harry Smith

Horticultural Photographic
Collection (HSHC); p69 t Clive
Simms; p95 tl HSHC; b/tr The
Garden Picture Library (GPL);
p96 br GPL; p98 br Clive Simms

(CS); p100m HSHC, tr A-Z
Botanical/Bjorn Svenson; p101
br GPL, tl Derek St. Romaine
(DSR), bl HSHC; p102 b HSHC;
p106 t DSR; p107 bl/br DSR;

p139 b CS; p111 b GPL; p172 l
Peter McHoy; p177 l HSHC, b
CS; p178t HSHC; p180 b GPL;
p183 t HSHC; p185 t CS; p190
t CS; and p196 t GPL.